D1617351

Ruins of Absence, Presence of Caribs

Florida A&M University, Tallahassee
Florida Atlantic University, Boca Raton
Florida Gulf Coast University, Ft. Myers
Florida International University, Miami
Florida State University, Tallahassee
University of Central Florida, Orlando
University of Florida, Gainesville
University of North Florida, Jacksonville
University of South Florida, Tampa
University of West Florida, Pensacola

Ruins of Absence, Presence of Caribs

(Post)Colonial Representations
of Aboriginality in Trinidad and Tobago

Maximilian C. Forte

University Press of Florida
Gainesville/Tallahassee/Tampa/Boca Raton
Pensacola/Orlando/Miami/Jacksonville/Ft. Myers

A record of cataloging-in-publication data is available from
the Library of Congress.

ISBN 0 8130 2828 0

The University Press of Florida is the scholarly publishing agency
for the State University System of Florida, comprising Florida A&M
University, Florida Atlantic University, Florida Gulf Coast University,
Florida International University, Florida State University, University
of Central Florida, University of Florida, University of North Florida,
University of South Florida, and University of West Florida.

University Press of Florida
15 Northwest 15th Street
Gainesville, FL 32611-2079
http://www.upf.com

To Allison, my angel,
and
to Justa May Werges (May 1, 1915–January 16, 2000),
Queen of the Caribs . . .
my queen
Eternal rest grant unto her.

Contents

Illustrations

Figures

Tables

Preface and Acknowledgments

... a great masquerade drama was being played out on the racist stage of White theatre, where indigenous denial and the ability to pass acceptance by Whites became the only route to social and economic success and survival. . . . The problems with identity are . . . deeply rooted in colonialism, slavery, racism, distorted or erased history, census rolls designed with political agendas, patron-client military alliances of the past, economic dominance designed to keep some people illiterate or to keep others in line as a serving workforce. All these factors, and more, left many in a genealogical-historical limbo that suggested they had no past, and without it, no future.

Arthur C. Einhorn, "Out of Pandora's Closet" (2002)

Let me begin with a few words about the title of this book. First, I wish to thank Kevin Yelvington for suggesting an inversion of Orlando Patterson's title for his 1967 novel, *An Absence of Ruins*. The "absence of ruins" notion suggests an absence of a historical presence of material relics of "the indigenous," the argument being that unlike, say, in Rome or Athens where one is surrounded by ancient monumental ruins that impede one from escaping consciousness of history, the absence of ruins breeds an ahistorical mindset. Indeed, with the exception of a few territories such as Puerto Rico, there is an absence in the Caribbean of the kind of precolonial indigenous monumentality that one often associates with Tikal in Guatemala or Machu Picchu in Peru. One of the goals of my book is to take up the issue of historical consciousness in the Caribbean: the fact that it exists and strongly so. Rather than assessing indigeneity in the Caribbean as a matter of a few physical relics from the distant past that point to something no longer present—indigenous peoples—I argue that even in their alleged absence, the indigenous still exercises a presence, even when that presence is constructed by nonindigenous others in symbolic terms alone, paradoxically with reference to a population presumed to be absent. The main themes of this book are therefore those of *presence* and the way that presence is established by actual historical actors in *representations*.

Like Arthur Einhorn above, I too endorse the critical reassessment of the role of modern scholarship in endorsing and perpetuating colonial and racialist myths of indigenous extinction in the Caribbean. It is, I believe, a vestige of colonial anthropology for scholars to preside as arbiters over the identity of their "subjects." I acknowledge "Carib" as both a presence and an analytical problem, as do my Carib hosts and colleagues in Arima, Trinidad.

In the social sciences, conventional depictions of the postconquest cultural development of the Caribbean are founded upon the absence of the indigenous.

However, groups such as the Santa Rosa Carib Community (SRCC) in the Borough of Arima, Trinidad, have begun to assert their identity and the traditions that they posit as emblematic of an Amerindian heritage. Furthermore, groups such as the SRCC have also received the recognition and support of the state and the attention of the national media. The figure of the Carib has increasingly acquired a valued place in nationalist discourses and local historical narratives. Thus, the questions that are addressed in this book are as follows: Why does "Carib" still exist as a category and as an available identity in Trinidad? What were, and what are, the conditions that make possible the reproduction of Carib as an identity and as a historical canon? What value does Caribness hold, and to whom, when, and why?

One purpose in writing this book is to bring attention to a field of Caribbean studies that has been severely neglected—contemporary indigenous peoples of the Caribbean—even though it is a field that is receiving new and undue interest since it challenges some of the analytical canons used to interpret and describe the Caribbean. In addition, the intent of the book is to redress certain gaps in anthropological studies of indigenous peoples by focusing on the political and economic processes that constitute and define "the indigenous," by locating the indigenous within a wider global and historical context, and by examining largely ignored revivalist groups in a region that was presumed to be lacking precisely such an indigenous presence.

A number of websites may be used as companions to various sections of this book. On the Carib Community of Arima, Trinidad, see the official website of the Santa Rosa Carib Community <http://www.kacike.org/cac-ike/srcc/> and First Nations of Trinidad and Tobago <http://www.centrelink.org/fntt/>. An information resource that contains online publications, personal testimonies, discussion fora, newsletters, and a comprehensive directory of websites is the Caribbean Amerindian Centrelink <http://www.centrelink.org>.

Since commencing this project in 1995 while I was an M.A. student at the State University of New York at Binghamton, I have received the assistance, encouragement, insights, and criticisms of numerous individuals. Beginning with previous teachers of mine in the Department of Anthropology at SUNY–Binghamton, I must thank my past supervisor, Richard U. Moench. Also while I was at SUNY–Binghamton, I was fortunate enough to have studied in the post-graduate courses offered by those associated with the Fernand Braudel Center, especially Immanuel Wallerstein. After completing the first year of my Ph.D. at Binghamton, I transferred to Adelaide University, where I was the beneficiary of the critical inputs of my supervisors, Michael Roberts and David Murray.

I am also grateful for the periodic feedback from various scholars, including Jonathan Friedman (Lund University), José Barreiro (Cornell University), and Joseph Palacio (University of the West Indies, Belize). I must also thank Gérard Collomb at the Maison des Sciences de l'Homme (Paris). I am grateful for the assistance, insights, continuing correspondence and reviews of my work, and supply of valuable research resources from Peter Hulme (University of Essex) and Kevin Yelvington (University of South Florida). I am especially thankful for the interaction I have had with my colleagues at the *Caribbean Amerindian Centrelink* and *KACIKE: The Journal of Caribbean Amerindian History and Anthropology.* In particular I would like to thank Jorge Estevez, Lynne Guitar, and Peter Ferbel, who have engaged me in intense discussions and have provided me with a wide range of valuable literature. Together, they have formed the daily network that has sustained my active interest in this field of inquiry.

Two reviewers of this work when it was still a doctoral dissertation, plus two reviewers of the current text selected by the University Press of Florida, provided many critical insights, suggestions for improvement, and important questions. Of the last two, I wish to especially thank Beth Conklin for her extensive and supportive commentary as well as that of an anonymous reviewer who engaged the material thoroughly and in great depth.

This research project would not have been possible without the financial support received from several sources since 1995. I am thus particularly grateful for a two-year fellowship from the Organization of American States (1994–1996), which allowed the project to get under way in the first place. In addition, I was extremely fortunate to be the beneficiary of a doctoral fellowship from the Social Sciences and Humanities Research Council of Canada (1997–2000). The award of an Australian International Post-Graduate Research Scholarship (1997–2001), a University of Adelaide Post-Graduate Award (1997–2001), an Adelaide University Research Abroad Scholarship (1998), and generous fieldwork funding from the Department of Anthropology at Adelaide University for the 1998–1999 period have been absolutely vital sources of aid.

In addition to all these critical sources of support and assistance, I must thank those individuals who made my fieldwork especially rewarding and memorable. In the Santa Rosa Carib Community, I therefore warmly thank Ricardo Bharath, Cristo Adonis, Jacqueline Khan, Susan Campo, Ricardo Cruz, the late Alexander Calderon, Catherine Calderon, the late Justa Werges, Clifford Carrera, and the late Elma Reyes. I thank Stacey Lezama for working as my survey assistant. In the Arima Borough Council, I was fortunate to have the assistance and amity of Mayor Elvin Edwards, Deputy Mayor Kelvin Seifert, and the councillor for Calvary Hill, Melan Garcia. I also wish to thank Susan Bhopa for being an excellent host during our stay in Arima for three years. I am grateful for the aid of President Cynthia Ross at the National Parang Association of Trinidad and Tobago. I am also indebted to Father Leo Donovan, O.P., at the Santa Rosa Roman Catholic Church for his patience and generosity in lending me antique church documents and baptismal registers to study at my leisure for over a year. Father David Oliveire was also a regular source of advice, insights, reflections, and wise commentaries. My in-laws—particularly my father-in-law, Edgar Diaz; my mother-in-law, Naomi Diaz; and my brothers-in-law Gerard and Richard—were especially helpful throughout my stays in Trinidad. In Dominica, I was very fortunate to benefit from assistance, especially on the part of Sylvanie Burton and Charles Williams; I am also thankful for the kindness of then-chief Hilary Frederick, Senator Kelly Graneau, former chiefs Faustilus Frederick and Irvince Auguiste, and James Frederick. I warmly thank the staff at the Documentation Centre of the Assembly of First Nations in Ottawa, Canada, for the range and depth of archival materials that they shared with me, and in particular I wish to thank Barry Simon for his generosity and Kelly Whiteduck, who was then director of the Documentation Centre.

Various local libraries and archives were of critical importance to my research. In this regard, I am indeed very grateful for the aid of the following individuals: Ricardo Forrester at the Archives of the Roman Catholic Archbishop, Port of Spain; Lirlyn Elliott and Mariella Pilgrim, at the West Indian Special Collection at the University of the West Indies in St. Augustine, Trinidad; Cheryl Cameron, librarian at the Securities and Exchange Commission Library, Port of Spain; and Denise Gonzalez, director of the Arima Public Library, and Beverly Williams of the Arima Public Library for their especially warm and cheerful assistance.

My wife, Allison Diaz, to whom this work is partly dedicated, has been of greatest help. I feel especially blessed to have her as my best friend and constant companion. While Allison worked at the Main Library of the University of the West Indies in St. Augustine during the period of my field research, she thus also helped directly with my library research.

Finally, I wish to warmly thank editorial and production staff members at the University Press of Florida for their extraordinary patience, dedication to detail, and wonderfully high standards of professionalism: Meredith Morris-Babb, Michele Fiyak-Burkley, Nick Eliopulos, David Graham, and Sally Bennett, an independent copy editor who did a fabulous job.

Abbreviations

ABC	Arima Borough Council
AFN	Assembly of First Nations of Canada
AMC	Assembly of Manitoba Chiefs
BWIA	British West Indian Airways
Caricom	Caribbean Community and Common Market
CDCC	Committee for the Development of the Carib Community (St. Vincent)
COIP	Caribbean Organisation of Indigenous People
CUFU	Communities United to Fight Underdevelopment
FSIN	Federation of Saskatchewan Indian Nations
HERBS	Herbal, Educational, Recreational, Biological Services
IBRD	International Bank for Reconstruction and Development (World Bank)
ILO	International Labour Organization
IMF	International Monetary Fund
JTTN	Jatibonicu Taino Tribal Nation of Boriken (Puerto Rico)
KTK	Kairi Tukuienyo Karinya
NAEAP	National Association for the Empowerment of African People
NAR	National Alliance for Reconstruction
NPATT	National Parang Association of Trinidad and Tobago
OAS	Organization of American States
PNM	People's National Movement
RC	Roman Catholic
SIFC	Saskatchewan Indian Federated College
SRCC	Santa Rosa Carib Community
TIDCO	Tourism and Industrial Development Corporation of Trinidad and Tobago
TTT	Trinidad and Tobago Television
UNC	United National Congress
UNCED	United Nations Conference on Environment and Development
UNDP	United Nations Development Program
UNEP	United Nations Environment Program
UNESCO	United Nations Educational, Scientific and Cultural Organization
URP	Unemployment Relief Program
UWI	University of the West Indies
WCIP	World Council of Indigenous Peoples
WIPO	World Intellectual Property Organization

Introduction

Reviving Caribs

Indigeneity in Trinidad and Tobago and the Dialectic of Aboriginal Presence and Absence

The first Amerindians disappeared hundreds of years ago and are no longer here. We are the descendants. We are not the same and we do not do the same things. Of course, we have some of the blood, but much has been lost. People must understand these things. Now with our associations and linkages with other groups, we hope to relearn our past traditions together. This is a learning experience for us.
Ricardo Bharath, president, Santa Rosa Carib Community, Arima, Trinidad (Friday, November 12, 1999)

Maori culture is not something that has been lost, it is the loss; being "a Maori" is struggling to be a Maori.
Steven Webster (1993:228)

I arrived at the Santa Rosa Carib Community Centre in Arima expecting to see it empty and quiet on this day. I had an appointment with Ricardo Bharath Hernandez, the president of the Carib Community, or the SRCC, as I will refer to it. He mentioned that we would be alone and have time to talk, after many attempted meetings that had to be called off because of Ricardo's intense schedule, given his work as an Arima borough councillor, his playing host to a delegation of Guyanese Amerindians, and his making cassava bread for sale. Instead of an empty building, what I found were four large groups of primary- and secondary-school students. SRCC members do not refer to this building as a shed; instead, they use a word that their Guyanese Amerindian visitors said is the correct Lokono/Arawak word, that is, a *benab*. Under the *benab*, four Guyanese Amerindian ladies, visiting with the SRCC on a four-week cultural exchange visit, were giving lessons and demonstrations of how to weave baskets using the *moriche* palm, one not commonly used for basketry in Trinidad in recent times. I had to venture inside the Carib Centre and witness the obvious, and audible, excitement for myself.

"Ricardo, you mind if I just stand at the side and look on?"

Ricardo replied, "Go right ahead, we're almost ready to start. . . . Sorry about the appointment; we only arranged this last night," and as he breezed past, he added, "We'll talk." An orderly group of about thirty-five girls below the age of ten, from the Arima Girls Government School, took their seats on the rows of benches facing the stage. Ricardo, looking like someone perfectly at ease in front of crowds, walked across the front row and said, "Good morning, everyone." Taking their seats, wearing crisp navy uniforms and holding little puffy white hand towels for wiping their foreheads, they softly replied, "Good morning, sir." Ricardo, hands joined at the fingertips, smiled—he impressed me as a friendly and welcoming teacher. He began right away: "I imagine many of you are from Arima, correct?" and most nodded. He then asked, "Well, as you are from Arima, or know about Arima, you must have heard of the Caribs, right?" Again, most nodded "yes." He then asked, "So if you know that there are Caribs here in Arima, what can you tell me about them?" The children smiled and wriggled on the benches—out of shyness, not for lacking knowledge, as it turned out. He then said, "Well, you have probably heard about the Santa Rosa Festival." They nodded again, and he continued, "So let me tell you a little about that. The Amerindians lived in a mission here in Arima, and were converted to Catholicism, so every year they celebrate this festival for their saint—Saint Rose—and as you see on this board, we also have a legend about her appearance. The Santa Rosa Festival is not an *Amerindian* thing as such, but we celebrate it because traditionally, it is said, it was up to the Caribs of the mission to prepare the decorations, the foods, and the festivities that followed. So we are still doing that, because it's what keeps us together as a community." Ricardo was following a script that had become familiar to me, reviewing the main traditions that he and others use to mark the identity of the Arima Caribs.

He turned to the subject of cassava. He asked, "How many of you know what cassava bread is?" Most of the children raised their hands. Then he asked, "So how many of you have eaten it?" Fewer hands went up. Ricardo then explained quickly how cassava bread was made. "O.K., you will see some cassava bread at the side here, and we have also prepared some cassava bread with coconut for you. The raw cassava, the root, looks nothing like that. It is big and rough; it has to be peeled, cleaned, and then grated. Traditionally we would use a grater like this one, which comes from Guyana, but we have not kept up this tradition, so instead we use modern steel graters."

He went on, "After the grating, we squeeze the cassava using this, what we call a *coulevre,* or what in some languages is called a *sebucán* or a *matapí*. Right, so it is suspended from the ceiling, and then a pole goes through the bottom and we weigh it down, so it stretches and contracts, and the juice runs out. You have to do this with poisonous cassava; it contains an acid, like cyanide. Then we sift the flour, and after that we bake it. This is one of our retained traditions, and we try to keep this alive, because anywhere you go, you will see this is an Amerindian thing."

Ricardo moved on, checking his watch, and he said he would tell them a little about the history of the Amerindians. "I don't know if you want to know about before Columbus, no?" Yet many of the girls nodded that, yes, they did. Ricardo briefly got a look on his face that suggested that was too much ground to cover. He talked about what Amerindians slept on, about how they hunted and fished, about their chiefs, and about how many different groups lived in Trinidad.

Ricardo then said, "We have a little time for a few questions." A forest of hands went up. One question was about what the Amerindians drank. Ricardo answered quickly: *paiwari* (made from cassava), *warap* (made from cane), and fruit juices. One asked about whether or not the thronelike wooden structure on the stage was "for carrying the cacique" (or chief), and Ricardo explained that it was for the statue of Santa Rosa. Another, also using the term "cacique," asked if the caciques really had thirty wives. Ricardo replied, "Well, no, I don't know anything about that. Of course—I hope he won't mind—but we have a scholar with us," and he looked at me, "who has probably studied this more in-depth, so you can ask him." Placed on the spot, I quickly interjected, "No, Ricardo, I have never come across that." Another girl asked, "Why were men scraped with human bones when they were made cacique?" Another, in the far corner, quietly asked, "Do Caribs still eat people?"

I didn't hear this last question. Ricardo pulled away with an amused look. Turning toward his Guyanese Amerindian guest, he said, "Hear the question that this one asked," and he repeated the question out loud. Ricardo turned and replied, "No, I don't know of them ever having eaten human flesh; people say this, but I don't know that to be true." Standing behind Ricardo was a blackboard. Ricardo, really rushing along now, announced, "Our brother from Guyana, who speaks the Lokono, or Arawak language, will teach you a few words." They learned the words for no, yes "ehei," boy "ichi," girl "ilonchi," and mother and father.

The children's schoolteacher, a tall and well-dressed woman, roughly late thirties in age, smiled throughout, seemingly proud of her pupils and enjoying the experience. Every now and again she would rise to photograph them. Afterwards, they filed through the new Carib Resource Centre, a series of displays of photographs and craftwork and a replica of a hut, made to look as if lived in, with a hammock draped between two of its posts. Later, the teacher told us on her own that she had not taught the girls all the things that they asked about, that they must have been learning all of this on their own, probably from the Internet, as many of them had computers at home. Ricardo was impressed, like me, that they even knew so much as to be able to ask those questions.

Here stood a representative of a minority presumed to be extinct by many social scientists, speaking of traditions said to have disappeared by other commentators, to a group of people that, in previous years of living in Trinidad, I had assumed would have little interest in indigenous issues. Ricardo was in fact standing at the interface between absence and presence: Caribs are framed within narratives that continually stress their impending disappearance, yet they constantly (even if not continuously) recur in wider social perceptions of the nation's

Amerindian legacy. Spokespersons such as Ricardo speak of the current revival of Caribbean Amerindian identities and retrieval of traditions against a backdrop of loss. Indeed, the central questions that I ask in this book are as follows: Why does "Carib" still exist as a category and as a legitimate identification in Trinidad? What were, and what are, the conditions that make possible the reproduction of the Carib idea? What value does Caribness hold, and to whom, when, and why?

In this introductory vignette the reader should see how brokers—intermediaries between the aboriginal past and the national present, between the current Carib Community and the wider society—play an active role in mediating and disseminating knowledge and awareness of Carib indigeneity in conjunction with interested institutions of the wider society, schools being one of the most important. These mediations of Carib indigeneity do not occur in a vacuum: they are mediated within a larger social and historical context where many actors, interests, and discourses are at work, even in contention, in framing the dialectic of Carib presence-absence. The modern mass media in Trinidad is another of these very important institutions involved in this process.

"The vanishing Caribs, yet surviving" or "the surviving Caribs, in the process of vanishing"—these are almost stock modes of narrating the Carib in the national media. "Carib customs are dying out" was the headline of a 1964 article by Peter Girwar in the *Evening News,* and it is worth reading one passage in full: "If the original Caribs were to come back to Arima they would be at a loss to know if their people still exist. Old customs are dying out and a new mode of life exists. Within a short while the last remaining relics of a tribe will be making preparations for the Santa Rosa Festival in Arima. . . . the Carib race is dying out and there are just a few families which bear the Carib name. . . . But despite the changing order, the Caribs live on." They are dying out, yet they live on; the world changes, yet they are the enduring "relics."

An editorial in the *Trinidad Guardian,* apparently from 1987 as it speaks of the death of Carib Queen Edith Martínez, was titled "Vanishing Caribs." Let us read some of the instructive words of the editor of the time: "The Caribs through centuries in this country have been dwindling, assimilated by other ethnic groups and if it were not for the ethnic pride of people like Mrs Martinez and the community's continuing links with Arima, every vestige of their existence here would have been lost. . . . It may be that to commemorate the Carib presence in Trinidad and Tobago we shall have to order official archivists to begin work early upon a definitive history of these aboriginal inhabitants of our country." The Santa Rosa Festival, according to the editor, is a "relic" or perhaps a "parochial social event." What seems to disturb the editor is the lack of documentation and thus the need for professional intervention: "it is doubtful that modern historians or anthropologists anywhere have continued to note or study their present day existence." Why is that? The answer speaks to Orlando Patterson's "absence of ruins" metaphor: "The reason for this may be the fact that they have left little to remember them by, no buildings, no imposing remnants of their heyday in the region." What to do about this absence, and the risk of losing awareness of the Carib presence? The answer is given by the editor: "Still, it may be left to us in Trinidad and Tobago to pay proper regard to the Caribs and to note their continuing, if vanishing, presence among us." Again, from a nationalist viewpoint, an article in the *Trinidad Express* (1982b) asserted, "The first people of this nation do have a relevant cultural contribution to make towards national development"—and here it is also important to note the use of the phrase "first people," a trope of both Trinidadian nationalist and indigenous internationalist modes of framing indigeneity.

If vanishing, the Caribs are also remaining, as suggested in an unsigned article, "Remains of the Caribs," in the *Sunday Guardian Magazine* for August 7, 1994. The writer quotes a member of the Carib Community: "'All real Caribs [are] dead,' says Judy [Julie] Calderon, an 80-year-old descendant of the Caribs. Calderon is not a full blooded Carib, but her father was." The relics are impure, now speaking to Trinidad's inherited colonial discourse of race and purity. Once again, the writer makes reference to the process of vanishing, which has been one of the standard tropes for framing Caribbean and Trinidadian indigeneity for at least the past two centuries: "The Carib Community in Arima is dwindling and the younger generations are reluctant to learn the traditions which their parents are struggling to preserve."

"No true Caribs left" is the headline of an article by Anna Walcott in the *Sunday Guardian* for December 12, 1992, where she labels Caribs "the first Creoles," speaking to a popular Trinidadian self-conception as a hodgepodge, multiethnic, and miscegenated society of locally rooted offspring of other continents. The pure Amerindian resides in the past, as implied by Walcott in quoting a local historian, Pat Elie, who makes a queer comment: "They remember they were once Amerindians." Walcott adds an important double-barreled argument that is also one of the dominant conventions for speaking of Trinidad's Amerindians: "There are no pure Amerindians left in Trinidad. But the stigma of being Amerindian during colonial times has been transformed into a patriotic need to establish the presence of a race that is quickly approaching extinction."

Patriotism, a national self-consciousness of the history of Trinidad not simply as a novel colonial creation but as a nation with ancient roots—this is what comes to the rescue of the Caribs as framed in these articles. Indeed, on the very eve of national independence in 1962, J. A. Bullbrook, a local archaeologist and author, wrote that it was necessary to go back to the island's aboriginal past to understand how Amerindian cultures are connected to the ideals of the present, to democracy and independence (1962:10, 12). It is not enough to wait for academic specialists to "save" the Caribs either: sometimes the very writers of these articles jump in and become actively involved themselves. One such journalist, Elma Reyes, became the SRCC's public relations and research officer for almost twenty years. In her March 21, 1981, article in the *Trinidad Express* headlined, "We are a forgotten people say Caribs," Reyes laid out all of the key practices marking Carib cultural survival: weaving using the *terite* reed and cassava bread, as examples. However, national rescue was an imperative, as "the Caribs are Trinidad's most ignored minority group"—and she called for a land grant to the Caribs. National rescue of a diminished group was also the concern of journalist John Kassie in his 1990 article titled "Focus on Our Surviving Caribs" in the *Trinidad Guardian*. The focus, he was happy to report, is slowly sharpening: "The Caribs' presence in Trinidad and Tobago took center stage last week with the observance of Amerindian Heritage Week at Arima." In terms that bring to my mind my introductory vignette, he added, "Hundreds of secondary and primary schools . . . were the target for the dissemination of historical information relating to the Caribs' ancestral linkages."

What we see from these examples is a divorced coupling of contending narratives: an absence of ruins, yet surviving relics in the flesh; forgetfulness, yet wider social interest and national commemoration; an alleged lack of interest, yet the active involvement of journalists and even politicians (Girwar 1964). We also see some dominant social conventions for framing indigeneity in terms of race and blood, ancestry and descent, purity and dilution. The political economic context is never far in the background, either: formerly, people of the SRCC received $70 TT annually from the Arima Borough Council (Girwar 1964)—today, they receive $5,000 TT annually from the same council, plus an annual subvention of $30,000 TT from the state. Lands are being scheduled for distribution to make up for the losses of the past and to save a "dying race." And in the midst of all of this is the active mediation of key brokers. So who are some of these brokers? Who are the Caribs of Trinidad, as presented by their primary representatives?

Representing the Caribs

Illustrative of the process whereby the society comes to know the Caribs through various mediated representations is the manner in which I first learned of them. My first knowledge and awareness of the Santa Rosa Carib Community of Arima came via Carifesta V in 1992,[1] pictures in state tourism brochures showing a procession of the Santa Rosa Festival headed by Ricardo Bharath, and newspaper articles on the SRCC's youth representative, Susan Campo, having won a scholarship to undertake Amerindian Studies at the Saskatchewan Indian Federated College in Canada. This was also the first way in which I was drawn into consideration of the dissemination and mediation of images of the SRCC, as well as state patronage for the group, and its international indigenous networking, all in one go.

What seems to stand out most about the SRCC (and perhaps this explains the particular slant of my own research, focused as it is on brokers) is the prominence and repeated appearance of key SRCC leaders in the national press and in public ceremonies. Rather than viewing an almost faceless mass of "indigenes," in Trinidad one quickly becomes familiar with the main actors who seem to dominate all circulated images of the SRCC. The three leading cultural brokers that are members of the SRCC are President Ricardo Bharath, Cristo Atékosang Adonis (using the title of shaman), and the Queen (Justa Werges during my 1998–1999 fieldwork period). I was thus attracted to this medley of representational facets, from the matriarchal authority of the Queen, to the modern corporate president, to an almost New Age spiritual-revivalist indigeneity: a politician, a singer and ecotour guide, and a grandmother—all acting in the name of tradition yet rarely in agreement on what that tradition is.

Ricardo Bharath, as I mentioned, is the president of the SRCC. While his father, who passed away when he was still very young, was East Indian as well as of Vincentian Carib ancestry, Ricardo has adopted his mother's maiden name, Hernandez, as a way of foregrounding a matrilineal Amerindian heritage that embeds him within a local clan of Carib-descended families. It may not be obvious, given that the surname is Spanish, but in Trinidad people of Amerindian ancestry frequently married individuals of Spanish ancestry or adopted Spanish names in the colonial mission context, so that a Spanish surname sometimes can indirectly act as a referent to this Amerindian past. Within the SRCC Ricardo acts as the central cultural broker (see Bharath 1995), since a significant part of the contemporary resurgence of the SRCC stems from his initiatives in reorganizing the group. A basic overview of his story is necessary for tracing the development of the SRCC, as he has led it for over a quarter of a century.

Ricardo's active involvement began when he was about nineteen years old, around 1973, after he returned from Detroit, Michigan, where he received his secondary schooling. Ricardo describes having been distressed on visits home from school by seeing how Arima's Santa Rosa Festival had declined, in terms of preparation and participation: "as a child, six, seven, eight years [old], I remember how bright and beautiful the festival [was]. That is how it [his interest in revitalization] started, . . . mainly concerned about that festival." He immediately adds, "The tradition as I knew it as a child was going to nothing, really nothing. . . . That is how it started, *not having any knowledge at that time* about Amerindian, Carib or Arawak, or the history of the people, or who was here 'first' or 'last' or whatever it is, but mainly concerned about that festival" (Bharath 1995, emphasis added). He was dismayed by the general state of disrepair and decline that the Santa Rosa Festival had suffered, especially its lack of "pomp and importance" (see also Almarales 1994:23). He called upon the Carib Queen and elderly members and said to them, "Let us do something. Let us form a group, a community so that we can preserve these things." Thus the current SRCC is, at the very least, a reformulated body, even if not an altogether new one.

Originally, as Ricardo explained, he considered entering the priesthood with the hope of becoming the parish priest of Arima. He lost interest, by his own admission, when he was informed that it was unlikely that he would be assigned anywhere permanently, let alone Arima itself.

Ricardo explains repeatedly and even emphatically (see also Almarales 1994) that when he began his career in Arima, it was never with the intention of leading an Amerindian revival. This forms one of the most dominant themes of his discussions of the Carib Community's development. I was drawn to this point since it seemed to indicate the possibility of Ricardo himself having his actions and outlooks reworked, reframed, and reinterpreted by the larger social and cultural contexts in which he found himself.

Ricardo's experience abroad, and his eventual reading of published materials about or inspired by the Caribs, played a role in shaping his interest in, and vision of, the SRCC. Ricardo told Beryl Almarales (1994:23), as he told me, that while he lived in the United States he was impressed by televised documentaries on American Indian festivals. Ricardo has also explained repeatedly to me and to others (Almarales 1994:23) that he was inspired to "restore the traditions and community spirit of my people" after reading F. E. M. Hosein's play, *Hyarima and the Saints*. Indeed, to some extent Ricardo plays an almost messianic role in the community, in part inspired by this work. As he stated in an early interview in 1995, "Well why me? Why am I in this? I am just doing it because I like doing it, I feel I need to do it. And then reading, reading history, . . . I saw that the last chief Hyarima said that . . . the remnants of his people that are scattered far and wide will in the end come back again, and that sounded so mysterious. So I said: 'Well probably what I am doing I have to do. I am motivated by some other force to do,' and I just go day to day with that." Ricardo says that he soon became interested in discovering how much of Arima's history was owing to the Carib presence, and he became interested in researching and then publicizing what he calls the "Amerindian contribution to the national foundation" and the Carib role in the Santa Rosa Festival.

The need for leadership, for someone to form a committee and rebuild a community, for representation to government ministries, for someone with valuable connections—for a broker—is a need that Ricardo sought to satisfy. The need for a new leader was also mandated by a prior breakdown of community gatherings arising from serious personal conflicts and by the fact, as Ricardo states it, that SRCC members were "so calm and docile" and did not push their claims. In becoming "better connected" with key local and national institutions, Ricardo ran for the People's National Movement (PNM), one of Trinidad's two main parties and long its governing party, and he became an Arima borough councillor on four consecutive occasions spanning 1993–2003. In 2003 he was appointed deputy mayor of Arima.

Most of those who have observed and participated in the life of the SRCC (over more years than I have) agree that prior to Ricardo, revival was never seen as a course of action (Almarales 1994:34). Ricardo has invested considerable labor in elevating what he sees as the hallmark tradition of the Arima Caribs— the Santa Rosa Festival—to something worthy of national notoriety. Nevertheless, even while claiming the festival as his special area of expertise, Ricardo has made an effort to include diverse interests in the development of the SRCC:

"everyone has their area of expertise. . . . someone might do or know something that I cannot do or do not know—likewise I can do or know something that they don't." Ricardo emphasizes that, above all else, "recognition is the key: with recognition everything else will work out."

For much of the 1990s, Cristo Atékosang Adonis was the unofficial number two man of the SRCC; Ricardo once referred to him as the vice-president. Cristo Adonis was a police constable in the early 1980s and then worked as a transport officer, an estate supervisor, and a construction foreman under the Labor Intensive Development Program and under its successor, the Unemployment Relief Program, as well as working as a nature tour guide for Paria Springs Eco Community and Rooks Nature Tours. Cristo—whom friends and family alternately refer to as Adonis or call him by his family nickname, Glen—described himself as the "ambassador at large" for the SRCC, alluding to the wide range of contacts and institutions with which he works and within which he promotes the SRCC.

Cristo embodies several tendencies all at once: panindigenous internationalism; shamanic practices; environmentalism and ecotourism; the relearning of Carib traditions from published ethnographic materials relating to contemporary Amerindians in South America and the Caribbean; and *parang* music. Like Ricardo, he maintains an active presence in the local campaigns of the People's National Movement (see also Forte 1999f). In some respects, his cultural practice and position within the Carib Community echoes that of Ricardo, while he extends himself with greater determination into the realm of what Ricardo calls "the recovery of ancient ways." Descriptions and representations of Cristo by various institutions tend to magnify these key themes of his cultural practice. A delegation from the United Nations' World Intellectual Property Organization described him as a "shaman within his community," adding that "he acts as his peoples' [sic] spiritual and medicinal healer and counselor." The WIPO representatives further added, reflecting Cristo's representational interests, that "he spoke about the need to safeguard the plants and other resources he views as indispensable for his work by protecting the environment. He referred also to the strong spiritual element of traditional healing in his community."[2] Cristo tends to eschew the value of the Santa Rosa Festival as emblematic of Carib indigeneity, stressing that, given its colonial origins and Catholic nature, it is "not indigenous enough."

Cristo also constructed what he sometimes called the "alternate Carib Centre" outside his home on Calvary Hill, Arima, the construction completed at roughly the same time as the current concrete SRCC Centre, circa 1996. This structure, referred to as an *ajoupa* before the recent adoption of the Guyanese Lokono name of *benab,* is quite important in the brokering process. It serves as a meeting place for the brokers who are also members of Katayana (a revivalist group). Journalists have regularly interviewed Cristo in his *ajoupa/benab.* Groups of schoolchildren are brought there when he is asked to lecture pupils on Trinidad's Amerindian heritage. Foreign visitors, researchers, and tourists on their way to the nearby Asa Wright Nature Centre also regularly stop there. It was also the home of his *parang* band, where practices and rehearsals were conducted. The ceiling of the *ajoupa* is decorated with stretched skins of deer that he hunted; small plaques of native wild animals decorate each post; carved calabashes and maracas that Cristo makes are on display; an "altar" with a platted palm backing and an earthen tabletop is also evident, flanked by spears, and featuring small bottles of herbal remedies, Taíno *zemis,* beaded necklaces, maracas, a feathered headdress, crystals, shells, seeds, and stones; and the rafters have dream catchers and medicine wheels hanging from them. At times as many as three hammocks are slung between the posts. All of these serve as a bold depiction of signs and symbols of indigeneity as conceived from within a modern context.

Prior to the return of Ricardo and the institution of a presidency, which came with formal incorporation as a limited liability company in 1976, the Queen was the sole authority over the Carib Community, and even then only during the period of preparations for the Santa Rosa Festival. Yet, despite what may seem in hindsight as a relatively minor degree of formalization prior to 1976, the Queen, like Ricardo, still served as a primary gatekeeper and broker with officialdom. I was told by key spokespersons of the SRCC today that historically the Queen was elected for her knowledge of Carib traditions, for her ability to pass on that knowledge and offer training in weaving skills among other things, and for her ability to deal with the public, receive visitors, and maintain a high standard of protocol on public occasions. With reference to Queen "Dolly" Martínez (sister to Edith, who reigned for a brief period), Elma Reyes, the SRCC's late research officer, explained to me that she was selected for the position since "her father was a white man, and she was 'fair.' . . . She was beautiful. . . . She could eat with a knife and fork, she could set a table in the European style, and she could deal with outsiders and foreigners." The recently deceased Queen Justa Werges was one of my primary informants on the subject of the rights and responsibilities of Queens. Justa Werges, with her patrician character and stately ways, was able to impress key SRCC patrons, such as former prime ministers, mayors, priests, bishops, and members of the press. In addition, her weaving skills have been held in generally very high regard.

While the president, shaman, and Queen are perhaps the three pillars representing the SRCC, there are of course issues, questions, and problems faced by the SRCC as a unit, as well as a history that the SRCC as a body either draws upon or has been shaped by. These individuals do not have the luxury of shaping their representations of Carib indigeneity within a vacuum, nor do they have the freedom to simply claim a history that has in fact been contested, controlled, and constrained by an all too wide array of institutions and actors over the centuries. Before we move on to some of the wider contexts and settings, over and above (yet containing) the individuals and particular events discussed thus far, let me first provide an introductory outline of the body called the Santa Rosa Carib Community.

The Carib Community in Focus

A Very Brief History of the Caribs

Amerindian peoples have existed in Trinidad for as long as six thousand years before the arrival of Columbus, making that island the oldest site of human settlement in the Caribbean; they numbered at least forty thousand at the time of Spanish settlement in 1592 (Boomert 1982; Newson 1976). They formed part of large regional island-to-island and island-to-mainland trading networks. The population consisted of almost a dozen different tribal groupings, many from the nearby mainland (Bordo 1976). With colonial occupation, and the differential legal rights and statuses accorded by the Spanish to Caribs (targeted for slavery) and Arawaks (singled out as allies), the plethora of labels for naming the Amerindians was gradually reduced to these two generic labels. In the 1600s the first Catholic missions were established, in an effort to "reduce" and "pacify" those tribes that remained in the island. In 1699 Amerindians at the Mission of San Francisco de los Arenales staged an uprising, eliminating key public figures including the Spanish governor, in what is now popularly referred to as Trinidad's first rebellion in the name of freedom. In the mid 1700s and again more permanently in 1785, the mission of Arima was formed. A number of tribes were pressed into Arima, which was the last mission in Trinidad. The Caribs in Arima had converted to Catholicism and were eventually represented by a titular Queen of the Caribs, responsible for overseeing communal preparations for the annual Santa Rosa Festival, a Catholic feast day that continues to play a special role in bringing together Arima's Amerindian descendants.

The advent of national independence from Britain ushered in nationalist reinterpretations of local history, including a revalorization of the history of the Caribs as most heroic for having fought colonialism. By the 1970s, return migrants from the United States, such as Ricardo Bharath, led the remnants of the Arima Carib Community through a process of revival and organizational formalization, initially centered on the Santa Rosa Festival as a key marker of the communal boundaries of the Arima Caribs.

Organization and Goals

The SRCC is an inwardly kin-based and outwardly formal organization that was incorporated as a limited liability company in 1976 in order to receive state lands. In that year, with the guidance and support of the Ministry of Culture, Joseph Pantor (a prominent attorney), and Andrew Carr (a local folklorist), the group was formally registered as The Santa Rosa Carib Community Company Limited. Elma Reyes often exclaimed, "This must be the only ethnic group in the world that is organized as a company." Ricardo explained that this option was imposed on him. This degree of formalization attracted my attention, as it represented another front on which the organization of the SRCC is reengineered by dominant social institutions.

The group's immediate needs, as spelled out in SRCC documents, are (1) "recognition by society and government as a legitimate cultural sector"; (2) "research to clarify their cultural traditions and the issue of their lands"; and (3) "support from appropriate institutions in their perceived need areas" (Reyes n.d.e). The working relationship that the SRCC has been able to establish with journalists and researchers has been critical to SRCC brokers' efforts at gaining historical material needed for representing Carib history.

One of the SRCC's primary aims over the past twenty-five years has been to acquire a land grant to build an Amerindian village. At one time this was to be called the "First Nations Botanical Park" and was meant to serve as a "cultural tourism facility" targeted especially at foreigners and as an "educational tourism facility" to educate nationals and visitors (Reyes 1995). The function of this re-created village is, in the view of leaders such as Ricardo, to provide a common residential space, combined with a jointly held economic base, for a continuous period of time, in order "to truly live as a community," to transform the current part-time practice of traditions into a more regular activity. For now, the SRCC's primary space as an organized body is that of the community center, built on land donated by the Roman Catholic Church.

Caribs and the State

The particular cultural politics of the SRCC are explicitly not of a segregationist sort; SRCC leaders do not engage in an overt critique of the postcolonial nation-state. Ricardo once exclaimed, when I asked him if the proposed re-created village might serve as a reservation, "It makes my blood boil that anyone should think we want to be separate and apart from everyone else." Indeed, SRCC leaders even refused to join in protests against the celebration of the five-hundredth anniversary of Columbus' landfall in Trinidad. The SRCC has never engaged in any public protests or demonstrations. One must remember that the SRCC is closely tied to the state (through funding arrangements and through Ricardo, who works in local government), the Catholic Church, the PNM, and various powerful interests. In this vein, Elma Reyes (1978) referred to the SRCC as being "on the peace path," adding, "the Caribs of the 20th Century no longer follow the ways of their ancestors, and they say their solution is not to attack with poison-tipped arrows and spears, but by the establishment of a representative body, through which they hope to acquire alternate lands." The leaders and members of the SRCC also struck me as keenly nationalistic and patriotic, and as some examples of this I recall their engaging in earnest discussions of how the national flag is to be held and raised, and how one should comport oneself during the singing of the national anthem. The largest number of members adopt "Trinidadian" as the self-descriptive label of choice, above "mixed," "Spanish," or "Carib," which are the other contending labels.

The SRCC has been relatively successful in gaining recognition and support from a variety of institutions. Most prominent among these have been the state and its constituent agencies and enterprises, the Arima Borough Council (ABC), the People's National Movement, the local media, and prominent individuals and small private foundations. In 1990 the government of A. N. R. Robinson, of the ruling National Alliance for Reconstruction (NAR), officially recognized the SRCC as "representative of the indigenous Amerindians" of Trinidad and Tobago and initiated an annual award of $30,000 TT. The ABC funds the SRCC with an annual subvention of $3,000 TT. When added together over the years, total state funding for the SRCC approaches $1 million TT. The SRCC as a group and some of its key members have also won numerous state awards over the last decade for cultural and community service. In 2000, Prime Minister Basdeo Panday of the ruling United National Congress (UNC) promised lands to the group, awarded over $150,000 TT for an international indigenous gathering, and proclaimed October 14 to be henceforth an annual "National Day of Recognition of Trinidad's Indigenous Peoples." The state has also been instrumental in funding the SRCC's international networking with other aboriginal bodies, evidenced by the provision of $250,000 TT in 1992 when the SRCC hosted indigenous delegates from across the Caribbean Basin, and by another $350,000 TT in 2000 for two gatherings, not to mention funds and labor for the construction of the SRCC Centre and its attached Resource Centre. Private companies, such as Carib Brewery, also sponsor the Carib Community, a fact that is not without a certain irony, considering that for the longest time the company's slogan was "In this country, a beer is Carib." With the upsurge in attention to the Caribs, and growing generalized pride in Carib ancestry by many Trinidadians not ostensibly connected to Arima, even the brewery has begun to use alternate slogans, such as "In this country, everybody has some Carib in them."

Caribs and Tradition

Among the goals of the SRCC, where traditions are concerned, maintenance and revival are the two most important objectives, in the words of its key brokers. The SRCC's practice of tradition is defined in the following terms, as set out in one of its publicly disseminated documents (Campo 1993):

> What the Santa Rosa Carib Community stands for: (a) To retain, publicize, and promote, in a respectful manner the tradition maintained by the Carib people of Arima, in honoring their patroness Santa Rosa de Lima, with

emphasis on the observance of the annual celebration founded through a mystical experience of their ancestors. (b) The establishment of agro-industries utilizing Cassava and other food-crop [*sic*] to be grown by co-operative effort on a commercial scale by members of the Carib tribe of Arima. (c) The establishment of a Cultural Centre to allow educational, recreational, and vocational training facilities; the setting up of archives, museum, and other relevant services designed to promote awareness and appreciation for the culture, history and traditions of the Carib people of Trinidad and Tobago. (d) The revival and practice of traditional handi-craft, utilizing natural, indigenous material and following the customs of the Carib people in Trinidad and Tobago. (e) To promote and develop in other relevant and positive ways the welfare of the Carib People of Trini-dad and Tobago, and the doing of all things that are incidental or conduc-tive [*sic*] to the attainment of the above.

In addition to these aims, the SRCC set out a practical agenda for its promo-tion of Carib tradition. In a "Proposal for a Centre for Amerindian Studies," the Research Unit of the Santa Rosa Carib Community (1998c) stated the main objectives as follows: "To retain, and when necessary revive, the survival [of] cultural systems which were evolved by the indigenous people of Trinidad and Tobago, for practical application in the late 20th and into the 21st century. To allow also, areas of job creation and career development, within the Santa Rosa Carib Community, and the wider society, through such activity."

This statement is an example of an instrumentalist facet of SRCC practice with respect to tradition, drawing my attention to the fact that remuneration is an important factor in the development of their various projects, even if not an absolute one. As Elma Reyes (1995) argued, the SRCC was "discriminated against," scorned, and ridiculed, because the Caribs "are at the bottom of the economic ladder," a situation that they seek to remedy. The need for money, Ricardo explained, is also important for building self-confidence and for increas-ing the appeal of the plans of the SRCC's leadership among potential members at the outer edge of the SRCC—as Ricardo stated, money "would be . . . a great support to whatever you want to do because you would be able to start putting the infrastructure [together]. The people will say: 'Well yes! Something is happen-ing! This is looking good'" (Bharath 1995). Ricardo observed that with increased funding, official recognition, and media coverage of the SRCC, more individuals are showing an interest in the group: "in the last few years, with the publicity, with the Community [be]coming a little more outright, and [our] people getting support from different areas, people are hearing with the printed media and other forms of communication to the wider society, people are learning more about the Community, that it exists, and you would find people coming now and saying: 'Hey, my grandmother, my grandfather or my father are Carib, and I'm part Carib or Arawak,' or as the case may be, and they [are] expressing interest"

(Bharath 1995). As instrumental as acquiring a sturdier financial base may seem, clearly it is an aim also designed to facilitate greater affective unity and interest.

The main "retained traditions" to be preserved come under the headings of food, house building, handicrafts, and the Santa Rosa Festival, as well as "traditional" or "bush" medicine to some extent. Traditions to be revived include the Carib language and weaving using a variety of local palms that had not been used in their current weaving. The SRCC is also intent on symbolically reclaiming certain traditions: *parang* music (or "*parranda*," a religious Spanish folkloric musical form that sweeps Trinidad for two months each year during Christmastime), the conventional "Red Indian" figures that appeared in Carnival parades, and other festival art forms.

The Santa Rosa Festival, which runs during the last week of each August, is considered of prime importance to SRCC brokers such as Ricardo, and it serves as the regular public announcement of "the Caribs' identity as a community" (Bharath 1995). The preparations for the festival, as Ricardo notes, are entirely in the hands of the SRCC, and "this keeps the community together" insofar as it is a collective production.

Revival, as SRCC leaders use the term, can blend in with their concept of retrieval, which entails instituting traditions learned from historical and ethnographic texts or reacquiring from elsewhere in the Caribbean and South America those traditions practiced in contemporary indigenous communities. The process of reacquisition entails what they call "cultural interchange" between themselves and these other communities.

Labels and Self-Identification

Not all Trinidadians who identify themselves as Carib or of Carib descent are members of the SRCC, nor does the SRCC represent all people of Carib descent outside of Arima. The Caribbean Organisation of Indigenous People claimed that there were two thousand "Amerindians" in Trinidad (*Caricom Perspective* 1991a:11). Peter Harris (1989b), a British archaeologist who worked with the SRCC, estimated that there are as many as twelve thousand people of Amerindian descent in northeastern Trinidad.[3] For its part, the SRCC formally determines membership in three ways: (1) what SRCC leaders term "recognizable surnames" (invariably Spanish) of "related families known to be of Carib descent"; (2) some history of residence in Arima, especially Calvary Hill; and (3) long-standing participation in the preparations for the Santa Rosa Festival.[4]

Identification as Carib is a problem that SRCC brokers such as Ricardo have had to grapple with. Among Trinidadians, it can be difficult to physically distinguish all members of the SRCC as being distinct. Ricardo, speaking of the intense miscegenation of the SRCC member families, notes that those individuals who have condemned them have done so "on the basis of purity," calling into question their Amerindian ancestry, but, he adds, it has been rare for them not to be accepted as Carib.

The label "Carib"—and how and why it is used—is an important issue for the key brokers of the SRCC, as both a resource and a constraint. On the one hand, brokers such as Ricardo say that as far as he knows the people who form the SRCC were "always referred to as the Santa Rosa Carib Community, referring to the people as descended from the Carib tribe." On the other hand, spokespersons such as Ricardo and Elma have stated that the descendants have different tribal origins, using the terms "Carib" and "Arawak." There is "mixture," but "because the people were referred to as the Caribs—the Santa Rosa Carib Community—the name remains, and when an outsider hears it, they would look at the people as direct descendants from the Carib tribe" (Bharath 1993). "First Nations" is a designation that SRCC brokers have adopted in recent years, arguing that this is the correct international designation and is endorsed by the United Nations. Given that the membership is the product of miscegenation and that the use of the Carib label is not fixed, Ricardo explains that which SRCC brokers instead do "hold fast to": "We know that our parents or foreparents on either side . . . came from that race, that Amerindian race who had certain traditions, who you know believed in certain things, . . . did certain things, and that was passed down, to a certain extent, to the generation today." The emphasis is on descent and especially the inheritance of traditional practices.

Yet Ricardo does not emphasize continuity, as he will repeat, "we've lost the language, the religion, and a lot of the traditions," even describing the Caribs as a group that is extinct or facing imminent extinction, in part due to their patterns of interethnic marital miscegenation. Phenotypical notions of race continue to be important in Trinidadian ways of assigning individuals to ethnic categories. In the case of the Caribs, perhaps the most widely repeated and longest held assumption in the wider society was that the only real Caribs are the pure Caribs, and the only pure Caribs are the dead Caribs. Bolstering one's identity as "an accredited incumbent of the relevant status" (Goffman 1990 [1959]:66) has been a challenge for SRCC representatives. Since race is not available as a clear marker of Carib identity, at least not given the dominant Trinidadian social conventions, brokers such as Ricardo turn to tradition. Since many of the traditions have been lost, as Ricardo says, revival becomes necessary. Instruments of official recognition of the SRCC as representative of Trinidad's Amerindians are also utilized by SRCC brokers to shore up the legitimacy of their identity.

Membership in the Carib Community

Determining the number of members of the SRCC is not an altogether straightforward task. Some of those whom the SRCC leaders refer to as members may appear only once or twice every couple of years, while others regularly attend meetings and functions. In 1976, Ricardo indicated that there were seven members of the SRCC executive and two hundred general members.[5] In 1995, Ricardo stated to the media that the SRCC numbered seventy-five registered members (*Sunday Express* 1995). Almarales (1994) spoke of forty active members divided into the following units: Research and Education, Building and Housing, Environmental Planning, Handicraft, and Food. This organizational definition also reflects the degree of formalization of the group and the way it mirrors the organization of the state bureaucracy. These units existed in a much more irregular fashion during the period of my fieldwork. Almarales (1994) also stated that the SRCC executive consisted of the Queen, president, secretary, youth officer, and public relations officer. During my fieldwork, regular members of the executive numbered three, with two occasional participants in addition, and one estranged member (the Queen).[6] Among the general membership that I saw regularly, the number fluctuated between fourteen and thirty-one, depending on the occasion. However, there may be an additional two hundred to five hundred individuals in the Arima area with whom Ricardo maintains contact and upon whom he can call for assistance and participation in various functions. In the three Santa Rosa festivals in which I took part (1998, 1999, 2002), I would see countless new faces of members I had never seen before.

The issue of numerical size is important, within limits. On the one hand, that such a relatively small body should garner the attention, recognition, and support that it has speaks to the power of "Carib" in Trinidad, that is, the symbolic value of indigeneity and the interest in Amerindian history and heritage generated in important circles beyond the SRCC, an observation that served to generate further interest on my part for the purposes of this research project. On the other hand, the small and diminishing size of the SRCC works to constrain any tendency toward a radical politics of opposition. Lastly, the diminishing membership affects the practical construction of practices that SRCC brokers identify as traditional (for example, the processing of cassava was to be mechanized, the group of ladies to be replaced by a mechanical grater). Some members jokingly called this the creation of "RoboCarib," another referring to the process as the downsizing of the SRCC, a result that they saw as the combination of an aging membership, defection to other faiths, and youth disinterest.

In a six-week survey that I conducted among thirty-one members of the SRCC in late 1998, I found that 48 percent of members use "Carib" as an autodenomination only if the term is preceded by a qualifying label such as "Trinidadian," "Spanish," or "mixed." Of this group, most prefer "Spanish Trinidadian" as an everyday mode of identifying themselves. Only 6 percent use "Carib" alone. At least 42 percent of the members are women over the age of forty, and many of those are over the age of sixty; overall, males constitute 29 percent of the membership. Over 90 percent of the members interviewed define themselves as earning insufficient income to meet all living expenses and debt obligations, and more than 75 percent indicate that they depend on allotments of temporary work under the Unemployment Relief Program. By most definitions, the majority of

SRCC members would qualify as working class, working poor, and even lumpen-proletarian. The overwhelming majority of members are related by blood or marriage, deriving for the most part from two main intermarried families: Hernandez and Calderon.

Apart from the internal limitations on the growth of the SRCC, there has been an increased, genuine interest from individuals and institutions in the wider society, with increasing numbers of individuals identifying themselves as being of Carib descent. This fact alone—which I have been able to corroborate independently and to a significant extent (especially via the written feedback from diasporic Trinidadian visitors to Carib websites, and from personal encounters)—ensures, I believe, that regardless of what may happen to the SRCC, there will be some foundation for continued attention to "the Carib" well into the future.

Expansion of Carib Cultural Practice

The global frame is one of great importance for many facets of the SRCC. The SRCC has developed relations with foreign and international indigenous organizations. The SRCC has been recognized and aided in different ways by Amerindian groups in Dominica and Guyana as well as Canada's Assembly of First Nations, the Assembly of Manitoba Chiefs, and the Federation of Saskatchewan Indian Nations. Links with Amerindian communities in Dominica, Suriname, and Guyana, in terms of educational exchange visits, are something the SRCC has maintained in the wake of Carifesta V in 1992, which brought several indigenous communities to Arima to share their cultural forms. Ricardo points out that the revival of Carib culture and identity takes place on a regional basis, as a relationship between the various communities. While not trying to reproduce North American Indian reservations, some SRCC members have broadened their knowledge of such communities, often through personal visits.

The Carib Community in Context

Trinidad—the southernmost island of the Caribbean archipelago—was, according to archaeologists, the first site of human settlement in the Caribbean, dating back over 7,200 years. The island of Trinidad, at the center of this study, covers a land area of 1,864 square miles, and the overall population of the twin-island Republic of Trinidad and Tobago numbered almost 1.3 million in 1997 (ECLAC 1999; UNDP 2001a). Port of Spain, the nation's capital and main port, is located on the northwest coast of Trinidad. San Fernando, the country's industrial capital, is situated in the south of Trinidad.[7]

Christopher Columbus named Trinidad after the Holy Trinity as he made landfall at the end of July in 1498. Other adventurers of fame to land in Trinidad were Amerigo Vespucci, Sir Walter Ralegh, Sir Robert Dudley, and Sir Lawrence Keymis. It was not until 1592 that Spanish settlement of Trinidad began. In 1797 the British seized Trinidad from the Spanish. Trinidad was thus subsequently ruled by the British, with Spanish laws in place (given the terms of the Spanish cession of 1802), and the majority of the population soon spoke French and French patois because of the waves of French Caribbean immigrants that started arriving in the late 1780s. With the emancipation of slaves in 1834–1838, migrant laborers were imported from Madeira, China, and especially India until the end of indenture in 1917, with additional numbers of Syrian-Lebanese and Palestinians arriving as well. Voluntary migrants from Africa, Caribbean islands, and Venezuela also arrived in increasing numbers throughout the 1800s. In 1946 universal adult suffrage was instituted, and the colony achieved internal self-governance in 1958. Arima, however, gained internal self-rule well before any other part of the Commonwealth Caribbean, in 1888. In 1958 Trinidad and Tobago joined the West Indies Federation, which it later abandoned, opting for full independence in 1962. The country became a republic in 1976.

Trinidad and Tobago is usually ranked as one of the more developed countries of the Caribbean, with Trinidad producing petroleum, natural gas, and chemical and manufactured exports while Tobago's economy is centered on agriculture and tourism. During the oil boom of 1973–1982, Trinidad and Tobago became one of the wealthiest countries in the Americas. Revenues from petroleum exports enabled the state to undertake rapid industrial growth, particularly via the nationalization of over eighty enterprises. At one point, the state was the country's largest employer. From especially 1988 to 1994, Trinidad and Tobago suffered a serious economic crisis and was forced to undergo internationally supervised "structural adjustment" programs organized by the International Monetary Fund and the World Bank. Neoliberal economic policies in the form of extensive trade and investment liberalization, divestment of state enterprises, an emphasis on export-led growth, cutbacks in social expenditures, and the floating of the exchange rate were instituted. Between 1994 and 1998, the country experienced steady growth in gross domestic product (GDP) of between 3 and 4 percent, while unemployment had fallen from 19.8 percent in 1993 to 14.2 percent in 1998 (ECLAC 1999). The country is undergoing another boom at present (1999–2001), being the highest recipient of U.S. foreign direct investment in the Western Hemisphere after Canada. Of a workforce numbering 521,000 people, 61 percent are employed in trade and services, 13 percent in construction, 11 percent in manufacturing, 9 percent in agriculture, and 4 percent in oil and gas (USDoS 1998).

According to the World Bank, 74 percent of the population is urban (IBRD 2000). Statistical breakdowns of the multiethnic population show 39.5 percent as African, 40.3 percent as East Indian, 18.4 percent as mixed, 0.6 percent as European, and 1 percent as other (USDoS 1998). This is also a multidenominational population, with 29.4 percent being Roman Catholic, 10.9 percent Anglican, 3.4 percent Presbyterian, 23.8 percent Hindu, 5.8 percent Muslim, and 26.7 percent listed as other (USDoS 1998).[8]

The politics of national unity versus ethnic segmentation have marked Trinidadian party politics over the past forty years. Organized politics in Trinidad and Tobago have usually been run along the lines of ethnicity, with Afro-Trinidadians mostly supporting the People's National Movement and Indo-Trinidadians supporting the United National Congress or its predecessors. In power, most parties have sought to cast themselves as national (as symbolized in the parties' names). The oldest party in Trinidad is the PNM, founded and led by Dr. Eric E. Williams from 1956 until his death in 1981 (the party ruling again during the periods 1981–1986, 1991–1995, and December 2001 until the present). In 1970 the country experienced a wave of protests and an army mutiny that have come to be known as the Black Power Revolution. Despite the name, the thrust of the protests was working-class oriented, seeking unity between Trinidadians of African and East Indian descent, and was strongly nationalistic and anti-imperialist. In 1986, the National Alliance for Reconstruction wed disaffected elements of the PNM and the major Indo-Trinidadian politicians in an alliance touted as a Rainbow party of "One Love." The NAR defeated the PNM in a landslide, promising the end of ethnic politics. While the outcomes were complex and contradictory, another organization challenged the established political order in the most forceful manner, with an armed rebellion in July of 1990. The Jama'at al Muslimeen—sometimes incorrectly designated as "Black Muslims" or misinterpreted as "black nationalists"—challenged what they saw as government corruption, illegitimacy, and alleged involvement in aiding drug cartels, though some argued that a land dispute with the state was at the root of its attempted coup. The group itself, similar to the government, combined members of both African and East Indian descent (see Forte 1996a). (Coincidentally, the Muslimeen were the first group that I researched in Trinidad.)

The decline in expenditures on education has resulted in a situation where "a large number of students now graduate without basic cognitive and numerical skills," according to the World Bank.[9] Figures of the World Bank nonetheless show a literacy rate of 98 percent, and they also show that for every 1,000 members of the population, there are 135 copies of daily newspapers circulated, 19.2 personal computers, 3.24 Internet hosts, and 318 televisions.[10] Radio, television, and newspapers, in that order, are thus the dominant means for disseminating news and images.

Arima, Trinidad's third largest urban area, is conventionally hailed as "the home of the Caribs" in the writings of Trinidadian authors (for example, Anthony 1988:2). Other writers note that up to the 1930s, most homes in Arima were constructed using Amerindian techniques and styles, and Amerindian utensils were common in homes (see Garcia 1991:50–51). Arima was established as a mission village in 1749 and again in 1784–85 (Wise 1938a:40). This was done to house Amerindian agriculturalists whose lands were earmarked for the new sugar estates to be founded by French Caribbean planters and their slaves, who were invited to settle in Trinidad by a 1783 decree. By a royal charter of 1888, Arima became a borough, entitling it to a certain degree of self-governance, with its own legislative body, its own budget, and its own tax base, anticipating internal self-governance at the colonywide level by sixty-eight years. Arima also once had its own bus company and its own waterworks (Garcia 1991:46–47), further enhancing its apparent self-containment within the colony.

Arima has undergone a series of population expansions since the demise of the mission in the 1840s, starting with large influxes of immigrants from Venezuela, voluntary immigrants from Africa and the West Indies, and indentured East Indians. During the Second World War, U.S. Army and Army Air Forces bases at Cumuto and Wallerfield, adjacent to Arima, were opened in 1941 and attracted people from across Trinidad and neighboring Caribbean islands (Garcia 1991: 34). The remaining sugar and cocoa estates required imported labor, since their "laborers left them in droves" (Garcia 1991:34). Large numbers of immigrants from St. Vincent, Grenada, and Barbados occupied different areas of Arima (Garcia 1991:35).

In line with Trinidad's and the wider Caribbean's development policy of "industrialization by invitation," whereby foreign-owned branch plants were rapidly set up in return for a series of incentives, Arima saw the establishment of the O'Meara Industrial Estate in 1960 on 235 acres of land (Garcia 1991:29–30). This industrial area has shrunk considerably, especially since the demise of Arima Textile Mills, where the Carib president, Ricardo Bharath, was once employed. Arima is still a mixed agricultural, industrial, and service economy and serves as the main transportation and commercial hub for the agricultural districts of northeastern Trinidad. My informants within the Arima Borough Council estimate that the majority of Arimians are employed outside of the borough; indeed, the long lines of commuters leaving Arima every morning seem to provide a rough indication of that. Four secondary schools are based in Arima, and most of those students come from outside of the borough. I resided in the central business district during my first stay (twenty-one months) and my second (nineteen months), and I found Arima to be a very busy and somewhat run-down area whose infrastructure was clearly taxed. While economically depressed, Arima still has all the main amenities one would see in a developed economy—supermarkets, nightclubs, restaurants, two cinemas, at least three Internet cafés, travel agencies, all the major banks, a post office, hardware and electronics stores, and a large shopping district that is still fairly well known for its clothing and shoe stores. Arima also has its own annual Carnival celebrations, on a smaller though no less raucous scale than the main activities in Port of Spain. Arima is also home to an increasing number of Venezuelan students who are in the country to learn English.

Arima today covers an area of approximately four square miles, at eight hundred feet above sea level. It is located sixteen miles east of Port of Spain. In 1971, the National Housing Authority began building homes for the working poor and unemployed, resulting in an influx of thousands of new residents (Garcia 1991:38–39). As a result, in 1980 the boundaries of the borough extended from one to the current four square miles. The environs of Arima are home to Santa Rosa Heights, Maloney Gardens, and La Horqueta, three large government-housing areas for the economically disadvantaged. The SRCC Centre is itself located in Jonestown, a district within Arima that came about as a result of extensive squatting on land owned by the Santa Rosa Roman Catholic Church. Jonestown is a fairly depressed area in economic terms and is known to be one of Arima's major zones of drug dealing.

Price (1987:1) notes that out of a population of 21,112 people in Arima, a census of 1980 registered 8,305 people as African, 74 as white, 5,030 as (East) Indian, 211 as Chinese, a massive 10,920 as mixed, 46 as Syrian-Lebanese, and 1106 as not stated (see also Garcia 1991:113). "Carib" does not appear as a category, especially when members of the SRCC itself chose such terms as "mixed," given their adoption of notions that to be Carib one must be racially pure. Out of that same total population in 1980, 15,558 people were professed Roman Catholics (Garcia 1991:108). In contrast with national figures, Arima is predominantly Roman Catholic and "mixed." Arima has experienced some of the main currents of globalization and creolization in the Caribbean: colonialism, missionizing, the cocoa economy, migration, world war, industrialization, and national integration. Yet this is still called "the home of the Caribs."

Questions of Absence, Debates of Presence

In much if not most of the social science literature on the cultural development of the postconquest Caribbean there seems to be a consensus that the indigenous has been absent or severely diminished to the point of virtual extinction. Moreover, in this state of postconquest construction, attempts at conceptualizing Caribbean indigeneity prove to be elusive, so the arguments go (compare Robotham 1998). In the case of Trinidad and Tobago, anthropologists have written that Trinidad "remained largely a *deserted island* until the last years of Spanish colonial rule, when in 1783 French planters and their slaves came and set up plantations based on slave labor" (Yelvington 1995b:37, emphasis added). As Yelvington (1995b:42) further notes, "social historians have investigated how the aboriginal population was virtually wiped out after contact with Spanish explorers who came after Columbus's voyage in 1498" (although this premise has not been investigated as much as repeated). Indeed, support for this argument has been forthcoming from the influential works of historians such as Bridget Brereton in Trinidad: "The modern history of Trinidad began in the 1780s, when the Spanish Government opened the island to settlement by French planters and their slaves. In the nearly three centuries following its discovery, Trinidad was a remote, isolated, and undeveloped outpost of Spain's vast American empire" (Brereton 1979:7–8).

Other anthropologists such as Lieber have utilized the deserted island thesis in explanations of the factors accounting for the distinctiveness of the Caribbean compared to other parts of the colonized world. Lieber (1981:1) thus states,

> as a sociocultural region the Caribbean developed in what may be called *a vacuum of indigenousness*. The earliest European settlers, through outright extermination and the introduction of Old World diseases, were remarkably successful in depopulating the area of its aboriginal inhabitants, leaving, here and there, marginal groups of Indians *whose impact on the cultural future would be nonexistent.* . . . imperialistic intrusion and expansion throughout the region could proceed as though the area were simply a cluster of lands, *without a human or cultural presence.* From the conquest on, the history of the Caribbean has been the history of *imported* peoples. (emphasis added)

Lieber therefore argues that with "no precolonial indigenous traditions available as partial models for the construction of a postcolonial society (as has been possible in much of the rest of the Third World), the attempt to forge an image of such a society is limited to reconstructions and elaborations of the *repertory set down by the colonial experience*" (1981:3, emphasis added). Similarly, Lewis argued that West Indians start on the road to "psychological independence" from inherited colonial complexes with "massive, even frightening handicaps," one of these being that "there is little left of the original culture in which to take pride, save for a few scattered artefacts," adding nevertheless, "the *Carib Queen of Arima* and the Carib reserve villages in St. Vincent and Dominica are about all that is left of the original populations" (1968:393, emphasis added). Aside from any reservations one might have with the thrust of Lieber's argument, he has at least effected a useful analytical coupling here, providing the duality at the heart of this book, which consists of understanding indigeneity at the wider social level as well as at the level of particular persons and their practices, rituals, and objects that are subsumed under the heading of "tradition." For his part, Lewis couples independence and national pride with the image of the Amerindian, an important connection that was also recognized by Lowenthal (1972) and is exemplified in some of the media quotes at the start of this chapter.

In terms of analyses affirming the decline or disappearance of the indigenes, or the impossibility of indigeneity, I would argue that there is nothing exceptional about the preceding statements when considered in the context of the mainstream social science literature. Indeed, as Palacio (1992) has noted, it has been common practice to teach students in the Caribbean that indigenous peoples were exterminated and are thus extinct (although even this has begun to change). Hulme further observes, "One debilitating consequence of the way in which the native Caribbean has been locked into an 'ethnographic present' of 1492, di-

vorced from five-hundred years of turbulent history, has been that the present
native population has been usually ignored: some seemingly authoritative accounts of the region even appear written in ignorance of the very existence of
such a population" (Hulme 1992:214).

Within that same social scientific literature, there has, however, been some
mention of the Caribs of Arima and the Santa Rosa Festival (Wood 1968:43–44),
as well as the "Carib Queen of Arima" (Lewis 1968:393), and only recently
Brereton (1996) has featured the current Santa Rosa Carib Community in her
text for history students. Much more mention of the Caribs of Arima exists in the
works of nonacademic writers, both Trinidadian and international, on both general and very localized topics concerning the Caribbean, written over half a century ago (for example, Luke 1930; Bullbrook 1960, 1940). Texts referring to
Amerindians in the mission of Arima, or after its demise, include colonial reports,
the writings of amateur historians, and the works of travel writers (see Borde
1883, 1876, Burnley 1842, Coleridge 1826, Collens 1886, Cothonay 1893; De
Verteuil 1858; Fraser 1896, 1891; Joseph 1838; Kingsley 1877; Wise 1938a,
1938b, 1936, 1934). The last category of literature residing outside of the institutional social sciences that makes some mention (in varying degrees) of the
Caribs of Arima or the Amerindians of Trinidad consists of locally published
texts in Trinidad, on various topics of Trinidadian history, culture, and society
(see Anthony 1988; Elie 1990; Harricharan 1983; Leahy 1980; Ottley 1955). In
summary, the Arima Caribs either have been featured in literature marginal to
social science research on Trinidad or have appeared only momentarily in some
of that social science research, again in varying degrees of acute marginality and
usually positing their imminent disappearance (Lewis 1968:19). For the most
part, the dominant view, across the array of social science research, is simply that
the native population was liquidated (see Williams 1970:41). There is, of course,
the occasional ambiguous exception in the social science literature, such as
Knight, who clearly speaks of the "rapid disappearance of the Arawakan population during the first century of Spanish colonization" given that "the arrival of
the three caravels from Spain in 1492 meant inexorable doom." While Knight
then states that although Amerindians did disappear, this "does not mean that
this group failed to have any impact on the future of the area" (1978:15, 22). This
is an opinion at variance with that of Lieber. This is the extent of the discussion
for Knight, even in the chapter devoted to Amerindians.

One of the givens in much if not most of the Caribbeanist literature in the
social sciences is that, in terms of the postconquest period, "Caribbean" and
"indigenous" (as in Amerindian) cannot usually go together except as a stark
contradiction of terms. The basic and widely accepted premise is that societies
such as Trinidad were artificially[12] instituted (Lowenthal 1972) for the purposes
of world capitalism, namely, the production of cash-crop exports (Mintz 1977).
The Trinidadian social order is in fact generally depicted as a nineteenth-century
creation (Brereton 1979; Wood 1968), a product of colonialism and the trans-

continental transplantation of peoples (Lewis 1968) in the service of monocultural production (Knight 1978; Williams 1970), and thus as a site marked by a dearth of indigeneity or primordial continuities,[13] a phenomenon that embodies ethnogenesis, hybridity,[14] invention, modernity, and migration. Nevertheless, the foregoing constitutes mostly one side of a debate between the two competing camps that Yelvington (2001a:232) identifies as the creationist[15] or creolization theorists and the neo-Herskovitsians. Even the works of authors who have tempered or argued against creationist analyses have been framed largely in terms of African and East Indian cultural continuities in the Caribbean and Trinidad specifically (see Herskovits 1941; Herskovits and Herskovits 1947; Klass 1991, 1961; Mintz and Price 1992; Warner-Lewis 1991) and thus are disconnected from an identifiable conception of indigeneity and usually discount continuities of an Amerindian, preconquest kind. If anything, the observation is that "as the [native] Indian population decreased, the African component increased" (Knight 1978:46; see also Williams 1964:7–9)—so that the presence of the latter is a function of the absence of the former. This sets historical processes in the form of a dichotomy. One alternative, increasingly necessary given the growing recognition of indigenous biological and cultural survivals in the region, is that Africans were imported since, after all, the aim of production is the maximum possible capital accumulation. Regardless of how many Amerindians were in place, they could never be enough, by definition, since there was no conception of "enough" in colonial accumulation to begin with.

The problem that is posed in assuming or arguing the absence of "the indigenous" is that it cannot give a satisfactory account for the presence and elaboration of two current phenomena: (1) the construction of nationalist discourses and representations of indigeneity in Trinidad, developed in part via the trope of the Amerindian; and (2) the current regionwide revival of Caribbean Amerindian identities and organizations both within Trinidad, as evidenced by the SRCC, state support and recognition for bodies such as the SRCC, and the holding of three regional indigenous gatherings in Arima, and at the regional level, as exemplified by the formation of the Caribbean Organisation of Indigenous Peoples, the growth of Caribism in Dominica, the international networking of Belizean Garifuna (the so-called Black Caribs), and the emergence of an array of new Taíno organizations comprising Puerto Rican immigrants in the United States (see Haslip-Viera 1999b).

However, having stated this problem we are not closer to any resolution, to the extent that two further problems are encountered: first, how "the indigenous" and "indigeneity" are defined and interpreted (when, where, why, and by whom); and second, how far one can go in framing this Caribbean Amerindian revival and concomitant attempts at developing national senses of indigeneity as forms of invention that occur in and through precisely the processes of postcolonial erasure of primordiality and the globalized creation of artificial societies in the Caribbean.

Problems are also posed by overstating arguments to the contrary of the absence/erasure theses in that these arguments run the risk of being contradicted by statements such as those made by Ricardo at the opening of this chapter. Moreover, in stressing presence in terms of an overcommunication of demographic and ethnic continuities, one runs the risk of (dis)missing observable contemporary constructions and reducing the suggestion of the existence of these constructions to a perceived moral accusation of fakery.

Indigeneity in a Globalized Caribbean

One of the main problems at the center of this project is the problem of indigeneity in a Caribbean location. This problem acquires greater focus with the recognition of the fact that the Caribbean is the site of the first European expansion beyond the confines of the Old World, combined with what many see as the fact that in sociological terms the Caribbean "owes its origins to . . . colonialism" (Yelvington 1995a:13). Trinidad, like the rest of the Caribbean, "is not on the margin of the 'so-called world system' but, historically, squarely in the system's foundation" (Yelvington 1995b:41). Given what some see as the genesis of Caribbean territories in globalizing capitalism, James thus observed that these territories "have a universal significance far beyond their size and social weight" (1980:173). As a result of the diversity of global inputs localized in the Caribbean, writers like Glissant (1989:xxxii) describe Caribbean consciousness as one marked by historical dispossession, caught between the "fallacy of the primitive paradise," "the mirage of Africa," and the "illusion of a metropolitan identity." Hall argues that it is this pervasive sense of "ruptures and discontinuities" that thus constitutes the "uniqueness of the Caribbean" (1994:394). My concern with indigeneity differs in some respects and is developed along two fronts: first, how in and through these very trends one can observe processes of developing a sense of Trinidadian national indigeneity, and second, the indigeneity associated with those identifying with an Amerindian heritage. The sense of having one's cultural identity either ruptured or discontinuous is a problem that some Trinidadians have sought to overcome—as C. L. R. James put it, "the West Indian, in searching for an identity, is expressing one" (quoted in Lowenthal 1972:292).

On the basis of the above arguments, various authors have stressed the lack or impossibility of primordial precolonial attachments in the Caribbean. For example, Lieber (1981:4) argues that "few regions on earth have been more affected by North American styles, demands, needs and other metropolitan images of the way life should be lived." Reminding us that "the history of the Caribbean has been the history of imported peoples," Lieber (1981:1, 4) adds that Trinidad "is virtually a satellite city of London and New York." Oxaal (1968:11) commented that the African roots of "part of Trinidad's lower class negro culture are today generally viewed as colorful but vanishing anachronisms," and C. L. R.

James emphasized that "these populations are essentially Westernized and they have been Westernized for centuries" (quoted in Oxaal 1968:1). Within this particular framework, active ongoing mimesis has thus been observed to be as much an aspect of Caribbean culture and society (see Naipaul 1969), exemplified in the importation of fashions from the metropole, as it is a defining element of Caribbean political economy (see Beckford 1975; Girvan and Jefferson 1971; Ramsaran 1989), evidenced by attempts at "bridging the development gap," "industrialization by invitation," and "becoming more like the North" (see Addo and associates 1985; Addo 1984). In this study I am interested in locating, paradoxical as it may seem, the Caribbean Amerindian revival within the same global and modern currents that many of the authors cited see as the decisive influences in shaping the postconquest Caribbean.

If we agree with the authors above, then we are faced with a problem in defining, locating, and analyzing indigeneity in the Caribbean. One approach is to take a long view of the cultural development of the postconquest Caribbean. "Carib" as a category emerged from within the confrontation between Europe and the aboriginal Caribbean, as Hulme (2000, 1992, 1990) has carefully detailed and argued.[16] This, we might say, was the original act of engineering, to construct and ascribe traits of the worst imaginable savagery (cannibalism), indiscriminately, to all aboriginal enemies of Spanish geopolitical expansionism. "Carib" is a world-systemic category insofar it emerges with European expansion (Hulme 2000). "Carib" is a powerful historical category and is enshrined at least as the starting point of all contemporary reconstructions of modern Caribbean history. Thus, in response to Lieber's analysis, one could note that the indigene is a constituent part of that same "repertory set down by the colonial experience," to use his words, a fact that can be observed in a variety of phenomena. Examples of the latter range from the naming of the Caribbean after the Caribs, to the colonial creation of special reserves in Dominica and Guyana, to the use of Amerindians as allies in the military and trade arenas, to the role of Amerindians in countering slave rebellions and hunting runaway slaves, to modern cultural nationalist reconfigurations of Amerindians as national heroes and as the first to suffer and resist European slavery. Even among those presuming their absence, Amerindians still exercise a presence, at the very least in symbolic and discursive terms.

Between Absence and Presence

There is something in between total absence and seamless continuity. That something, I argue, consists of phenomena that can be understood as constituting revival, resurgence,[17] or, as I will explain, the reengineering of indigeneity from within certain political economic contexts. It is this in-between approach that I call, with reference to the literature cited above, a creolist approach to the Carib presence. However paradoxical, a key subject of concern for this study is how indigeneity is defined, developed, and disseminated in and through the processes set out in the creolization perspectives.

One underlying intent of this project is to take up a challenge issued by the Trinidadian anthropologist John Stewart in *Drinkers, Drummers and Decent Folk* (1989:20), where he wrote that while the anthropological literature emphasizes that Trinidad is a "migrant and therefore non-indigenous society," few treat "the struggle to establish indigeneity as a significant problem." By indigeneity I take Stewart to mean some primordial sense of belonging to place or some mode of self-identifying as uniquely Trinidadian. As early as the start of the 1970s, Lowenthal observed that the Amerindians play "an important symbolic role in the West Indian search for identity. . . . Cultural nationalism throughout the Caribbean today promotes the search for Arawak and Carib remains" (Lowenthal 1972:186). Williams thus titled one chapter "Our Amerindian Ancestors" in his *History of the People of Trinidad and Tobago* (1962).

I will thus describe and analyze the development of a national sense of indigeneity via the symbolic device of the Amerindian, as a contextual complement to my research on the SRCC in Arima and this organization's attempts to define and promote Trinidad's Carib heritage. Part of the background of this book's focus is necessarily that of increased recognition and institutionalization of the Carib in narratives of national history, as well as the state's nation-building efforts in seizing upon the proclaimed Carib "contribution to the national foundation." I therefore highlight modern Trinidadian attempts to reconstruct the indigene, the Carib, in a nationalist and anticolonialist light, while utilizing the symbolism of Amerindian indigeneity as a device for creating a sense of local primordiality and of territorial continuity with antiquity. Taking into account dominant texts, state recognition and rewards, and the impact of the national media in promoting certain representations of Trinidadian society, we seem to be facing a process constituted of elements of the wider society (and often the classes that dominate it) rediscovering Carib heritage. Authors working within the "vacuum of indigeneity" perspective miss the contemporary practices of states and intellectual elites in the Caribbean in forging a sense of national indigeneity, in part and sometimes indirectly, via the figure of the heroic Amerindian, the first root of the nation, the territorial predecessor even if not the biological ancestor of the true national, as detailed in this book. When this assumption is coupled with efforts by individuals to assert and articulate their Amerindian ancestry and the value of their traditions, we see a dual process at work: national elites and culture brokers discovering a general Trinidadian indigeneity via the symbolic archetype of the Amerindian, while the newly recognized and self-identified Amerindian discovers his or her indigeneity in the wider society.

In the case of the SRCC, elites and institutions situated within Trinidad and abroad have vested diverse interests in the development and promotion of Amerindian heritage or in the deployment of the label "Carib." The impact on the

SRCC, in terms of producing representations of Caribness that are partly managed and orchestrated by diverse brokers and institutions in accordance with different valorizations of the Carib and of indigeneity, is that as a group the SRCC bears and enacts multiple and even divergent meanings, representations, and organizational projects and goals. Furthermore, the joining of the emergent sense of national indigeneity with the revivalist efforts of SRCC brokers in defining and promoting Amerindian indigeneity has resulted in the powerful translation of the Carib into the "First Nations," the "First Trinidadians," and the "First Peoples," a translation that enhances nationalist reinterpretations of Amerindian history while also intersecting with increasingly powerful globalized discourses of indigeneity.

It is striking to witness the multilaterality of various cultural brokers and patrons engaged in affirming and displaying the value of indigeneity at the crossroads of the local, the national, and the global. Traditions are created, maintained, reworked, and publicly presented by the SRCC in conjunction or in conflict with a variety of local and global institutions and agents. Hence, of special concern is the work of cultural brokers and gatekeepers both within and without the SRCC. One of my aims then is to understand why, and explain how, certain practices and objects evoking indigeneity are organized, reformulated, reinterpreted, and articulated for particular audiences in the contemporary period and as shaped by history. In the articulation of Carib indigeneity I look at how some of the brokers act as *bricoleurs*, forming a local-global bricolage[18] of indigenous symbols and meanings, and even reinfusing or objectifying non-Amerindian originated practices with indigenous symbolic properties. The twofold nature of this work thus entails focusing on structure and agency, on wider normative frameworks and particular interpretations, on larger bodies of practice and particular actions, and on brokers maneuvering within certain structures. The emphasis selected in this work is, in the end, perhaps a little more on structure than on agency: I do not see random, voluntaristic aims as having that much sway in this particular case and given the conditions that I will discuss. Different levels of analysis are involved in developing a comprehensive understanding of the problem, ranging from the local (Arima) to the national (Trinidad and Tobago) and the global (the wider Caribbean and the world system), though not necessarily in that order. The three analytical axes of this study are thus structure-agency, past-present, and local-global.

The Work of Cultural Brokers

One of my most basic analytical and methodological premises is that the study of indigeneity cannot be the study of indigenous peoples alone. One of the approaches that I found useful in developing this study is Antoun's "social organization of tradition," which includes his focus on culture brokers and their reinterpretation of tradition. The "reinterpretation of tradition" perspective sees brokers as responsible for accepting, rejecting, reinterpreting, or accommodating customs and traditions (Antoun 1989:17). The "social organization of tradition" is defined by Antoun as a process that is to be found when communities become linked to "overarching political, economic and religious structures and implicated in the concomitant processes of debt, politics, social control, and the quest for salvation" (Antoun 1989:17). I would add that the social organization of tradition, in definitional terms, would be altered by the historical and social contexts and the sorts of traditions we study as ethnographers, but Antoun's definition is a good starting point. The work of the culture broker "involves the necessary selection from and interpretation of tradition"; culture brokers interpret a message "for a particular clientele at the same time that they deal with political and religious hierarchies [among others] whose norms and aims [may] differ from those of both the culture broker and his audience" (Antoun 1989:4–5). The culture broker is, in Antoun's perspective, a translator, intermediary, interpreter, and marshal of tradition. One could also add that brokers promote, publicize, organize, and add value where secular traditions are concerned and at times even where sacred traditions are involved, such as the Santa Rosa Festival in Arima.

The focus on cultural brokers is important, as Jean and John Comaroff (1999:295) argue: "Without human agents, without specified locations and movements and actions, realities are not realized, nothing takes place, the present has no presence." This perspective can be used to highlight the importance of the work of brokers in realizing both the presence of specific traditions and their value. Peace (1998:274), looking at trade in popular culture at the national and international levels, sees brokerage as "located between the core areas of global production on the one hand and semi-peripheral areas of popular consumption on the other" and notes that "brokers do much more than merely trade in culture. They define its meaning, they establish its significance in the overall order of things, they endow it with particular kinds of power." In addition, Peace argues that "the concept of broker emphasizes above all the importance of conscious and calculating social agency in what can be too easily and mystifyingly represented as an impersonal marketplace driven by forces of supply and demand"; in his view, "brokerage underscores the point that regional-global articulation is, first and foremost, a complex, socio-politically mediated constellation of relations, not just a matter of mere economics" (1998:278). He also adds that processes of endowing cultural productions with special value "have to be calculatingly *engineered*, carefully fabricated, and that is always and everywhere the forte of cultural intermediaries" (Peace 1998:279, emphasis added). While I favor the broad outlines of this approach, what is problematic here is the implication that brokers create value mostly through their own agency and not as conditioned by historical forces or constrained by powerful institutions or conventions.

Reengineering and the Political Economy of Tradition

"Carib" as a category and as an identification, with diverse traditions that are represented at different times as emblematic of Caribness, is being actively organized, reinterpreted, and promoted. This introduces questions of who are the actors and institutions involved in these processes, when do these processes materialize, and where and why they become evident. One may perceive that this label and the emblematic traditions are maintained and revived by a variety of actors and institutions because they have some importance, that is, value. Values of whatever kind are historical (rising, stabilizing, and declining), which means that they fluctuate, and over the past twenty years the positive valuations of the label "Carib" have been increasing once again. The latter is due in large part to the work of cultural brokers operating in receptive circumstances, working within an established framework of patronage and clientelism, and actively organizing and adapting meanings while promoting (or even demoting) particular traditions.

One way of analyzing what cultural brokers do with the Carib idea is to argue, as I do, that they are reengineering Caribness. The notion of reengineering, as I employ it here, refers to multiple interests vested in redesigning, constructing, or maintaining Amerindian traditions for various purposes, all of which are purposes valued in different ways by different interested agents. The concept is one of multilateral management, organization, and even design to a limited extent. The term "reengineering" is intended to bridge concepts of construction in a manner similar to Mark Rogers' stress on the "dialogic coproduction of 'indigenous' rhetoric," involving a group's selective interaction with national and global contexts (Rogers 1996:79). The ethnographic case here is not unidimensional—no single concept will embrace its multifaceted nature, the multiple and divergent interests vested in the Carib revival, and the multiple representations of Caribness.

I refer to the context in which these cultural brokers operate in terms of a number of phenomena encompassed under the heading "the political economy of tradition." The two main elements of this are (1) the politics and economics of associating certain values with particular cultural representations pertaining to individuals marked as members of specific peoples; and (2) legislated recognition and rewards for groups engaged in often competitive and even conflicting cultural display.

This idea of a political economy of tradition is used here to make reference to the way certain practices and objects achieve, maintain, or even lose value, in line with specific material and ideational interests. Moreover, in viewing indigeneity as socially organized, we begin to consider what makes certain identities possible, valid, or even useful. We are thus led to consider how certain identities are communicated (or made communicable) and understood. This is another way of seeing the indigenous as not just, or even primarily, self-defining, self-constructing, or self-inventing. Thus the approach I follow is based on seeing indigeneity as not just personal but a complex and difficult process to site. One of the reasons for this complexity is the network of institutions, interests, and actors engaged in articulating indigeneity. The involvement of an array of interests is also indicative of the value of indigeneity. Deciphering what that value is at any given point can be complex when considered historically and when one takes into account the range of interests and meanings involved.

In societies such as Trinidad and Tobago where the state has been the primary provider of employment and goods and services for most of the country's postindependence history, the state can also act as an important cultural arbiter. Brackette Williams' analytical framework brings the state into the question of how groups organize and legitimate their power or their quest for it. Williams views the state as a set of power-brokering apparatuses, and she sees state intervention as a factor in establishing the material and symbolic conditions for the production of ethnic groups (B. Williams 1989:406, 427). Tambiah also notes that the state, as the central political authority, "is now, after years of escalating ethnic divisiveness and pluralistic awareness, counseled to be a 'referee' adjudicating differences and enabling regional cultures and societies to attain their 'authentic' identities and interests" (1994:436). He also links the "state as referee" phenomenon to the bolstering of ethnic strategizing in making claims on state resources, which he sees as inevitably reinforcing the "patron/client networks, bossism, and patronage structure" (Tambiah 1994:436). It is at this juncture between power, patronage-brokerage, and the political and economic implications of the role of the state in managing diversity[19] that we can discern a political economy of tradition.

History and the Carib

The temporal dimension of reengineering processes highlights at least three themes that are central to this work. To begin with, Amerindian revivalist groups in the Caribbean, such as the SRCC, do not just invent themselves in either historical or social isolation, or on terms entirely of their own choosing. Instead, their self-representations are products of mediations between their own interests and beliefs, historical texts, and social institutions upholding and legitimating particular representations. In addition, the temporal dimension of reengineering runs counter to the finality of the perspective that argues that a dearth of indigeneity is a feature of modern Caribbean cultural development, by highlighting the fact that even the once commonly assumed absence of an actual group does not preclude at least the presence of its historical imagination and the activation of its symbolic value. History forms a critical cultural resource in the mediation and development of current representations of Amerindian identity in the Caribbean. Lastly, the temporal infrastructure of ideational and institutional sources engaged in the current interactions that make "Carib" valuable is part of a process that Haslip-Viera (1999a) and Dávila (1999) identify as the construction of a canonical status for Caribbean Amerindian identities. Dávila argues that "the old Puerto Rican nationalist canon" has "created new memories out of forgetting," and in her work she outlines "the transmutation of the Taíno from a recognized group and a living population into a symbol to be revived, romanticized and manipulated" and the subsequent transformation of the Taíno from symbol to living reality (1999:12, 14).

A further reason why I have chosen to use the term "*re*engineering" is as a means of pointing to the history involved in the construction and valorization of "Carib," processes that neither ceased in 1492 nor developed out of thin air over the past two decades. In fundamental ways it is history that gives "Carib" its cultural weight as an evocative idea. It is also difficult to miss the extent of historically oriented self representation that occurs among Caribbean Amerindian revivalist groups such as the SRCC. One of the primary features of their discourse is that of history, embedded in concepts of tradition, ancestry, heritage, cultural loss, and cultural retrieval. In broader terms, some argue that the historical processes that informed the Caribbean's ethnic heterogeneity produced a historical consciousness among Caribbean peoples, "a consciousness which many anthropologists could not (or would not) recognize" (Yelvington 1996:87).

The Concept of Tradition

Tradition acts here as the central entry point to the discussion of the articulation of indigeneity in Trinidad. Tradition is at the very center of the programs and projects articulated by the SRCC's own cultural brokers and those associated with it. In addition, I am also trying to bring attention to the tradition of certain people being called Caribs, at different times and places and for different reasons. Tradition is conventionally identified as a key component of heritage in Trinidad. This approach is also called for because traditions are the basis for the public demonstration of ethnic heritage and a critical basis for making claims on state patronage in Trinidad and Tobago (compare Ryan 1997). "Tradition," like most folk concepts and keywords in anthropology, is a problematic term; it does not simply denote a set of givens. I treat "tradition" as comprising texts, practices, rituals, and objects representing what actors believe to be representative of a particular cultural history and what analytically we can perceive as implying repetition, regulation, and institutionalization (compare Antoun 1989).

One of the dominant themes in the literature on tradition over the past two decades has been the renewed debate between essentialist and constructionist perspectives occasioned by the "invention of tradition" approach and its diverse anthropological variants. The SRCC represents a complex mix of possibilities that render dichotomous analyses problematic. Both sides of the debate assume that people attach themselves to certain traditions, with the result that neither side attempts to concertedly explain why or how traditions are lost, forgotten, or deliberately abandoned.

Numerous concepts in anthropology and the wider social sciences have dealt with the reactivation and revival of traditions and identities in different ways and contexts, resulting in what Sissons (1993:97) observed to be a "bewildering variety of terms." Indeed, Linton's concept of "nativistic movements" (1943) and Wallace's closely related concept of "revitalization movements" (1956) both speak to forms of ethnic politicization where cultural markers are consciously deployed as tools in interethnic contests.

Of especial import to anthropologists working in a constructionist framework has been the "invention of tradition" perspective developed by historians. The notion of "invention" is defined by Hobsbawm (1983:1) as the rapid institution of traditions, as well as actually inventing and constructing outright and then seeking to formally institute these novelties. Specifically, he says, "'Invented tradition' is taken to mean a set of practices, normally governed by overtly or tacitly accepted rules and of ritual or symbolic nature, which seek to inculcate certain values and norms of behavior by repetition, which automatically implies continuity with the past. In fact, where possible, they normally attempt to establish continuity with a suitable historic past" (Hobsbawm 1983:1). Hobsbawm notes that inventions occur in accordance with certain "overtly or tacitly accepted rules" that we can logically assume are in existence prior to the invented tradition.

Hobsbawm carefully qualifies and limits the applicability of his concept, a fact often lost in the more polemical critiques of this approach (for example, Sahlins 1993). First, Hobsbawm says that when one finds cases where "the old ways are still alive" and where "traditions need be neither revived nor invented," then his approach cannot be used (Hobsbawm 1983:8). In addition, his work makes it clear that the agents responsible for invention are states themselves. Furthermore, he does not indicate whether revival of tradition is to be equated with invention. I see the invention of tradition as a useful starting point and at the very least as a valuable counterpoint to the essentialist "billiard ball models of culture" critiqued by Wolf (1994, 1990, 1984, 1982), which do little to account for change, agency, and interaction.

Some anthropologists have applied Hobsbawm's concept of invention while disputing precisely the notion of old, continuous traditions that Hobsbawm's approach permits, in arguing that even traditional culture is increasingly recognizable as more of an invention constructed for contemporary purposes (see Hanson 1989). Some anthropologists likewise speak in terms of the ongoing reinvention of traditions. Handler and Linnekin (1984:273) argue that tradition is invented because "it is necessarily reconstructed in the present, notwithstanding some participants' understanding of such activities as being preservation rather than invention," adding that while "traditional action may refer to the past . . . to 'be about' or to refer to is a symbolic rather than natural relationship, and as such it is characterized [as much] by discontinuity *as by continuity*" (Handler and Linnekin 1984:279, 276; emphasis added). Unlike Hobsbawm, Handler and Linnekin also address the question of revival, stressing that "cultural revivals change the traditions they attempt to revive," since "to do something because it is traditional is already to reinterpret, and hence to change it" (Handler and Linnekin 1984:276, 281; Linnekin 1983:241). Wallerstein also developed a concept of reinvention, noting that when groups seek to establish their particularities, "they reinvent their histories. They look for 'continuities' which at that moment in time will be congenial" (1984a:63). This approach is one that I value for opening up the discussion to wider contexts and the roles of structures and a variety of agents in helping to shape that which is particularly congenial. As Cohen (1989:99) states this case, "The manner in which the past is invoked is strongly indicative of the kinds of circumstances which makes such a 'past reference' salient. It is a selective construction of the past which resonates with contemporary influences."

Thomas (1992) outlined a bundle of concepts referring to ways traditions can be utilized, shaped, and reconstructed. Thomas' primary principle is that "self-representation never takes place in isolation and . . . it is frequently oppositional or reactive" (1992:213). His second principle is that the "reform and reformulation" of tradition involves an "immediate strategy" for dealing "both with what is inadequate in intersocial relations and with what seems unsatisfactory or backward in one's own situation" (Thomas 1992:228). His concept of articulation, unlike invention, involves cases where "something already present becomes explicit or is made explicit in new terms that alter its content, valorization, and ramifications" (Thomas 1992:220). Another of Thomas' concepts is the "objectification of tradition": the organization of a "neotraditional culture" organized primarily in novel and oppositional terms; reifying practices and characteristics of an "emblematic way of life" signifying the distinctiveness of a community; and where identity and tradition are "part of a broader field of oppositional naming and categorization" (Thomas 1992:215, 216).

Critiques of the matrix of invention-construction concepts have been issued on a number of fronts. Some would argue that these approaches introduce other problems by implying that there are authentic traditions somewhere or at some point that act as the benchmark or baseline by which to determine that something is invented or reinvented in the first place. There is always the historicist temptation to be overzealous in showing that what is done *now* is not quite the same as it was done *yesterday,* while missing the broader, more interesting cultural and sociopolitical implications.

Some authors argue in favor of drawing a distinction between invention and construction (for example, Mato 1996). Mato's view is that Hobsbawm's "invention" can be differentiated from "the general social dynamic of making representations, which may be said to involve social practices that vary in their degree of conscious and formal intent" (1996:63). Mato's emphasis suggests that constructions may be conducted unconsciously while inventions are fully conscious constructions (Mato 1996:63). I appreciate Mato's focus on construction as not asserting itself as opposed to anything that may be considered more real—"from this point of view, the dilemmas 'real vs. imagined,' 'authentic vs. false,' or 'genuine vs. spurious,' are simply not pertinent" (1996:64).[20] Perhaps, as some contend, the problem is that one of the anthropological biases underlying the desire to preserve the Other by diminishing change and dispelling contradiction is an attachment to the assumption that "real culture" is eroded by invention, strategic mimesis, and so forth (Moore 1994:366). Jackson explained the problem in similar terms, saying that "in order to be thought of as good, culture must not be seen as invented or created, except over a long period of time" (1989:127).[21]

Others argue that "invention" and cognate approaches fail to take into account preexisting social and cultural realities that make the invention possible. As one author puts it, "traditions are invented in the specific terms of the people who construct them" (Sahlins 1999:409). The "experiential substrate" perspective employed by Smith (1993:31) and Friedman (1994:13) counters invention by arguing that there must be a substrate of shared motivational and interpretive fields underlying what superficially appears as complete novelty. As Smith argued, "'inventing' ethnies, like creating nations, requires certain preexisting elements and appropriate conditions. Otherwise, the 'inventions' will fail to take root among the designated populations" (1993:31).

An additional problem concerns what seems to be analytical selectivity in terms of the agents of invention in much of the literature, some focusing on states, others on select ethnic groups or communities, and both often in isolation from each other. The problem is either one of structureless agency and the notion of man making his own culture, or that of a top-down approach to culture. In focusing on the display of indigenous heritage, my interest lies in examining the role of presentation to others in the constitution of selfhood. There is insufficient discussion in the approaches outlined above concerning how a tradition is socially organized and valorized, or contextually placed, with a multiple vesting of interests in the act of coproduction (Rogers 1996).

If not for the alliances the SRCC has cultivated and the assistance it has received, the suggestion that such a small group could single-handedly win the degree of support and recognition that it has gained from the state, the media, and various international bodies would strain anyone's credulity. One of the ways in which the SRCC has attracted this attention and support has been to speak through the dominant social conventions of Trinidadian society, a cautious strategy not without its contradictions and burdens. There has been an accretion of images and resultant expectations in Trinidad, as elsewhere, concerning what constitutes a true indigene. SRCC leaders are aware of these presumptions. They play to some expectations, but sometimes only half-heartedly, with the aim of slowly challenging some of the more unreasonable desires that they conform to images of Indians in early colonial chronicles (hence Ricardo's almost acidic antiessentialist statement at the outset of this chapter). If brokers are intermediaries, then, by definition, this necessitates situating their agency within a wider social and cultural context, mindful of power relations and key institutions (the state, political parties, churches, and so forth) and patrons that reward certain representations and practices.

In the final analysis, one of the more useful conceptualizations of neotradition for this work comes from another study of indigeneity and creolization in the Caribbean. One of the lesser-known anthropological concepts dealing with the construction of traditions emerged from the study of the Garífuna ("Black Caribs") of Belize. Gonzalez (1983:157) spoke of neoteric traditions, where "neoterics" describes "a type of society which, springing from the ashes of warfare, forced migration or other calamity, had survived by patching together bits and pieces from its cultural heritage while at the same time borrowing and inventing freely and rapidly in order to cope with new, completely different circumstances."

The Concept of Indigeneity

"Indigeneity" is another challenging term that is used repeatedly in this work in an admittedly slippery fashion, as a matter of both design and necessity. The term seems to have only randomly and sporadically surfaced in the literature, mostly within the past ten years, and there is as yet no apparent consensus on how best to define the term. Indeed, how "indigeneity" is to be defined (much like the term "indigenous") is a contentious issue and forms part of the problem addressed by this text, even while forming part of the vocabulary of the text itself. For my own part I use it as an open term, meant to be distinguished from "indigenousness," which can connote a static state of being, or "indigenism," which has specific Latin American connotations of elitist romanticism and state incorporation projects known as *indigenismo* (see Díaz-Polanco 1982; Field 1994), which contrasts with *indianidad* (or "Indianity") as indigenism from below (see Berdichewsky 1989:25–26; Varese 1982), or what some call "radical *indigenismo*" (Bollinger and Lund 1982:20).

In broader terms, the value of the term "indigeneity"' is in its avoidance of the sometimes confusing distinctions among various concepts related to "the indigenous." Its value then lies in its generalizing denotation of the theory and practice *of, by,* or *for* "the indigenous," that is, as a bundle of discourses and practices for representing the indigenous. "Indigeneity" can be also be used to refer to some notion of being locally rooted in a particular territory, of being either "first here" as expressed in the First Nations idea (an idea of ancient, prenational precedence) or the "true local" as expressed in the "sons of the soil" idea (an idea of local birth, national citizenship, and thus legitimate residence), although these two senses often overlap.

In the Field

My research began with a pilot study of the SRCC in 1995. I noted two strong themes in the statements that individuals made to me, especially by individuals who would become my key guides later on. One of these was their desire to receive greater recognition, locally and abroad. The second, very much related to the first, was their constant emphasis on networking with a wide array of institutions and actors, locally and internationally, in seeking greater recognition, support, and funding. The group had developed, and sought to further develop, a critical mass of documents, written representations of the group, project proposals, letters, historical statements, and so forth, on the group itself and in connection with its wider networking. These observations seemed to suggest the following: that much of their time is spent in formalized activities of brokerage, and that much of their work consists of formal documentation, and thus writing and graphic forms of self-representation were paramount. My future guides and collaborators also made it clear that they expected researchers to be of some assistance to them, to not "just come and take."

As I was about to begin my two years of doctoral fieldwork in 1998, I struggled to outline areas of possible cooperation between informants and myself, as well as envisioning the appropriate modes of participant observation. As far as I could see, two of my strengths were my training in writing research reports and my access to funding that permitted me to acquire computer, video, and photographic equipment. Becoming an "insider," acting in some ways as an intern or even a consultant in terms of their brokerage processes seemed to be a valuable means of gaining knowledge of this group. I was invited to assist in writing project proposals, letters, and so forth, as a form of participant observation. In addition, I developed certain collaborative writing and representation exercises that would allow me further access to the ways in which they perceive themselves, construct their identity, and articulate their self-representations with a wider public. One of the platforms for collaborative writing was my proposal that we develop websites about the group, to further some of their aims for greater recognition and to gain feedback from a wider audience, both locally and internationally (see Forte 2003a, 2003b).

My fieldwork took place in three stages. The first was the pilot study that I conducted in June–July 1995, when I met some of the key spokespersons for the Santa Rosa Carib Community (Ricardo Bharath, Elma Reyes, and Ricardo Cruz), along with an elderly medicine man associated with the SRCC (Ian Capriata Dickson). I conducted formal recorded interviews and engaged in several informal conversations, and began a collection and analysis of SRCC documents, newspaper reports, and general historical literature on the ethnohistory of Caribbean Amerindian populations, along with materials on Trinidadian history. The second stage lasted from February 1998 to November 1999, followed up with online media research lasting until July 2001. I began the second stage with a round of formal, structured and recorded interviews of five leading members of the SRCC and two leading ex-members. I met all the members of the SRCC, and I conducted a survey of the group to gain a sense of a socioeconomic profile of the SRCC membership and members' attitudes and opinions on a wide range of subjects: ethnicity, religion, politics, money, tradition, identity, leadership. I spent many weeks on Calvary Hill, where most members reside, just "liming" with members. My own apartment became a field site insofar as certain key informants regularly visited and discussed a wide variety of subjects, and on a couple of occasions that same apartment served as the site for some of the events that I observed. The third stage of my research, far more informal, lasted from December 2001 to July 2003.

I attended meetings in the Carib Centre from 1998 through 1999. I also aided in the drafting of a proposal for a land grant and further state funding (see SRCC 1998c),[22] designing two websites in conjunction with the SRCC and Los Niños del Mundo (Forte 1998g, 1998h), and writing an article for a newsletter (Forte 1999f). In addition, I assisted in producing an annual report of SRCC expenses, activities, and projects for the Ministry of Culture (SRCC 1998a, 1998b, 1997), in the process also gathering past reports and letters (Bharath and Khan 1997a, 1997b). I also assisted in the drafting of letters to corporations and press releases for leading SRCC members (Bharath and Khan 1998). I attended key meetings between select members of the SRCC and external brokers (that is, politicians and business persons). Moreover, I also attended non-Carib functions and events, such as political party meetings and rallies, and festivals in the company of select SRCC members.

One of my analytical and methodological premises is that the study of indigeneity cannot be the study of indigenous peoples alone. Neither an ethnography of contemporary Caribs nor a history of colonial Caribs can effectively be a study in which Caribs appear alone. Hence, I conducted participant observation within state structures at the local level, attending statutory meetings of the Arima Borough Council, interviewing and conversing with a number of councillors and the mayor, preparing letters for the SRCC president in connection with his constituency work, and even working on a joint project[23] with Kelvin Seifert, the deputy mayor, who also brought me on a working tour of Arima with some of his staff. In the course of my research I regularly interacted with at least four members of the Arima Borough Council, which also gave me a firsthand introduction to party politics, the local workings of the People's National Movement, and led to my meeting the PNM leader (who is now prime minister), Patrick Manning.

My rounds of interviews and conversations extended to priests in the Catholic Church, both within Arima and outside Arima. In addition, my research also took me to another Arima-based institution of some public magnitude (and with connections to the SRCC), the National Parang Association of Trinidad and Tobago, whose events I attended, along with select SRCC members, on a number of occasions.

In September of 1998 I traveled to the Carib Reserve in Dominica. There I mostly conducted formal recorded interviews with five key informants and met and spoke with several former chiefs, including the man who was then chief (Hilary Frederick) and his current successor (Garnette Joseph), one senator, three members of the Carib Council, and the head of a Carib nongovernmental organization. In total I conversed with and interviewed fifteen individuals. The main purpose of this research was to follow up on leads and connections that I had acquired from SRCC members in Trinidad. Similarly, in June 1998, I traveled to the Assembly of First Nations headquarters in Ottawa, Canada, where I carried out research in the documentation center of the AFN.

Discussions and even interviews by e-mail were conducted with ex-Arimians in Miami, New York, and London, as well as some of the SRCC's Taíno associates in New York and New Jersey. Guest books and visitor surveys collecting online visitors' responses to select questions was another method, albeit unscientific, by which I also gauged public reactions and estimations (more details on this are in Forte 2003a, 2003b, and 1999b).

Lastly, I also benefited from a deeper grounding in Trinidad than that afforded by formal fieldwork alone, having lived there for several years. I resided and studied in Trinidad from August 1990 until September 1993, enrolled at the Institute of International Relations at the University of the West Indies and being taught by former government officials and state technocrats (the university often functioned as an employment backup for members of the "out" party). This served to immerse me in the thinking and practices of policy makers and technocrats, a virtual type of participant observation in state structures.

Overview of Chapters

The chapters follow a flow from past to present and from colonialism to nationalism and then contemporary globalization. In chapter 1, "Canonizing the Carib," I bring in history by highlighting the contexts, processes, and interests behind the construction and reproduction of the figure of the Carib, with a special focus on Trinidad and beginning with European colonization. In that chapter I focus on the political economy of identity construction with reference to Caribbean Amerindians in the colonial period, the original phase of engineering Caribness, thus building the temporal and ideational field of interaction encompassing this identity construction.

Chapter 2, "Placing the Carib," continues the historical analysis but with especial concern for the spatial dimension of emplacing Carib identity. Both this and the previous chapter are also intended to reveal the modes by which the label "Carib" came to have a value and how that value has changed, by highlighting the manifestations of the historical and spatial recurrence of Carib identity. The aim of this chapter is thus to spotlight the modes by which Arima has come to be popularly referred to as "the home of the Caribs" and how the Carib came to be localized within Arima via at least two previous revivals of the presence of the Amerindian in Arima, in both demographic and symbolic terms.

Chapter 3, "Writing the Carib," is an almost inevitable distillation and application of the previous two chapters that points to the continued presence and influence of influential colonial discourses on indigeneity in Trinidad, the contemporary extensions of these discourses, and the role of modern texts and cultural displays in adapting or responding to these earlier texts or, in some cases, simply reproducing them. My intention here is to track the enduring influence of historical texts on contemporary reinterpretations and articulations of the presence of the Carib. Additional attention is paid to the position of the Amerindian in the colonial hierarchy of race, as reflected in select colonial texts. While each of the texts was produced at a given historical moment (like my own)—reflecting circumstances, changes, and concerns particular to that moment—what is important to note is that in the present, all of these texts are flattened out and collapsed into one another in an often confusing and contradictory repertoire of themes and ideas on indigeneity in Trinidad, a confusion that is at once both constraining and troubling to contemporary actors and yet provides some representational freedom.

In chapter 4, "Nationalizing the Carib," my aim is to substantiate, describe, and analyze the articulation of the Carib (by non-Carib social institutions and actors) in Trinidad's search for a national sense of indigeneity. I thus outline the key ways in which the Carib has been appropriated as a symbolic anchor for mooring modern articulations of Trinidadian and Arimian identity. I direct attention to the ways in which colonial discourses of indigeneity are replayed in contemporary Trinidad via certain nationally sponsored traditions and institutions. The contemporary political economy of tradition with respect to cultural politics in the modern Trinidadian nation-state is also brought to light here, updated from its earlier colonial counterpart as presented in chapter 1. I believe this to be a critical chapter insofar as this dimension of modern Trinidadian and Caribbean cultural development in the Anglophone Caribbean has been almost completely neglected and overlooked.

Chapter 5, "Reproducing the Carib Locally," underscores the role of the cultural broker in promoting and shaping the meaning and value of the Carib. I focus on contemporary patterns of cultural brokerage and the construction of indigeneity in Trinidad, highlighting the structural field of sociocultural interaction underlying the current reengineering of indigeneity. The primary aim of that chapter is to provide a description and analysis of the relevant patterns of cultural brokerage while examining in depth the network of contemporary interests at work and the main actors and institutions that were at the heart of my ethnographic research.

Chapter 6, "Representing the Carib," involves an ethnographic focus on the ways that contemporary brokers publicly articulate representations of Carib indigeneity, and especially how they manage events and publicly perform rituals and traditions for the wider national audience. The Santa Rosa Festival, the smoke ceremony, and some of the traditional offices of the modern Carib Community are discussed in detail. In addition, this chapter examines those aspects of the SRCC's approaches to tradition (as outlined in the preceding ethnographic synopsis) that involve symbolically reclaiming as "Amerindian" certain practices located within the wider Creole cultural setting, and then their subsequent reappropriation as indigenous in contemporary constructions of national history.

Chapter 7, "Globalizing the Carib," features the global dimension of current reinterpretations and valuations of the Carib in Trinidad. I therefore outline the extent to which the contemporary SRCC constructs and reinterprets its indigeneity in and through a network of globally organized representations of aboriginality. Furthermore, I bring attention to the legitimating and value-adding impact of the SRCC's international associations within the Trinidadian social context. To emphasize the impact of the insertion of the SRCC within globalized discourses and networks of aboriginality, I focus on the development of new SRCC traditions that embody and enact the Caribs transformation into internationally defined "First Nations."

In the conclusion, "Reengineering Indigeneity," I bring this text to a close with a consideration of the overall transformations in the processes and practices of representing and reinterpreting Carib indigeneity. The key element of the closing chapter is a discussion of how we go about theorizing indigeneity, how we are to analytically locate indigeneity, and ways of addressing indigeneity as a theoretical and ethnographic problem. Finally, I reflect on some of the problems and prospects facing the SRCC in its practice of representing and promoting Carib traditions.

1

Canonizing the Carib
Colonial Political Economy and Indigeneity

The historical reconstruction of Caribbean Indigenous Identities can be exemplified by the chronological sampling featured in table 1 below. The various quotations demonstrate that, on the one hand, Carib as an idea was loaded with powerful connotations that have enshrined the label in historical narratives of the Caribbean for the past five hundred years. On the other hand, "Carib" exists in tension with other labels, such as "Arawak," and is set against ideas of docility and friendliness. Drawing on the works of Hulme[1] we may well agree that this is one of the central historical paradigms underpinning most constructions of indigeneity in the Caribbean in the postconquest period. But why do these constructions even matter today? How are they made to matter?

The ethnographic is historical: SRCC brokers today are often careful to reference or otherwise adapt ideas, data, and meanings from influential historical texts, producing representations that are mediated by allied historical researchers. More than that, SRCC brokers are called upon to account for who the SRCC Caribs are and why they are still here, in historical terms. Historical processes and their textual distillates thus weigh heavily on SRCC brokers' reinterpretations and articulation of Carib identity, and that history serves as a resource in their quest to affirm their cultural presence and their contribution to the national foundation.

Historical processes of political economy and identity construction have been central to framing the figure of the Carib in particular ways and at particular times, for a variety of purposes. One of the intended outcomes of this chapter is to highlight the figure of the indigene—whether symbolically constructed or demographically recognized—as a presence that is actively mediated in Trinidad's postconquest cultural development. What we must first examine is how colonial elites in their interactions with Caribbean natives set about establishing a field of signification that would first institute and then condition the subsequent deployments of the label "Carib." We are thus dealing with the construction of what Archer (1988) calls the propositional register.[2] The colonial experience generally and the creation of Caribness in particular have produced the field from and within which current Caribbean Amerindian identities are developed and delim-

Table 1. Identifying Caribs: A Chronological Sample

1493　"an island which is *Carib* . . . which is inhabited by people who are
　　　regarded in all these islands as very ferocious, who eat human flesh. They
　　　have many canoes with which they range through all the islands of India, rob
　　　and take whatever they can. . . . wearing their hair long like a woman . . .
　　　use bows and arrows of the same cane stems. . . . ferocious among these
　　　other people who are cowardly to an excessive degree."
　　　—Christopher Columbus (1992 [1493]:14–15)

1500　"We knew that they were of a people called *cannibals* and that most of them
　　　live on human flesh; and of this you can be certain Your Magnificence. . . .
　　　Of this we were certain in many parts, where we met such people, because we
　　　immediately saw bones and skulls of some they had eaten, and they do not
　　　deny it; moreover their enemies, who are always afraid of them, also say so.
　　　. . . These people we knew to be cannibals and that they ate human flesh."
　　　—Amerigo Vespucci, letter to Lorenzo de Medici of July 18, 1500, on his
　　　landing in Trinidad (Vespucci 1963 [1500]:43–44)

1518　"In the island of Trinidad . . . the Indians are as good and kind as any
　　　to be found in all the Indies."
　　　—Bartolomé de las Casas (the "Apostle of the Indies"), 1518 (quoted in E.
　　　Williams 1962:24)

1902　"Cuba, San Domingo, Jamaica, and the other islands in the West Indies,
　　　appear to have been inhabited, at the time of their discovery, by a mild and
　　　timid race, generally called Arouagues by Labat, Du Tertre and other French
　　　historians of the 17th century. The smaller islands, stretching from St.
　　　Thomas to Tobago, seem, on the contrary, to have been peopled, at that
　　　period, by a warlike and indomitable race of savages, collectively known as
　　　'Charaibes' or 'Caribs,' who heroically resisted every attempt at
　　　colonization on the part of European intruders. . . . stubborn was the
　　　persistence offered by these dauntless savages. . . . [with their]
　　　indomitable spirit[,] untameable nature [and] their remarkable passion for
　　　human flesh."
　　　—Henry Hesketh Bell, British governor of Dominica (1902:3, 4, 5, 7); also
　　　on the Internet at <http://www.delphis.dm/caribs2.htm>

1938　"Caribs were an intractable and warlike people; they were proud and
　　　dominating and preferred death to subjection. Throughout history the Caribs
　　　have always been indomitable and implacable opponents of all invaders. The
　　　early Conquistadors . . . found in the Caribs valiant and worthy opponents,
　　　and only too often the Spaniards suffered disastrous defeats."
　　　—K. S. Wise, *Historical Sketches of Trinidad and Tobago* (1938b:76)

1960　"I am combating a tradition [that of believing that Caribs were the
　　　indigenous people of Trinidad] which is deep rooted and hard to destroy, yet
　　　it must be destroyed if people of Trinidad of today are to understand their
　　　history."
　　　—John A. Bullbrook, *The Aborigines of Trinidad* (1960:54–55)

2000　Carib: "American Indian people who inhabited the Lesser Antilles. . . .
　　　Their name was given to the Caribbean Sea. . . . The Island Carib . . . were
　　　warlike (and allegedly cannibalistic). . . . Raids upon other peoples
　　　provided women who were kept as slave-wives; the male captives were tortured
　　　and killed."
　　　Cannibalism: "The term is derived from the Spanish name (Caríbales, or
　　　Caníbales) for the Carib, a West Indies tribe well known for their practice
　　　of cannibalism."

(continued)

Arawak: "They were driven out of the Lesser Antilles by the Carib shortly before the appearance of the Spanish."

Trinidad and Tobago (the people): "The original inhabitants of Trinidad were chiefly Arawak. Although there are inhabitants of the town of Arima who claim descent from Carib royalty, it is doubtful that the land was settled by Caribs."
—*Encyclopaedia Britannica* <http://www.britannica.com>

ited—a field that is represented by examples of the range of positions on the indigenes set out in table 1.

My focus here, following Archer, is on those elements of the cultural system that are constructed (as a result of previous cultural elaborations) and act to condition actors in their social interaction, resulting in a causal consensus that precedes further cultural elaboration (Archer 1988:xv–xvi).[3] By focusing first on colonial constructions of the meanings and value of "Carib," we are then better positioned to understand the subsequent localizations of the Carib within Arimian history and identity and in nationalist constructions of Trinidadian indigeneity. The objective here is to first map the wider field of interpretations and constructions of the meanings and value of "Carib" and "Amerindian" more generally, since they act to condition the contemporary practice of SRCC brokers.

I do not wish to unduly privilege the temporal dimension at the expense of the spatial, the latter being more the concern of the following chapter. Ultimately, the two are deeply intertwined, as best expressed in Wallerstein's term "TimeSpace" (1991b). Exemplifying this spatiotemporal duality, the temporal dimension of this chapter highlights the Caribbean as the place of the Caribs, and much effort was invested by colonizers in constructing that place and in defining and redefining particular places as either Carib or not. Nevertheless, the spatial dimension involved in the making of Arima as the *last* place of the Caribs is one that is set out in temporal terms, of rise and fall, resurgence and memory, legacy and tradition. By assuming this spatial-history orientation, I am highlighting the past-present axis of the reengineering concept underpinning this work.

The Colonial Construction and Consumption of "Cannibal" Capital: Classifying Caribs versus Arawaks, 1492–1498

"Carib," as a classification applied to certain groups, emerged from the confrontation between Europe and the aboriginal Caribbean and was the first attempt at some measure of ethnic specification after the initial deployment of the generic term *indio* (Indian). *Carib* was a pejorative native term that was not used as an autodenomination by any group at the time of the first European incursions; indeed, all we can be sure of is that there is no record of any native ethnic self-ascription in the Caribbean at the time of contact (Hulme 1993:200; also 1992:57).[4] The seminal act of categorical construction and imposition is the original act of engineering: constructing and ascribing traits of the worst imaginable savagery (cannibalism) to all aboriginal enemies of Spanish geopolitical expansionism, in contradistinction to the construction of the image of the peaceful and settled Arawak. "Arawak" itself was a word "never used by any Caribbean Amerindians" as an ethnic self-ascription; indeed, "neither Arawak nor Taíno were ever, as far as we know, self-ascriptions" (Hulme 1992:59, 61).[5]

The earliest writings by Columbus and his contemporaries, in the 1492–1498 period, attest to an uncertain probing, with multiple questions of designating language, place, or customs in connection with native identities, endless mistranslations and doubts, and constant redefinition and improvisation. However, this strategic European discourse soon became a reality "on the ground" within the Caribbean, when conflict and cooperation between Europeans and natives opened the door to specific and clear purposes motivating particular designations. The earliest reengineering, at least at the nominal level of self-identification, lies in later native subscriptions to the "Carib" label; in the shifts in deployment of the label by various European powers in contest with each other; and in the labor invested in redefining, reassigning, and reinterpreting the labels (and their presumed ethnic constituents and their traits). This is a project of categorization that has yet to cease.

"Carib," a former cognate of "cannibal," had, at best, indeterminate ethnographic substance. It was primarily a political label, deployed with real economic consequences. Applications of the label from the late 1400s have been flexible and open to manipulation. Interests were vested in this labeling process, as momentarily glimpsed by the often divergent and fluctuating ascriptions that lead to contradictory assertions about the Carib versus Arawak presence in Trinidad (see the quotes from 1500 and 1518 in table 1). Along with a great degree of necessary ethnographic obscurity, this label of convenience helped to establish elements of the ideational framework within which current groups such as the SRCC navigate, both by constraint and by choice. The portability of the products of these historical processes, stemming from the valuation of the Amerindian in colonial political economy, lies in their being enshrined in accessible and, indeed, widely disseminated and taught texts and, ultimately, in being seized upon and reproduced in the nationalist imaginary.

The earliest phase involves the engineering of categories by which Europeans were to interpret and remap the Caribbean. We can speak of the institution of "Carib" through globalizing processes such as colonialism and then localized as the appellation of particular communities in specific locales. With respect to this seminal construction of the label "Carib," Hulme challenges us to question "the frequently-made assumption that new human groupings first come into being—and are then categorized," noting that "the Caribs may in some sense themselves have been a 'new people,' created in the context of the sixteenth-century Caribbean" (2000:2, 9). The colonial reinvention of the Carib has "proved remarkably successful: colonial discourse may misrecognise, but it also has the power to call its categories into being" (Hulme 1992:213). Indeed, it is this dual process of categories of (mis)recognition that then assume a living reality which forms the ideational thrust of the reengineering process in the colonial era.

European geopolitics and the imperatives of capital accumulation played leading roles in European constructions of the native that are still in use today. For the Spanish, allies were Arawak, enemies were Carib. Enemies were any natives that contended with the Spanish in dominating the region. These two labels characterize the European perception of the native Caribbean. Todorov explains that "nomination is equivalent to taking possession" and that Columbus, among others, was not concerned with knowing what a name signified in Indian terms (1992:27, 29). In fact, it is this process of appropriating "Carib," without its aboriginal social or cultural substance, that permits us to speak in terms of invention. Todorov (1992:30) argues that labeling "good versus wicked" teaches us only that labeling depends on the point of view adopted, since the labels "correspond to specific states and not to stable characteristics" and derive from the pragmatic estimate of a situation.[6]

"Arawak" resides within the same discursive framework as "Carib." Arawak, as the other half of the ascriptive equation utilized by European colonizers, was caught within the same web of interests as Carib. "Arawak" and "Taíno" were treated by the Spanish as synonymous, with the Taínos being a specific group of Arawaks inhabiting the Greater Antilles. Neither "Arawak" nor "Taíno" was an ethnic self-ascription (Hulme 1993:199).[7] The friendship term, *guatiao*, utilized between these aboriginals of Hispaniola and Columbus also assumed a synonymous stance with Taíno. In Peter Martyr D'Anghera's 1587 classifications of natives of the islands, those who welcomed the Europeans were called *taíni*. Martyr described the meaning of "Taínos" as "good men" and set off the group as "noble men" in opposition to the cannibals (Roberts 1999:60; Hulme 1992:202–203).

The central point here is that Taíno was deployed as meaning "not Carib," and *guatiao* as "friend"—and since both Taínos and the Spanish were interested in identifying themselves to each other as friends, in opposition to the Caribs, the native transference of *guatiao* to the Spanish acted as a means by which Indians conferred native status on Spaniards, thus establishing a bond of friendship (Roberts 1999:61; also Hulme 1992:201). The stark contrast between Taíno and Carib became elevated to the heights of a mythic construct that would last for centuries. In contrast to the warlike Caribs, the Taínos thus became "the prototype of Rousseau's 'noble savage,'" and this "constant reiteration of the same adjectives—docile, sedentary, indolent, tranquil, chaste—from one author to another acquires ritual and mythical connotations" (Duany 1999:39).

The term "Arawak" is, however, saddled with additional interpretive difficulties that are not addressed when most contemporary commentators critique the label "Carib." For example, some assume that since there was a town in the Orinoco delta called Aruacay, identified as such from the earliest Spanish records of the region,[8] that Aruacas, or Arawaks, naturally must have been naming themselves after their place of origin. The resultant legitimation of Arawak, and deconstruction of Carib, in academic debates is problematic today even for the SRCC when commentators confront them with the charge that they are Arawak and not Carib.

There is little evidence to suggest that the label "Arawak" is any less problematic than "Carib." First, some writers have argued that *aruac* was used as a pejorative term as well: "the word 'Aruac' is not the name given by these people to themselves; it is a Carib word meaning 'Meal Eaters,' and used contemptuously by the Caribs" (Wise 1934:11). Indeed, apparently the only self-designation used by some so-called Arawaks was Lukuni, meaning "The People" (van der Plas 1954:3, Wise 1934:11). Second, there are also place names in the Orinoco-Guyana region, such as Little Canniballi and Caribana ("from the *Arawakan* meaning 'place of the Carib'" [Whitehead 1988:104, emphasis added]) that could be used to validate the label "Carib" as originally rooted in a place name as well—that is only if in the cases of both Aruacay and Caribana we forget to question who recorded these terms and at what stage of the colonizing process. Third, there is also evidence to suggest that Aruacay was likely to be identified as Carib and not Arawak: (1) the shaman of Aruacay was identified as a *piache*, a term belonging to the Cariban linguistic family (Oviedo 1959:398); (2) the people of Aruacay were identified in early reports as "very close friends with the Caribs" (Oviedo 1959:397); (3) Aruaca also happened to be the name of a Carib chief from the Santo Tomé region (Whitehead 1988:84); and, above all, (4) there is no evidence that the natives called the town Aruacay, since early reports state that it was "also known as" Huyapari (Whitehead 1988), the same term as Uriaparia, which refers to the Orinoco River and not to a people as such. This is a mere glimpse of the confusion and ambiguities that we all face in navigating through often arbitrary designations, in addition to the fact that original political arbitrariness has also become scientific convention, as when linguists speak of Cariban and Arawakan linguistic groups or when they argue that the Island Carib language was actually Arawakan (Hulme 1992:63; see also Davis 1992; Davis and Goodwin 1990).

Slavery and the Early Colonial Value of Carib in Trinidad, 1500s to Mid-1600s

By the 1600s, the ambiguity and tension between ascribing "Carib" or "Arawak" to certain native groups continued. This period reflected multiple strategies and outlooks on the part of both Europeans and aboriginals, before the colonial enclaves achieved stability (Hulme and Whitehead 1992:45). Spanish designations of certain groups as Carib were motivated by the desire to secure slave labor in ways consistent with the wishes of the Spanish Crown and with the drive for capital accumulation (see Davis and Goodwin 1990:38). In 1503, with the growing demand for slaves in Spanish-occupied territories such as Hispaniola, Queen Isabella issued her edict authorizing the capture and enslavement of the Caníbales, swayed by accounts of anthropophagous savages propagated by slave traders (Honychurch 2002:10; Hulme 1992:70). Only Caribs could be enslaved under this edict and similar edicts, which overtly proscribed the enslavement of natives.[9]

If and when Trinidad's own Amerindians were deemed to be "real Caribs" was a question framed within the dominant concerns of colonial political economy, with debates raging as glimpsed from the quotations in table 1. From the early 1500s, the trade of Trinidad Amerindian slaves to Margarita and Cubagua to work in the pearl fisheries had begun, with some also sent to Puerto Rico and Santo Domingo (Joseph 1970 [1838]:132). This first phase of colonial political economy thus centered on slave trading and pearls. Given that it was legal to enslave Caribs only, due to their alleged state of irredeemable savagery, slaves were thus actually branded with the letter "C" on their thighs.[10]

Diego Columbus began a trade in Amerindian slaves, in 1509, from Trinidad to Margarita (Ottley 1955:2–3; Wise 1938a:7). However, it was not then fully settled whether Trinidad's Amerindians were Carib or not, for, as Newson (1976:18) noted, "in 1510 it was said that there were no peaceful Indians along the whole coast of the Tierra Firme, except in Trinidad." Indeed, a royal decree of June 15, 1510, addressed to Diego Columbus, ordered a stop to the Trinidad Amerindian slave trade.[11] The situation was not so quickly stabilized, however, given intense lobbying by slave traders, inflammatory firsthand reports by partial observers, and changing strategies. Under this kind of pressure from the colonists of Santo Domingo, clamoring for an increased labor force (Whitehead 1988:11) on December 23, 1511, the king then issued a *real cédula* legalizing slavery again.[12]

Viewed in retrospect this series of edicts produced a bizarre series of assertions and reversals of previously established "truths." In 1510 Trinidad was not Carib; in 1511 it was Carib; and by 1512, once more Trinidad was not Carib. Orders to cease the enslavement of Trinidad's Amerindians "were repeated in 1512 to San Juan and the Royal Officials were urged to take immediate steps to verify the Indian reports of valuable gold deposits in Trinidad" (Wise 1938b:8). The promulgation of the Ley de Burgos in 1512, stipulating the end to Indian slavery, also decreed that "Indians were to be paid just wages for their labor" (Bisnauth 1996:18). Yet, as the search for gold proved unsuccessful, "interest in Trinidad thereupon lapsed except as a place for enslaving Indians to be sold at Cubagua and San Domingo" (Wise 1938b:8–9). Therefore, if the labor of Trinidad's Amerindians was needed elsewhere, as in the pearl fisheries or in Santo Domingo, they were labeled as Caribs and enslaved; if their labor was instead needed in Trinidad, for possible gold mining or for a peaceful trade in pearls given the generalized anti-Spanish hostility of tribes in the area, they were to be freed and declared non-Carib. The calculations behind these formalized proclamations of identity were, apparently, simple and tightly geared toward efficient capital accumulation in tune with the realpolitik of the early colonial aboriginal arena.

The need for some consistency in definitions became salient especially with the increasing outcry from members of the Dominican Order, such as Friar Bartolomé de las Casas, and during the reforms of Cardinal Cisneros in Spain: "the distinction between 'Carib' and 'non-Carib' populations became a serious concern for the Spanish Crown, and, in 1518, Rodrigo de Figueroa was appointed a judge, with plenary powers, to produce *a definitive classification of Amerindian cultures*, throughout those territories known to the Spanish" (Whitehead 1988:9, emphasis added). Three centuries later, the traveler/explorer Alexander von Humboldt wrote of Figueroa and his report, "His ethnographic piece, called *El auto de Figueroa*, is one of the most curious records of the early conquistadores' barbarism. Without paying attention to languages, any tribe that was accused of eating prisoners was called Carib. All the tribes that Figueroa called Carib were condemned to slavery" (Humboldt 1995:277). Following the protests by Las Casas (see the 1518 quote in table 1), Trinidad was excluded from Figueroa's classification of 1518, "though . . . as in the meantime gold had been reported from the island, the change in the status of Trinidad's Amerindians might be seen as reflecting a desire to preserve a native labor force, *in situ,* for use in future mining operations" (Whitehead 1988:11).

Though Trinidad was thus declared an island not occupied by Caribs, this situation seemed in doubt when slave traders once again petitioned the Crown for permission to enslave Indians on the basis of their being evil, warlike cannibals (Newson 1976:18–19). In a pattern that should be familiar to the reader by now, "when the *gold failed to materialize* and Antonio Sedeño was given permission to colonize the island in 1530, Trinidad was, once again, declared 'Carib,' by a *Real Cédula* of the 13th of September of that year" (Whitehead 1988:11, emphasis added). In addition, the strategic value of Trinidad was increased in this period by Spanish attempts to penetrate the Orinoco region in search of the mythical land of Meta (the province of the famed El Dorado), making an unhindered occupation of Trinidad highly desirable (Whitehead 1988:11).

The accusation of cannibalism, it seems, was also sometimes wielded by Trinidad's Amerindians against the Spanish. When Antonio Sedeño, Trinidad's first governor, arrived in Trinidad in 1532 and "with the aid of a contingent of 80 men proceeded to punish the Indians, 'putting them to fire and sword and inflicting severe penalties,'" it was recorded that in this fight "the Indians refused to surrender, choosing rather to die in the flames, than to be made captives by Spaniards who, they had grown to believe, *ate all their prisoners*" (Ottley 1955:6, emphasis added). As Las Casas also wrote, "because they [their fellows] did not return to their lands they would say that they [the Caribs] ate them. They believed the same thing about the Christians and about the admiral [Columbus] the first time some of them saw them" (Las Casas 1992b:18). Writing in the

1530s, and repeating some of the negative caricatures highlighted in table 1, Gonzalo Fernandez de Oviedo y Valdés (a Spanish traveler who spent decades in the early colonial Caribbean and interviewed many of the leading Spanish conquerors) wrote that "the island of Trinidad . . . is populated by Carib Indians bearing arrows. . . . They are a very bellicose people, naked and idolatrous, and they eat human flesh, and beneath these vices one must believe that they have many others" (Oviedo 1959:387).

Apart from the persistent desire to imagine the Caribs as even worse than the evil they were already known to manifest, Oviedo's writings provide a glimpse of early Trinidad aboriginal tactics in actively subscribing to these same negative depictions when it was convenient, that is, when striking fear into the hearts of Spaniards seemed appropriate. Oviedo described the following situation faced by a small Spanish landing party in Trinidad. "Returning to the river . . . three or four Indians arrived . . . who appeared to be Caribs, and the Christians told them they came in peace and if they could get something to eat; and they [the Indians] responded that *if there would be any eating to be done it would be Christians that would be eaten,* if they [the Spanish] would wait there another day since many Indians would come" (Oviedo 1959:395, emphasis added).[13]

For approximately sixty years after the departure of Sedeño in 1534, Trinidad remained in the hands of the Indians, who developed a brisk trade in tobacco, corn, and other foodstuffs with the many adventurers who came to the West Indies in search of riches (Ottley 1955:9). The problem with this situation was that the Spanish were eager to appropriate Amerindian trade networks as another source of capital extraction in addition to more direct forms of accumulation. They were equally eager to secure these trade networks for themselves, to the exclusion of new contenders in the region such as the Dutch, the French, and the British. More often than not, those local polities that were identified as Carib were those that still controlled an independent trade in valuable commodities such as tobacco. Unsurprisingly, in 1547, "the King of Spain gave special permission to the inhabitants of San Juan to make war upon the Caribs and to enslave them. . . . The natives of Trinidad, Guadeloupe, Martinique (Matinino), Dominica, and Santa Cruz were specially aimed at. These islands appear to have always been the chief strongholds of the Caribs" (Bell 1902:6). In the same period, in 1550–1551, Las Casas engaged Juán Gines de Sepúlveda in Valladolid in a debate over Spain's waging war against the Indians as a step toward Christianizing them (Bisnauth 1996:18). According to Sepúlveda, the Indians were "so uncivilized, so barbaric, contaminated with so many impieties and obscenities. . . . [They are] little men (*hombrecillos*) in whom you will scarcely find even vestiges of humanity" (quoted in Bisnauth 1996:19).

Claiming real or imagined attacks by savages against Spanish populations could also have been used as a justification by more sanguine colonists, thus serving to build a mystique around Carib military prowess even while providing a basis for the conquest of the Caribs. The heroism and tenacity of Carib resistance and their warlike nature is treated as a matter of fact in today's texts and in conventional depictions produced in contemporary Caribbean societies. It is this heroism that is often seized upon in contemporary nationalist reinterpretations of the aboriginal past, as well as by Carib activists today.

By the end of the 1500s, when the indigenous population of Trinidad declined, colonists turned to the Orinoco as a new source of slaves (Whitehead 1988:29). Pointing to documents from the end of the 1600s, Whitehead tells us that when all the slaves on Trinidad were released as a result of the Spanish Crown's ordering a cessation of the armed conquest and the holding of personal slaves, "some 2,000 Caribs, mainly from the Caura and Cuchivero Rivers, were given their freedom at this time . . . although the legal provision for the slavery of 'rebel' Caribs remained in force until 1756" (1988:29).

The Trinidad that the Spanish first encountered was one that had long been a hodgepodge of Amerindian groups from the Caribbean islands and northern South America, a virtual transit station in long distance trading networks between the islands and the mainland, with various languages and tribal identifications recorded by subsequent European explorers. Spanish entry into a complex local political situation had a considerable impact on the local state of affairs described by colonial chroniclers, "introducing another player, of obvious power if markedly ignorant, whose presence and actions had immediately to be factored into all native calculations, responses, and words" (Hulme 1992:211). That some groups would be classified as cannibal (Carib) in order to justify their legal conquest and thus displace them as competitors for local labor power would also serve to facilitate alliances between the Spanish and Amerindian rivals of the so-called Caribs.

With greater penetration and with the passage of decades, the map of labels changes and begins to diversify considerably, as preexisting native complexity became enmeshed in a system of fluctuating ascriptions among competing European powers intertwined in contending networks of alliances with aboriginal groups. Thus, beginning with the term "Carib" itself, we have a dizzying array of cognates (from which today's communities freely choose): from the Spanish— Caribal, Caniba, Canibal (Cannibal), Calinago, Califuna, Carifuna, Cariña, Caliña, Caliponam, Carini, Carinepogoto, and Camajuya; from the French— Caraibe, Charaibe, Callinague, and Galibi; and from the British—Carib, Caribbee, and even Caribou. Beyond this, the accounts written by the famed English adventurer Sir Walter Ralegh relating his raid on Trinidad in 1595 identified Arawak settlements and, near San José de Oruña (the Spanish capital in Trinidad), the Carinepagotos, "probably a Carib group" (Whitehead 1988:15). Other groups named by Ralegh were the "Yaio (. . . Yao, a Carib-speaking group), *Arwaca* (. . . Lokono, or True Arawak), *Saluaios* (?), *Nepoios* (. . . Sepoios, another Carib-speaking group)" (Figueredo and Glazier 1991:238). Other writers in the early 1600s such as Vázquez de Espinosa stated that the "Indian tribe of the island of Trinidad" was "Nepuya by name" (Espinosa 1968:37), a label that has surfaced as a contender for legitimacy as an alternative label for today's SRCC in Arima. Others speak of Lokono (Arawak) villages in Trinidad, noting that Trinidad was the major link in the Arawak–Island Carib trade relationship (Boomert 1986:10). Espinosa spoke of Caribs who were called Garinas, as dominant in the Orinoco delta, with Trinidad positioned at its entrance (1968:72), echoing the writings of Amerigo Vespucci and Alonso de Ojeda, who also insisted on the Carib designation in 1499–1500 (Whitehead 1988:12). Also in the early 1600s, Robert Harcourt wrote, "the Caribs had only recently driven out other Amerindian groups from parts of Trinidad" (Whitehead 1988:17). Writing in the mid 1600s, the Dominican cleric Jacinto de Carvajal identified among "the Kalinago groups fleeing the Antilles . . . the Galeras, who had invaded the Punta de Galera on Trinidad, the Dragos, who had settled islands in the Paria Gulf and Orinoco Delta, and the Tobagos, Kalinago from Dominica and Grenada living on Tobago" (Whitehead 1988:16). "Carib" today acts to reduce and simplify this complex map, even though elements of the map itself are still available at present in contemporary texts.

Whitehead argues that the fact that the documents of Ralegh and his contemporaries, some of whom are cited above, do not always square with one another is due to the fact that with greater European penetration came greater discernment, and thus more denominations were revealed (1988:17). As Whitehead notes, "by the 1620s, the Spanish were no longer referring to 'Caribe' groups on the northern coast of Venezuela at all but, *more correctly*, to Cumanagotos, Parias and Guayqueris" (1988:17, emphasis added). I believe that it is too great a leap of faith to pronounce any label as correct from our present vantage point, that is, as we look back at such overt chaos and as we are forced to breathe such ethnographically thin air. Moreover, the notion that European penetration would reveal—more than it would change, shape, or provoke that which was presumably revealed—is also debatable. Thus one could argue that with greater penetration also came further displacements, diverse reactions, changed cultural fields, and even altogether new names. I agree with Whitehead when he later reflects, "the European presence itself had already affected the situation considerably" (1988:18). Indeed, as with the previous examples of Trinidad's Amerindians playing up the mystique of being man-eaters, Amerindians themselves engaged this field of contested and motivated multiple naming, thus marking the deepening and widening of the reengineering of indigeneity.

Natives in the Early Reengineering of Indigeneity

Starting in the 1600s, cultural transformations of aboriginal polities were already being recorded, along with evidence of pragmatic native appropriations of dominant European ascriptions. Even before Spanish rule had been consolidated in the Caribbean, the Caribs were miscegenated to some degree and even multiethnic in a sense, that is, consisting of a mix of peoples from the Americas, Europe, and

Africa. As a Carib man told a French visitor in 1665: "Our people are becoming in a manner like yours, since they came to be acquainted with you; and we find it with some difficulty to know ourselves, so different are we grown from what we were here-to-fore" (quoted in Honychurch 2002:1, 10). Island Caribs in this period were reputed to have assimilated foreign captives, and inevitably some mutual acculturation must have occurred.[14] The chaplain to the Earl of Cumberland found Caribs in Dominica and reported in 1598, "they speak some Spanish words" (quoted in Hulme and Whitehead 1992:59), which presumably could have been learned from their captives. In the mid 1700s in Dominica, runaway slaves made "common cause with the Caribs" in order to defend their forests (Bell 1902). Others note that acculturation must have begun at an early date, as shown by the Caribbean words of Spanish origin included in Father Raymond Breton's famous dictionary of 1665 (Taylor 1992 [1941]:315; see Breton 2001 [1665]). This process of cultural creolization could only be amplified through trade, marriage, and military relations with Europeans, the impact of Christian evangelization, and other processes such the Caribs' incorporation of African slaves, as in St. Vincent (see Le Breton 1998 [1702]; van der Plas 1954). By the start of the 1600s, then, already much had changed, with the Amerindians having incorporated not only items of European culture but even some Europeans themselves.

Some analysts perceive some strategizing in auto-denomination on the part of Caribbean Amerindians, of seemingly subscribing to European ascriptions for very specific purposes. As Whitehead put it, "'Carib-ism,' along with its historical counterpart, 'Arawak-ism,' . . . represented alternative political responses, on the part of the Amerindians, to the European invasions" (Whitehead 1988:189). In terms of the Arawak label, Boomert believes it "was rapidly adopted, possibly by several Amerindian tribal groups, due to the protection the name gave against Spanish slave-raiding expeditions," especially after Rodrigo de Figueroa's report of 1520 mentioned previously (Boomert 1986:13). Boomert outlines groups that called themselves Arawak yet traded and intermarried with the Kalina (Mainland Caribs), whose languages possessed items of mixed lexical origins and who could position themselves as either Arawak or Carib, depending on the context and the prospective partners in question. Boomert also states that by about 1600, "the name Arawak had become a generic term undoubtedly including not only *Lokono* . . . but other, smaller ethnic groups in especially Trinidad and the Lower Orinoco area as well" (1986:10).

By the late sixteenth century the inhabitants of the Lesser Antilles probably considered themselves as an ethnic unit and called themselves Carib.[15] Father Adrien Le Breton, who lived amongst the Caribs of St. Vincent between 1693 and 1702, echoed this in his writing: "For me there is absolutely no reason to find it surprising that this word calls to mind courageous and warlike men" (1998 [1702]:18). Some chroniclers recorded native subscriptions to the Carib label as early as the 1530s, noting that for some, "Carib" signified brave and daring (see

Campbell 2001:1). The adoption of this badge by aboriginals may have served to promote their own value as worthy military allies in the eyes of various European powers contending for supremacy in the region in their struggles against Spain. Therefore, what also stemmed from these native responses and appropriations of Carib was a conditioning of further European responses to the ways aboriginals positioned themselves.

The Carib label, as an aboriginal auto-denomination, began to spread; this is substantiated by various sources. Rouse wrote that when "the English explored the Guianas at the close of the 16th century, they found Indians living there who called themselves Carib" (Rouse n.d.). Additional testimonial evidence of groups actively adopting the Carib label is found in 1734, in a writer's account of the rebellion by Chief Taricura, which mentions that the chief persuaded parties of Guaraunos (Warao)[10] and Arguacas (Arawaks) to become Caribs (quoted in Whitehead 1988:117). Boomert also observes that the serious decline of the Amerindian population in coastal Guiana during the contact period resulted in "the amalgamation of numerous groups whereby especially smaller ethnic unities were absorbed by the larger tribal groups, a development which can be reconstructed from the gradual disappearance of various Amerindian self-denominations from about 1650 onwards" (1986:12). Boomert says that by the mid 1600s, the original self-identifications of the original inhabitants of the Windward Islands "had in fact long been forgotten" (1986:13). Others have also found that on the mainland, with Carib monopoly of the trade with the Dutch in Essequibo from the 1620s onward, a variety of groups began to adopt the Mainland Caribs' auto-denomination (Whitehead 1988:190).

These were early processes in the reengineering of indigeneity, that is, of interests vested in the creation and projection of particular identities, a process whereby power brokers such as Amerindian chiefs and European colonizers mediated in the articulation of Self and Other and the ways these were denominated. Moreover, the products of these early processes, filtered out of their original contexts, condition current articulations of Carib indigeneity, thereby achieving a status as truths.

Valiant Allies

Imperial contests, and the texts that were produced in that context, subsequently achieved a prestigious if not legislative authority for historians and today's revivalist groups alike. Imperialism and its impact is a necessary part of our consideration if we are to avoid the "ethnomyopia" criticized by Gonzalez, meaning the failure to take into account global struggles for hegemony played out between various European actors in the Caribbean (Gonzalez 1983:145; see also Whitehead 1988:92). How European powers were positioned against each other and the ways Amerindians positioned themselves in turn had serious consequences for all the European colonizing projects insofar as they were heavily dependent on Amerindian support (Whitehead 1988:2). Unfortunately, the voluminous details of the complex histories of these multiple alliances far exceed the scope of this volume.

In colonial peripheral zones such as Trinidad, the Orinoco delta, and the Guianas, Amerindian allies were vital to the success of colonial projects, especially as such zones produced no taxable flows of bullion. For the Caribs, such alliances gave them a preferential access to highly valued items, such as metal manufactures, thereby enhancing not only the status of individual aboriginal leaders and traders but also, through their associated kin networks, that of Carib groups generally (Whitehead 1988:104). While Trinidad itself was no longer considered a probable source of gold by 1600, it had a strategic and economic importance in other respects, primarily in terms of Trinidad's location as a base for searching for El Dorado; the cultivation and trade in tobacco, the first lucrative cash crop of the Caribbean; and, later, the export of cocoa, the second valuable agricultural commodity to be produced in the Caribbean (see Noel 1972: 13). In the early colonial period (pre-1800), the search for El Dorado from Trinidad and the production of tobacco both dominated from the late 1500s to the early 1600s. Cocoa became prominent from 1670 to 1725. The Amerindians themselves maintained a significant hold on the tobacco trade even into the 1600s. Dutch, English, and French vessels illegally traded manufactured goods for tobacco in Trinidad in the early years of the 1600s (Wise 1936:17).

Trinidad became imbued with a special myth of place associated with El Dorado, pointing to the promise of great wealth even if it was never actually realized, a place where fantasy and ideology, discovery and conquest, pragmatism and idiosyncratic compulsions became fused in a type of "magical rationalism" (see Ramos Perez 1973). From 1583, with Antonio de Berrio's inheritance of the title to the provinces of El Dorado, there began a new phase in the occupation of the Orinoco, and in this period Trinidad became "the forward base for this penetration" (Whitehead 1988:80). Governor de Berrio thus sent a letter to Spain "to inform His Majesty of these new territories, how well-peopled they were with savages, and that they lay close to the provinces of Omagua, or El Dorado, about which, and their great wealth of gold and silver, many reports were in circulation" (quoted in Espinosa 1968:55). In addition, the increasing presence of the English, French, and Dutch in the Caribbean made it "a matter of utmost importance that the Orinoco be secured for the Spanish Crown," and accordingly it was from this date (1583) that Carib populations began to experience "the full effects of a permanent European presence" (Whitehead 1988:81; see also Ramos Perez 1973:646). Sir Walter Ralegh's attack on the Spanish capital of Trinidad in April of 1595, immediately followed by his exploration of the Orinoco in search of El Dorado, served to galvanize Spanish policy in the region.

When Trinidad was finally settled by the Spanish in 1592, Governor de Berrio obtained Amerindian laborers and began to cultivate tobacco, thus breaching Amerindian control over labor and the trade in tobacco, and the Spanish colonists suffered their attacks as a result (Ottley 1955:11). Succeeding his father in 1597, Don Fernando de Berrio had largely failed to conquer and penetrate the Orinoco region, and "he therefore built an ajoupa at San José de Oruña [St. Joseph, the capital of Trinidad at the time] and occupied himself in the cultivation of tobacco, in which task he received the assistance of his Indian slaves" (Ottley 1955:16). The aims of the Spanish in Trinidad at the start of the 1600s were not to engage in the total armed conquest of all of the Amerindians in the area; rather, the interest was in gaining a foothold in the illicit tobacco trade with the English, Dutch, and French, as well as maintaining a bridgehead into the Orinoco (Ottley 1955:15).

The Spanish had Amerindian allies in these various ventures, that is, groups competing with Carib access to European goods. How were these allied groups classified by the Spanish? One early designation was simply that of "Christian Indian" (see Espinosa 1968:87; Oviedo 1959:391). In other cases, the allies were referred to as Aruacas (Arawaks) even though in 1603 there had also been alliances with the Warao,[17] who were dominant in the Orinoco and Trinidad (Wise 1936:13).

One might ask if having Arawak allies would inspire any confidence, given that the Spanish had invested so much labor in constructing the Caribs as the true warriors and Arawaks as docile cowards. Would the Crown not frown upon the poverty of such an alliance? This is where a rupture with the previous dichotomy became mandatory, with the resultant transformation in the traits associated with the Arawaks. Writing in the early 1620s, Espinosa thus certified: "The tribe of the Aruaca Indians is among the most valiant. . . . feared for their bravery by their neighbors and adjoining tribes, they are envied by the Indians of other tribes; they were always very loyal friends of the Spaniards, and when the latter came from Spain in the year 1595, they helped, served, and assisted them in all their needs" (1968:68). The Arawaks of 1620 were no longer defined as the Arawaks of 1492, at least not when it was necessary to forget the classifications of yesteryear.

From the 1500s onward, the Spanish "formed strategic alliances with the Arawak (Lokono) of the Orinoco and coastal Guyana; both for economic reasons, especially the supply of food to Spanish settlements, and for political ones, specifically to gain a bridgehead into the Amerindian polity" (Whitehead 1988:18). As expressed by Espinosa above, the Spaniards heavily favored the Orinoco Arawak over other Amerindians, even exempting them from the general liability to enslavement. The Arawaks gained great prestige through their early dominance of the trade in Spanish goods, especially the trade in metal tools, which the Caribs were to successfully challenge in the 1600s through alliance with the Essequibo Dutch (Whitehead 1988:18). A further expression of the value Arawak allies held for the Spanish is evidenced by the Spanish giving African slaves to the Arawaks to labor on tobacco plantations that the Arawaks had set up in the Orinoco basin, as well as to work mines on the lower Caroni River.

The Spanish also gave the Arawaks intermittent military support as they occupied the lower reaches of rivers in what is today western Guyana, notably the Essequibo, Moruca, and Pomeroon, and parts of Trinidad (Whitehead 1988:18). After the 1620s the Dutch established an alliance with the Caribs in what is today eastern Guyana, with the marriage of Groenewagen, a Dutch West Indian Company representative, to a local Carib woman. This early glimmer of the subsequent privileging of Amerindians within European colonial projects shows the development of affective ties even if strategically motivated (or perhaps one could rephrase this as strategic ties with an affective insurance policy).

In the conflict with the Spanish and their Arawak allies, the Dutch and the English became allies of the Caribs. In various parts of the region the Caribs supported British settlements; along the Essequibo River, the Caribs and the Dutch jointly manned a fort (Espinosa 1968:77; Whitehead 1988:85–86). In 1629, both the English and the Dutch established themselves in Tobago and joined themselves with the Caribs (Whitehead 1988:88). On Trinidad, Sir Thomas Bridges planted a group near Toco, "helped by the Indians on the North Coast" in the 1670s; in the 1680s, "the Dutch too, had made an alliance with the Indians in the South and had settled near Moruga about that same time" (Ottley 1955:22, 23).

The Dutch-Carib alliance produced an episode featuring a Trinidad chief who, in the 1990s, would be resurrected by researchers associated with the SRCC and hailed as a national hero: Chief Hyarima. Very little documentary evidence is available concerning Hyarima, and this mostly consists of two letters written by don Diego Lopez de Escobar, governor and captain general of Trinidad, in 1636 (Wise 1934:52–55). Hyarima is identified as a Nepuyo, a tribe belonging to the Cariban linguistic stock. A summary of these letters tells us the following: "The Nepuyo Indians whose Cacique was Hyarima lived three leagues (nine miles) to the east of St. Joseph, evidently at Arima. They had offered the Dutch as hostages all the old men, women and children of the tribe in return for the assistance of 80 men with arquebuses" (Wise 1934:58). In 1637, Hyarima joined the Dutch in a campaign up the Orinoco River and against St. Joseph, the Spanish capital of Trinidad (Wise 1934:70).

Affective relationships between European colonists and Amerindian ruling groups became the norm in the post-1600 Caribbean. Spanish colonialists had developed systems for establishing kinship ties with Amerindian groups as a basis for forming alliances, through marriage and friendships (see Hulme 1992:71). In the case of what became British Guiana, it has been noted that Caribs were the ones who had the closest relations with Europeans and who still continue to maintain favorable stereotypes of Europeans as their benefactors (see Sanders 1976:119, 134; also J. Forte 1996). Amerindians in Guyana also played an active role in maintaining the slave regimes of the 1700s and 1800s.[18]

In an even more critical manner, these competing alliances and their impact on

Trinidad led to serious changes in Spanish policy. As part of the attempt to restore Spanish control of the Orinoco, in 1686 Trinidad's Governor Tiburcio de Aspe y Zuñiga gave orders to abolish, "in the Province of Trinidad and Guayana, every sort of bondage contract of Indians, in order that they might enjoy their liberty" (quoted in Whitehead 1988:101). *Encomiendas,* the Spanish institution for coercing and administering Amerindian labor, were abolished throughout the Spanish empire by 1716 (Whitehead 1988:100). The Spanish turned instead to missionaries in securing Amerindian allies and co-opting Amerindian trade networks.

The geopolitical utility of these previous alliances for the Europeans would necessarily decline somewhat, especially with the reinforced détente with the Caribs begun by the Spanish in 1639, an example of this being the governor of Trinidad baptizing "one of the most important caciques of the Orinoco, Macuare . . . 'Don Martin, General'" (Whitehead 1988:91). Moreover, in 1649 Spain signed the Peace of Westphalia with the Caribs' allies, Holland. In the 1700s, there was a further decline in Carib power, with the Dutch turning to sugar, establishing stable relations with Spanish neighbors, and reducing their trade relationships with Amerindian groups (Whitehead 1988:107).

The Undoing of Carib Power, the Making of the Mission Indian, and Cocoa in the Late 1600s to Early 1700s

In 1642 King Philip II of Spain ordered that the armed conquest cease, and in a royal decree of that same year he initiated the mission system, given that military invasions had largely failed to subdue Amerindian groups (Whitehead 1988: 132). In addition, by the early 1700s, the Spanish sought to undercut and obstruct Carib trading patterns by offering European goods apparently for nothing (at first), thus reducing Carib influence among Amerindian peoples of the Orinoco (Whitehead 1988:106). With indigenous populations held in one place, access to them secured, and men's labor for the priests' agricultural projects paid for in European goods, the mission system was thus designed to effectively undercut Carib dominance (Whitehead 1988:106). The king of Spain issued orders to the Capuchin fathers to establish missions in Trinidad in 1686. The official justification was a civilizational and evangelical one, as seen in the king's letter to the governor of Trinidad dated February 14, 1686.[19]

Father Tomás de Barcelona, prefect of the Capuchins, arrived in Trinidad in 1686. As was to be expected, he found "most disconcerting of all the grave disinclination of the native peoples for labor in the tobacco and cocoa fields" (Ottley 1955:24). We can surmise that the reason for this was that, for the natives, it would mean loss of control over their production and trade in these goods. As the Spanish were interlopers in Amerindian trade networks, they also suffered constant attacks against their missions by Amerindians from the nearby mainland, most often the Warao (Ottley 1955:29). It would be relatively easy then for the colonists to reduce this struggle to one of civilized Amerindians (and their protective Fathers) versus the savage Warao.

The mission Indians were seen by the Warao and other Amerindian rivals of the Spanish as "relations of the Spaniards" (Whitehead 1988:117). In effect, from the 1700s to as late as the mid 1900s, and within the very localized sphere of Trinidad and eastern Venezuela, the Warao began to stand in for almost everything the Caribs had come to symbolize at the wider Caribbean level: warlike, engaged in fierce resistance, untamable, independent, elusive. To this day, in parts of Trinidad, one can hear of individuals perceived as wild or gypsylike in their behavior being referred to as Warahoons. In addition, the Warahoon became enshrined in the annual Carnival celebrations in the figure of the Wild Indian. The "raiding Warao" is still a figure common in many stories emanating from southern Trinidad in recent times, relating to Waraos entering yards at night and stealing clothes off of drying lines or even snatching babies.

At this localized level of Trinidad, the Nepuyos, identified by the Spanish as a subtribe of the Caribs, were allies of the Spanish missions—yet another rupture with the early paradigm of fierce Carib enemies and docile Arawak friends. The Amerindians of the missions of San Agustín de Arauca (today's Arouca), San Pablo de Tacarigua (Tacarigua), and the Partido de Quare (Caura) were noted by one historian to be of "the Nepuyo Nation, a part of the Carib stock who had generations before migrated from the Lower Orinoco and settled in the northern part of Trinidad and particularly between San Josef and Matura" (Wise 1938b:87). This latter reference is indeed very important since, along with the passage on Hyarima the Nepuyo chief (above), it has found its way directly from Wise to SRCC leaders via historic notes written for the SRCC by Peter Harris (1989a, 1989b) and has led to a nascent reinterpretation of the "true Carib" as being fundamentally a Nepuyo, as the SRCC secretary and current research officer, Jacqueline Khan, asserted in an interview with me.

In the 1730s, Spanish municipal officials in Trinidad wrote to the king to impress upon him the loyalty and service of the Nepuyos. They wrote: "we have the greater reason to keep the Indians happy and contented, especially these Nepuyos, who are the only Indians who will supply men to oppose the enemies of your Royal Crown and who are always in the forefront of battle"; and further, "we know well from experience the loyalty and zeal with which they have always served Your Majesty," hence the need, they stressed, to "foster the best interests of these Indians" (quoted in Wise 1938b:87–88).

In the wake of declining aboriginal power and shifting alliances with the Spanish, the Capuchin priests succeeded in founding the cocoa industry by establishing plantations in their missions at San Fernando, Savana Grande, Montserrat, Santa Anna de la Savonetta, and San Francisco de los Arenales, with cocoa becoming the major cash-crop export by the 1700s (Stephens 1985:10–11; Wise

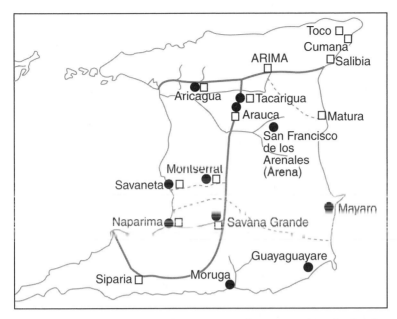

Figure 1. Map of missions in Trinidad.

● Missions of the Catalan Capuchins, 1687–1708.

☐ Missions of the Aragon Capuchins of Santa Maria, 1758–1837.

(Adapted from Rétout 1976:xx)

1934:32). Mission-owned cocoa plantations were subsequently established in Arima, Toco, Salibia, Siparia, Matura, and Point Cumana (figure 1).

Amerindian chiefs, under the control of the Spanish, acted as internal rulers within missions (de Verteuil 1995:53–54). These co-opted chiefs functioned to bolster the civil, economic, military, and geopolitical purposes of these missions, a fact that would also differentiate them from nonmission Amerindians and thus would serve to develop differing perceptions and valuations of mission versus nonmission Amerindians in the eyes of the colonial elite. Each mission was organized as a *pueblo*, the same as a Spanish town with its *cabildo*, or town council. As a document of the period explained, the priests, in order to ensure "regular subordination in the villages and civility among individuals, . . . elect from the most diligent and reasonable Indians a certain number of officials and ministers of justice . . . so that the Indians should obey them and be ruled by them" (quoted in de Verteuil 1995:58). Chiefs became the instruments of collection of tribute and the organization of labor and were given the title of "don" (de Verteuil 1995:67). Special insignia were granted to these aboriginal officials, and special places were reserved for them in church, in order to add to their prestige. An Indian council administered its own justice; Amerindian leaders would even run jails—"in fact *much of the actual controlling of the Indians was done by the Indians themselves. . . .* this was the only way the two Capuchins in each mission in the island could control the hundreds of Indians" (de Verteuil 1995:58, emphasis added). Moreover, as civic leaders, these officials were ascribed a higher status, with the cacique (chief) and shaman exempt from labor (de Verteuil 1995:67). Ultimate authority lay in the priests' hands, however: "the power of the priests was absolute but their government was paternal" (de Verteuil 1995:59; also Noel 1972:20).

The Capuchins also had their Amerindians trained in military matters, and in Trinidad each mission had its captain and lieutenant with uniform and insignia. Amerindians in Trinidad were allied with the Spanish against the Dutch, forming an Indian-Spanish army, and in some quarters were even referred to as "Spanish Caribs" (de Verteuil 1995:67–68; Whitehead 1988:190). Companies of Indians to defend missions were also established with the intent of countering repeated Warao raids (de Verteuil 1995:68).

As a result of the establishment of missions in Trinidad, the church became an economic magnate in the colony, controlling almost all the labor as well as leading the production of cocoa for export, one of the world market's lucrative agricultural commodities of the time. Even Trinidadian historians with a predisposition to favor the Catholic Church reluctantly admit that "the mission was organized almost on a commercial basis" (de Verteuil 1995:57). All aboriginals in the missions were subject to the missionaries for a period of ten (some say twenty) years, "during which time they worked free of charge in exchange for their board and the protection of their bodies" (Ottley 1955:26). At the end of this period of indenture and in keeping with their new status as freemen, "a tax . . . was imposed on each of them" (Ottley 1955:26). The priests were also authorized to distribute the Amerindians for monthly service at a wage on private *encomiendas*. Nevertheless, with the expansion of the missions' cocoa fields, within a short time "the missions absorbed all the available labor and little was left for the Spanish planters" (Ottley 1955:26). Thus the missions paid virtually nothing for labor and exported a crop of great remunerative value, inevitably boosting the dominance of the mission in the colonial economy.

An indirect result of this church monopoly was the emergence of a local debate over categorizing aboriginals as civilized or savage. By 1701, planters in Trinidad sent a petition to Governor don Felipe de Artieda, seeking the release of Indians from missions to supply labor for expanding their own cocoa cultivation (Ottley 1955:35). At this stage, the planters were anxious to stress that the Amerindians were "already civilized" and thus required no more bondage to missions (Ottley 1955:36). It is unsurprising, given the patterns we have seen thus far, that as missionaries abandoned the island after the king's *cédula* ordered them to the mainland, the planters would anxiously report that the Amerindians went back to forest areas and "continued 'the idolatrous practices of their fathers,'" and thus, once more, they were uncivilized and needed to be conquered (Ottley 1955:

37). At this stage, civilized versus noncivilized and mission versus nonmission became the dominant dichotomies in Spanish colonial attempts to sort out native enemies and allies. The Carib-Arawak dichotomy, once a categorical monopoly, thus was transformed and began to fade altogether.

By the end of the 1600s, Capuchin missionaries had brought more than 5,000 Amerindians under their control, incorporating them into agricultural settlements producing cocoa for export (Harricharan 1983:21). In the view of some historians, by 1716 "the great majority of [Trinidad's] Indians had become 'Hispanized'; that is, Christian, Spanish-speaking, . . . [and] organized into villages under some degree of control by the Church, . . . [by] the Government," and by Spanish settlers who used them as laborers on their estates (Besson and Brereton 1991:36). By 1765 there were 1,277 Christianized Indians in a total population of 2,503 (Brereton 1981:4). In that same time, the Amerindian subsistence economy had been replaced by commercial estates; land was increasingly privately owned; Amerindians were moved into urban settlements; aboriginal religious beliefs declined in favor of monotheistic Catholicism; and aboriginal kinship systems became progressively Europeanized (Newson 1976:4, 229).

In 1786 a mission town was formed in Arima, drawing aboriginals from various settlements throughout Trinidad. This occurred after the proclamation of the 1783 *cédula de población*, which called for Catholic migrants (French planters and their slaves escaping French territories in turmoil) to settle Trinidad and transform its economy into one producing sugar. The Amerindians were cleared off of the productive lands that were to be used by these new settlers. The remaining Spaniards, according to British governors coming into Trinidad after the British takeover of 1797, were found to be few in number, impoverished, and virtually indistinguishable from the Amerindians in terms of lifestyle (Brereton 1981:20; Newson 1976:194). By 1797 the Amerindian population, it was claimed, had fallen to 1,082 individuals (Brereton 1981:6, 20). Seemingly, the Spanish and the Amerindian declined together and were often culturally and socially likened to each other by the new colonial elites, providing yet another take on the Spanish-Indian categorization.

The categorical transformation of the Carib was thus almost complete. The Caribs, former foes of the Spanish, became interim friends and then dependent subjects and wards. By this time, the term "Arawak" had been virtually dropped from the dominant local lexicon of ethnic ascription—it was no longer necessary, as acknowledged Caribs (Nepuyos) joined the Spanish and the dominant foes became the Warao. Above this layer of ethnic labeling, there was a layer of value-based labeling: Hispanized and civilized Indians. The Carib-Arawak dichotomy has been fraught with contradictions, convenient manipulations, and changing contexts of usage. When the products of these periods (that is, the actual texts) are all "flattened out," like books on a table, a dizzying array of possibilities as well as constraints are available for the choosing by contemporary Carib brokers.

The Changing Political Economy of Ascription and Valuation of Indigeneity

The ways that Europeans perceived Amerindian responses to their expansionism conditioned the manner in which Europeans classified Amerindian groups. The labels they ascribed would then condition perceptions of the home audience, future writers, adventurers, explorers, and even modern scholars. This situation of apparent morphostasis (Archer 1988), that is, of labels conditioning perceptions that reinforce the choice of labels, would have continued were it not for a number of discontinuities. One of these was the change in colonial powers' motivations in ascribing labels, shifting from early colonial denunciations of the man eating savage to late colonial preservation schemes designed to favor the remnants of noble savages. Secondly, the same material interests were not at work in the ascription of these labels over the long term; the political economy underlying the tradition of ascribing particular labels itself changed. Thirdly, Caribbean Amerindians underwent serious demographic displacement and socioeconomic incorporation. Following the creation of the Carib-Arawak dichotomy, labels multiplied in meanings with time.

Using the material presented thus far, I have mapped out transformations and developments in both colonial perceptions and valuations with respect to the Caribbean case, and that of Trinidad in particular (figure 2). Figure 2 outlines how Spanish colonial perceptions of Trinidad's Amerindians have shifted over time: the gray boxes illustrate the dominant forms of political-military relationships between the Spanish and Amerindians, and the white boxes indicate the commodities of greatest value to the Spanish in a given period. The gray boxes are organized chronologically, their widths meant to depict duration. The white boxes are instead placed around the point in time in which they were relevant. The position of the gray and white boxes, above and below the positive/negative axis, is merely a graphical necessity and is not intended to suggest that gold was held to be in low value in 1510, as an example. This graphical representation also presents a summary overview of main themes, devoid of some of the subtle details presented in this chapter (for example, how even the Spanish would come to designate certain Caribs as friends after the mid 1600s, that is, the so-called Spanish Caribs and the Nepuyo).

Presenting broad brush strokes, the chart outlines a select list of labels ascribed by the Spanish, sorted according to their valences, as perceived and written by Spanish explorers, ecclesiastical and military officials, and chroniclers as cited herein. The Amerindian perspective is largely absent, even though in many cases it seems to have been an inversion of the Spanish perspective (that is, adopting the Carib label to inspire fear in the Spanish, and later, friendship with Spain's enemies). The intention here is to present a map of the political economy of naming, attendant to issues of power, production, and accumulation. The cyclicality shown is not synonymous with repetition, in that the specifics of each phase do not replicate those of a previous phase.

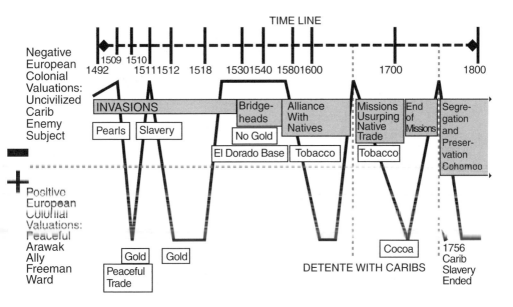

Figure 2. A summary overview of the political economy of naming, with special reference to Trinidad.

While retaining some graphic inexactitude, figure 3 is a distillation of figure 2, with my first aim having been to chart the ebb and flow in ascriptive valences according to a more evenly measured time line (figure 2 presents a time line that gives generous space to the 1500s while squeezing the remaining centuries). Figure 3 demonstrates considerable early instability and rapid fluctuations, as supported by earlier discussions outlining the European entry into a politically and ethnographically complex situation, seeking ways to gauge native responses and endeavoring to sort out potential allies and enemies, as Hulme and Whitehead explained. Eventually, a certain measure of stabilization emerges in this chart, with the ebb and flow appearing to be more or less regular. What is remarkable here is the apparently close correspondence between Spanish ascriptions of hostile intentions and negative attributes to specific Amerindians in peak periods of successive inter-European struggles for hegemony in the region. In other words, when local Amerindian groups became aligned or collaborated with rival European powers, Spanish ascriptions and valuations tended to stress their nature as savages. Whereas figure 2 depicts a political economy of naming, figure 3 highlights, albeit tentatively and approximately, a geopolitics of ethnic ascription. It is thus noteworthy that figure 3 should approximate the long-waves and cycles of European hegemony regularly featured in the works of Modelski and Wallerstein (see Overbeek n.d.).

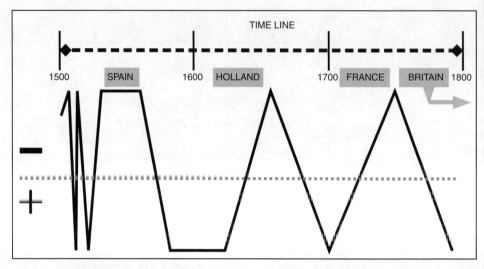

Figure 3. Spanish perceptions and valuations of Trinidad's Amerindians in geopolitical context.

In summary, indigenous identities were engulfed in expanding and contracting phases of colonial political economy and European struggles for hegemony in the Caribbean. Labels also became fairly simple and standardized devices for naming and controlling indigenous populations, to the extent that we can virtually chart cycles of these naming strategies. The point is that we are not dealing so much with being as with presence, and with perceptions of that presence. Colonialism developed a field of signification for describing that presence, a field that has been inherited—by and large, though, in bits and pieces—by the contemporary brokers of the Arima Carib Community.

If the Caribbean (and Trinidad within it) has been constructed in a manner that canonizes the Caribs, how then were such identities and histories played out and focused within particular places? Here I am concerned with Arima, nowadays usually announced in Trinidad as "the home of the Caribs."

2

Placing the Carib

The First Two Resurgences and the "Gens d'Arime" in the Nineteenth Century

Toward the end of the era of European colonial expansion in the Caribbean in the 1700s, and with the decline of Caribs as a geopolitical force in their own right, Caribs began to receive the respect accorded to "noble savages" whose integrity and identity had to be preserved and protected, as a special people, with special rights vis-à-vis the relative newcomers to the Lesser Antilles and Guyana: African slaves and, later, indentured East Indians. Unlike these newcomers, Amerindians would be the only group next to the Europeans whose labor was not to be coerced. However, Amerindians in Trinidad held little economic power or political clout, apart from the lands they occupied in the missions. These realities would serve to shape how they would be depicted and treated by colonial authorities. The strategic shifts between negative and positive valuations remained.

What I wish to do here is to first describe the processes by which Amerindians attained an important symbolic status within the colonial order in ways that ensured the perpetuation and reproduction of discursive valuations (both positive and negative) of their presence. The second objective is an extension and application of the first: I want to establish how Amerindians became enshrined in the quest for a local sense of identity, especially at the level of Arima, that is, the localization of wider processes of valuing the Amerindian figure. Both of these aims are an important part of explaining the bases for current revaluations of the Carib presence in Trinidad.

First, I outline the nature of what I loosely call the first resurgence[1] of Arima's Amerindian community, roughly from 1813 to 1828, under the auspices of Governor Sir Ralph Woodford and the Protector of the Indians in Arima, Captain William Wright. Second, I highlight some features of the racial specialness of Amerindians within the colonial hierarchy of the nineteenth century and discuss this concept's impact on current ways of perceiving Amerindians. Third, I present evidence of the symbolic institutionalization of the Amerindian in the dominant historiography of Arima, a process that gained momentum with the demographic decline of Arima's mission Amerindians and the eventual displacement of a large number of them from Arima. I argue that both this upsurge in symbolic valuations of the Amerindian and the assertion of the centrality of the Amerindian in Arima's history and identity stem from a second resurgence that apparently occurred between 1870 and 1920.

I see this second resurgence as resulting from a variety of converging processes: (1) late colonial romance, as reflected, in part, in writers' depictions of mid- to late-1800s Trinidad as an "Indian Paradise"; (2) the dissemination of news about North American Indians in their last stands to protect their lands; (3) a sort of reindigenization-by-substitution with the importation of large numbers of mixed Spanish-Amerindian cocoa laborers from Venezuela who themselves created and popularized new depictions of Amerindians in Trinidad, while also becoming amalgamated into Arima's local Spanish-Indian historiography; (4) the creation of an Arima identity from the late 1800s, relying in part on its unique position as the last seat of Amerindians in the country and spurred by interelite competition between Spanish and French Catholics versus British Anglicans; and (5) the 1870s–1920s cocoa boom that renewed the fortunes of old Spanish and French Creole families in Arima, itself a center of the new boom, accompanied by a revival of interest in local church and mission history and the development of ritualized and textual commemorations of the Indian mission past. The emplacing of the Amerindian occurred as an outcome of processes that both displaced and re-placed Amerindians in Arima.

The Mission of Santa Rosa de Arima and the Ranking of the Amerindian

The Contemporary Politics of History

The history of the Arima mission is not one that is locked in the past, that is, left unexamined and inactive in the cultural politics of the present. The story of the mission is one that continues to be told, and retold, as the consequences and interpretations of Arima's mission history are played out and elaborated in both current rituals and historical narratives. For example, for the high mass of the August 1999 Santa Rosa Festival, Bishop Malcolm Galt of Grenada (a former parish priest of Arima) stressed "the facts" of the Arima mission's history during the homily he presented as chief celebrant and did so in a manner that was almost pointedly didactic and authoritative in tone, while the members of the Carib Community and their president sat in silence in the front pews of the church. Bishop Galt stressed that the mission was founded in 1786 by Father Reyes Bravo, who named the mission in honor of Saint Rose on her two-hundredth birthday, and that he led Amerindians to Arima from other missions. There is some tension between the church and the SRCC over which of the two can lay greater claim to rights to the Santa Rosa Festival. What is almost an official history within the SRCC, as told to me on various occasions, was also told to a writer from the regional *Caricom Perspective* magazine: SRCC leaders stress that the mission was founded in 1759 by Capuchins, adjacent to an existing Carib village, thereby stressing some degree of continuity with the times of Chief Hyarima. In their account, in 1783 Governor Chacón closed down "all other Mission villages in Trinidad," and Christian Amerindians were sent to the Santa Rosa Mission. More importantly, SRCC spokespersons add, "the Santa Rosa festival was established in 1759 and is the oldest continuing local festival in Trinidad." The devotion to Santa Rosa began with her apparition to three Carib hunters and her urging them to convert to Christianity, as enshrined in a local legend retold by members of the SRCC. The SRCC leaders stress that Caribs are responsible for the preparations for the festival and have always been the ones to decorate the church (*Caricom Perspective* 1990:46). The slants of these two narratives—that of the church and that of the SRCC—differ not merely on a matter of historical detail but on the interpretation of who can claim a paramount role in the Santa Rosa Festival, an argument fully immersed in attempts to historicize representations.

Producing the Indian Mission of Arima

Following the formal proclamation of the legal end to Carib slavery in 1756, Trinidad underwent a second wave of missionary efforts by the Capuchin order (Noel 1972:34). Adding to the seven missions that survived from the previous campaigns (see figure 1), the Capuchins founded six new ones: at Arima, Toco, Siparia, Matura, Punta Cumana, and Salibia (Rétout 1976:xviii–xx). Amerindians had undergone significant Hispanization in the process of missionizing generally. By as early as 1699, one historian has noted, "most if not all [of the Amerindians] were Christians (with Spanish names), the plantain had become 'the most important fruit of the land,' and oranges were grown; the Indians raised pigs and goats and chickens" (de Verteuil 1995:55). However, to a significant extent, up to the 1780s Trinidad remained "essentially an Amerindian society" (Brereton 1991b:36), at least in terms of demographic predominance. As Noel (1972:24) explains, following the 1725–1727 cocoa blight and subsequent economic collapse, "the Hispanic element of the population did not reach a sufficiently large enough size again in order to ensure a nucleus for another Hispano-american community"; during the mid 1700s there were only 50 adult white males, 200 adult black males, and "thousands" of Amerindians. The degree of alleged Hispanization is of course open to debate, especially as the evidence presented above is somewhat circumstantial and does not speak well to complex cultural processes underlying the constitution of identity and meaning.

Certainly by the 1780s momentous changes had begun to occur in Trinidad. After a succession of European peace treaties, Trinidad decided to open its doors to French Caribbean immigrants and their slaves in an effort to revitalize the Trinidad economy by entering into lucrative sugar production and thereby also increasing the island's population. These French immigrants were also seeking to

flee from wars and uprisings affecting various French territories in the Caribbean. Hence in 1783 the *cédula de población* was promulgated, stipulating that
the new arrivals must be Roman Catholic and bring property with them. These
transformations would have immediate impacts on Trinidad's Amerindians, as
similar European treaties of 1783 would have on Caribs in the wider Caribbean,
which consisted primarily of schemes to place aboriginal groups on reservations
and to institute Christianization and assimilation campaigns (see Gregoire and
Kanem 1989:52). Furthermore, in 1797 the British seized Trinidad, which was
formally ceded by Spain in 1802. The transformation of the space that was
Trinidad, and the relocation of diverse groups to Trinidad, would also serve to
provide the new relational framework within which Amerindians would be defined, characterized, and valued.

By 1785, the last Spanish governor of Trinidad, José María Chacón, consolidated the northern villages of Tacarigua, Arauca, and Cuara at Arima (Leahy
1980:102). The Amerindian population of Tacarigua was 193 and that of Arauca
was 297 (Noel 1972:97). In total, 632 Indians, led by Venezuelan Father Pedro
Reyes Bravo, were transferred to Arima (Moodie-Kublalsingh 1994:13). Perhaps
the very fact of relocating aboriginals to Arima might in itself signal the very first
resurgence of the Arima Caribs, whereby Arima gained a new or larger Amerindian population.

The reason for amalgamating in Arima the Indians from the quarter of Taca-
rigua/Arauca was probably twofold, argues Leahy, a Trinidadian historian who
belongs to the Dominican Order: "to give their lands to the new colonists, and to
segregate the Indians, for their own good, from the newcomers" (1980:102; also
see Wise 1938a:40; Collens 1886:115). Hence, Arima was to be the place of the
Amerindians.[2] Collens also supports the fact that "each head of family [had] his
own *conuco* or allotment" of land to cultivate (1886:115).[3] The mission of Arima
was dedicated to the first saint of the New World, Santa Rosa de Lima, born in
1586 in Peru, of Spanish parentage (Rétout 1976:46). Various authors give different dates for the founding of this new settlement (ranging from 1784 to 1786),
with few disagreeing with the proposition that it was formally established in
1786, on the two-hundredth anniversary of Saint Rose's birth (Rétout 1976:46).
The first entry in the baptismal register is for January 15, 1789; Father Reyes
Bravo was in charge from 1786 until 1819 (Rétout 1976:46). As was the case
with all the other missions in Trinidad, festivities were held on the feast day of the
patron saint of the mission, and thus the Santa Rosa Festival was born.

It seems clear that at this time Trinidad's Amerindians were not particularly
valued in the overall political economy of the colony and indeed were moved out
of the way. This was, as some have put it, the era of King Sugar, and the lands the
Amerindians had occupied were suited to sugarcane, whereas Arima is located in
a hilly area more suited to cocoa cultivation. By 1793, sugar had become
Trinidad's main industry (Stephens 1985:12). In 1809 sugar was responsible for
68.7 percent of the total cultivated acreage in Trinidad; sugar production in-

creased from 4.2 million pounds in 1802 to 25.95 million pounds in 1809 (Stephens 1985:13). Cocoa, however, faced a glut in the world market by 1827, and prices fell by 90 percent (Stephens 1985:14). Cocoa, we must note, was the primary commodity cultivated by the Amerindians in the Arima mission. Not only did this decline in the commodity's value lessen the economic importance of Amerindians in the colony, there was also an associated decline in the fortunes of their patrons,[4] Trinidad's remaining Spanish landed oligarchs. Following the influx of vast numbers of wealthy French and free colored planters from 1783 onward, along with the formal takeover by the British in 1797 (adding yet another stratum of higher-ranking elites), the Spanish found themselves progressively marginalized. In 1802, Governor Thomas Picton stated that there were only six or seven Spaniards of "any respectability" in Trinidad (quoted in Newson 1976:194). Of course, this may well have been a deliberate overstatement as a means of minimizing the importance of the previous ruling class in the new, and now British, Trinidad (especially as the new British rulers sought to grab land by claiming that Trinidad was virtually *terra nullius*). During this process "the old Spanish Creoles of St. Joseph, *impoverished and isolated,* lost all influence over the affairs of their native island. . . . a number relapsed into poverty and obscurity, and *disappeared from the historical record. This destiny was to be shared, ultimately, by the Amerindians*" (Brereton 1981:20, emphasis added). This was yet another means by which the Spanish and the Amerindians became virtually fused as one in historical narratives.

Trinidad's Spanish elite was the primary sector that had interests in the Amerindian missions of the late 1700s and in the early years of British rule. Governor Chacón himself is said to have taken a personal interest in the formation of these new missions, having personally named the mission of San Juán de Aricagua (Rétout 1976:6). Don Cristóbal Guillén de Robles, a royal officer of the treasury who had been in office from the 1750s to the 1770s (Noel 1972:45), was responsible for granting land for the mission of Arima.[5] Don Manuel Sorzano, who had held the post of *contador de ejercito,* or "treasurer of the military chest," under the Spanish government (Fraser 1971 [1896]:15), is said to have actually founded the Indian mission in Arima and to have acted as *corregidor* (administrator) of the Indians until 1815 (see Governor Woodford in Fraser 1971 [1896]:101).[6] His son, Martin Sorzano, was also *corregidor* of the Indians (Joseph 1970 [1838]:102). In addition, it seems possible that the prominent Sorzano family, whose name is permanently inscribed on one of Arima's streets, may also have been responsible for instituting the office of the Queen of the Caribs. According to Douglas, "Adhemar [de Verteuil, another leading family in the Arima oligarchy] . . . married the first Carib Queen of Arima, Francis Sorzano" (1999:20). Spanish families in Trinidad retained, along with a paternal interest in the welfare of Amerindians (their workforce), significant tracts of land devoted to cocoa production, with a concentration of these in and around Arima.

Some demographic statistics for the Amerindian population of Trinidad, and

Table 2. Trinidad Amerindian Population Statistics, 1782–1838

Year	Amerindian total	Trinidad total	Amerindians as percentage of Trinidad total
1777[a]		3,433	
1782[g]	2,082		
1784[a]	1,495		
1786[a]	1,391		
1787[a]	1,414	11,533	12.26
1788[a]	1,428	11,722	12.18
1789[a]	2,200[g]/1,432[a]	13,053[a]	10.97[a]
1790[a]	1,408	13,247	10.63
1791[a]	1,398	12,009	11.64
1792[a]	1,195	14,009	8.53
1793[a]	1,268	14,744	8.60
1794[a]	1,144	11,119	7.17
1795[a]	1,070	15,279	7.05
1797[g,b]	1,082	17,718[f]	6.11
1799[g]	1,148		
1800[g]	1,071		
1801[g]	1,212		
1802[g]	1,166	28,477[f]	4.09
1803[g]	1,416		
1804[g]	1,416		
1805[g]	1,733		
1806[g]	1,697	30,043[f]	5.65
1809[d]	1,647	32,095[f]	5.13
1812[e]	1,804		
1819[d]	850	39,935[f]	2.13
1821[e]	956		
1824[c]	893	41,120[f]	2.17
1828[d]	727	41,020[f†]	1.77
1838[e]	520	39,328[f]	1.32

Sources: a. Noel 1972:94, 96, 103, 104.
b. "Plan for the Isle of Trinidad made from actual surveys in the year 1797."
c. *Trinidad Almanac* for 1824, quoted by Coleridge (1825) in Besson and Brereton 1991:123.
d. Fraser 1971 (1896):211.
e. Wood 1968:43–44.
f. Burnley 1842:110.
g. Fraser 1971 (1891):288, 289.
† Figure is for the year 1829
Historical Notes: 1797: British capture of Trinidad
1802: Spanish cession of Trinidad
1808: Abolition of the slave trade
1824: Transfer of slaves from one British colony to another was prohibited
1834: Emancipation of slaves, start of apprenticeship
1838: End of apprenticeship
1849: Dissolution of the Arima mission

Table 3. Baptismal Statistics for Amerindians in the Arima Mission, 1820–1852

Time period	Total number of Amerindians baptized	Total number of people baptized	Amerindians as a percentage of the total
1820–1835	192	1,511	12.71
1835–1840	51	497	10.26
1840–1852	7	1,446	0.48

Sources: Baptismal registers of the Mission of Santa Rosa, Arima: Book 1 (1820–1835), Book 2 (1835–1840); baptismal register of the Church of Santa Rosa, Arima: Book 3 (1840–1852).

Arima itself, were maintained. I have amalgamated diverse surveys to show the size of the registered Amerindian population in all of Trinidad for the period from 1782 (before the influx of French Caribbean immigrants) to 1838 (when most missions were more or less disbanded), as shown in table 2.

According to Coleridge (in Besson and Brereton 1991:123), the Amerindian population of the Arima mission in 1824 consisted of 278 people, comprising 60 men, 77 women, 81 boys, and 60 girls. Martin Sorzano, the *corregidor*, testified that the Amerindians in the mission "never exceeded 600, and have now [in 1841] fallen off to less than half that number" (in Burnley 1842:109). From my own research of the baptismal registers of the Santa Rosa Roman Catholic Church, I compiled statistics on the number of people identified as Indian who were baptized during the period 1820–1852, as shown in table 3. It must be noted that these statistics can give one only a rough impression, at best, of what the total Amerindian population of the mission might have been, assuming that all children born were also baptized. What is also noteworthy is that the priests involved always noted the race of those baptized. The designation of *indio* for Amerindians continued to be written in only until the start of the 1850s, when it abruptly disappeared, roughly at the same time as the mission of Arima declined (thus when the group lost the legal status assigned to classes of laborers ordered in terms of the racial hierarchy). The central shortcoming of these statistics is that they apply only to those Amerindians who actually lived within the confines of the missions, and that in turn was determined by racial considerations. In other words, these figures tell us nothing about those who were of mixed parentage, with an Amerindian parent, who were released from the missions, thereby diluting the overall picture of Trinidad's Amerindian demographic and even cultural presence.

The Social Organization of the Mission of Arima

In spatial terms, the mission of Arima, like most missions, was structured around the church. A central square dominated the mission, with the church located on the east side (where the sun rises) and the homes of the Amerindians located along the other sides, along with orchards, a small market, and, later, schools.

The remnants of this spatial organization are still evident in Arima, in Lord Harris Square, located just about two hundred meters north of the modern center of Arima.

The mission was under the governance of a municipal council headed by Amerindians of the mission, and under the control of the priest (De Verteuil 1858:300). In addition, under the British, a *corregidor* was appointed as well as a "protector" to whom the Amerindians could appeal against any arbitrary act of the *corregidor*. After the Spanish cession of Trinidad in 1802, the British vowed to uphold Spanish laws and institutions, in line with the terms of the cession.

All the Amerindians of the mission who were fit for work were obligated to work two days of each week for the support of the community, employed in such tasks as cleaning the village and farming common lands. Each head of family had his own personal allotment of land (De Verteuil 1858:300). The Amerindians of the mission were not subject to taxation but were bound to serve as a public workforce when ordered by the *corregidor* and had to accompany the latter when required and were paid wages in return (De Verteuil 1858:300). The Amerindians were not entitled to sell or otherwise dispose of their property, which descended to their heirs. As De Verteuil argued, "the Indians were considered in the light of minors," and this measure was in force to protect them since "the moment they became emancipated, they sold what property they had for a mere trifle" (De Verteuil 1858:300). Indeed, De Verteuil's suggestion here is that this is one reason why Arima's ex-mission Amerindians would eventually depart from Arima. Of course, such a suggestion also masks the fact that local elites wished to acquire their lands and certainly went some way toward covering up the facts of how aboriginals lost their hold on land.

The church was the center of the social, political, and religious organization of the mission. The church building itself was in fact originally constructed by the Amerindians (De Verteuil 1858:300): as noted by Governor Woodford, writing in 1817 on extant churches in Trinidad, "St. Rose of Arima: A thatched house built by the Indians" (quoted in Leahy 1980:37). This too forms part of the written history seized upon by current SRCC leaders such as Ricardo, in stressing the Caribs' role in the foundation of the parish, which entails some measure of necessary "respect and recognition." The church and the ceremonies enacted within it were critical parts of mission organization: "the missionaries very skillfully played upon every conceivable natural desire. They emphasized the externals of their religion—the ceremony, the music, the processions" (Whitehead 1988:141). We thus see a number of patronal feasts celebrated throughout the various mission towns of colonial Trinidad, with records for the 1750s speaking of the festivals of Saint Augustine (San Agustín) and Saint Paul (San Pablo), patron saints of the towns that bore their names, and governed by "the corregidor of the *Nepuyos*, Gabriel Infante" (Noel 1972:36–37, emphasis added).

The Racial Status of the Amerindian in Mission Times

The alleged intent of the church was to preserve the racial and residential integrity of the Amerindian community under its control. Friars had "prohibited 'mission' Indians from contact with 'bush' Indians, Negro slaves, mestizos or other Spaniards and kept them confined to the missions" (Harricharan 1983:22). Noel argued that one of the successes of the Capuchins "seems to have been the partial preservation of the Indigenous race as agricultural workers under the external guise of living a Catholic life" (1972:18). Nevertheless, even within Arima, Amerindians were a minority and contact was inevitable. Venezuelan immigrants were also encouraged to settle in Arima from the earliest days of the mission: "In an effort to maintain the dominance of Spanish customs, language and traditions, Padre Bravo encouraged Spanish speaking planters and peons from Venezuela to settle in and around the mission. These migrants from Venezuela brought their strong Catholic traditions, language and customs and so the dominance of Spanish culture in the mission continued unabated" (Ahee 1992:25). Moreover, the arrival of large numbers of these peons—"laborers and backwoodsmen of mixed Spanish-Amerindian-African descent," a term that in the Trinidadian context is reserved exclusively for the Venezuelan peasant laborers also known as Cocoa Panyols—in addition to more prosperous Venezuelan immigrants resulted in the formation of "a considerable Spanish-speaking community in many parts of the island, *reinforcing* the dwindling numbers of indigenous Hispanized Amerindians" (Brereton 1979:8; emphasis added).

The status of the Amerindian should also be understood within the context of the valuative and comparative race hierarchy upheld in colonial society. In the early 1800s in Trinidad, the population consisted largely of whites, blacks, Amerindians, and Venezuelan peons. Only blacks were enslaved and thus, perforce, occupied the bottom rung of the colonial race hierarchy. The Amerindian occupied a relatively privileged position in this hierarchy. Censuses of the 1800s in Trinidad eventually included Amerindians in the "white" category (Leahy 1980:104). In terms of physical traits the Trinidadian Panyol or peon, "with his mixture of three races—black, white and Amerindian—was, according to the ideals of the Trinidad society, in a favorable position: his hair was straight or wavy, and his skin was light" (Moodie 1983:5). The intermediate status of the Amerindian category derives from its relational position between the stigma of blackness and the superiority of whiteness.

Labels and the Mission Amerindians of Trinidad

By 1820 Trinidad was (once again) declared an island not occupied by Caribs, according to the sources examined by Newson (1976:18–19). In the baptismal registers of the Arima mission, starting in 1820 with the first book available for examination, only once did I see the designation Indio Caribe (Carib Indian), with priests invariably using the term *indio*. "Indian" was also the only designation used by the British colonial authorities in Trinidad in the early 1800s. By 1869, referring to the remaining ex-mission families in Arima, Father Louis Daudier spoke of "my little Indians and their mules."[7] *Indio* was generic, nontribal, and homogenizing in its conception and application.

It is also likely that *indio* and "Indian" had different meanings for the Spanish and the British respectively. As Leahy argues, the designation "Indian" often had a wider meaning for the British than the Spanish: "for several years it included *peons* or free laborers from the mainland, possibly because the *peons* were usually employed, like the Indians, in clearing forests for cultivation, possibly too because some of the *peons* may have been Indians" (Leahy 1980:104). Even today, the labels "Spanish" and "Carib" are conflated in popular usage in north eastern Trinidad, the two treated synonymously, with labels such as "mestizo" (the offspring of an Amerindian-European union) having disappeared from local usage by the mid 1850s.

Under the Spanish, *indio* became a category that signified a state of cultural loss. Speaking of colonial Mexico, Turner explained that "the term 'Indio' is highly ambiguous. . . . It cannot . . . be applied to any kind of tribal group with an indigenous political system and religious and other customs handed down from pre-Columbian times" (1974:138). Later usage of *indio* in the 1700s and 1800s, Turner argued, seems to refer to all the depressed and underprivileged masses, including mestizos (1974:138), in a manner that parallels the use of "Indian" to include the peons in early British Trinidad. In all of these cases, from colonial Mexico to Spanish and then British Trinidad, the *indio* classification also related to "a very real economic category" (Turner 1974:139). In the Trinidadian case, this category was that of free labor, engaged in peasant production. In addition, belonging to this category allegedly entitled the Indians to certain privileges, as explained by Martin Sorzano, the ex-*corregidor* of Arima: "they were even exempted from taxes paid by other free classes in the community, and had medical attendance furnished to them gratis" (Burnley 1842:109).

So what did the Amerindians of Arima call themselves? There is not much written evidence to answer this question. The only account from the time of the mission is that of De Verteuil, who witnessed the Arima mission in its last decades and attended its festivals. He wrote, "The Indians of Arima called themselves *Califournans*" (De Verteuil 1858:300). This source has occasioned further investigation, especially among the researchers who have aided the current SRCC (see Harris 1989b:9), suggesting that these must have been French-speaking Caribs from St. Vincent, where the name Califuna was in use. In fact, Arie Boomert found that "throughout the eighteenth and 19th centuries Amerindian groups from the mainland and Lesser Antilles went to live in Trinidad, with or without consent of the government," and in 1786 "Governor Chacón granted some land to a group of Kalinago (Island Carib) from St. Vincent. They settled in the Salibia area of northeast Trinidad. Most of them returned home in 1795 but other Island

Caribs came to Trinidad after a volcano eruption had destroyed their settlements in St. Vincent in the early 19th century. They were granted land near the Arima mission" (Boomert 1982:37–38). Leahy found that "though in Toco and Cumana the Indians were or had been Chaimas," in later years, "when the parish of Toco, which included all the former Indian villagers as well as colonists, was regularly supplied with a priest, the name 'Carib' seems to have been the popular name for all Indians in the parish as the baptismal register (dating from 1837) invariably describes an Indian mother as 'Caraibesse'" (Leahy 1980:103). It is therefore at least possible that some member of the family of cognates of "Carib" survived at this level even at this time. What is also interesting is the increasing revelation of the cosmopolitan nature of the Arima mission indigene of the early 1800s, comprising groups from across northern Trinidad, Venezuela, and St. Vincent.

Sir Ralph Woodford and the First Resurgence of the Arima Amerindian Community, 1813–1828

The mission of Arima, from its inception until the mid 1800s, was relatively inconsequential to the overall developments occurring in Trinidad, that is, the transition to British rule, the development of the sugar economy, and the importation of slaves. Indeed, as one local historian writes, "as early as the 1800s it was easy to see that the British paid no attention to the missions, for from the time they had taken over, all the missions began to disintegrate" (Anthony 1988:300). This was largely true, until the arrival of Sir Ralph Woodford in Trinidad on June 14, 1813, as the new governor of the colony. As an acquaintance of the governor and writer of the time noted, Woodford "regarded himself not as representative of a constitutional British sovereign, but as a Spanish viceroy, armed with the most absolute authority" (Joseph 1970 [1838]:248). As late as 1838, the Spanish colonial code known as the Laws of the Indies, compiled in 1680, remained in force in Trinidad to some extent (Joseph 1970 [1838]:111). One of the titles inherited by the British governors of Trinidad from their Spanish predecessors was that of "Royal Vice-Patron of the Holy Roman Catholic Church" (Fraser 1971 [1896]:10). This title had been held by Spanish colonial governors as representatives of the Spanish Crown, with the Spanish monarch having been conferred the title of "Royal Patron of the Church" by Pope Julius II in a papal bull dated July 28, 1508 (Fraser 1971 [1896]:10). In line with this, one historian explained that "the office of Vice-Patron was not only one of dignity; it possessed many well defined powers and duties which Sir Ralph Woodford exercised with more strictness than any of his predecessors, whether Spanish or English" (Fraser 1971 [1896]:10–11). One of these duties was to uphold the Roman Catholic Church, Spanish laws, and the Indian missions. Symbolic of Woodford's role, a monument in the Roman Catholic cathedral of Port of Spain commemorated Sir Ralph Woodford as "Founder of the Church" (Collens 1886:79–80).

As royal vice-patron of the Holy Roman Catholic Church, Woodford took a special interest in the mission of Arima, and it was he who largely reconstituted it for its final two decades in Trinidad.[8] In 1818 Woodford appointed Captain William Wright to take charge of the mission. The following is a statement issued by Sir Ralph Woodford in this regard; the rare voice of this long-past actor is worth quoting at length:

> The Governor and Captain General being desirous of *re- establishing* the Mission of Arima in the *rights* and *privileges* which *the Laws accord to the Indians,* and of contributing by all the means in his power to its *improvement and prosperity,* has decided to name as its Corregidor an Officer of His Majesty's Forces who possesses all the qualities needed for such an important post. . . . In Don William Wright the Indians will find all *aid* and *protection,* their person and property will be under his immediate care; he will ۷۰۰۰ن۰۰۰ ۰۰۷۰۰۰۰۷۰ ۰۰۰۰۰۰۰۰ ۰۰۰ ۰۰۰۰۰۰۰ ۰۰۰۰۰ ۰۰۰۰۰۰۰۰۰۰ ۰۰ ۰۰۰۰۰ selves, so that their children following the example of their activity, may be useful and virtuous, and the lands which the Law allows them may be constantly kept in cultivation by the able-bodied amongst them. . . . The Governor hopes that the Indians on their part will co-operate in his good intentions on their behalf by obeying all that the Laws enjoin upon them, by being sober and industrious, and carrying out their respective duties as submissive fathers, wives and children, and especially by seeing that the latter attend regularly to hear and to learn the Christian Doctrine so strictly enjoined by the Law, on the days and hours fixed by their venerable Parish Priest. . . . The above notice is to be communicated to them and put up on the Casa Real of Arima—Ralph Woodford, Government House, St. Ann's, Trinidad, 27 June 1818. (quoted in Fraser 1971 [1896]:102, emphasis added)

The original mission had set aside 1,000 acres for the use of the Amerindians. According to a late *corregidor* of Arima, Martin Sorzano, testifying on July 16, 1841, in front of the Burnley Commission, more was granted to the Amerindians: "559. Do they [the Indians] not hold a tract of land set apart for their own use?— [Sorzano:] Yes, a tract of about 1,000 acres, granted to them by the King of Spain, to which Sir Ralph Woodford added afterwards 320 acres, in consequence of their complaining of a want of provision grounds" (Burnley 1842:109). Hence, 1,320 acres were granted to the Amerindians.

The developments occasioned by Woodford's command can be characterized as a first resurgence of the Arima Amerindian community insofar as he sought to renew the rights of the mission and of the Amerindians' hold on their lands, as well as shoring up their uniqueness as a separate population and preserving them against many of the changes sweeping Trinidad. This was a top-down affair, of course, not a resurgence from below (that is, from the Arima Amerindians themselves), nor did it ever assume the form of what might be called a nativist cultural revival (at least, as far as we know, which can indeed be very little). While reaffirming the laws governing the mission, Woodford also reinforced the subordinate position of the Amerindians, shielding them from the power to determine their own future as much as he shielded them from the incursions of self-serving (would-be) land barons.

Woodford took charge of segregating the Amerindians as much as possible, to safeguard their racial integrity, in a manner that presaged later British colonial preservation attempts in Dominica. In a letter to Captain Wright, Woodford instructed the latter to execute the following commands, as quoted in Fraser (1971 [1896]:102–104). First, upon taking charge of the "Village of Arima," Wright was to obtain a general return of the Indians from his predecessor. Second, Woodford instructed Wright to "proceed to make a return of them by families, shewing [sic] their lineage or descent as well as their trades, and if intermixed with other than Indian blood." Third, Wright was to examine all dwellings of the Indians, noting their state, and make plans for their maintenance (in the case of widows, the elderly, and the infirm) by demanding a "general contribution of labor" or to compel the idle to fix their own homes. Fourth, Woodford instructed Wright "to inquire into the tenures of the houses built by others than Indians of which many have been introduced into the Mission without my knowledge or concurrence," to examine titles in order to learn if lands were purchased from Indians, and then to take action given "the laws expressly forbidding and annulling any such sales." This suggests that the mission was much more heterogeneous than the Church first proclaimed and that perhaps even the stated goal of preserving them as a race may have been less important than simply removing them from valuable lands. Fifth, Wright was to "call upon all persons not being Indians, residing in Arima, to show my [Woodford's] permission for the same, and in default of their possessing it," he was at liberty "to order them to quit the Mission within a reasonable time to be fixed according to the nature of their establishment; for those having none a very short notice will suffice." Sixth, Woodford requested that Wright "cause all strangers to be apprehended that enter the village not being furnished with my permission to reside in this Island" and to prohibit "any person henceforward to reside in Arima that has not my express authority for that purpose." Nevertheless, Woodford added, it may be "desirable to attract respectable inhabitants and useful artizans [sic]; the former may be encouraged and the latter permitted to exercise their trades upon condition of teaching the same to one or more young Indians under the usual stipulations of apprenticeship." Seventh, Wright was to formally delimit the boundaries of the village and to command the Indians to plant a lime fence along its boundaries. Eighth, Wright was required to "inspect with the greatest attention and care the *conucos* or provision grounds of the Indians situated within the limits of the Mission, . . . notifying all persons encroaching therein to justify themselves before you in the first instance." Ninth, Wright was commanded to "not allow any of the Indians to work abroad until you shall receive further orders for your guidance, and you will order back to the Mission those who now may be employed abroad." Tenth, the Indians were to be ordered to maintain the public infrastructure of the village, and their presence at mass on Sundays and the great holidays was to be enforced. Thus Woodford set about enforcing and consolidating the mission of Arima possibly to a greater extent than had been done before.

Woodford never failed to support the cabildo, the municipal council of Arima, in any move aimed at "guaranteeing Arima as Amerindian territory" (Anthony 1988:3). Indeed, Woodford took a leading role in preserving Indian rights over the territorial integrity of the mission. Three individuals with commercial agricultural interests complained to Governor Woodford about the steep rents they were asked to pay for the use of lands in Arima. In reply, Governor Woodford wrote (and this is worth reproducing in detail):

To the Marquis del Toro, Don Francisco Toro, and St. Hilaire Bégorrat, Esq.:—Gentlemen, I have received and considered your representation on the 12th ult. and in reply have to observe that the ground rent which the Indian Cabildo of the Mission of Arima have [sic] imposed on the lots occupied in the village by others than Indians received my consent and approbation. . . . As regards the right of the Indians to impose this charge, the existing documents prove that the land of Arima was given to them (the Indians) as their property in community, with an exclusive and untransferable right to the employment thereof to the best advantage for their general benefit, and as I am not aware of their having by any act forfeited their right to claim rent for any land belonging to them in common, I am advised that it was competent to them to impose a ground rent on lots belonging to them in Arima. . . . As regards the transfer of lots, it is within my knowledge that Don Manuel Sorzano who established the Mission, never permitted any transfer but of the houses, and not of the lots themselves, and Mr. Goin and Mr. Francisco Febles have declared the same; they could not indeed legally authorize the transfer of any portion of the Mission lands or of the property of that establishment. As to the occupation of these lots since 1783, and the invitations given by the Spanish Government to strangers to resort to Arima, I have to observe that in 1797 only two white persons and nine colored men (married to Indian women) were then living in the village, and notwithstanding every search I remain quite ignorant of any regulation of Governor Chacon or of His Catholic Majesty that might have altered the Law regarding the settlement of strangers in an Indian Mission—I have, &c., &c., Ralph Woodford, Government House, 26th October, 1819. (quoted in Fraser 1971 [1896]:101)

Both Woodford and Wright assumed a patronal role with the Amerindians of the mission of Arima. In the case of the latter, very little is written except that I found evidence in the baptismal registers of the Church of Santa Rosa that Wright became a formal godparent to at least one Amerindian child. Wright also married a local "white" Spanish woman, Serafina de Orosco, which resulted in a child born on November 12, 1825.[9] On Woodford's role more has been written. For one, Woodford assumed the right to appoint or dismiss the Amerindian cacique (or village headman) at the head of the cabildo (see letter of January 18, 1819, by Woodford in Fraser 1971 [1896]:100). In addition, Woodford stipulated guidelines for the corporal punishment of disobedient Amerindians, generally stressing that the prelates of the mission should avoid this, yet advising the following as a form of compromise: "it appears to me that although it is a troublesome business to manage the Indians, their natural indolence and their submissive nature requires that the rule should be severe in appearance but mild in reality" (quoted in Fraser 1971 [1896]:100).

Woodford also controlled Arima's Amerindians as a type of public works labor crew to carry out some special projects of his own (Fraser 1971 [1896]:97). One of Woodford's key projects was the settling of ex-soldiers of the disbanded Third West India Regiment in 1822 along the way from Arima to the east coast, with Amerindians of the mission of Arima opening up a road in that direction (Anthony 1988:140). Woodford did much the same in southern Trinidad with the Amerindians of the mission of Savana Grande (Anthony 1988:229). These ex-soldiers had fought for the British during the War of 1812. They formed the Fifth Company Village and, at first, depended on mission Indians for food (Anthony 1988:92).

Woodford's indulgence in ceremoniality, maintaining a keen interest in the annual Santa Rosa festivities of the Arima mission, was perhaps his most prominent role as a patron. In general, Woodford went to lengths to encourage elaborate ceremonies of state and public processions. While it is difficult to determine to what extent he may have influenced the development of the Santa Rosa Festival's ceremonial forms, it is largely acknowledged that the festival had begun in very modest ways, with the simple saying of novena prayers and a mass, and to have later developed into a public feast celebrated with more pomp and splendor, with longer and longer processions and the decoration of the church in a gay fashion (see Garcia 1991:3–4; Harricharan 1983; Rétout 1976:46). What we also know is that Woodford had a "fondness for show and ceremonial. That he was so is undeniable; but it was not from personal vanity, but because he considered a certain amount of display to be necessary to his position" (Fraser 1971 [1896]:53). As Fraser added, "Sir Ralph Woodford was not only a man of rank and influence, but he lived in days when it was expected that the Governor of a Colony should maintain the dignity of his position and be really what his title implied" (1971 [1896]:52–53).

Fraser also offers us a description that, insofar as it is in any way an accurate representation, can provide some telling clues as to the development of some of the key ceremonial procedures of the Santa Rosa Festival in terms of today's public processions and the prominent role of officials of the Arima Borough Council and the occasional visiting prime minister or president:

On grand occasions, such as New Year's Day, and the Festival of Corpus Christi, he attended the celebration of High Mass in State, accompanied by a brilliant staff, by the Members of the Council, and of the Illustrious Cabildo, and the effect produced on these occasions is yet spoken of by the few survivors who remember those days. . . . the streets leading from [Government House] to the Catholic Church . . . were lined with troops, both Regular and Militia. A Guard of Honour was drawn up in front of Government House to receive the Governor, who arrived from his residence in a carriage drawn by four horses, preceded by out-riders and accompanied by mounted aides-de-camp. Assembled in the Council Room, were the Members of Council, the Board of Cabildo, and the principal Public Officers, all in uniform, robes of office, or Court dress. A procession was then formed which was closed by the Illustrious Cabildo headed by the Governor with his wand of office as perpetual Corregidor. In this order the procession went through the streets, the troops presenting arms as the Governor passed. At the door of the Church the Governor was received by the clergy and conducted to a Chair of State prepared for him. At the Elevation of the Host the troops presented arms and a salute of twenty-one guns was fired from the Sea Fort Battery, and at the conclusion of the ceremony the procession returned to Government House in the same order. (Fraser 1971 [1896]:11)

Woodford also regularly patronized the Santa Rosa Festival. As Anthony (1988:4) found, "Woodford never failed to journey to Arima for the feast of Santa Rosa, celebrated on August 31. Woodford, referred to as 'Gouverneur Chapeau Paille,' because he always wore a straw hat, cut a merry figure on those occasions, enjoying himself with the Amerindians during this festival of dancing, sport, fruit and flowers." Of especial interest is the following passage by De Verteuil given that at the time of Woodford's attendance at the Santa Rosa Festival De Verteuil was a boy living in Arima and was an eyewitness to the festival, according to Rétout (1976:46):

After mass, they performed ceremonial dances in the church, and then proceeded to the Casa Real, or royal house, to pay their compliments to the corregidor, who gave the signal for dancing and various sports—among others, that of archery, in which the men exercised themselves until a prize was adjudged to the best marksman. People from all parts of the country would resort to Arima for the purpose of witnessing the festivities, which were invariably attended by the governor and staff. Sir Ralph Woodford, in particular, always took the greatest interest in the mission, and every year would distribute prizes to the children of both sexes, who deserved them by their good behavior, and their improvement at school. (De Verteuil 1858:301)

Woodford's presence created a discontinuity of sorts between what was in place prior to his arrival and what came after, hence leading me to speak of his actions with the Arima mission as amounting to a resurgence of the mission at least, as a formal institution. Prior to Woodford's arrival in 1813, the Arima mission seemed to be, at best, of localized interest to certain members of the declining and allegedly dwindling Spanish oligarchy, receiving little or no attention from the first British governors of Trinidad. The instructions and plans outlined by Woodford for reconstituting the mission are also, indirectly, an indication of the extent to which the mission was in disrepair and, indeed, barely possessing structural or communal integrity that would distinguish it as an Amerindian mission. Following Woodford's departure in 1828, the Arima mission entered a precipitous decline into almost total disregard and obscurity and eventual dissolution.

The Demise of the Mission of Arima and the Dispossession of the Amerindians

Speaking in 1841, Martin Sorzano, the former *corregidor* of the mission of Arima, had these replies to questions posed by the Burnley Commission on the current state of the mission:

> 563. Is the mission, then, broken up?—[Sorzano:] Virtually it is so. No regulations are now enforced, and those who remain there follow orders, because they have the benefit of the crops of cocoa belonging to the mission. . . .

> 564. As they appear to have emancipated themselves from the regulations of the mission, do you think they have any legal claim to either the cocoa or the land at present?—[Sorzano:] I should think not; but it is a legal question, which I am not competent to answer. (quoted in Burnley 1842:109, 110)

Note that the commission made it plain that it had an interest in ascertaining whether increasingly lucrative cocoa lands in Arima were open to acquisition, with another eye on the potential problems that could be caused by descendants making land rights claims. Another Arimian wrote that "in the year 1830 there still existed 689 survivors of that race; the ratio of mortality among them being, in the same year, 3.49, and that of births 3.75 per cent. At present there cannot be above 200 or 300 Indians in the colony, so that the aborigines may be said to be almost extinct" (De Verteuil 1858:172). Though it may be a conspiratorial thesis, one might argue that the statements made before the Burnley Commission (relying on racial statistics as evidence) may have been designed to minimize the presence of Amerindians and to diminish their legal ties to the mission in order to produce justifications for the seizure of their lands, the latter eventually having occurred. What is more clear is that aboriginal descendants in Trinidad, unlike any of the other major groups who performed servile labor, were to be denied any rights to independent and compensatory parcels of lands once their period of labor service was ended. In addition, unlike the Africans and East Indians, aboriginals were deemed to be extinct if they produced miscegenated offspring, the logic being that if the race is impure then the race is no longer a race, and those with aboriginal ties to the land no longer exist.

The decline of the Arima mission occurred in a period that merits the designation of being post-Woodford, given that most of his concerns and interests in the mission were largely swept aside by his successors (Anthony 1988:229). After Woodford died en route back to England in 1828, "Arima was not preserved as a mission", instead, "the Governors who came immediately after Woodford— Lewis Grant in 1829 and George Fitzgerald Hill in 1833—did not seem to care about Spanish-founded missions which in fact were missions for converting the Amerindians to the Catholic faith, a faith which the British did not profess." As Anthony observes, "in any case these were the years just before the end of slavery, and the Governors mentioned were much too busy making preparations for that crucial period" (Anthony 1988:4; see also Ahee 1992:26). The Spanish laws that Woodford was careful to uphold were retained only until the period between 1832 and 1840, and the mission was effectively terminated, as some argue, in the 1840s (Moodie-Kublalsingh 1994:156)—although in the case of Arima, at least, there is no evidence to suggest that such termination was ever de jure. Arima was opened up to other parts of the colony and became structurally more integrated into the colony's communication and commercial networks. In 1828, the "Indian Track" between Arima and the L'Ebranche Road was opened as a public road (Williams 1988:10). In 1834, a stipendiary magistrate was appointed, and thus "the Indians were brought under the common law, and the corregidorship was abolished" (De Verteuil 1858:300; Williams 1988:10).

Encroachments on the land base of the ex-mission Amerindians of Arima occurred in a variety of ways. First, the law under the British began to posit pre-British Trinidad as a virtual *terra nullius*. Even Woodford had been advised by Mr. Huskisson, secretary of state for the colonies, in a dispatch: "Immemorial possession in the strict and absolute sense of the term seems indeed to be acknowledged as a valid title. But *it might perhaps be difficult to rest any title upon that ground* with reference to Lands situate in a Colony which *within a period comparatively recent was an unoccupied wilderness*" (quoted in Fraser 1971 [1896]:222–223, emphasis added). The "deserted island" thesis thus in fact seems to have been articulated for the first time in order to justify the dismissal of aboriginal and pre-British land tenure. Worse yet, the uncritical acceptance of statements plucked from their original contexts, time periods, and intended audiences can help to legitimate what was in fact a calculated argument for the colonial usurpation of aboriginal lands and the dispossession of aboriginal heirs.

Second, the administration of Governor Lord Harris (1846–1854) reorganized and defined geographic boundaries in Trinidad, thus creating ward boundaries in 1849 and embarking on the collection of ward rates for public works development; however, those who could not pay the new ward rates or did not understand the law had their lands confiscated and sold (Anthony 1988:323). Formal title to lands had to be demonstrated, or land deeds registered, which worked against Arima's Amerindians, who either possessed no such written deeds, were not informed as to the new policies, or in many cases could not read (Moodie-Kublalsingh 1994:6). Self-described as Arima's "sturdy beggars," some cocoa planters vowed to fight new taxation laws that also militated against established landownership in Arima.[10] In 1849, after the passing of a new territorial ordinance, "the lots in the village were put up for sale at an upset price — a measure the legality of which is highly questionable, as far as the Indians were concerned, since the lands lost in the mission had been granted to them as a compensation for property of which they had been deprived" (De Verteuil 1858:300). Thus the Amerindians became the only group in Trinidad whose freedom from bondage was rewarded with the expropriation of their lands. All of this happened comparatively recently, not in 1492.

The whole process conducted by Governor Lord Harris was quite ironic given that he—next to Woodford—was the alleged favorite of the Amerindians of Arima. Father Louis Daudier learned from the few remaining elderly Amerindians of Arima of how Lord Harris Square came to acquire that name:

> It carries the name of Lord Harris only because this Governor, having the greatest interest in the Indians living at Arima and having deigned to put himself into good and amicable relations with Père Sanchez [former prelate of the mission], often came to Arima, and gave on Santa Rosa's Feast day innocent amusements to the Indians, on this square; and he had trees planted to beautify it but not to take possession of it, nor to change the order of things. So, in gratitude the Indians called the square Lord Harris and the name became official.[11]

By this time, too, Father Sanchez is said by Father Daudier to have become senile, the implication being that he could not have been too astute in dealing with a duplicitous governor. Perhaps it is also ironic that the only surviving Amerindian place-name within Arima itself is named after a non-Amerindian, Lord Harris.

Third, the land base of Arima's ex-mission Amerindians became of interest to squatters as well, and Amerindians themselves apparently drifted away from Arima in search of plots on which to squat, moving thus to districts to the east and south of Arima prior to 1870 (Moodie-Kublalsingh 1994:5; Stephens 1985:27). "As the population of Arima grew," notes one historian, "the Caribs retreated into Calvary Hill and other outlying districts," and "as the town became more populated they moved to places where abundant land for planting, rivers for fishing and forests for hunting were available" (Garcia 1991:8). Following the emancipation of slaves in 1838, increased squatting on Crown Lands became a "huge problem" (Moodie-Kublalsingh 1994:5); this would facilitate the development of the cocoa industry, with most squatters found to be engaged in cocoa cultivation (Stephens 1985:14). In the 1850s new cocoa fields were thus being opened in Tacarigua, Chaguanas, and Arima (Stephens 1985:14–15).

The combined result of these various laws and developments from 1828 to 1849—affecting the Arima Amerindians' land tenure, as well as the laws that worked to undermine the mission—was the dislocation of most Amerindian families from Arima and the economic depression of the few that remained. Writing in the 1850s, De Verteuil related his meeting with some remaining Arima Amerindians. He began by noting that "few of them are now alive" and then proceeded to describe an elderly couple he had met:

> the patriarch (about one hundred years old), and his wife, are good specimens of the race or tribe. The old man is short and square-built, with high cheek bones, small eyes, and straight, white hair: his wife presents a similar appearance, and both are borne down by the weight of years. Pascual is always gay, and seems satisfied with his lot; he is fond of spirits, and becomes drunk whenever an opportunity is afforded; he is otherwise most honest and peaceable. The old man has sold his *conuco,* and now depends upon the *padre* or parish priest for his maintenance. (De Verteuil 1858: 300–301)

De Verteuil also mentioned two schools, one for boys and another for girls, that "were once maintained for Indian children, but, owing to the paucity of attendance, are no longer so" (1858:301). Speaking to the question of their economic dispossession, Father Daudier noted, "As to the indigenous population, they are ruined without means by the last fiscal measures of the Government, and there is nothing to hope for in any way."[12] The general picture is that of drastic socioeconomic decline but not extinction.

Donald Wood wrote in his 1968 history of Trinidad of how the missions had been in a state of decline since the British takeover. Wood noted that while a smallpox epidemic had killed some of the Amerindians, others "had been debauched by the rum that became available to them as the missions had become more and more secularized"; indeed, he observed that "the expenses of the Arima mission were defrayed from the profits of a liquor store at the settlement" (Wood 1968:43). I too routinely noted announcements in the local press posted by the *corregidor,* Martin Sorzano, for the sale of liquor licenses for the mission of Arima.[13] Wood also believes that a number of Amerindian families would have intermarried, especially with the peons of Venezuela (1968:43–44)—a view corroborated by my Carib informants in Arima. Moreover, as Wood indicated, "by 1846 the best of their lands at Arima, where they held 1,000 acres from the King of Spain and 320 acres from Sir Ralph Woodford, were deserted and only nine families remained" (1968:44). A yellow fever epidemic swept Trinidad in 1817, and in 1854 a cholera epidemic struck the Amerindians of the north coast and is said to have "decimated the Amerindian population living in the hills around the old Arima mission" (Joseph 1970 [1838]:253; see Goldwasser 1994/96:15; Brereton 1979:130). In the 1870s a smallpox outbreak again afflicted parts of Trinidad, including Arima. Perhaps one of the starkest overviews of this decline is provided by the Trinidadian historian Bridget Brereton, although not in terms I would necessarily agree with:

> One other racial group was swiftly passing away: the Amerindians, the aboriginal inhabitants of Trinidad. By 1870 only a few pure-blooded Amerindians survived. . . . Their numbers declined very fast as Trinidad entered the mainstream of plantation development after the 1780s. By 1885 there were only perhaps a dozen half-caste Amerindian families on the north coast. . . . In Arima the story was the same. In 1840 there were only about three hundred Indians of pure descent in the old mission, mostly aged. Occasionally surviving members of a group of Chayma Indians used to come down from the heights beyond Arima to the Farfan estate, to barter wild meats for small household goods. But after 1854 they were seen no more: cholera had extinguished the Chaymas. Indeed, by 1850 there were said to be no more than four hundred Indians of pure descent in the whole island; by 1875 only a handful survived, and of the people of mixed Amerindian-Spanish-African descent, very few knew anything of Indian languages or ways. They all spoke Spanish. The "half-caste" Amerindians, living mostly in the valleys of the Northern Range behind Arima, were simple peasants and hunters, living in *ajoupas*, often preserving Amerindian arts of basket-weaving. (1979:130–131)

One should also question Brereton's persistent and apparently uncritical proclivity for using folk concepts of race, blood, and purity—concepts whose usage ought to be explained rather than being used as analytical terms. Nevertheless, this is yet another valuable indication of the kind of discursive haze through which current SRCC leaders are forced to navigate, even though Brereton herself has abandoned the extinction thesis in very recent times.

Similar transformations in the nature of the Santa Rosa Festival were also recorded. De Verteuil himself observed that the "30th of August is a holiday still, but bears quite a different character," and then he explained how different: "people still crowd to the village from different parts of the island, but there are no more Indians, neither are their oblations to be seen adorning the church; their sports and their dances have passed away with the actors therein, and, in their stead, quadrilles, waltzes, races, and blind-hookey are the present amusements of the village" (1858:301). Wood found that, as governors of Trinidad customarily attended the Santa Rosa Festival, in 1857 "only seven Indians could be found to present him [the governor] with a flag. After this time the Amerindians appear only fleetingly. . . . The festival of Santa Rosa de Lima became an excuse for a holiday rather than a commemoration of the earliest Trinidadians and the mission to the Americas" (1968:44). In 1868, when Father François Esteva, then parish priest of Arima, invited the monsignor to "the feast of Santa Rosa," he wrote, "On one hand, I regret to make you disturb yourself for so few people"—people that he calls Spanish—and he added, "we will have a fête, all Dominican, very simple and very frugal," suggesting that the festival had become smaller, simpler, and particular to the Dominican Order.[14] Traveling through Arima in the 1880s, Collens (1886:115) noted in his guidebook, with respect to postmission Arima, "'times are altered,' the Indians at least are gone, and the once famous fête is now chiefly commemorated at any rate by the bulk of the people, by the annual races, coupled with not a little extra gambling and drinking." Indeed, a variety of sources have recorded the secularization of the Santa Rosa Festival by the late 1800s, as it became noted for its famous horse races (the annual races at the Santa Rosa track are still popular with elites to this day) and for the new fashions for ladies to display when attending the events.

By the 1880s and 1890s, a near total transformation of Arima since the end of its mission days was commented on by local observers, historians of the time, and travel writers. Fraser (1971 [1896]:104), said of the Amerindian presence, "now little more than a few names and half-forgotten traditions mark their former sites." Wood went so far as to compare the Arima Amerindians to the aboriginals of Tasmania in the same period, and, as I argue against in this entire project, he also committed the error of stating that they were replaced by "peoples with little interest in the preservation of their culture" (1968:44). Some observers of the time instead had direct access to the people in question; one of the few detailed personal accounts of a visit with Arima Amerindians at the end of the 1800s comes from a Belgian priest, Father Marie-Bertrand Cothonay, who later would become active in resurrecting Trinidad's mission history. In his journal, published in France in 1893, Cothonay wrote the following on November 30, 1888:

> I need to say a word on the ancient inhabitants of Trinidad. Bit by bit they were forced to disappear, for the most part dying of misery or moving to the coasts of South America. A certain number resided in the interior of the island, and mixed with the Spanish, forming a type which is very recognizable. . . . It is in the parish of Arima where one finds them, most of all. Messieur le curé [Father Louis Daudier] believes to have from 70 to 80 of pure Indian blood and around two hundred with mixed blood. I went to Arima, a few weeks ago, and he showed me a whole family that I examined and interrogated at my ease. . . . The Indians of Arima are all Catholics and speak nothing other than Spanish. . . . They have some franchises and rights which the government concedes to them; but, since ten years ago, they sold their lands, because, it seems, they were not cultivating them anymore. Today they live isolated in the forests and will one day soon be extinguished. M. le curé of Arima wanted to take up their cause with the govern-

ment, but he was not able to succeed with these plans. . . . Up to our time, these poor people have conserved a *simulacrum* of a king. The last, called Lopez, died this year. . . . As he had no one to inherit from him, all the Indians gathered together and chose as king the relative nearest to the deceased. I have no details about him, but I know that he is a poor Indian who lives in a hut and has nothing royal to him except the title. . . . What a strange country is ours! Not so? (Cothonay 1893:98–99)

Thus Cothonay presents us with an indication of the structure of the surviving Amerindians of Arima (as they did in fact exist, contra Brereton's assertion), their king, their relative dispossession from Arima, and their fusion with the Spanish. What this passage also manifests is the fixation on racial types, mixture, purity, and blood quanta. This is an indication of the way that the ascription and definition of indigenous identities were structured in nineteenth-century Trinidad. Nevertheless, while eroding the racial basis for certain individuals to be defined as Amerindian, such discourses nevertheless permitted and enabled certain practices to continue to be defined and spotlighted as Amerindian traditions, regardless of the racial identity of those performing the traditions. This is critical, for as we shall see later, it permits the nation to claim a heritage of Amerindian traditional practices regardless of whether or not an actual Amerindian demographic presence is recognized or asserted. Moreover, this implicit distinction between racial purity and heritage also allows the current SRCC to claim Amerindian indigeneity via traditions, even more than via race.

The Second Resurgence of the Amerindians of Arima, Late 1800s–1920s

If we accept that a major demographic dislocation and decline of the Arima Amerindian population had occurred by the 1860s, after they were dispossessed of their mission lands and faced with a cocoa economy in crisis, then how and why is it that by the 1920s–1930s we see the reappearance of the Carib, the Amerindians of Arima, and a Santa Rosa Festival closely associated with an Amerindian group and its history? I see the answer as necessarily lying in a second resurgence having occurred from the late 1860s to the 1920s—*something* certainly must have happened to reinstall the Amerindian as a central feature of Arima's publicly performed identity.

What lies within that period is Trinidad's second cocoa boom of the 1870s to the 1920s, which can easily be classified as Trinidad's longest economic boom to date. In that period, Arima flourished and, astonishingly, acquired internal self-government decades before any other polity in the Commonwealth Caribbean and before Trinidad itself, which won this status only in 1956. I see this context and its features as central in trying to answer this question. I also want to outline how Amerindians became enshrined in the quest for a local sense of identity at the Arima level, that is, the localization of wider processes of valuing and representing the figure of the Amerindian, and the ensconcing of Amerindian images and symbols in the postmission period.

The Cocoa Boom, 1870s–1920s

One of the reasons the colonial authorities invited French sugar planters to settle Trinidad was the fact that throughout the 1700s Trinidad suffered repeated failures of its cocoa crops. In 1787, Trinidad's sugar exports were worth 65,360 pesos, while cocoa exports were worth only 8,400 pesos; by 1795 805 *fanegas* were under sugar cultivation, and only 142 were under cocoa (Noel 1972:114). The Arima mission was thus of marginal value to colonial authorities and the Trinidad economy, and by the 1830s world prices for cocoa—the mainstay of the mission's economic production—began to plummet, indeed, by almost 90 per cent (Stephens 1985:14).[15] Spain, at the time, was Trinidad's largest market for cocoa, and along with the fall in Spanish demand, Spain imposed high duties on cocoa imports from non-Spanish colonies, with even higher duties charged if the cocoa was transported in non-Spanish ships.[16] In addition, crop failures were reported for three consecutive years, from 1836 through 1838.[17] Between 1846 and 1850, Governor Lord Harris authorized the selling of 96 plots of land in Arima, and some Amerindian families had secured formal title to only 9 of these, followed even there by an apparent sell-off later on.

Perhaps as many as 200 Amerindian families found themselves in a depressed economic environment, without land, and without work. By 1849 the mission came to an apparent end, according to most sources. There was a migration of squatters to districts to the east and south of Arima, presumably including many of these displaced Arimian families. Laborers often deserted for the higher wages available on sugar estates, thus setting the stage for the eventual labor shortage that areas such as Arima would face during the subsequent cocoa boom.[18] An influx in immigrant laborers showed a pronounced presence in the baptismal registers of Arima, as I detected without difficulty.

Afterwards, however, a combination of high prices, high yields, and low wages set the stage for the cocoa boom of the 1870s–1920s. Demand for cocoa in Europe and North America expanded tremendously (Brereton 1991a:317). In 1870, 8.5 million pounds of cocoa were exported, constituting 14.33 percent of export value; by 1920, cocoa reached 62.7 million pounds exported, or 43.39 percent of total export value (Stephens 1985:17; see also Brereton 1979:19–20; Collens 1886:225; Moodie-Kublalsingh 1994:1). In the 1870s, a total of 19,000 acres of land was under cocoa cultivation, increasing to 200,000 acres in 1920 (Stephens 1985:17). Land in the traditional cocoa areas was in immediate demand (Stephens 1985:18). Indeed, in the 1860s, 80 percent of the 16,020 acres under cocoa cultivation were in the north (Moodie-Kublalsingh 1994:7), around where Arima is located. From 1899 to 1920, the number of cocoa estates grew from 450 to 966 (Stephens 1985:64–64). Trinidad became the fourth largest producer of cocoa in the world, and in 1898, for the first time in the history of British Trinidad, cocoa exports exceeded those of the sugar industry in value (Moodie-Kublalsingh 1994:1).

The cocoa boom not only gave the traditional cocoa centers such as Arima a new lease on life (Brereton 1991a), but also spawned the creation of new towns, added to a vast influx of imported laborers. The nineteenth century, as argued by most historians of Trinidad such as Wood (1968), was the foundational century for a modern Trinidad insofar as these narratives posit that what Trinidad is today owes a great deal to that post-Spanish century, especially evidenced by the importation of vast numbers of laborers from different parts of the globe. Towns such as Río Claro were new creations (Monrique 1987:5). The town of Caigual came into being in 1894, founded by an individual who cleared land to establish a cocoa estate (Anthony 1988:23). The village of La Verónica, in the vicinity of Arima, was established in the late 1800s and was populated by Spanish-Amerindian peons from Venezuela (Anthony 1988:38). The town of Lopinot, founded by these settlers of Caura, still bears the very strong influence of this Venezuelan presence. The town of Comuto (Cumuto), immediately adjacent to the eastern side of Arima, came into being in 1900 (Anthony 1988:60). It was not until the 1880s that Sangre Grande emerged into what is today a large town east of Arima; it was populated by cocoa peasant settlers (Anthony 1988:263). The famous Mission of San Francisco de los Arenales, the site of Trinidad's biggest mission Amerindian uprising in 1699 (which later became the town of Arena, then became Tumpuna, and finally today's San Rafael), was brought to life by Manuel Luces, who owned the San Rafael cocoa estate from 1892 onward (Anthony 1988:280). Tabaquite, at Trinidad's geographic center, emerged from the colonization of the area by cocoa planters in the 1870s–1920s period (Anthony 1988:314). Cocoa not only made the previously missionized northeast of the island wealthy, it also empowered some of the region's older families and ushered in renewed Amerindian cultural ties.

The Rise of the Cocoa Panyols: Amerindian Substitutes?

Along with the renaissance of old cocoa centers and the creation of entirely new communities, there was also the importation of vast numbers of laborers to meet new demand. Many of these came from Venezuela, from where previous generations of migrant laborers had come since the late 1700s (some of whom had settled in Arima, as mentioned before). These immigrants came to be known in time by a variety of labels, from "Spanish" to "peons" to "Cocoa Panyols." The term "peon" has fallen out of use; "Cocoa Panyol" is seen as a derogatory term by those who are referred to as such; and "Spanish" remains the most popular of these terms to this day. In the North Trinidad context, and in the context of ex-mission areas of Trinidad, "a Spanish" refers to persons of "mixed Venezuelan,

Amerindian, and sometimes African blood" (Goldwasser 1994/96:6n.7; Moodie-Kublalsingh 1994:1). Ties between Venezuela and Trinidad were considerable throughout the nineteenth century (Fraser 1971 [1891]:355).

The "Spanish" peasant, whether of Trinidadian or Venezuelan origin, was the central figure in the expansion of cocoa (Moodie-Kublalsingh 1994:1). Wood described the "Spanish"/"peons" in the following terms: "The peons prized their freedom and were scornful of field labor on sugar estates during the time of slavery. . . . From the Spaniards they had inherited their language and their religion; from the Amerindians they had derived the art of weaving baskets and cassava-strainers, they ate cassava, unlike other Trinidadians, and slept in bark hammocks like the Indians of the Orinoco" (Wood 1968:34). Here is an instance of the peons and Amerindians being perceived as overlapping cultural and racial entities, a conflation of sorts that has also had considerable longevity in Trinidad. The peon was a convergence of the Spanish and the Amerindian, as Brereton (1981:22) put it: "in general, the Arawaks and Caribs influenced the life-style of rural Trinidadians in the 19th and twentieth centuries, particularly the people of the Spanish-speaking community of Venezuelan origin, called 'peons' in the island."

These latter statements lead us to something fundamental, that is, the Venezuelan peons reinforcing the dwindling numbers of Trinidad's Amerindians, acting virtually as substitutes for the latter and enhancing the presence of this Catholic Spanish-Amerindian and cocoa-cultivating mélange within which the Arima mission Amerindians and the peons were amalgamated within conventional public discourses in Trinidad, both then and now. This is the closest we will come to a virtual demographic resurgence of the Hispanic-Amerindian presence in Trinidad in the late 1800s.[19] As Moodie-Kublalsingh explains, the "Venezuelans settled alongside the existing local 'Spanish' population. . . . in British Trinidad the two groups merged to form a Spanish minority within a plural society" (1994:4; see also Brereton 1979:132). Brereton also writes that the "peons from Venezuela brought Spanish elements to reinforce those contributed by the original Spanish settlers and their descendants, and by the Hispanized Amerindians" (1979:152). The influence of these arrivals was very significant insofar as one can argue that it is probable that, were it not for these contract laborers, little of the Hispanic-Amerindian presence would have remained (Moodie 1983). One of the preferred locations of the new arrivals of Venezuela was the Northern Range, in towns and villages near Arima (Brereton 1979:165).

Fortunately, a rare personal testimony written by one of these Spanish peons exists for us to examine. Pedro Valerio was born around 1880 in Tortuga, a small village in Trinidad's Central Range, and was (as Brereton put it) "the son of a light-skinned Spanish-Amerindian father and a dark-skinned African-Carib mother"; his parents "were both born in Trinidad, but their parents had emigrated from Venezuela some time in the early nineteenth century" (Brereton 1979:133). Pedro Valerio observed that "the section of the country in which we lived at that time was newly settled" (Valerio 1991:323), an area that had been opened by cocoa cultivators. In his autobiography Valerio gave the following account of his family:

> To the villagers, my father and mother were known respectively as José Tiburcio Valerio, and Eleonore Valerio; both being natives of the island. From them I have inherited a natural legacy, which it is perhaps the privilege of comparatively few people to fall heir to, and the possession of which I dare say the majority of them would be only too willing to ignore. This legacy consists of a mixture of three strains in my blood: the Caucasian, the Indian and the Negro. My father, a man of small stature, was born of white and Indian parents, and, in color and other external characteristics, would have had no difficulty in passing for a white man. My mother, a dark-skinned woman, also of small size, and very kindly disposition, is descended from the Negro and the Carib Indian; the latter being now almost extinct on the island. (Valerio 1991:322)

This segment is valuable on a number of fronts. First, it indicates a consciousness of race—a blood legacy—associated with Amerindian ancestry. In addition, use of the term "Carib Indian" suggests that the label possibly remained or came back into local use sometime in the late 1800s. (Valerio's account was written circa 1920.) The text also reinforces the constant theme that the Carib is "almost extinct," an assertion routinely made in Trinidad and the wider Caribbean for at least the past two centuries, and this can be double-edged: highlighting the specialness of "those few Caribs that survive" yet also imposing a burden of proof on those claiming to be Carib.

On three occasions, Valerio wrote that although he was personally proud of his natural legacy, there was a desire to leave this behind: he referred to the "miserable little thatched hut" in which he was born (which he later described in detail as a Carib hut); he said that most people who possessed this legacy would have been only too happy to ignore it; and he chose to become a doctor in the United States. Valerio explained his choice: "The wretched condition in which my parents lived, the grinding toil and poverty, the hardships and sufferings of my childhood, had aroused in me the strongest sort of determination to better my condition. . . . I must acquire an education, and, if possible, a profession, a physician for choice, because of the terrible suffering, due largely to ignorance, which I had seen and experienced among the class of people into which I was born" (quoted in Brereton 1979:133). The current SRCC leadership finds itself struggling against this very theme: the desire to abandon tradition on the part of those whom the SRCC leaders class as Carib descendants, mixed with their alleged sense of shame, their striving to be seen as something other than Carib and to live a life free from poverty.

At the elite level, the cocoa cultivator and the Spanish were almost always cast in favorable racial terms. One must remember that in colonial Trinidad each people was associated not just with a color and place of origin, and possibly a religion and language as well, but also with a crop. In the case of the Spanish this crop was cocoa, just as it was for the mission Amerindians. Though he seethed at what he saw as the lethargy of the mission Amerindian, H. N. Coleridge, a travel writer who visited Trinidad in the 1820s, had this to say of cocoa cultivation:

> If I ever turn planter . . . I shall buy a cacao plantation in Trinidad. . . . The cane is, no doubt, a noble plant, and perhaps crop time presents a more lively and interesting scene than harvest in England; but there is so much trash, so many ill-odored negros, so much scum and sling and molasses that my nerves have sometimes sunken under it. . . . Sugar can surely never be cultivated in the West Indies except by the labor of negros, but I should think white men, creoles or not, might do all the work of a cacao plantation. (Coleridge 1826, 77)

At the time, sugar was vital to the economy; yet cocoa was for the racially favored. Coleridge's enthusiasm overflowed when he spoke specifically of Spanish women in Trinidad.[20] Joseph agreed with Coleridge on the noble value of the cocoa cultivator: "Most of the inhabitants of Arima are cacao planters. The cultivation of the cacao tree is well adapted to the habits of the Creole Spaniard— people who are not destitute of vices, but in general possess noble qualities; they may be sometimes injured, but never insulted with impunity. In their ordinary intercourse with mankind, they are the politest of acquaintances, the most good-humored of associates, and the most faithful of friends" (Joseph 1970 [1838]: 103).

A local newspaper editor, writing in 1847 on the condition of the Spanish cocoa cultivators, stated, "Here were a large number of people free from their birth, some of them natives of the Colony, many more, immigrants from the Spanish Main. . . . who will blame the pride that forbad them to work side by side with slaves," and he continued by saying:

> if they have now become attached to these pleasant though remote spots— if they have established their small plantations of Cocoa and Coffee, which, insignificant as their return may appear to the cane-grower, yield them a small nett [sic] income, and maintain them in an honest independence, let the dry and cold expounder of political economy pause a moment before he drives these fine, healthy, athletic, . . . moral and religious people to expatriation, especially when our only present source of immigration [India] offers so glaringly deficient a substitute.[21]

In this passage we see a whole nest of attributes and valuations of the "Spanish," which includes natives of Trinidad. First, they were free, and thus socially higher than slaves but also better than the East Indian immigrants who were then beginning to enter Trinidad. Second, they inhabited pleasant and remote spots. These people were also independent, of strong moral fiber as much as they were

Table 4. Broad Trends in the Spanish-Surname Population of Arima, 1840–1916

Time period[a]	Total number of Spanish surnames[b]	Total number of children baptized	Spanish as a percentage of total baptized
1840–1852	762	1,446	52.70
1866–1876	603	1,586	38.02
1877–1887	633	2,560	24.73
1887–1899	999	3,819	26.16
1900–1910	641	2,666	24.04
1910–1916	431	2,042	21.11

Sources: Baptismal registers of the Church of Santa Rosa de Arima, 1840–1852, 1866–1876, 1877–1887, 1887–1892, 1892–1899, 1900–1906, 1906–1910, 1910–1916.

Notes: a. Not all are divided into decade-long periods; instead, the divisions follow the years covered by individual books of baptismal registers.

b. Includes all children baptized with any surname that is identifiably Spanish in origin.

of prime physical condition. In addition, the editor was indirectly combating the interests of the sugar planters, possibly because he may have had cocoa interests himself or was allied to these. Such positive valuations could only be reinforced when cocoa itself became King in the later 1800s.

The baptismal register of the Santa Rosa Roman Catholic Church of Arima reflects some of the demographic shifts of this period. By the 1850s all notations of *indio* vanish from the registers,[22] and at the same time there was a pronounced decline in the numbers of children baptized with devotional types of surnames, which were the surnames often (not always) carried by mission Amerindian families. Interestingly, the overall percentage of Arimians with any kind of Spanish surname is also seen to decline in a marked fashion from the 1850s onward. The surnames of families who are current members of the SRCC, surnames that appeared only rarely up to the 1870s (and often designated as white, colored, and mestizo), make a relatively massive appearance by the 1870s, with surnames such as Hernandez, Gonzalez, Medina, and Calderon suddenly multiplying. To provide a glimpse of some broad trends, a statistical test of data found in the baptismal registers should suffice (see table 4). If we assume that all immigrants from Venezuela carried Spanish surnames—keeping in mind that all those with Spanish surnames included more than just these Venezuelan immigrants (that is, ex-slaves, ex-mission Amerindians, descendants of Iberian settlers, and so forth)—then the total number of Spanish surnames can be taken as the maximum-sized container within which all Venezuelan immigrants can be found.

This table shows that there was in fact a progressive decline in the number of children with Spanish surnames being baptized in the Roman Catholic parish of Arima. This fact is also a hint of the degree to which families, such as those of Pedro Valerio, sought cheap lands in other parts of Trinidad, rather than an indication of a drop in the high annual numbers of Venezuelan immigrants reported by Moodie-Kublalsingh (1994).

With time writers began to associate Venezuelan Spanish/peon/Panyol immigrants with Caribs, and the terms could then be used interchangeably. Of this group of terms, "Spanish" has achieved the widest popularity in Trinidad. One ex-Arimian informant (residing in London, England) told me in an e-mail interview that his family was from Venezuela, where he still has relatives, and that "all of the people on my father's side were referred to as Spanish (or 'payol' short for Español) when I was a boy." Carib is sometimes conflated with Panyol as well. On a drive to La Pastora, a village beyond Lopinot, to meet an informant, Sylvia Moodie-Kublalsingh encountered the informant's wife and wrote of her, "She was 'Carib,' Amerindian, with some sprinkling of creole African blood; a true, true panyol" (1994:33). The conflation of Panyol and Carib, on the one hand, and the renewed Amerindian/mestizo presence effected by immigration from Venezuela, on the other hand, both served to bolster the recognition and validation of the Amerindian heritage of Trinidad in elite narratives and popular conceptions.

Amerindian Masking

The production of cultural forms on the part of the Venezuelan Panyols would play an influential role in the dissemination of Amerindian images and symbols in the late 1800s and through the 1900s. One of the most prominent of these ways of representing and popularizing the image of the Amerindians was the development of Amerindian masking in Carnival, from the mid 1800s onward, which in their detailed study Bellour and Kinser (1998) explain as the product of Venezuelan settlers and the dissemination of stories and depictions of American Indians via the U.S. news media. Exposure to U.S. media, and to the dissemination of accounts of indigenes in neighboring and distant regions, began from a very early period, as I found in my research of Trinidadian newspapers of the 1800s.[23]

The Panyols were instrumental in the earliest portrayals of the "wild Indians" of their nearby homeland. The first description of Amerindian maskers in Carnival is provided by Charles Day, an English visitor to the Caribbean between 1846 and 1851. He witnessed a Carnival parade in Port of Spain in 1848 that included maskers portraying "Indians from South America." These maskers were "'Spanish peons from the Main, themselves half Indian,' a racial extraction exhibited in their 'small feet and hands.' They retained a sense of Warao hunting and trading practices, as seen in Day's description: 'Daubed with red ochre' and, proceeding in parade, they carried 'real Indian quivers and bows, as well as baskets; and, doubtless, were very fair representatives of the characters they assumed'" (Day quoted in Bellour and Kinser 1998:2). Bellour and Kinser also argue that newly emancipated Afro-Trinidadians took up Amerindian masking, with its connotations of savagery and wildness, as a means of challenging the elites by deliberately playing to their worst fears and stereotypes; thus, "Carnival street festivals, with

Amerindian masking among its features, became one of the few ways in which Afro-Trinidadians could protest or at least pretend to momentary liberation from the status quo" (Bellour and Kinser 1998:3). In the midst of the allegedly scarce presence of Amerindians, the figure of the Amerindian was prominent in popular culture. As Bellour and Kinser add, "the festival which many regard as Trinidad's national emblem offers honored status to Amerindian maskers" (1998:1).

Amerindians in eastern Venezuela also continued to exist in large numbers in the 1800s and well into the 1900s, retaining their contacts with Trinidad. We should avoid taking an insular view of Trinidad in forgetting, for example, that Venezuela is clearly visible in most parts of Trinidad, being only seven to fourteen miles away. Accounts of bands of Warao Indians who had come to trade were common not just in the literature of nineteenth-century Trinidad, but even up to the 1950s and later in some cases.[24]

Carib-Panyol Traditions and Popularized Depictions of the Amerindian

The Venezuelan Panyols also continued a variety of traditions and practices that current SRCC leaders, associated researchers, and other local brokers highlight when enumerating items in the inventory of Carib traditions. Among these are the ways of making dwellings with earthen walls and floors and palm-thatched roofs and internal partitions (Valerio 1991); local town celebrations for the birth of a child, involving the firing of guns or fireworks to announce the moment of birth (Valerio 1991:323); special prayers, still known as *oraciones* and feared by some; as well as a host of roles that modern writers label "shamanic," such as those played by medicine men using prayers and herbal cures and the roles played by their female counterparts, the *parteras* (midwives) (Moodie-Kublalsingh 1994:10). In addition, writers speak of the community events of the Panyols— centered on christenings, weddings, and funerals—as a means of gathering scattered groups of individuals and families, as well as their collective labor arrangements (known by the Amerindian word *gayap*) and the communal contribution to the needs of the sick, elderly, widowed, and orphaned (Moodie-Kublalsingh 1994:10). Indeed, among my various non-SRCC informants I detected a fair amount of nostalgia for these old communal lifeways of the country folk, some emphasizing that country people are always the most hospitable and generous, since "they have values." The valuations of these Panyols is often what one would expect of people represented and perceived as the salt of the earth.

The Panyols also fostered festivals and performances in which they either highlighted Amerindian motifs or decorated themselves as Amerindians. The *sebucán* dance is one example, *sebucán* being the Amerindian term for the cassava strainer. The interesting feature of this dance is that it is metaphorically woven into a Maypole dance, since, as some argue, the resultant weave of ribbons around the pole looks like the cassava strainer, as put by one of my elderly Venezuelan-Trinidadian informants in Arima. I took the opportunity to observe and document a nationwide Maypole Festival held in Arima in May of 1999, and all of my observations corroborate those of Moodie-Kublalsingh. Her research especially details this dance, which, she explains,

> depicted an Amerindian ceremony. A tall pole (*palo* or *horcón*) was placed in the ground. From the top of the pole hung fourteen multi-colored ribbons which were woven by boys and girls as they sang and danced around the pole. They sang as they wove the ribbons into the shape of a *sebucán*. There was a captain and a queen carrying her sable and a maidservant. The maidservant gave the boys and girls *guarapo* (cane juice) from a *totuma* (calabash gourd) and shared *cazabe* [cassava bread] from a *taparo* (calabash cut in half). When the dancing ceased, the pole looked like a pretty *sebucán*. (Moodie-Kublalsingh 1994:94–95)

Moodie-Kublalsingh also notes that there has been "confusion especially the origin of the *sebucán* which greatly resembles the European maypole"; however, regardless of this, she points out that "it is significant that this is the only instance in Trinidad where the *panyols* actually chose to disguise themselves as indigenous characters in the performance of a song or dance. In Venezuela the dance has been performed to the accompaniment of a song about Maremare, an old Indian of legendary fame" (1994:95). (In the SRCC, Cristo Adonis also sings a song titled "Los indios de Maremare.") In addition, she writes, "It seems that the *sebucán* was a favorite with the Arima Indians. Today, the Arima area is regarded as a 'Spanish/Carib' district *par excellence*" (Moodie-Kublalsingh 1994:95).

One of my informants, an elderly Arimian of Venezuelan parentage, spoke of another dance in which the performers dressed as Amerindians. This dance, the *guarandol,* involves the figure of a bird (with a man, arms held straight out to the side, stepping around a circle, imitating the movements of a bird walking), a hunter (a fellow often wearing a grass skirt and armed with a bow and arrow), and a shaman (a man shaking maracas and wearing a feathered headdress). The dance depicts the hunter stalking and killing the bird, followed by the shaman bringing the bird back to life. In Trinidad, this dance was accompanied by *parang* music.

Venezuelan immigrants also fostered the development of *parang* music, sung in Spanish and accompanied by stringed instruments and maracas, as practiced by roving groups of nighttime male revelers (for more detail, see Allard 2000; Marquez 1979; Moodie 1983; and Taylor 1977). This musical tradition has become ensconced in Arima, as symbolized by the location of the headquarters of the National Parang Association of Trinidad and Tobago (NPATT) in Arima. NPATT actively disseminates what it portrays as the Carib heritage of *parang* and often works to support the current SRCC. Part of *parang* festivals of the past were dances depicting animal figures, with one popular dance being that of the *burroquita,* featuring a donkey figure that was once a popular Trinidad Carnival

motif (Moodie-Kublalsingh 1994:66). This too has become part of the amalgamated Arima-Venezuela, Carib-Panyol matrix.

The Tradition of the Indian Mission and Interelite Conflicts

Simply listing the phenomena outlined above does not immediately suggest how
identities were produced, defended, elaborated, or deployed in relation to other
identities, even though hints of this have been provided at different points earlier
in this book. That which weaves these phenomena into a politics of identity is
competition between and among "raced" groups and classes for a variety of
resources, especially lands, income, and local political control.

The dominant classes in Trinidad were divided in the late 1800s and in competition with one another. As Wood indicates, the "free classes" were divided by
religion and language, to a degree that set Trinidad apart from the older British
colonies in the Caribbean (1968:1). Wood points out that the underlying tensions
between the older Spanish and French Creoles and the British, both expatriate
and Creole, "came to a head after 1840 when an aggressive English party sought
to mould their fellow-citizens in their own image," and that "as with Boer and
Briton in South Africa, so also in Trinidad did the relations between two sets of
Europeans sometimes take precedence in their own minds over their relations
with those of other races" (1968:1).

One of the media for this conflict was that of religion, especially when the
distribution of state resources (that is, funding for schools, property ownership)
was at stake. In the late 1800s the majority of Arima's inhabitants were Roman
Catholics (Collens 1886:114). However, the Catholic Church faced growing
competition from the Anglican Church and found itself in a conflict with the
governor's office over its properties in Arima and over school funding. In 1891,
out of a population of 8,500 in Arima, 4,500 were Catholic and as many as 2,000
were Protestant, with 2,000 listed as other (Cothonay 1893:448). For Trinidad as
a whole, a religious census of 1891 (and the fact that this would be conducted is
significant) showed a total population of 73,733 Roman Catholics, followed by
64,413 Coolie and Chinese (presumably meaning Hindu, Muslim, Confucian,
and Buddhist) and 46,920 Anglicans as well as 6,312 Wesleyans (Brereton
1979:12). As early as 1843 the Anglicans built their first church in Trinidad, in
Tacarigua, adjacent to Arima (Rétout 1976:10). While the dividing lines were not
neatly drawn, in broad terms Roman Catholics tended to be led by Spanish and
French Creole families who, in many cases, dominated the cocoa economy; Anglicans, by contrast, tended to be mostly British and to have large investments in
sugar production. Both competed for labor, for quotas of immigrants, and for
state subventions.

Competition between Catholics and Protestants in Arima surfaces in some of
the internal Catholic Church correspondence of the late 1800s. The departure of

the parish priest in 1867, added to the deterioration of the old church building, led some estate owners to lament the apparent neglect of their parish, and they warned the archbishop: "Our enemies, the Protestants, surround us on all sides. They profit from this abandonment to thus implant themselves in the parish, and then it will be difficult to get them out."[25] Catholics felt the need to be on guard against Protestant incursions, as reflected by a letter to the archbishop from the parish priest of Arima, who complained that the "Parish Priest of Arouca insists that his parishioners give him in advance at least one dollar for the baptism of each child they bring to him, without which he refuses baptism. . . . it would not be astonishing that several persons, under this practice, should refuse to baptize their children in the Catholic Church and bring them to the Protestant church."[26] By 1885, the Anglican Church of St. Jude was established in Arima. One might suspect that, in this environment, competing groups might feel the need to justify themselves and secure legitimacy at the expense of each other.

The question of the Catholic Church's hold over lands in Arima was a hotly contested issue that reached boiling point on several occasions over a period from the 1870s though the 1880s. It is on this plane that we see the history, and even the presence, of the Arima mission Indians take center stage once more. The fact that the church backed its claims to lands by rooting its proprietary history within the mission, an Indian mission, served to fuse the interests of the church with those of the Indians it claimed to protect. Indeed, at one point the parish priest would argue that the mission never ceased to be and that he was still "protector of the Indians" into the 1880s. Starting in 1871, Father M. Rouger wrote to the archbishop about the "application which I am making to Government to obtain for the church in Arima the title to several lots of land which it occupies from *time immemorial*" (emphasis added), thus using the language that one might associate with indigenist discourse.[27] From that point, his successor in Arima, Father Louis Daudier, a Parisian and a prolific writer and campaigner, took over the contest. Père Daudier wrote emphatically in 1873:

> The Catholic Church possesses land here since the last century. It is the Catholic Church itself which founded the locality, under the name of the Mission of Santa Rosa de Arima. The lands had been given to it by a Spaniard of the name of Cristova [*sic*] Robles, to establish a mission for Indians. The lands belonged to the Church, and around the Church the priests gathered the Indians; and the old certificates of baptisms have these words 'I, parish priest of Santa Rosa de Arima, and proprietor of this village.'[28]

Daudier also explained that "since then, by a change in the administration [of the island], Government took possession of one part of these lands, and even those which remained in the possession of the Indians, and above all of a part of the square on which the church was situated." Daudier thus also entered a campaign to gain formal title to Lord Harris Square. In addition, echoing the quasiindigenist language of Father Rouger, Daudier wrote, "May I add that the creation of the Mission of Arima is *much older* than the measure which the English Government took to relegate the Indians of the plains to the heights of Arima and to give them lands there" (emphasis added).[29] With respect to the Indian lands on the "heights of Arima" (the foothills leading north, also known by the Spanish as *cabezeras* and today known as Calvary Hill, the residential home of many SRCC member families), Daudier was probably referring to the additional 320 acres of land granted to the Amerindians by Sir Ralph Woodford.

How would Father Daudier prove his case? The question of sources of information and verifiability was at issue. Daudier stressed that "everybody is of the opinion, and knows by tradition, that these lands belong to the Church." However, he also admitted that "it would be difficult to arrange to have affidavits signed, not only because witnesses are either all dead or infirm, but also because their affidavits would affect some deep-rooted interests." The latter is in itself a very curious statement since it suggests the possibility that interests within Arima would also be compromised by Amerindian testimonies.[30]

How did Daudier know about the origins of the mission given the lack of "evidence on parchment," as he put it? His answer was, "I was not able to invent it, knowing nothing of the country on my arrival in Arima. It is therefore by tradition that I found it out," a tradition attested to "by the oldest Indians."[31] Moreover, Daudier quoted an unnamed government employee who, he said, had told him the following: "Basically it is certain that you have rights, but Government, having begun to sell the Mission lands, cannot admit it for, once admitted, you will have the right to demand restitution."[32] Daudier had won a partial victory by the late 1870s, with the colonial government granting the church formal title to more than six acres of land.[33] The battle over additional lands continued nonetheless; indeed, in response to further agitation by Father Daudier, the government simply responded, in "reference to certain old Indian lands at Arima," that "His Excellency [the governor] had decided that these lands were liable to public competition."[34]

Daudier brought the question of history, tradition, and Amerindian rights to the forefront of this debate, not just over lands the church claimed, but also over lands for the remaining Amerindians. In response to a plan to outline the church's land claims in Arima, detailing sizes and historical interpretations, Father Daudier concluded firmly, "there is nothing of substance to this matter other than the fact that it was an Indian area and that there were two authorities both having rights in this area. Those of the Church have never been destroyed; that is precisely the question to be settled."[35] In a noteworthy letter of considerable length,[36] Daudier expounded on these questions with great emphasis. He said of the Government's counter-claims (that is, that no formal titles were in evidence, and thus lands could be alienated and taxed), "I think that they exaggerate the rights of the State to the lands of the Mission." Daudier harkened back to Spanish laws in arguing, "the Spanish government generally exempted these lands from taxes, which was the case in Arima, and that made the land unalienable." Daudier also argued that the government "cannot deny at least that this land was Indian land or dedicated for use by the Indians," and he repeated, "an Indian land, because all the documents subsequent to the Spaniards, in the archives of the government, show this evidence."

Daudier made his argument of continuity in church proprietary rights by referring to living traditions, and he explained that, by and large, Arima was still a mission, and that he was, in effect, a missionary. He thus stated, "On arriving in the parish of Arima, I found myself involved in a traditional network. The priest, from old times, has been regarded . . . by the Indians . . . as the Protector of the Indians and as the representative of the Mission; my predecessors have done like I have, . . . the authority of the Missionary has suffered from time and circumstances, but it has never been destroyed by any official act—it could be denied but it could not be destroyed as long as there are Mission lands and Indians."[37]

Daudier played the role of broker—as he explained, "by tradition and custom, each time that the Indians are in trouble it is to me that they come, to be their intermediary before the Government in their difficulties; and several Governors have accepted my petitions to make the pursuit against them as squatters cease."[38] In return, the Amerindians also performed labor service for the priest: "as a sign that they recognize the power of the church on them, there is the obligation that they have maintained towards me of coming every Monday to work for the church. It is I who have begun to abolish this custom. However, if I call them for work, they come. Also, if they need a liana [vine] or some wood on the Mission lands, it is to me that they have always asked for permission. . . . These facts also give witness to tradition."[39]

Daudier's logic is that if he is recognized as the Amerindians' broker, and if he still serves as their proprietary Father, and if the government has previously recognized this state of affairs at least tacitly, then the mission is still in place and the laws governing the rights and legitimacy of the church's hold on mission lands, as decreed by the Spanish, were thus in effect, and therefore the problem is resolved. In these arguments, it is of especial interest to see the degree to which he engaged in representation of Amerindian mission history, the oral history of the "oldest Indians," and the parallel or backup argument that, at the very least, these were still "Indian lands."

Father Daudier was thus active in campaigning on a second front, that of Indian rights over mission lands. Daudier revealed that this position was not winning him any friends in government: "They accuse me, in the Government, of mixing myself up too much in this affair of the Mission and the Indians of Arima. . . . I have always thought that I was fulfilling my duty."[40] In this same letter, Daudier wrote that letters "sent by me to the Government, at the request of the Indians" were returned unanswered.

Daudier had joined, or perhaps led, a campaign by Amerindian parishioners to obtain formal recognition over lands they claimed in Arima. Daudier's argument was that "what remains for the Indians of this Mission land is so little, that I cannot understand the hesitation to recognize such a real right." Even though "a part of this land has been alienated through the passage of time and the vices of the Indians," Daudier asked, "why take away the rest?" Daudier also spoke of the fact that on Calvary Hill, "several Indians asked me to let them build their houses there, and I allowed them; and nearly all saw their houses sold, after they had cleared the land which was in high woods, they were thus obliged to buy land that they could regard as their own," and he added, "it is a new undertaking for the buying of lots on this land, possessed by the Indians which is the cause of all this correspondence." He explained, "the Government could give to the Indians according to whatever scheme they wished, be it collectively as inalienable land, or be it individually and dividing it as private land, whatever remains of the Mission lands," subsequent, of course, to the fulfillment of the church's claims. As to the "cultivable lands petitioned for by the Indians," Daudier emphasized that there were "two motives that oblige the Government to concede: (1) their status as the old Indian owners of the area, and the interest which they must inspire in their claim; (2) a kind of justice to compensate them for the Mission lands which they have lost when these lands should have remained intact."[41]

Thus we see Daudier helping to put in place, as early as 1881, a discourse of indigeneity and indigenous rights and of the need to respect and recognize indigenous citizens. The rights of those who were "here before you" were paramount; the older the claims, the more legitimate. The logic here is that written evidence to substantiate claims is not necessary where tradition persists. The vital point is that in order to justify its claims before outside intruders, the church utilized the Amerindian as a means of planting its metaphorical flag in Arima, thereby laying the basis for enshrining the Amerindians as a definitional feature of the uniqueness of Arima's history.

These arguments were extended into the issue of the government's proposal to establish a market in Lord Harris Square. Daudier noted, "several times I have had to fight for this savannah."[42] Daudier again reminded the government that the square "was created by the missionaries, then the real proprietors as in all the places which were under the missionaries, before the arrival of the English, and it was created with the object of protecting the Catholic worship from the noise and to surround it with the respect which it merits."[43] The government, one can infer from the text of his message, had reminded Daudier that it was the ward, and not the church, that was responsible for the upkeep of the square, thus eroding the credibility of the church's claim to the square. Daudier replied that, although that had been true since the English took the island, "on the eve of great Feasts, if the square was too dirty, the Indians cleaned it, and this happened two or three times since I became Parish Priest."[44] Daudier also informed the government that the square was church property, as evidenced by the fact that the very first chapel of the mission had been built there: "The chapel on the square existed until the construction of the new church which was begun in 1789. I can still find,

not witnesses of the existence of this chapel, but witnesses of the tradition received from their ancestors that the first church was there, on the Lord Harris
Square itself."[45] Daudier pleaded that the government show respect for the sanc-
tity of church services that would be interfered with by noise from the market,
and he framed this in Catholic versus Protestant terms: "For though not believing
in the presence of Jesus Christ in the Eucharist, you know that we Catholics
believe in it."[46]

From a certain point of view, Father Louis Daudier was successful in inculcating certain main points of his arguments, later to be routinely recycled in historical reflections by Arimian parishioners. Thus, as one example, a letter signed by
a group of prominent parishioners to the visiting archbishop in 1909 recites what
has become a virtual article of faith at the local level: "Arima was one of the first
Catholic parishes in this country; it has existed since the time of the Spanish
Missions, and on the list of its parishioners are many of the oldest Catholic
families in Trinidad."[47]

Both sides—the Catholic-French-Spanish and the Anglican-British—had divergent economic interests. As Brereton (1979:20) indicates, cocoa was dominated by the Spanish and French Creoles and was "the backbone of their prosper-
ity in the 1880s and 1890s"; moreover, unlike sugar, cocoa estates were entirely
locally owned. Indeed, the "economic basis for the recovery of the French Creoles
after 1870 was cocoa" (Brereton 1979:49). Brereton also points out that in 1875,
out of 29 cocoa estates listed, 22 were owned by "French Creoles," increasing to
26 out of 29 in 1880, 82 out of 111 in 1885, and then 146 out of 172 estates by
1890 (1979:50). The only industry in which British capitalists had significant
interest was sugar, and as Brereton found, "there was a distinct bias to sugar [in
the government administration]. . . . In 1870 out of eight Unofficials [in the
legislative council], five were sugar planters, one was a doctor with interests in
sugar and cocoa, and two were barristers. . . . Members were appointed to 'represent' cocoa, when that crop became as important as sugar, but often they also
had interests in sugar" (1979:26). The cocoa industry not only brought economic
recovery to the French Creoles, "it also improved their political status which was
reflected in their nomination to the Legislative Council during the 1880s and
1890s" (Stephens 1985:24). While this division of interests served to set dominant elites apart, within the cocoa fraternity a tightly knit system of association
and intermarriage developed. Indeed, the clannishness of the cocoa elite in Arima
was seen in the following description by a local writer: "And this was good old
Trinidad. The land of the red cocoa pod. Where Ganteaues spoke only to de
Verteuils. And de Verteuils spoke only to God" (P. E. T. O'Connor quoted in
Douglas 1999:8).

Class Competition and Ethnic Differentiation

Competition between ethnic groups at the level of the working class also occurred in the cocoa growing regions. While thus far the role of the Cocoa Panyols in this industry has been stressed, the fact is that since at least 1878 some cocoa estate owners had begun using indentured laborers from India, with cocoa estates on the whole beginning to apply consistently for East Indian laborers from about 1884 onward; in 1890 cocoa estates applied for 244 East Indian immigrants, rising to 692 in 1911 and 560 in 1917, at the end of indenture (Stephens 1985:21–22, 45–47; Brereton 1979:181).

With the sugar depression of the 1880s and 1890s, the flow of East Indians into the cocoa zones increased (Stephens 1985:22, 40). Free labor from West Indian islands also began to arrive (Stephens 1985:22). East Indians not only worked on cocoa estates, they eventually founded their own cocoa plantations, and they increased their purchase of Crown Lands, gaining between 1,500 and 1,800 acres of land per year in the early 1890s (Stephens 1985:23). By 1916, East Indians owned 97,962 acres, and out of this, 59,239 acres were in cocoa cultivation, which stimulated requests for further numbers of East Indian laborers given that time-expired East Indians who owned large estates tended to employ indentured East Indians (Stephens 1985:59). The influx of workers of diverse backgrounds changed the composition of the Arima workforce: "In 1888 in Arima there were French and Spanish speaking contractors, a few Portuguese, Madeirans, Cape . . . Verde Islanders, African creoles, Barbadians and free East Indians, supplying labor in one way or another to the cocoa areas" (Stephens 1985: 43–44).

The fact of diversity alone is not what would lead to competition or even conflict. However, differential positions within the colonial race hierarchy and the impact on wages resulting from inflows of new laborers are two forces that could foster competition and conflict. As we saw, both Panyols and their local Spanish-Amerindian counterparts were cast in an intermediate position within the race hierarchy, as nearly white, and certainly not as low as blacks or East Indians. As for the impact on wages, the introduction of indentured East Indian labor in the cocoa zones "meant a reduction in the rates of pay per task" (Stephens 1985:48). In addition, as indentured labor became more readily available, some cocoa estate owners simply refused to hire free labor (Stephens 1985:53). By the 1870s, over 2,000 Venezuelans and West Indians arrived every year; with the arrival of East Indians, "competition for employment was characteristic of the period, whereas previously there had been competition for laborers" (Moodie-Kublalsingh 1994:7–8).

However, estate-based labor was only one form of income for most peasants, who had their own plots and simply supplemented their incomes with seasonal contract work on estates. The Spanish peons frequently owned small cocoa farms and were employed on the big estates as skilled workers, usually on contract or task work (Stephens 1985:58–59). Other peasants found participation in road works a particularly important source of additional income, and virtually all groups except the East Indians were favored for this kind of employment.

By 1920, when the cocoa industry began to decline once more, 60 percent of the industry was in the hands of peasants, and about 26 percent in the hands of ex-indentured East Indians (Stephens 1985:60). Another ingredient in this setting of interethnic competition was the figure of the shopkeeper. Shopkeepers were sources of supplies for estates and workers, as well as of loans to assist peasants in acquiring new holdings (Stephens 1985:33). Shopkeepers tended to be either Europeans or, in many cases, Chinese.

The result of these processes, as Moodie-Kublalsingh explains, was a further consolidation of a sense of group difference among the Panyols. As she puts it, "among the panyols (including the mixed descendants of native Amerindians) there was a strong group consciousness. To a certain extent it was that who continued, in the post-Spanish-colonial era (after 1797), to identify with the earlier dominant Hispanic culture. They were, therefore, a distinctive group among the native creole folk" (Moodie-Kublalsingh 1994:xi–xii). According to Moodie-Kublalsingh, the Panyols showed "disdain and antagonism towards other subordinate groups" (1994:xi–xii).

One conclusion that may be distilled from this set of tendencies is that—combined with religious self-defense, a feeling of being encroached upon by others, and local competition for resources—symbolic alignment with an Amerindian heritage served to bolster and even enshrine indigeneity at the Arima level. When the figure of the Amerindian became imbricated with a diverse set of forces (from the reaffirmation of the paternal and proprietary interests of Catholic and Spanish elites in Arima, reinforced by the cocoa boom, bolstered by the arrival of the Panyols and concretized in interelite and interethnic competition, followed by examples of how Arimians later defined themselves in the face of the wider society), then the Amerindian—far from suffering erasure—became a canon in the construction of an Arimian identity.

The Catholic Boom of the Late 1800s

The 1870s–1920s cocoa boom renewed the fortunes of Spanish and French Creole families in Arima, which became a center of the new boom. This was accompanied by a revival of interest in local church and mission history and the development of ritualized and textual commemorations of the Indian mission past. The Catholic Church and its constituency invested great labor and financial resources into maximizing the Catholic presence, a concomitant process of establishing its legitimacy if not its primacy, and this formed one important feature of the wider context within which renewed elite interest in the mission Indians was articulated.

One result of the cocoa boom and the efforts of cocoa elites to preserve and enhance their status within the wider society was the greatly increased expansion and construction of churches in this period. From 1870 to 1923 (the period of the cocoa boom), new churches, or ones renovated at great expense using imported Italian marbles, were recorded as having been funded by cocoa barons or peasants. These included the church of La Verónica, erected in the heart of the northern cocoa district; the church of Maraval; Rosary Church; the Roman Catholic church at Laventille; the Church of St. Michael in Maracas; the Tunapuna church; and the church in Erin (Moodie-Kublalsingh 1994:14; Rétout 1976:63, 99, 102, 106, 116, 118). Of course it is also during the cocoa boom, in 1869 (under Father Louis Daudier), that the Church of Santa Rosa de Arima was reconstructed and expanded; in 1882, Arima's church was further enlarged under Monsignor Charles de Martini (Rétout 1976:17).

Of even more significance was the effort to resurrect a church in the place of the old Mission of San Francisco de los Arenales, site of the 1699 Amerindian uprising, which resulted in repeated historical accounts, tales, songs, and even media-oriented commemorative activities well into the present. In 1877 Father José Perdomo (a member of the local Venezuelan elite, being a relative of the Bermudez family) established the parish of San Rafael near the site of the old mission;[48] funds for the construction of the church "came from estate owners who donated towards it the money of their first crops of cocoa," and "for many years this gesture became a tradition for the people of the village" (Rétout 1990:7). It was also during this period that a number of priests, such as Father Buissinck and Father Marie-Bertrand Cothonay, began to research and publicize the mission histories of Trinidad, in a manner not unlike Father Daudier's research on the oral history of the Arima mission.

The Emergence of the "Gens d'Arime"

By the 1850s Arima had already begun to expand enough to be seen as one of Trinidad's key urban areas. In adducing evidence some cite the fact that a postal service was inaugurated in Arima in 1851, the same year that postal services of any kind were instituted in Trinidad; in the same year Arima received one of the first ward schools established by Lord Harris (Anthony 1988:5). With the advent of the cocoa boom in the 1870s, Arima underwent important transformations, evidenced by the establishment of the first railway line on the feast day of Santa Rosa on Thursday, August 31, 1876 (Anthony 1988:6). By 1881, the government had opened two new schools in Arima (Anthony 1988:6).

Observations written at the time provide testimonial substance to these recorded transformations. Writing in the mid 1880s, Collens observed, "Arima is fast blooming into importance with its multifarious streets, shops, post office, cabs, &c." (1886:114). His entry for Arima in the 1890s read thus: "*Arima*—The third borough; is a flourishing little town, an hour's journey from Port of Spain by rail. On Santa Rosa day, the 31st [of] August, Arima is always *en fête* with races and festivities" (Collens 1896:20). The editor of the *San Fernando Gazette*, writing in November of 1889, observed "droves of donkeys, heavily laden with provision and produce," and he saw Arima "as a commercial center of the largest and most important agricultural districts in the colony" (quoted in Garcia 1991:7).

By the 1910s, some of the most prominent cocoa barons emerged in Arima, with the mean size of estates being 357 acres (Stephens 1985:36). A number of the most prominent members of the cocoa elite were behind agitation to secure borough status for Arima; these included Arimian magnates such as LeBlanc, Cleaver, Strickland, Warner, Sorzano, Sanchez, Farfan, DeGannes, Quesnel, and Lopez (Williams 1988:11; Garcia 1991:4). Streets in Arima still bear the names of most of these plantocrats. The objective of securing the royal charter (which was applied for on Queen Victoria's Jubilee in 1887 and granted on August 1, 1888) was the "desire for some degree of self government and a chance to separate themselves from the Ward to which the town had given its name" (Garcia 1991:4–5), a fact that would also allow the new borough to collect taxes for itself and free it from some of the administrative control exercised by Port of Spain, the source of much bane for Father Daudier. Beyond this legal fact, which has largely been forgotten, the royal charter became a great symbolic asset in the construction of an Arima identity with a sense of its uniqueness within Trinidad; the achievement of this status is still celebrated on an annual basis. As Anthony noted, "it was the first and only town in the Colonies that Queen Victoria had so honored" (1988:7).

In the process, the French phrase "gens d'Arime," meaning "Arima folk"—a phrase that is still in popular use among members of the older generations in Arima—shifted from simply describing a class of French planters that arrived in Trinidad from 1783 onward, to "a representation of civic pride, a distinctive identity," which also grew into "a strong feeling of independence after the actual handing over of the Charter of Incorporation in 1888" (Douglas 1999:1). Arima became a small motherland (akin to the Spanish *patria chica*), at the very least a self-ruling regional capital well before the colony of Trinidad itself achieved self-rule.

Currently, some definitions of the "true Arimians" include recitation of the belief that it is Arima that not only was the last seat of the Amerindians in Trinidad but also "retains the last surviving links with the Amerindian past" (Ahee 1992:21). In justifying the xenophobic tendencies of some members of subsequent generations of Arimians, as especially demonstrated against the influx of immigrant laborers from Barbados in the 1940s and the resettling of low-income tenants on the outskirts of Arima from the 1970s, one historian has argued, "Arima, it should be remembered, evolved from a mission settlement. In the 18th Century, the Indians were discouraged from mixing with outsiders" (Garcia 1991:56n.37; see also Douglas 1999:2). The elaboration of the contents of this Arima identity is an ongoing process, usually enunciated as an inventory of disparate items—Spanish, Amerindians, French, the mission, *parang* music, the royal charter, and so forth—culminating in a statement of difference within the Trinidadian framework, for example: "As a gen d'Arime myself . . . I [am] inherently proud of the city in which I was 'born and bred' and which possesses a distinct history and identity" (Douglas 1999:2). It is not surprising that we see the cultural products established from the time Arima was an economic center, a dominant local metropole at the crossroads of various ethnic encounters occurring within a class hierarchy, with differential rewards for a labor force differentiated by color, having become part of the ideological reservoir deployed by certain Arimians when convenient.

The Late Colonial Romance of the Amerindian and the Institutionalization of the Encounter between Columbus and the Natives

In addition to the utilization of the figure of the Amerindian as a vehicle for Arimians to establish and define their sense of local rootedness, distinctiveness, authenticity, and legitimacy, the 1870s–1920s period also saw the newest phase in the positive revaluation of the indigene in the Americas. This was the period in which the largely defeated American Indian was romanticized and museumized and broadcast to the world with the subsequent rise of the United States in world politics and its achievement of hegemonic status within the western hemisphere. Some priests also began a historical search for the remains and the histories of old Amerindian missions in Trinidad in what may be seen as an upsurge in interest in local history as whole, as evidenced by the number of books on Trinidad published in Europe in the late 1800s. Moreover, this period also saw the celebration of the fourth centenary of Columbus, the cocoa boom in Trinidad, and the establishment of reservations for Amerindians in different parts of the Caribbean.

Trinidad, in the minds of some members of the colonial elite, was likened to a paradise, sometimes with reference to the Amerindians. Caura, with its cocoa estates and Venezuelan Panyols, was hailed as "a perfect paradise" by De Verteuil, and according to Moodie-Kublalsingh (1994:13), "Caura fitted in well with the Europeans' romantic vision of tropical exotica." In his entry for January 18, 1885, Father Cothonay wrote for his French audience, "The inhabitants of this earthly paradise are not in effect Indians, as would seem to be indicated by the [place-]names in this country; they are descendants of the Spaniards, more or less mixed with the Indians [Amerindians] and the blacks" (1893:241–242). Why did Cothonay feel the need to write this clarification? It is probably in response to the way that local elites referred to Trinidad, from the mid 1800s onward, as "this Arawak island" (Anthony 1988:117) and as "our Indian paradise."[49]

The impact and coverage devoted to the Columbian quincentenary of 1992 was significant; 1892 likewise received important media coverage and was the subject of various commemorations and festivities in Trinidad and in other parts of the Americas. In 1881, a statue of Columbus was erected in Columbus Square in Port of Spain, east of the Roman Catholic cathedral, and Collens wrote (1886:71), "The fountain, which was presented by the late Mr. Hypolite Borde, a wealthy cacao proprietor, is surmounted by a bronze statue of one whose memory should be perpetuated in this Colony—Christopher Columbus." Perhaps this was the beginning of a story that Trinidadians continue to repeat to themselves in popular culture and the media, that of the first encounter, of Columbus and the Caribs.

For the fourth centenary in 1892, the *Port of Spain Gazette* gave great play to the commemorative celebrations held then in Spain, in Genoa, and in New York. While the paper appreciated the holding of a Solemn Mass of Thanksgiving to the Most Holy Trinity for the occasion, followed by a celebration in the cathedral, it regretted the lack of additional pomp and ceremony, "especially as our connection with the memory of Columbus [who named Trinidad] and the discovery of America is of a close kind . . . we do not think that an official and a popular demonstration would have been *de trop* in the matter." The paper was envious of "the mighty nation to the north, which has imported such pomp and circumstance into the Columbus celebration" and lamented that West Indian governments did not band together to mark the occasion. The paper then detailed the events of the mass, from the presentation of arms, to a military band striking up "God Save the Queen" and a sermon highlighting Columbus' religious virtues.[50] Discovery Day, commemorating Columbus' arrival, came to be celebrated on an annual basis. In 1938, the *Port of Spain Gazette* called attention to the fact that that year's Discovery Day was special not only for being the 440th anniversary of the discovery of Trinidad by Columbus, but also for being the golden jubilee of the grant of a royal charter to Arima. Once again, the *Gazette* complained of insufficiencies in the celebrations: "The second happening [Arima's Jubilee] might at least have inspired us to observe this year's celebration of Discovery Day with certain *éclat*"; indeed, the paper added, "it sounds strange to say that in this year's celebrations there seemed to be lacking . . . the public consciousness of the event as a National affair."[51] As to Discovery Day itself, the paper indicated that "this bit of legislation declaring 31st July—Discovery Day, a public holiday was the outcome of persistent efforts by certain prominent [nameless] public spirited men of this island extending over a period of years. It became an accomplished fact in 1931 and has been held as an annual event since that date."[52]

Processes of transforming the Amerindian into an object of ceremonial commemoration, as well as the prior institutionalization and textualization of the Amerindian in Arima's mission history and in nineteenth-century texts respectively, worked to place today's SRCC within the phenomenon that is the construction of an Arimian identity. These processes have done more than create an object of commemoration: they have also enabled living actors to claim the identity and history being commemorated.

3

Writing the Carib

Debates on Trinidad Indigeneity from the 1800s through the 1900s

As I witnessed throughout the course of my fieldwork, texts (including, inter alia, schoolbooks, history books, journal articles, academic mimeographs, newspaper articles, and self-publications by local authors) left an imprint on Carib brokers' thinking, sense of self, and public self-representations. Most of the SRCC brokers possess an acute sense of the weight of history, both in explaining themselves to others who wish to know their history and in discovering that history for themselves. History, as most of the Carib and allied brokers see it, is encoded in written documents. The documents are the facts. There was a real hunger for accumulating more of these documents—documents are treated as capital, they have value, they can reproduce truth, and they can be challenged only by other documents. Not all that was in print was treated as truth—these are not simpletons—but an assortment of documents could be sifted for those facts that could then be reassembled in what seemed to be a plausible history. Research support— one of the main stated needs as officially expressed by the SRCC—was critical in discovering, sifting through, and assembling these facts. Within the SRCC, calling on elders' memories for the period covering the past eighty years or so was almost as important as documents written by those whom the society at large would acknowledge as authorities, professionals, and objective analysts.

Much of this processing of history was impressed upon me. To deepen my own rapport with leading members of the Carib Community, I too did my part in providing information that was often of greater interest to them than it was of relevance to my research project. Not always did I comply, however, as in the words of one SRCC member who virtually chastised me: "You really ought to be researching the medicinal plants and providing this information." I recall, for example, afternoons with Cristo Adonis in my apartment as he excitedly read through the pages of books such as Besson and Brereton's *Book of Trinidad* (1991), seizing upon reproduced Amerindian folk tales and legends, or the 1997 volume edited by Brecht, Brodsky, and Farmer, *Taíno: Pre-Columbian Art and Culture from the Caribbean,* which Cristo found captivating for its wonderful images of Taíno artifacts. He asked me to make photocopies in the hope that a wood sculptor could reproduce some of these items for him. Other documents of interest, to both them and myself, ranged from denials by Spanish chroniclers that the Caribs were anthropophagites, or that Caribs ever inhabited Trinidad, to old nineteenth-century depictions of the Santa Rosa Festival by eyewitnesses, to the apparent mystery of how the Amerindians of the mission of Arima could one day have inalienable lands and the next day lose them.

As a result of my assisting in their continued navigation through historical sources or contemporary ethnographic accounts of neighboring indigenous groups and their practices in search of that which may be deemed retrievable, certain subtle changes, of which few subsequent researchers would know the origins, took place. For example, in prior smoke ceremonies or discussions about Carib religious beliefs, it was the norm for Carib brokers to speak only in terms of "the Great Spirit," without ever providing a less generic, more ethnically specific, or, let's say, more authentically indigenous name. At one stage, Cristo advanced the name Akourouka, but I personally never saw this in any of the literature that I read, nor was I blunt enough to simply ask, "Where did you get that?" Once he read in a Guyanese Amerindian creation myth (Besson and Brereton 1991:9) that their name for the Great Spirit was Yacahuna, this became the standard name still in use in smoke ceremonies today, as when Ricardo will say, "We make these offerings to our Great Spirit, who is God, and whom we call Yacahuna" (sometimes also called Yocau, and who is the creator of cassava). Not for lack of modesty, I relate here one of Adonis' statements to a group of family members and neighbors speaking of his relationship with me, as it voices his own thoughts on the outcomes of our many "limes": "The friendship we have . . . has helped to engineer in me a deep appreciation and understanding of old things I knew, and new things. . . . whenever we get together, we could talk about anything, laugh and lime, but you can be sure that at some point he will start talking about something academic, about history, about knowledge I never had, and so I always learn from him. And that is my only friend about who I can say that."[1] A possibly less charitable view of the effect of my presence, as one critical colleague put it, was that I was "extending, justifying, and legitimating" their own (presumably objectionable) identity claims. To some extent this must be true; after all, how many students would travel from the other side of the planet, enhanced by support from funding agencies, to devote their entire doctoral research to this relatively small group? That in itself is an act of recognition, validation, and legitimation of the SRCC. Nevertheless, they continue to exist with or without me and to have their own agendas and their own minds.

What I wish to underline in this chapter is the overall importance of the text in the making of current Carib self-representations and in highlighting certain practices as traditional. Of critical importance to SRCC brokers is the question of naming, that is, how aboriginals were labeled (if and when they were even deemed to exist, the two issues often going hand in hand). Finally, I wish to demonstrate the extent to which Carib and Amerindian acquired a doxic status

(Bourdieu 1977:164) and serve as canons of dominant Trinidadian reflections on the island's history and identity, either as a symbol of the past or as a living reality.

The Carib Tradition

European conflicts and alliances with Amerindians resulted in certain ideational products that, filtered out of their original contexts, continued to be mediated in subsequent historiographies, educational texts, and conventional public reflections on Trinidadian history as written or voiced by teachers, historians, journalists, and politicians, among others. These ideational products consisted of the various European ways of labeling Amerindians, the ways Amerindians reportedly labeled themselves, and the belief that specific cultural traits could be associated with each group, whether termed people or nation. In addition, certain valences were attached to each label and have proven to be remarkably persistent in their general outline.

The ideational products of colonialism would be reproduced, appropriated, or reconfigured both by Trinidadian nationalists and by intellectuals in laying out the history of Trinidad's Amerindians and Trinidad's Amerindian heritage. They would also serve as definitional guideposts for the leaders and brokers of the SRCC, who are always forced to answer to these labels and historiographies, to give an account of themselves in defining their identity and ancestry, and to even respond to charges that Arawaks were essentially cowards and Caribs were cannibals, and that maybe SRCC members are either one people or the other, or even neither. By and large the SRCC leaders have taken on board the various assumptions underpinning the trait lists accompanying each label, while trying to find some room for maneuver between the various labels. What I wish to focus on right now are the elite and colonial constructions of narratives on Trinidad's Amerindian history in the late colonial period, as a means of rounding out the historical dimension of this text.

One of the primary debates about Trinidadian indigenous history centered on whether Trinidad's Amerindians were either Arawak or Carib, continuing in the either/or tradition founded in early Spanish colonial discourse. The search for a single denomination for all of Trinidad's remaining Amerindians seems to have begun in earnest in the late 1700s, at a time when they were marginalized in the colonial economy in favor of sugar plantations and African slavery and thus reduced to a protected, if dispossessed, minority confined to missions. In 1788, a British parliament report referred to Trinidad's Amerindians as "Yellow Caribs," a term hitherto reserved for the St. Vincent context (Lewis 1983a:5). Alexander von Humboldt attested at the dawn of the 1800s, "the native tribes of Trinidad, and the village of Cumana, are all tribes of the great Caribbee nation" (quoted in Ober 1894:301). E. L. Joseph, an English writer who resided in Trinidad in the early 1800s, instead insisted: "that the Caribes had no footing in Trinidad, may be learned from Las Casas. . . . such enmity existed between the Caribes and the other races, that they never could have resided in the same island" (1970 [1838]:118–119). Joseph thus extracted Las Casas' assertions from the context in which they were written, thereby obscuring Las Casas' motivation to fend off slave traders preying on groups conveniently designated as Carib, while also perpetuating the binary opposition of Carib versus Arawak. A prominent French Creole historian wrote that, when first discovered by Columbus, "Trinidad was . . . then inhabited by Yaos, Caribs, Chaymas, and other tribes of the Carib-Tamanaco family" (De Verteuil 1858:172). Two decades later, a priest in Siparia wrote, "only a few years ago the Carib Indians, or Waraoons (as they are called by these different names) lived in the woods of Siparia," one instance where Carib and Warao were thus conflated (quoted in Goldwasser 1994/96:046). Adding yet another twist to this sequence of arguments, a French historian of Trinidad wrote that seven tribes occupied Trinidad, including the Arnacas, Chaimas, Tamanaquoo, Chaguanoo, Salivoo, Quaquao, and Caraibes (who were further divided into four subtribes: Nepoios, Yaios, Carinepagatos, Cumanagotos) (Borde 1876:40). As Borde explained, "while the other islands of the Antilles, even the largest, were inhabited by only one or two, or at most, three Indian tribes, Trinidad had an agglomeration of the greater part of those found on the neighbouring continent" (1876:39). However, even while highlighting this diversity, Borde posited Carib dominance: "Carib was the dominant language in the country" (1876:42).

Of the whole array of European and Euro-Creole historians of Trinidad in the nineteenth century, Joseph, De Verteuil, and Borde are three of the most regularly cited in contemporary Trinidadian literature and research on the country's Amerindian history. This fact is important insofar as they represent the complete range of established positions on the question, Who were the natives of Trinidad?

In the 1930s, historian K. S. Wise wrote and delivered a series of public lectures on the island's history, producing materials that are still circulated among leaders of the SRCC via research papers prepared for them by individuals such as Peter Harris (archaeologist) and Patricia Elie (local historian). Wise noted the dominant conception that the aboriginal name for Trinidad is Iere. After combing through the word lists of various Amerindian languages he argued that the only possible name was Kairi, which is the Aruac word for island, rather than Iere, which was commonly understood to mean "Land of the Hummingbird" ever since Joseph wrote it in 1838 (Wise 1934:7–9, 11). What is interesting to me (more than who got what wrong or right) is that such debates should even engage the local intellectuals of the time. Wise (1938a:87) was also responsible for emphasizing that the Amerindians of the last missions to be established in Trinidad were all of "the Nepuyo Nation" and that these were all "of the Carib stock." Nepuyo has in fact enjoyed a resurgence with SRCC brokers during the 1990s, based on historical materials cited in the previous chapters.

In opposition to theses that Trinidad Amerindians were Caribs, another author of the time, John A. Bullbrook, a British geologist and amateur archaeologist, became prominent. Like Wise, Bullbrook was affiliated with Trinidad's Royal Victoria Institute and the Trinidad Historical Society, and also like Wise, he delivered and wrote a series of public lectures on the aborigines of Trinidad (Bullbrook 1940, 1960). Bullbrook spoke critically of the Carib presence thesis and cast doubt on the ancestry of the Arima Caribs (thereby also indicating that by the 1930s this is how they were indeed known in Trinidad): "To this day we speak of the Queen of the Caribs at Arima, yet I doubt if there is much—if any—Carib blood in her or her race" (Bullbrook 1940:4). Bullbrook's argument, stated briefly, is that Caribs were never dominant in Trinidad. Why? His excavation of shell middens failed to reveal any number of arrowheads, and, given that Caribs were "known to be" warlike savages, this absence would in turn point to the absence of the people (Bullbrook 1940:4, see also Bullbrook 1949a, 1949b). He described the true Trinidad indigene in opposite terms: "the Trinidad Arawak was a mild, inoffensive person" (Bullbrook 1949b:14). Later, Bullbrook also called on early colonial chroniclers: "I have had the opportunity of reading extracts from the young Columbus (son of the Admiral)[,] Dudley, Raleigh and Père Labas [*sic*]. All agree that from the time of the Discovery at least until 1700 AD there were no Caribs in Trinidad" (1960:4). Seeing himself as "combating the Carib tradition," Bullbrook emphasized in his critiques: "Such a tradition, once firmly rooted, would not be lessened by time, nor easily be killed, unless some unusual event brought its fallacy to public notice. Such an event has not yet happened, and, so, Trinidad still has a 'Queen of the Caribs'—probably without a drop of Carib blood in her. Nevertheless, I hail the Carib Queen, for even *fallacious tradition* is better than none at all. At least, it affords basis for research" (Bullbrook 1960:57, emphasis added). Bullbrook argued that this baleful belief in the Carib tradition arose as a result of the royal edict of 1503 permitting the enslavement of Caribs (as discussed earlier), thus leading slave traders to cause Amerindians to revolt in order to then name them Caribs (1960:55). Rejecting that position, Bullbrook seems to have opted for the other polar extreme.

Though Dr. Eric Williams wrote quantitatively less material on this topic, his published work is of special importance. Dr. Williams was the founder of the People's National Movement (of which SRCC president Bharath is a member and elected representative) and the first and longest ruling prime minister of Trinidad. Williams, an Oxford graduate, was for a long time Trinidad's leading historian and published a number of seminal texts that are still prominent in Trinidad today. One of these texts, *The History of the People of Trinidad and Tobago*, was published by the PNM itself in time for the granting of independence. In the first chapter, titled "Our Amerindian Ancestors," Williams wrote, "The Caribs tended to settle for the most part in the North and West, around what is today Port of Spain; two of their principal settlements were located in Arima and Mucurapo [west Port of Spain]. The Arawaks seem to have concentrated above all in the southeast, and it is recorded that on one occasion the Arawaks took Tobago from the Caribs" (Williams 1962:3). The import of Williams' statement lies in two key facets: (1) it legitimates and underscores the view that the Amerindians of Arima were Caribs, and (2) it also helps to recast the Arawaks in a more heroic light—not as victims of the fierce Caribs but as capable of vanquishing the Caribs.

In more recent decades, the published work of academics has also supported the designation of aboriginal Trinidadians as Carib. A map produced by Arie Boomert, a Dutch archaeologist and former lecturer at the Trinidad campus of the University of the West Indies, shows Trinidad and Tobago as inhabited by South American Kalina ("Mainland Caribs") circa 1650 (Boomert 1986:4). Taking a position similar to that of Boomert, two anthropologists wrote recently that "in 1772, 'Nepuyo' is listed as the common language of the mission Indians" (Figueredo and Glazier 1991:238). Generally speaking, then, the Carib label persisted through these debates, with some significant changes in meaning (for example, the "heroic Carib," in the light of nationalism) and alongside the development of new terms (such as "First Nations"), as well as the resurgence of labels that were previously buried in archives (such as "Nepuyo").

Pathetic Primitivism: Depictions of the Indian Character in the Early Nineteenth Century

While the phenomenon of non-Amerindians unilaterally assigning the Carib label itself became a tradition, the meanings and expectations attached to the label have clearly changed and fluctuated over time. By the 1800s in Trinidad, Amerindians once depicted as warlike had come to be often cast as childlike. In terms that are very relevant here, Janette Forte sums up these transformations with respect to neighboring Guyana, which saw similar transformations: "Looming domination was disguised first by stories of the armed, belligerent, intractable natives, to be followed later, when the natives had been reduced to a shadow of their former numbers, by descriptions of child-like, somewhat sub-human, beings, akin to the flora and fauna of the interior, and thereby banished from the coastal areas [of Guyana] when the European economy no longer required their services" (1996:6).

We can detect at least four major themes in the depictions of Trinidad's aboriginals in colonial European writings of the early 1800s, depictions that offer a rough index of how the aboriginal peoples were valued within the colonial social hierarchy. The first such theme can be summarized as Amerindians languishing in a perpetual state of indolent torpor. The second theme stresses cultural loss through dilution of tradition and the lack of a conscious identity. Third, Amerindians were often depicted as children, in a state of historical and cultural infancy as well, deprived not just of power but also of cultural self-knowledge. The fourth theme involves casting the Amerindian as untrue to his or her race through the abandonment of Amerindian marital bonds, and viewing the resultant mixture as something that led to the approximate extinction of the true Amerindian. In contrast to romantic primitivism, these characterizations amount to a form of writing and thinking about Amerindians that we ought to call *pathetic primitivism*, as oft expressed by the phrase "these poor Indians," especially with reference to these apparently post-Carib creatures hospitalized within their missions. These writings reflect and narrate a uniquely transitional period in Trinidadian history, of a colony in transition from Spanish underdevelopment (according to the self-justifications of Trinidad's new colonists and later generations of national developmentalists) to one that aimed to be a thriving part of the world economy and a colony uncertain about its mode of exploiting the lower classes (after all, this was a cloudy period when abolition and emancipation loomed on the horizon) and thus uncertain about the comparative value of free men such as Amerindians versus that of African slaves.

H. N. Coleridge, a cousin of the more prominent Samuel Coleridge, spent some time in Trinidad and wrote about his various journeys throughout the island, including visits at its various Amerindian missions. "Every one, who goes to Trinidad," Coleridge wrote, "should make a point of visiting the Indian missions of Arima and Savana Grande," in order to witness these "poor dear Indians" (1826:82, 90). Joseph too stated that "Arima is a neat village, and is interesting, because in and about it reside the largest assemblage of the remnant of the aboriginal Indians anywhere to be found in the island" (1970 [1838]:102). With reference to the Arima mission, which Coleridge visited in 1825, he described the Amerindians as sitting for hours in motionless silence (1826:94). Yet far more telling was his description of the Amerindians of the mission of Savana Grande:

> Nothing seems to affect them like other men; neither joy or sorrow, anger, or curiosity, take any hold of them; both mind and body are drenched in the deepest apathy; the children lie quietly on their mothers' bosoms; silence is in their dwellings and idleness in all their ways. . . . The Indians were all summoned forth, and the *alcalde* and the *regidores* stood in front with their wands of office. These were nearly the only signs of life which they displayed; they neither smiled or spoke or moved, but stood like mortals in a deep trance having their eyes open. . . . The governor [Sir Ralph Woodford] gave a piece of money to each of the children, which was received with scarcely the smallest indication of pleasure or gratitude by them or their parents. . . . The amazing contrast between these Indians and the negroes powerfully arrested my attention. Their complexions do not differ so much as their minds and dispositions. In the first, life stagnates; in the last, it is tremulous with irritability. . . . I know nothing more delightful than to be met by a group of negro girls, and be saluted with their kind 'How d'ye, massa? How d'ye massa?' their sparkling eyes and bunches of white teeth. . . . It is said that even the slaves despise the Indians, and I think it very probable; the latter are decidedly inferior as intelligent beings. . . . Indeed

their history and existence form a deep subject for speculation. The flexibility of temper of the rest of mankind has been for the most part denied to them; they wither under transportation, they die under labor; they will never willingly or generally amalgamate with the races of Europe or Africa; if left to themselves with ample means of subsistence, they decrease in numbers every year; if compelled to any kind of improvement, they reluctantly acquiesce, and relapse with certainty the moment the external compulsion ceases. They shrink before the approach of other nations as it were by instinct; they are now not known in vast countries of which they were once the only inhabitants. . . . [They are] destined to be swept from the face of the earth. (Coleridge 1826:122–123)

Coleridge's depiction is special insofar as it is one of the few that cast Amerindians as inferior to Africans and claims that Amerindians avoided contact with the other races—indeed, the consensus among later writers is that just the opposite was true: miscegenation was intense.

E. L. Joseph also produced a characterization that mirrors Coleridge's for its incessant emphasis on the lifeless character of the Amerindian. In this regard, Joseph wrote the following:

Children of the island they are, in more than one sense of the word. They are as thoughtless, although not as lively, as infancy; left to themselves, they would become wanderers of the wood, or would starve in their encampments. . . . their total want of mental and (unless violently excited) bodily energy is beyond credibility; the greatest earthly good of the poor Indian of Trinidad seems to consist in crouching on their haunches and remaining in a state of waking torpor or of somnolency, and it is not easy to tell the difference between the torpor and the sleep of the Indian. . . . The glorious robe in which nature is arrayed delights not his eye; the charms of beauty have little influence on him—he views these as an ox regards a flower-garden, who merely looks amongst the blossoms for objects for the gratification of his appetite. . . . let him drink to excess, and he calmly crouches with his thighs doubled up and the whole weight of his frame resting on his heels; in this Simian posture he sleeps off the fumes of his tranquil inebriety. (1970 [1838]:102)

To some extent, depictions of the indolence of the Amerindian seem to have stuck, insofar as Arima continues to be referred to as "a sleepy village" by public speakers such as politicians, journalists, and writers. As early as the 1830s, Joseph wrote, "I have often thought that the somnolent inactivity of the poor Indians is contagious, and has in some measure communicated itself to many of the inhabitants of Arima" (1970 [1838]:103). Recently a Trinidadian historian wrote of Arima as that "sleepy mission village that the Capuchins founded"

(Anthony 1988:8). Likewise, a Trinidadian historian of Arima wrote, "Before 1940 Arima was a sleepy, agricultural community, greatly influenced by the Spanish-Amerindian heritage. . . . It was a town developed through the adaptation of Amerindian influence" (Garcia 1991:iii). At a rally of the United National Congress (UNC) that I attended in Arima during the July 1999 local government elections, the member of parliament for Arima, Dr. Rupert Griffith, pleaded that voters give the UNC a chance in Arima so that they could transform "that sleepy town" into a "modern city." This is more of a persistent way of thinking about Arima than it is an adequate reflection of the reality of the town as the busy, crowded, and noisy hub of northeastern Trinidad that I experienced.

The theme of cultural loss and vanishing traditions commonly recurred in descriptions of Arima's Amerindians. One 1833 account of the Arima Amerindians portrayed them as numbering around 200, speaking only Spanish, and having no ancestral traditions: "still less are they aware that the whole island was formerly theirs," and "their little world is now limited to Arima" (in Lewis 1983a:29). This alleged state of being without identity or tradition was repeated even more emphatically by Joseph after his visit to Arima. He wrote that "little information has been obtained from themselves" concerning their origins, and he added, "as to the Indians of the present day, their tradition extends not even as far back as the time when the Spaniards first visited their island" (Joseph 1970 [1838]:118). Joseph thus emphasized that "the Arawaks of the present day are not in the same situation that they were when these islands were discovered. During the last three and a half centuries, their national spirit was broken, their arts lost, and yet they have learned nothing of civilization but its vices and its crimes" (Joseph 1970 [1838]:120–121).

In addition to indolence and loss of tradition, European colonial accounts of Trinidad's Amerindians in these early decades of the 1800s also stressed the theme of the Amerindian as a child. Joseph wrote in this vein about the "harmless and inactive children of the island" (1970 [1838]:102). Writing much later, but with reference to this period, Fraser (1971 [1891]:3), told that "when the English became masters of the Island, the few Indians who remained were little better than 'hewers of wood and drawers of water.' To a great extent this was due to the laws enacted for their protection, which by *treating them as children who never came of age*, crushed out of them all feelings of independence" (emphasis added).

The fourth major way of characterizing the Amerindian, one that would prove fairly resilient, relates to the question of whether the Amerindian even existed by this time; the character issue involved is that of the Amerindian who was untrue to his own race, with a recurrent focus on the notion of approximate extinction by interracial mixture, a theme that is currently vibrant not just in Arima, but across all Island Carib communities in the Caribbean today. Thus, Joseph wrote, "this indolent harmless race is here fast merging on extinction—from no fault of the local government, nor from any disease: the births amongst the Indian women exceed the deaths in the usual ratio." Instead, he says the reason for this is "that the Indian men, since they are obliged to live in society, choose mates of other races, and the women do the same (Mr. Coleridge was misinformed when he stated that the Indians will not intermarry with other races), hence out of every seven children born of an Indian mother during the last 30 years, there are scarcely two of pure blood, as I have been informed" (Joseph 1970 [1838]:102). Joseph thus concluded that "this will of course decrease their population; for those of the mixed race, whether they be Samboes (between Negroes and Indians), or Mustees (between Europeans and Indians), or the countless castes that the admixture between the African, European, and Indian tribes produce, *they are not the real aboriginal race*, and leave the inactive community of Indians as soon as they reach the age of discretion" (1970 [1838]:102–103, emphasis added).

This is one of the first written statements associating the "real Indian" with the "pure Indian," a logic that dogs the current SRCC, if not the whole subject of indigeneity in the Caribbean, as well as those otherwise critical contemporary scholars who write of the absence of an indigenous presence. Colonial legislation governing the missions basically resulted in this formula: the real Indian is tied to the mission, and the mixed Indian is free. In line with Joseph, the ex-corregidor of the Arima mission, Martin Sorzano, before the Burnley Commission, engaged in the following exchange: "562. To what, then, do you ascribe the gradual and rapid diminution in their number?—[Sorzano:] Chiefly to the gradual mixture of the races. As *pure Indians* they were compelled to remain at the mission, and conform to the regulations; but the children born of Spanish and Creole fathers could not be so classed, and would not submit to the restraint of remaining there" (Burnley 1842:109, emphasis added). De Verteuil, writing not too long afterwards, also added that while

> it is highly probable that many did seek a refuge and home in the virgin forests of Venezuela . . . I also coincide in opinion with some judicious observers, who trace the *approximate extinction* of those tribes to the marked presence manifested by the Indian women towards the negroes and the whites, by whom they were kindly treated, whilst they were regarded by their husbands, of kindred race, more as slaves and beasts of burden, than as equals or companions. As a consequence of those connections, there exists at present, in the colony, a certain number of individuals of *Indian descent,* but of *mixed blood.* (1858:172, emphasis added)

We thus observe the launch of a discourse that persists almost as strongly today as it did in the early 1800s, that the mixed Indian is not pure and that Trinidad only possesses people who can at best be classified as of Indian descent rather than Indian proper, thus demonstrating the full racialization of indigeneity in the nineteenth-century Trinidadian context. Moreover, racializing and spatially placing the Amerindian are concomitant processes, as mixed offspring were free to leave the missions, while the nonmixed were forced to remain. This way of writing about Amerindians in racial-spatial terms continued into 1877, when, in his popular *At Last: A Christmas in the West Indies,* the travel writer Charles Kingsley lamented, "At present, there is hardly an Indian of certainly pure blood in the island, and that only in the northern mountains" (Kingsley 1877:74).

In the end, these arguments of the approximate extinction of the Amerindian may also have been motivated by a desire to usurp the mission lands of the Amerindians, especially as some of the writers belonged to the local landed elite (for example, De Verteuil) or wrote their texts in consultation with the old, established families of the area (for example, Joseph). Were they motivated to "write out" the Caribs in order to mask or legitimate the practice of displacing the aboriginal people from the mission lands in Arima? It is a possibility.

The Extinct Carib, the Mixed Carib, the Spanish Carib

Thus far I have covered the most prominent works on the Carib-Arawak debate from the nineteenth through the twentieth century. However, two other conceptions of Trinidad's Amerindians have also gained considerable currency since the end of the 1800s. One of these is that Trinidad's Amerindians simply became virtually extinct, that is, reduced in numbers or racially diluted through mixture, thus no longer exercising a presence as a race. The operative principle here is that the only real Carib is a pure Carib, and the only pure Carib is a dead Carib. The second major thesis, which does not contradict but rather refocuses the first, is that Amerindians and Spaniards had become mutually assimilated and miscegenated (in other words, one may have some aboriginal ancestry by virtue of being "a Spanish."

Starting with the prominent thesis that Trinidadian Amerindians became virtually extinct, De Verteuil commented that the Amerindians of Arima had "finally sunk under the ascendancy of a more intelligent race" (De Verteuil 1858:172). In a passage that is circulated in various texts of today (for example, Anthony 1988; Moodie-Kublalsingh 1994), De Verteuil also wrote:

The few aborigines yet remaining in the colony are leading an isolated life in the forests, depending for their subsistence upon hunting and fishing, using the bow and arrow in preference to the fowling-piece, and, in short, retaining their savage ancestral habits precisely as if the light of civilization and the sun of Christianity had never beamed on their lovely island of *Jere.* A few families of Indian descent are still, however, to be met with in different parts of the island, all speaking the Spanish language and having preserved Spanish habits—fond of smoking, dancing, and all other kinds of amusements, but above all, of the *dolce far niente.* They are, generally, possessors of *conucos,* that is to say of a few acres of land, which they cultivate in provisions and coffee, but particularly in cacao. (De Verteuil 1858:174–175)

De Verteuil thus provides a snapshot of nested themes that are still part of the conventional register for describing and conceiving of Trinidad's Amerindian descendants: rural, linguistically if not culturally Spanish, essentially indolent, and cultivators of coffee and, above all, cocoa—an almost classical trait list for what today is conventionally referred to as a Spanish, a Cocoa Panyol, or a Carib, these terms often used interchangeably within the northeastern Trinidad context. The importance of De Verteuil's writing is that he had been raised in the Arima district when it was still a mission in the early half of the 1800s (Rétout 1976), and his widely quoted text is a cornerstone of Trinidad's nineteenth-century historical literature, which is also some of the first published literature from or about Trinidad. What is also significant is his claim that some still retained an aboriginal culture, in isolation—people who have been left almost completely out of the historical record.

Extinction via mixture and regular allusions to the American Plains Indians also featured in texts of the latter half of the century. In the 1880s, an author of a series of handbooks on Trinidad wrote that, "as in most other similar cases, persecution or civilization, perhaps both, have driven before them these wild children of the plains, until they have become, so far as Trinidad is concerned, all but extinct" (Collens 1886:7); an interesting point is that we see another hint of the influence of the North American setting in designating Trinidad's Amerindians as "wild children of the plains." In the same period, and again referring to North American Indians, L. M. Fraser wrote that "there are few traces left of those to whom the hills and forests once belonged. As in North America the Red Indians have gradually disappeared before the encroaching white races, so in Trinidad the Aruacas and the Chaymas, the Tamanacos and the Cumanagotes have little by little faded away out of the community, and are now barely represented by a few families of mixed descent" (Fraser 1971 [1891]:1). The latter is, like that of Collens, an argument of virtual extinction, based on a conception of extinction via miscegenation, which in turn is logically rooted in notions of racial purity.

Fraser's argument has a remarkably contemporary resonance, representing perhaps one of the most dominant ways of thinking about Caribs today, one that would even be subscribed to by some SRCC leaders. During my fieldwork, Ricardo told a journalist that "there are no true Caribs anymore, what we now recognize as Carib is the mixed descendant of an extinct Amerindian race," with the journalist adding, "he explained that interbreeding with other races throughout the years has depleted the original Carib stock in Trinidad" (McLeod 1998a).

Histories written in the 1900s extend some of these themes. In a public lecture and book produced under the auspices of the Trinidad Historical Society, Dominican Father McArdle wrote that by the mid 1600s, with the complete emancipation of Amerindians, it was "too late to save them from extermination as a Race in the West Indies" (McArdle 1936/37:10), further endorsing the extinction thesis. Ottley, in a text that was widely used in secondary schools in Trinidad, commented that by the 1750s, "Toco, Matura, Point Cumana, Salybia, and Siparia, in all of which at that time the remnants of the proud and ancient race of first Trinidadians, whose fathers had controlled the colony centuries before the white man came, were struggling for survival against the inroads of the many disintegrating forces which the white man's world had brought to them" (Ottley 1955:54–55).

In the 1970s, Lowenthal's still-influential history text noted that in the wider Caribbean, "however defined, only about 50,000 Amerindians inhabit the West Indian culture realm, a small fraction of the one or two million living there at the time of Columbus"; moreover, in Lowenthal's estimation, "the surviving remnants are dwindling, socially demoralized, progressively less Indian in character" (1972:179). Lowenthal points out that sources claim that by the end of the eighteenth century the Arawaks were all extinct and that the few remaining deindigenized Caribs were in a state of cultural and ethnic deterioration (1972:32). A seminal text on Trinidad's aboriginal history also claims that "few if any" indigenous inhabitants remain in Trinidad (Newson 1976:3). Eradication and extermination are the key descriptors here (see Lowenthal 1972:31, 32). Contemporary Trinidadian historians claim that by 1797 all of Trinidad's Indian villages had virtually disappeared; moreover, isolated Indians who had not been brought under colonial control must have been an insignificant minority that also disappeared (Brereton 1981:7, 16, 20, 21). As Brereton wrote (in contrast to her subsequent writing for school texts, as we shall see later), "the Amerindians gave way to newer and sturdier people. Their day was nearly done, and they had no role to play in the development of Trinidad by the later nineteenth century" (1979:131).

We thus see race as a salient theme that now asserts itself in the contemporary ethnography. The unavailability of race as a resource for modern Carib identification stems from the weight attached to positions outlined above and from SRCC brokers' subscription to these positions. Claiming to be a descendant of Caribs is a much more likely contemporary stance, adopted by a wider number of Trinidadians beyond the SRCC alone, than is the stance of simply asserting, "I am a Carib." Carib was, apparently, a special race, whose dilution resulted in impurity, according to the conventions of colonial race discourse.

As noted in De Verteuil's passage above, and as will be discussed later in this work, there is also a common association between Spaniard and Amerindian both in contemporary northeastern Trinidadian racial discourse and in ways of thinking about Spanish colonial history. Writers portraying the progress of Trin-

idad from the Anglocentric perspective often stress that the Spanish were as indolent and backward as the Amerindians and that, indeed, the two could be considered as one. Writing of the "era of Spaniards and Indians" (Ottley 1955:41) and
focusing on the 1725–1727 collapse of Trinidad's cocoa economy, when Trinidad
entered a long, dry period of absent trade and commerce and was forced to resort
to a survival economy of basic self-sufficiency, Ottley wrote, "The handful of
Spaniards, who had built *their houses of mud and wattle,* at St. Joseph, *struggled*
on. They managed to eke out a *precarious existence* from the surrounding coun-
tryside. Since there were however, no exports, and no trade to speak of with the
outside world, *their life differed little from that of the native peoples.* With their
Indian wives and half-breed children, they *gathered* the fruit, fish, and game of
the country" (1955:40, emphasis added). Ottley further described, with a slight
hint of revulsion, how Spaniards slept on straw beds, clothed themselves in
"guayaco [guahuco] (Indian rough cloth)," and ate out of calabashes (1955.47).

Creating an Interest in the Caribs

Once an idea—the Carib presence—is not just studied and taught but actually
celebrated, then one can firmly speak of that idea becoming socially distributed.
In other words, we are no longer speaking of possibly esoteric literature but of
social values, related by agents in elaborating mythical histories of a society and
presenting these back to the society, which then reproduces and circulates them.
This type of commemoration then becomes a part of the local cultural repertoire,
helping anchor the meaning of a place (Arima) in a people shrouded by both
heroic tragedy and sanctified continuity.

One example of this celebratory commemoration is the play titled *Hyarima
and the Saints,* published in 1931. It was written by F. E. M. Hosein (1880–
1936), an Oxford graduate, former mayor of Arima in the late 1920s, and a
member of the legislative council. Hosein explained that his miracle play "was
actuated by the sole desire to preserve whatever there was of historical interest in
the Town which I so deeply love" (1976 [1931]:4). Hosein particularly concerned himself with the Caribs of Arima, with their history, their current descendants, and the Santa Rosa Festival. He was the first to formalize an annual pay-
ment for the community and even secured a cannon from the British for a
ceremonial firing to announce the start of the Festival.

Hosein was possibly the first in a series of local politician-researchers who
seized the image of the Carib as a token of Arima's heritage. In opposition to
absence or cultural irrelevance, Hosein was not only commemorating the Carib
presence, but was also casting the Caribs as heroic, even legendary figures. It is a
double-edged commemoration: Hosein, himself an ardent Christian convert, was
keen to hail the role of the Catholic Church in converting the Amerindians and in
bringing them into order. The play is based on the events of the 1699 uprising at
San Francisco de los Arenales, where Amerindians of the mission led a planned

rebellion that resulted in the killing of the three Spanish priests in charge and, stunningly, the governor of Trinidad and members of the ruling elite, who were all due for a celebration at the mission. However, Hosein mixed various stories into this one event, which, as mentioned before, has been the subject of songs and tales especially during the period of Spanish dominance in Trinidad.

In the play, the chief protagonist is Chief Hyarima, leading the uprising. Hyarima was in fact not in that mission and had died well before then, the actual leader being Cacique Bustamante (De Verteuil 1995). Hosein also borrowed from the history of early colonial wars against the Taínos of Hispaniola, so that, in the play, one of Hyarima's three daughters is named Anacaona, apparently after the queen who ruled over eighty chiefs in Hispaniola and was known for her songs and poems (this legendary heroine was hung by the Spanish). Saint Rose of Lima also makes an appearance in the play, in line with the local legend surrounding her apparition to three male Carib hunters in exhorting them to convert to Catholicism, except that here she appears to Anacaona. In literary terms, the play seems to echo Henry Wadsworth Longfellow's *Song of Hiawatha*—Hiawatha, like the dying Hyarima in this play, urged peace between his people and the Europeans.[3]

The play has been reinterpreted by some members of today's Carib Community as an actual history, with at least one of the spokespersons publicly insisting that the first Queen of the Caribs was indeed Anacaona. Hosein himself explained the degree to which history informed his play:

> I have not written with any pretensions to strict historical accuracy. No one knows that better than Dr. Wise to whom I am entirely indebted for whatever of Carib History appears in my Play. That History, it is true, was meager. But it was the most that could be had. And from that little I feel that I am justified in placing Hyarima in the lime-light. That little revealed that he was altogether too big to be lost. "The great Nepuyo Chieftain" is undoubtedly our national Hero. At least, such is my conception of him. (Hosein 1976 [1931]:4)

This perhaps suggests that in the 1930s there was an emergent sense of nationalism, of a nation in search of a national history and its national heroes. It is not surprising to me that such an emergent nationalism should emerge in a place that, after all, had tasted some measure of internal independence well before the rest of the colony.

The play has also been drafted into the actual making of history. Recall how Ricardo claimed that this very play had inspired in him the sense that he must lead a revival of the Caribs. The evocative words spoken by an imagined yet nonetheless emotionally potent Chief Hyarima are routinely recited by the current SRCC president in his public speeches and paraphrased in interviews. It is worth reproducing that particular passage of the play:

I see the remnants of my people scattered far, in numbers few, in strength diminished. . . . I see the now oppressors of my race, in turn themselves subdued and driven forth from blessed Cairi and all other lands. . . . I see their places taken by a race 'mongst whom the light proceeding from the Flaming Cross shines forth in greater brilliance. And two such men I clearly see. The one shall gather what remains of all my people under his protecting arms here in this place where I was the Chief, and through His love and pity and by favors shown shall gently lead them on to reconcilement and assuage the pain of being conquered. The other coming next shall rescue all my people from a dark oblivion. And he by gracious acts of courtesy and Love and Sympathy for a fallen and a broken race shall then create an interest in my unhappy people not felt before, a people who were always here, and met Columbus when he landed on their hospitable and friendly shores. Hail potent, glorious Chiefs from foreign climes! (Hosein 1976 [1931].26–27)

Hosein highlights the role of chiefs in reviving the Caribs, chiefs who come from foreign climes. Why two chiefs, I do not know. However, the two Ricardos of the SRCC—Ricardo Bharath, the president, who returned from Detroit, and Ricardo Cruz, a young shamanic figure, returned from New York—would seem to be obvious candidates in a play that some SRCC members see as an idealized script for real life. These chiefs act to bring about a revival of these sanctified people, the moral owners of the land, thus revived from oblivion by chiefs who "create an interest" in them. Arima—"this place where I was the Chief"—is inevitably singled out as the seat of indigeneity, the prime locus of those who "were always here, and met Columbus."

Lastly, the play provides an almost mythological explanation for a practice that is so minute that most observers of today's Santa Rosa Festival might not notice it: the fixing of a silver cross to the top of the pole that is used to carry the flag of Santa Rosa during the procession. Carib spokespersons today depict that cross as symbolizing the cross handed by the dying priest of the mission to Hyarima's Anacaona, following the uprising, when he tells his daughters in the play, "You shall keep it daughters as the sad yet happy memory of eternal sacrifice." For the dying Hyarima, too, the cross looms large: "To thy almighty influence I surrender. The Cross! The Cross! The Flaming Mystic Cross. The Power of Light and Strength! Bathed in thy rays my vision wider grows." The play ends with the surviving Amerindians urged on to reconcilement with the Catholic Church via the figure of Saint Rose, who appears to Anacaona in a dream alongside her father Hyarima.

The Contemporary Reinstitutionalization of the Amerindian Legacy

Stereotypical notions of the Carib have their roots in Columbus' first voyage. The apparent longevity, institutionalization, and perpetuation of the labels and trait lists emerging from the colonial period demonstrate, as Hulme puts it, "the quite spectacular success of the process of hegemonization, in which even such a potentially disruptive notion as identity of ethnic origins has been controlled from the center of political power" (1992:66). Institutionalization of what Bullbrook called "the Carib tradition" has occurred via the education system in Trinidad, in public discourse, and in established or legitimate sources of information. In this section I present a basic sample of some educational[4] sources that are of contemporary relevance and in current circulation, sources that also act as indices of the myriad ways in which the figure of the Amerindian is constructed, represented, and valued. This sample includes encyclopedias, anthropology handbooks, and school texts in Trinidad and should be seen as a further layer on top of the historical texts on Trinidad already cited and discussed.

Encyclopedias continue to be the most regular source of recycled assumptions stemming from the early European encounter with Caribbean aboriginals. In most of the cases that I surveyed, the depiction of Arawaks as settled and peaceful and suffering from the attacks of the fierce and cannibalistic Caribs goes virtually unrevised. In the case of the entry for Trinidad and Tobago in the *Encyclopaedia Britannica,* authored by Bridget Brereton, her suggestion is that the Caribs of Arima are most likely Arawaks and that their identity claims are thus erroneous. The entry under "Carib," authored by Nancy Owen (1974), in the *Encyclopedia of Indians of the Americas* opens with mention of the warlike nature of the Caribs, a statement that is repeated in an identical entry in the *Dictionary of Indian Tribes of the Americas* ("Carib" 1993). The entry for "Caribs" in *The Catholic Encyclopedia* not only labors the above points, but also blames the Caribs (and not the Catholic Spanish conquerors) for the decline of Arawak numbers (Bandelier 1999b). These charges are repeated in the author's entry for "Arawaks" (Bandelier 1999a). Similarly, in *The Columbia Encyclopedia,* the entry for "Caribs" states: "Extremely warlike and ferocious, they practiced cannibalism and took pride in scarification (ritual cutting of the skin) and fasting" ("Caribs" 2000; see also "Cannibalism" 2000). *The Columbia Encyclopedia* also claims that Arawaks were the occupants of Trinidad and that they became extinct, in part due to Carib attacks ("Arawak" 2000). The most modern of these types of sources, the Microsoft Network's *Encarta Online Encyclopedia,* posts the following depictions in the entry for "Carib": "The Carib . . . were noted for their ferocity. The tribe practiced cannibalism. . . . Carib men valued exploits in combat above all else. . . . Male captives were tortured and eaten" ("Carib" 1997–2000). For the "Arawak" entry, the same encyclopedia states that the Arawaks have been extinct for several hundred years and had been subjugated by the Caribs. The Arawaks are depicted as skilled potters, weavers, and wood- and

metalworkers, noted for that since pre-Columbian times, a description the encyclopedia does not offer for the Caribs, who are depicted as nomads ("Arawak"
1997–2000). All told, we see these key themes being repeated in these various
encyclopedia sources: Carib cannibalism, ferocity, and nomadic savagery; Arawak docility and skill in handicrafts; extinction; and confusion over whether the
Arawaks or the Caribs dominated Trinidad and its surrounding region.

Handbooks written by anthropologists have not produced much that is different from those sources. Irving Rouse, the noted archaeologist of the region, writing in Julian Steward's *Handbook of South American Indians,* described the
Arawaks as suffering from the incursions of the Caribs; this description follows
along the lines of the Carib-Arawak binary opposition (1948a:545). The same
confusion over whether Trinidad was Arawak or Carib finds some moderation in
Julian Steward and Louis Faron's *Native Peoples of South America* with their
statement that "the island Carib occupied all of the Lesser Antilles and part of the
island of Trinidad" (1959:322).

Having a more immediate presence are the school texts used to teach history
and social studies to secondary-school students across Trinidad.[5] One of those
reflecting on these teachings is Kim Johnson, a journalist with the *Trinidad Express.* Johnson expresses the core of this discussion of the ways historical characterizations and ascriptions have become institutionalized, and the substance and
weight of these teachings, in the following manner:

> The story of the Arawaks, the Caribs and the Spaniards is a well known tale
> told to every Caribbean child. We all, from the least educated to the most
> widely read, accept it almost instinctively that there were, before the Euro-
> peans landed on these our islands, a peaceful and gentle tribe of Amerindi-
> ans called the Arawaks who had inhabited the entire Caribbean archi-
> pelago. So generous and guileless were these people that they embraced the
> Spaniards and provided every comfort for them, only to be repaid by being
> mercilessly slaughtered so that within a few decades not one Arawak was
> alive. (Johnson 2000:part 1)

With respect to the other half of the dichotomy, Johnson adds that "there was
another tribe, a ferocious one called the Caribs, who were on the verge of pounc-
ing on the Arawaks and putting them to an even more horrible end. These Caribs
were, you see, eaters of human flesh. Following hard on the heels of the Arawaks,
they had gobbled their way up the Caribbean archipelago, settling on each island
like a swarm of locusts in a field, and only moving on when they had gorged
themselves on every available Arawak" (Johnson 2000:part 1). Johnson thus
simultaneously highlights two features that are vital for this study: (1) depictions
of the orthodoxies that are widely taught, as picked up from colonial discourses
on Caribbean aboriginals; and (2) the questioning, reinterpretation, and reworking of these discourses in the modern context, guided by specific interests and
widely communicated via modern media.

Savagery and extinction are ambivalently countered by modern texts taught in schools, in ways that are important to the contemporary SRCC. We have already examined some material from Ottley's *Account of Life in Spanish Trinidad* (1955), which was once a commonly taught text in Trinidadian secondary schools. Ottley made a significant statement in that text that served to endorse the extinction thesis yet made an exception for the Arima Carib Community, whose continuity and cultural influence Ottley validated: "but for a handful of them at Arima, these first inhabitants of Trinidad have gone. We have, however, inherited from them certain skills which today still serve us in as good stead as they did those from whom they originated. The technique of making Carib baskets, of manufacturing fishpots of bamboo, the preparation of cassava bread on hot stones, are all of them cultural remains" (1955,4).

Bridget Brereton's *Introduction to the History of Trinidad and Tobago* (1996) and Jack Watson's *West Indian Heritage: A History of the West Indies* (1982) are the two main texts now used in secondary-school history classes. Both begin with the mandatory chapter 1 on the Amerindians. While the latter feature may suggest specialness (for being first), in a history text following a linear chronological order it also suggests the acute degree of pastness associated with Amerindians. Watson (1982:8) asserts that "the Europeans eventually destroyed the Arawaks, and their way of life can only be pieced together by archaeologists and historians." He also casts the Arawak within the same noble savage framework encountered previously, noting, "the search for wealth and the aggressive pursuit of power were not characteristics of the Arawak civilization" (Watson 1982:9). As for the Caribs, Watson unsurprisingly declares that "they were cannibals, who from time to time fed on the Arawaks" (1982:9). Watson ends this chapter in the school text by saying that only a very few Caribs survive in some parts of the Caribbean, owing to their fierce and protracted resistance, whereas all the Arawaks were dead by 1600 (1982:25, 39). Indeed, this is yet another orthodoxy added to the rest we have discussed, that is, of directly linking Arawaks with extinction while enabling the Carib to be associated with survival and resistance.

Brereton (1996) differs from Watson in some respects in her school text. First, unlike in her earlier writings, she tends to avoid the Carib and Arawak labels and instead sticks with the generic label "Amerindian," even while noting that the Yao, Carinepagoto [*sic*], Shebaio, Arawak, Nepoio, and Kalina occupied Trinidad and Tobago. Second, Brereton's text does not insist upon either the extinction thesis or the standard traits associated with Caribs and Arawaks, as Watson's does. Instead, Brereton's text offers a more nationalistic reinterpretation of Trinidad's Amerindian history and makes specific references to the contemporary Santa Rosa Carib Community. Her chapter is titled, significantly, "The First Trinidadians and Tobagonians," following Williams' (1962) designation of "Our Amerindian Ancestors." She repeatedly uses phrases such as "the first people" and "the first Trinidadians" throughout her chapter (Brereton 1996:1). The resistance theme appears in her text as well, without discriminating between

Arawaks and Caribs: "Amerindians resisted . . . strongly. The Amerindians were good fighters and it was not until 1592 that the Spaniards could actually make a permanent settlement" (Brereton 1996:3). Instead of arguing that Amerindians became extinct, Brereton opts for the view of Amerindians declining in numbers (1996:4). Brereton also covers some details of the history of missions in Trinidad, up to the 1800s with respect to the then-remaining Amerindian missions in Arima, Toco, and Savana Grande (1996:4). The Amerindians may not have been extinct, but Brereton explains, "In the end, however, nearly all the Trinidad Amerindians accepted the Catholic faith, and by 1793 most of them spoke Spanish. By then there were few Amerindians left in either Trinidad or Tobago" (1996:4).

Equally significant, if not more so, with respect to the contemporary context, are Brereton's statements pointing to both the Trinidadian search for a national indigeneity and the special position of the modern SRCC. Brereton explicitly speaks of "our Amerindian heritage" in the following passage of her school text:

> Only *a few* people in Trinidad and Tobago today have Amerindian *blood,* but *we should all be proud of our first people. Their legacy is all around us.* We can see it in many words and place names, reminding us that *these people made the islands their own by settling down* and naming places, rivers, bays, districts and things. We can see it in roads which date back to their paths. We see it in ways of cooking, especially dishes made with cassava. *We* also *have* a community in *Arima,* who call themselves "Caribs" and are very proud of their culture. They are working hard to make us all more aware of *the heritage of our first people.* (Brereton 1996:4, emphasis added)

I must flag this particular passage as one that neatly and concisely summarizes and condenses the core of current, dominant Trinidadian nationalist thinking on the Caribs and indigeneity in general, expressing at the same time all the prevailing themes internal to that thinking. It is, in this sense, an epitomizing statement, and it is instructive for being used to teach school pupils. Brereton suggests, as a supplemental study activity at the end of the chapter, "Visit the Santa Rosa Carib Community in Arima, and speak to community members about their activities, taking notes on what you learn" (Brereton 1996:6). It is thus not surprising that one of the dominant year-round activities of leading SRCC members such as Ricardo and Cristo is the holding of lectures and displays for visiting schoolchildren.

In line with the sentiments outlined by Brereton, in 1989 the Arima Public Library established its Carib Corner. Librarians established this display as part of an effort to showcase the local histories of each of the locations of the various branches of the National Library System. In this instance, however, the Arima

Table 5. Historical Phases in the Perception and Classification of Trinidad's Amerindians

Historical position	Classifications
Colonial enemies/allies	Caribs, Arawaks
Imperial subjects	Remnants of Caribs and Arawaks
Protected populations, wards	Christians, noble savages (second to whites?)
Ending of missions	Indolent, inferior laborers, passive, child-like
Postmissions	Extinct, mixed/not pure, peasants, Cocoa Panyols
National independence	Caribs as heroic warriors, resistance fighters; Arawaks as noble; or elements of national folklore
Postindependence	descendants of Caribs
Present	First Nations, indigenous, Amerindian descendants

Public Library obtained national press coverage for the launch of its display (see Kassie 1989). The display, much like Brereton's passage above, underscores the Amerindian heritage in terms of place-names, a history of Caribs, and Carib traditions in food and weaving, as well as highlighting the current Carib Community and its Santa Rosa Festival. In addition, schoolchildren were asked to submit sketches and paintings of how they pictured typical Amerindians. The latter is one of a number of school exercises that inculcate the Amerindian legacy in the minds of schoolchildren; these exercises also include an annual "Know Arima" quiz for primary-school children organized by the Arima Borough Council. The Carib Corner, according to the librarians, also serves as the main focus for the many children that I regularly saw crowding the library, and the associated materials are also heavily consulted by children for their various projects and essays.

Positioning Perceptions of Presence

These first three chapters have been focused on the history of political economic and ideational modes of constructing the Carib, laying the foundation for a meaningful map of the transformations of ways of ascribing identities and traits to Caribbean aboriginals, as well as apportioning various statuses to them at different times. My attempt at a summary is presented in table 5.

Accompanying these historical phases, and in conjunction with the social and political ranking of aboriginals and their stances toward various contending powers, is the following overview of the range of labels that have been deployed in an attempt to handle Caribbean aboriginals. Table 6 is derived from the literature specific to Trinidad. We can thus see the fluctuations between generic labels

Table 6. Temporal Range in Perceptions and Designations of Trinidad's Indigenes

Time period	Designation
1492	*Indio*[a]
1500–1600s	Carib vs. Arawak
To mid1600s	Dutch Carib vs. Arawak
To late 1600s	Dutch Carib vs. Spanish Carib
Early 1700s	Warao vs. Nepuyo
1708–1756	Christian Indian vs. Wild Indian
1786–mid1800s	*Indio*, Indian
Late 1800s	Indian, Cocoa Panyol, Spanish peon
1920s–1970s	Carib
1980s–1990s	Carib, Nepuyo, Amerindian, indigenous, First Nations

Notes: a. *Indio* is the starting point in European ways of labeling the Amerindians in Trinidad; this is not like "Carib" is similar to later periods. The horizontal line in the table marks the transition from Spanish to British rule of Trinidad.

(Indian) and specific ethnic labels (Nepuyo), between allied and opposed groups, and between Spanish and British control, and finally, with many of these diverse labels assorted and conflated in the present. In the final analysis, the result is a very complex map that constrains (in that culturally legitimate choices are finite) and yet provides great room for representational maneuvering.

4

Nationalizing the Carib

The Indigenous Anchor of a State in Search of a Nation

In staking their claim to Amerindian heritage, the SRCC does not aspire towards racial purity, but to establish Amerindian cultural practices as being as important to the brewing perception of national identity as those who were introduced at a later date.
Trinidad Guardian, **August 25, 1993, p. 16**

You will find everybody claims to have some little Carib blood in them.
Ricardo Bharath, president, Santa Rosa Carib Community

The Carib has been increasingly privileged in nationalist discourses as the bedrock of the nation, as the territorial precursor if not the biological ancestor of the modern Trinidadian, thus acting as a trademark of locality whereby Trinidad's Amerindian heritage imparts antiquity to the concept of a Trinidadian nation. Nationalism has motivated the reinterpretation of the Carib in line with the development of a sense of national indigeneity that is anchored within the Amerindian past and articulated via the symbolic device of the Carib. John Stewart (1989), a Trinidadian anthropologist, has challenged us with the argument that the anthropological literature on Trinidad emphasizes its migrant and nonindigenous character while largely neglecting the struggle to establish a (Trinidadian) sense of indigeneity. In addition, David Lowenthal (1972) found that at least since the 1970s Amerindian history has played a key symbolic role in West Indians' search for national identities, framed by an emerging cultural nationalism. Thus we witness in Trinidad the increased recognition and institutionalization of the Carib in narratives of national history, added to the state's nation-building efforts in seizing upon the proclaimed Carib contribution to the national foundation. In general terms, Rhoda Reddock observes that recently there has been "increased acceptance of aspects of the 'folk' culture as 'national culture'" across the Caribbean (1996a:3), even though the figure of the indigene in reworked nationalist narratives remains neglected in the social scientific research of the Commonwealth Caribbean.

Indigenization

A sense of national indigeneity, along with globalized discourses of indigeneity—joined with the revivalist efforts of the SRCC in defining and promoting their own Amerindian indigeneity—have jointly produced a powerful translation of the Carib into the "First Nations," the "First Trinidadians," and the "First Peoples." This contemporary translation receives the validation of internationalized discourses of indigeneity embodied by agents that have made their presence directly felt in Trinidad. The concept of indigenous in Trinidad is also split between its dual applications as signifying either national or Amerindian. At the Arima level, one commonly finds a dual distinction between local and aboriginal: "We are all citizens of Arima and its environs, but not all of us are original inhabitants" (Williams 1988:6).

Beyond Trinidad and the Caribbean, nationalism has loomed large in the construction of a folk culture. Tambiah observed that with decolonization in the 1960s, the emphasis of nationalists was on nation making, strengthening national sovereignty, and creating national culture and national identity (1994: 435). It is from within this national identity paradigm that we find the earliest attempts at reinterpreting the Amerindian legacy in terms of local authenticity, independence, and the primordial constitution of nationhood. The search for national identity involved highlighting rural folklore and creating inventories of national traditions. This lends some credence to arguments positing that in nationalism, "the traditional has been associated with small-scale communities located within peripheral areas of the state, whose seemingly changeless culture is identified with the cultural roots out of which modern nation-states have grown," hence it is "in the fringes of the nation-state" that nationalists find "remnants of its cultural heart" (Olwig 1993a:89; see also Beriss 1993:114). Similarly Duany argues that the "quest for native origins is a common discursive practice to 'narrate the nation' by including certain 'autochthonous' ideological elements and excluding 'foreign' ones" (Duany 1999:31). The history of the Caribs is taught as the history of the nation, thus acting as a local and autochthonous anchor for modern nationhood.

Tying in with the dualistic nature of reinterpreting and articulating the Carib (that is, caught between the national and the ethnic) is the question of the duality of nationalism on the subject of ethnicity in Trinidad. Yelvington sees nationalism and ethnicity in Trinidad as characterized by two opposing yet related processes: "On the one hand, there is the conflation of nation/state/ethnicity to construct a 'non-ethnicity,' in which there are 'Trinidadians' and 'others,' that is, 'ethnics,'" and on the other hand, "there is the construction of ethnic and cultural differences to prove and justify contribution, authenticity, and citizenship" (1995b:59). The reengineering of the national position of the Carib, whether on the part of the state or the SRCC, directly confronts this problem. The state, acting as an arbiter among competing ethnic groups, also treats the SRCC as

Table 7. The Annual Cultural Calendar

Month	Public holiday	Commemorative day
January	1 New Year	
	30 Eid ul Fitr (Muslim)	
February	23 Carnival period begins	
March	30 Spiritual Baptist/Shouter Liberation Day	Sunday after full moon—
		Phagwa (Hindu)
April	10 Good Friday	13 Easter Monday
	12 Easter	25 National Rapso Day
May	30 Indian Arrival Day	25 African Liberation Day
June		11 Corpus Christi
		19 Labor Day
July		
August	1 African Emancipation Day	
	31 Independence Day	
September		24 Republic Day
October	19 Divali (Hindu)	14 Amerindian Heritage Day
November		1 All Saints Day
		2 All Souls Day
December	25 Christmas Day	
	26 Boxing Day	

Note: Some of the dates, such as Eid, Phagwa, and Carnival, are specific to 1998.

another of these groups. The state has now taken on the commitment of providing the standard menu of rewards: land, funds, and a day on the calendar. The SRCC, for its part, while working to articulate the meaning of Carib identity and traditional heritage, does not do so only for the use value of the exercise, that is, to satisfy themselves about maintaining traditional cultural practices for their own private satisfaction. The SRCC's aim is also to affirm the position of these practices within the inventory of cultural contributions to the foundation of the nation, an argument that has accompanied the request for recognition and rewards.

A similar national-ethnic duality emerges with respect to the cultural calendar. By the cultural calendar I mean the allotment of different parts of the year to the commemoration and celebration of certain events, festivals, and special days. Here too we see a certain balancing act being performed on the part of the state. The calendar is almost evenly divided between those holidays and commemorative days that are of a universalist, non-ethnic, and inclusively national nature and those holidays and commemorative days that are particular to ethnic and non-Christian groups, as shown in table 7 (see NALIS 2000d; Ryan 1997:20).

Given the preponderance of Anglicans and Catholics, and the fact that dominant elites belonged to these faiths, even Christian holidays were taken for granted as being national, a character that has been questioned only in recent years. Significantly, of the twenty-two days listed, nine are particular to either a specific ethnic group or a non-Anglican/non-Catholic denomination. I noted that in the April–May period of 1998, government ministers would appear in the appropriate ethnic costume for Shouter Liberation Day and Indian Arrival Day, hailing Trinidadians' attempts to "rediscover roots" and "celebrate their ethnic heritages" and feel "ethnic pride." Sometimes, television news anchors also appear in African costumes for select national days, whether they are of African descent or not.

Prime Minister Basdeo Panday in public interviews and appearances applauded the head of the Emancipation Support Committee, Kafra Kambon, for "revitalizing interest in African roots." Yet by December 1998, Panday had placed concerns for cultural heritage, race, and ethnic pride on the same plane as "division, insecurity, inferiority complexes and hatred." December is also the Christmas season, and Christmas is increasingly becoming the "season" for social awareness in Trinidad, especially with prominent media-organized charity campaigns. There is thus an almost periodined tension between national welfare and ethnic selfishness.

The seasonality characterizing the mode in which various cultural performances, events, rituals, and festivals are allocated national attention (that is, by government and the media) is widely commented upon in Trinidad, and sometimes resented. There is a Carnival season, a Calypso season, and a Parang season (itself tied to the Christmas season), manifesting the way certain cultural manifestations are confined within the boundaries of particular national time slots. As one of my non-SRCC informants commented, "it's as if some mastermind decided to extract diverse ethnic traditions and sequester them to select times on the calendar."

While this seasonality helps to spotlight particular episodes in the cultural life of the country, focusing attention on elements in the inventory of cultural contributions to the national foundation, it just as easily serves to remove ethnic expressions from public view for most of the year in a kind of ritualized forgetting. This is something that Ahee also observed in his thesis on the Arima Caribs: "It is only during the month of August when the Santa Rosa Festival takes place that the group is given a small measure of prominence. The media dutifully accords them some exposure and attention when these festivities are held, however, once these are over, the descendants of the Caribs return to their humble existence, forgotten, only to be remembered again the following year" (1992:32). This is a syndrome that some local commentators have called "fête and forget."

In connection with the temporal dimension of the dualist nature of articulating and valuing the Carib, there is also a spatial dimension. The symbol of the Carib belongs to the space of the nation when commemorated as the ancestral bedrock of the nation. However, the Carib belongs to the place of Arima when articulated as a local ethnic group, represented by the SRCC as a body and by the notion of Arima as the "home of the Caribs." Similarly, October 14 (Amerindian Heritage Day) is a national time; August 23 (the Santa Rosa Festival) is an Arimian time.

One context of these processes is a postcolonial political economy of tradition, one that differs in key respects from what was outlined in chapter 1, and which can be sketched using the following four features. First, we are now dealing with the making of a modern, independent nation-state, with familiar problems of identity and nation building common to many of the decolonized states of the post–World War Two era. Second, starting in the late 1960s, there has been increased political agitation in promoting the learning and appreciation of local history and local customs, in a generalized sense of local pride that was spawned by independence in 1962 and further encouraged by both the 1970 Black Power Revolution, with its dual cultural nationalist and ethnic pride orientations,[1] and the post-1973 petroleum boom. The latter period led to increased local wealth and was accompanied by economic nationalism articulated through a "Third Worldist" political philosophy and enacted in the policy of nationalizing foreign-owned industries.[2] Third, from the late 1980s and through the 1990s period of neoliberal structural adjustment policies, adopted by all Trinidadian governments under the guidance of the International Monetary Fund and the World Bank, there was increased state emphasis on three main areas of policy: increased "self-reliance,"[3] the "marketing of cultural products,"[4] and the development of community-based cultural components in new national tourism policies. Thus once more there was emphasis on local customs and culture, albeit for different purposes than in the 1970s. Fourth, as a controlling force in a multiethnic society—one where each of the main ethnic-based political parties endeavors to appear as nationalist, inclusive, and patriotic as possible—the state has often acted as an arbiter between competing ethnic groups, funding displays that emphasize diversity while ostensibly supporting the national ideology of "where every creed and race has an equal place," words enshrined in the national anthem. It is especially at this level of state patronage of cultural representations, of making investments in the symbols of national unity, that I see a key foundation for thinking of a postcolonial political economy of tradition. Taken together, these four main factors manifest some of the intersections where politics and economics are intimately tied to questions of locality, identity, modernity, and globalization.

"Our Amerindian Ancestors": The Articulation of the Carib in the Search for a National Indigeneity

Starting from as early as the 1930s, there is evidence of a renewed and growing prominence of reflections on the indigenous history of Trinidad, and on the figure of the Carib, in some of the elites' writings of local history. As K. S. Wise wrote in his *Historical Sketches of Trinidad and Tobago* in 1934: "No one can live long in Trinidad without being told that Iere was the aboriginal Indian name for the Island. . . . so much so that this name has become part of the traditional history of Trinidad and has been adopted as a place name" (1934:7).

The Carib gradually attained the status of a primordial hero in the struggle against colonialism. Again, from as early as the 1930s onward, writers and public lecturers such as Wise played a role in disseminating the proud and heroic attributes of Caribs as valiant warriors of resistance (see Wise 1938b:76). Arima, which since the end of the 1800s had been cast as the last remaining seat of Trinidad's Caribs, also figured prominently in new constructions of the anticolonial valor of the Amerindian (and even their postcolonial resurgence), as in F. E. M. Hosein's *Hyarima and the Saints*.

The view that holds Arima as a special locus of Trinidad's Amerindian heritage has been validated and disseminated by local scholars. This view of a surviving Amerindian heritage that privileges the place of the Arima Caribs as the anchor between the present and the long-term past found renewed expression in Ottley's *Account of Life in Spanish Trinidad*, a text formerly used in Trinidadian secondary schools. Ottley (1955:4) wrote of the survival of Trinidad's first inhabitants in Arima and of the inheritance of Amerindian household practices that had come to form part of the national patrimony, speaking in particular of basket weaving and the making of cassava bread. These two "cultural remains" are also two of the practices promoted as hallmarks of "maintained Carib traditions" by SRCC brokers such as Ricardo. Brereton also points to the national inheritance of various Amerindian practices:

> Techniques of preparing food were also influenced by the Amerindians. Rural folk of diverse racial origins in Trinidad adopted Amerindian foods and cooking methods. . . . From the [native] Indians, later Trinidadians learned the techniques of making bark hammocks and weaving baskets; log mortars and wooden pestles for pounding maize, cocoa or coffee, until recently still found in rural kitchens, were probably Amerindian survivals. The Indian *corial*, or canoe, made from a single tree trunk, continued to be used. In general, the Arawaks and Caribs influenced the life-style of rural Trinidadians in the nineteenth and twentieth centuries, particularly the people of the Spanish-speaking community of Venezuelan origin, called "peons" [Cocoa Panyols] in the island. (1981:22)

In the sunset years of British rule in Trinidad, one may perceive another side to the valuation of the indigene as the ancestor of the nation. This is a case of the Amerindian holding not a positive value in the articulation of a sense of modern nationhood but rather an important negative value: as a foil for measuring the progress of modern Trinidad against a historical background constituted by the Amerindian past, which is typically portrayed as primitive and backward. There is thus a double-edged value of indigeneity: a positive sense of local primordiality and locality, and a contrast between the traditional primitive and the modern progressive. In metaphorical terms, the nation salutes its first cornerstone while in the process of erecting a modern edifice on top of it. One modern Trinidadian discourse on the pre-British "era of Spaniards and Amerindians" accuses the Spaniards and their Amerindian kin for their failure to "develop" the colony, a fact owing to the Spaniards' laziness and lethargy and the Amerindians' indolence and primitivism. The languid backwardness of Spain's inertial imperialism and the unprogressive sloth of the colony's Spaniards are seen as having led them to adopt Amerindian ways. Ottley reinforced and disseminated the modern Trinidadian prejudice toward the pre-British era: "Time marched on but Trinidad slumbered serenely," its residents living an "indolent life of poverty and social inactivity"; in the 1740s, "Spaniards in St. Joseph and Indians in the forests had once more fallen completely asleep"; "the Spanish word manana [*sic*] (tomorrow) became household"; "the people of Trinidad during that era, sat quietly on their rickety doorsteps, waiting philosophically for their fairy to turn up and wave her golden wand to change the face of things" (Ottley 1955:48–49). Appropriated by the late colonial and postindependence ideology of progress and development, the Amerindian still served a function, but as a reminder of how far Trinidadians had come (or had yet to go).

The figure of the Carib is also embedded within mediated representations and ritualized reenactments of the foundation of postconquest Trinidad. The landing of Columbus on Trinidad in 1498 is a story that is replayed annually on the first of August (formerly the date of the Discovery Day holiday); the village of Moruga on the south coast of Trinidad, the presumed site of Columbus' landfall, takes center stage for these occasions, at least since the revival of Moruga's celebrations in 1963. The event serves to reinforce the place of the Caribs in national history even while commemorating their succumbing to European colonizers. As one of the organizers of Moruga's Discovery Day celebrations for 1998 emphasized: "Trinidad's *development* in the *modern* world began in 1498" (Gobin 1998, emphasis added).

In recent years, especially for the 1998 quincentennial of Columbus' landing in Trinidad, the celebrations have drawn some protest from Africanist organizations. Even here the figure of the Amerindian occupies an important part of the stage, as a journalist wrote of the protests: "the grouse lies in the fact that the arrival of Columbus brought ensuing hardships for the Amerindians, the people Columbus met living here" (Gobin 1998). The annual event has reportedly gained new interest since it began to feature its reenactments of Columbus' landfall and his encounter with the Amerindians. This encounter has also been the subject of extensive attention in the print media (see, for example, Milne 1998a, 1998b; Ramlakhan 1998; *Trinidad Express* 1998d).

Amerindians are privileged within narratives of the foundation of the nation in that the act of foundation is seen as emerging from the crucible of the European encounter with the natives. The nation builds on but also seeks to surpass the Amerindian substratum. The entry of the nation into the modern world is epitomized by the arrival of Columbus, a moment that is fixed within Trinidad and Tobago's national coat of arms.

The ambivalent treatment of the Amerindian as a symbol of the antiquity of the roots of the nation and as a primitive savage at one and the same time is a complicated phenomenon. Narratives of the Amerindian as a savage predate the rise of cultural nationalism in Trinidad. These narratives survive in texts and are also drafted in the construction of a modern nationalist sense of progress. Narratives of Amerindian savagery can be enduring, especially among elites and members of the older generations in Trinidad. As an example, Gaylord Kelshall, a former head of the Coast Guard and a prominent white Trinidadian, allegedly exclaimed at the opening of the Chaguaramas Military Museum, "'The Amerindians were left behind by time, about 5,000 years. . . . It was a clash of cultures. . . . It was not brutal conquistadores destroying a way of life. The Amerindians had to die.' He suggested that members of the . . . audience . . . would have lent a hand in killing Amerindians too had they walked into a temple and met one of them, his teeth filed, hair greased with human blood, and knew his job was to rip human hearts out of the chests of living sacrificial victims. 'You too would have killed him'" (Johnson 1998a). This statement derives its strength from the earliest colonial texts depicting the Caribs as horrendous man-eating beasts. The occasion for the remarks was the museum's commemoration of the five-hundredth anniversary of the arrival of Columbus in Trinidad, as well as three hundred years of Spanish rule, the types of commemorations that can serve to perpetuate the Amerindian as a critical actor in the foundation of Trinidad, even while reaffirming colonial perspectives.

The presence of the Amerindian in modern reflections on Trinidadian national history and identity became increasingly indispensable. Researching the Amerindian heritage, and colonial history, garnered new interest throughout the 1900s. One argument for the contemporary importance of researching national history was made by Ottley on the eve of Trinidad's achieving internal self-government in 1956: "If we are to understand the present we must know the past, for the present is but an extension of the past, with sundry changes wrought by the hands of circumstances" (1955:ix). One of Ottley's primary objectives in the "connecting up of the Trinidad of today with that of yesterday" was to highlight the history of what he called the "early Trinidadians—the Indians" and to describe the lifeways of "the First Trinidadians" (1955:x, 1). Indeed, Ottley may have been the first writer to refer to the Amerindians in this manner.

Intersecting issues of modernity, class, locality, national identity, and self-reliance can also be found in local theses that seek to recoup the native in Trinidad's cultural legacy. For example, in studies of Trinidad's architectural history, the late John Newel Lewis, a prominent upper-class Trinidadian architect of considerable repute, played a key part in highlighting the "Amerindian architectural legacy" in the form of the *ajoupa,* also the title of his volume on the subject (1983a; see also 1983b).

Lewis argues that the *ajoupa* has never been absent as a basic structural model in the construction of homes in Trinidad, tracing its continuities from precolonial times, through colonialism and the homes built by slaves and indentured East Indians, into modern times. Indeed, he sees many of the basic forms of the built environment of Trinidad as a simple substitution of materials laid over a basic Amerindian form (Lewis 1983a:14). For Lewis, the Amerindians were the "first great architects of Trinidad," having produced the "prototype," the "leitmotif," the "basic vernacular form" that is the "purest expression of Trinidad architecture" (1983a:23, 25). His argument also resonates with populist class themes at certain moments, discrediting the alien constructions of the snobbish upper class, with all their imported materials and environmentally inappropriate designs, while praising the "defiance" of the working classes and rural dwellers. Coupled with his own form of class critique is his critique of modernity: "the growth of all middle classes discredits the achievements of vernacular architecture" (Lewis 1983a:85). In contrast, he writes that "many country people have defied the prefabricated timber systems and continued to use jungle wood. In spite of all the imported technology and in spite of the fact that the rest of the Caribbean has been hooked on the standardized system of the timber houses for centuries, in *Trinidad, many people just continue to do what the Arawaks did*" (Lewis 1983a:85). Lewis called for the "revival of indigenous culture," where city dwellers should draw upon "the countryman's natural simplicity, taste and good sense," emphasizing that "we should salute our roots and understand its achievements" (1983a:85).

Turned into a symbol, the Amerindian dwelling also has certain nationalist political connotations. The walls of the *ajoupa* were often made of *tapia,* a mixture of mud, grass, and pebbles pasted onto a wooden frame or bamboo lattice, left to dry, and then perhaps coated with plaster. The *tapia* inspired Trinidad's critical dependency theorists of the 1970s, such as Lloyd Best, an economist and political activist who heads the Tapia House Movement.

The figure of the Amerindian has been appropriated as an interethnic bridge in contemporary Trinidadian nationalist discourse, where indigeneity subverts the bipolar divide between Africans and East Indians. Burton Sankeralli, a columnist for the *Daily Express,* wrote, "These Amerindians, whom we call 'Caribs,' are the primordial tribe, the red[5] ancestors of all 'Trinibagonians.' They are the first children of our earth" (1997:29). More than that, speaking of Trinidad's dominant ethnic groups today, Sankeralli declared: "We here need to note that all four tribes consider themselves indigenous. This land is home for all of us. Hence these tribes are all descended from the primordial tribe—the Amerindians" (1997:31). He thereby fused the two senses of indigeneity: native as in those born here, and native in the sense of those who were here first. In defining the locus and genesis of Trinidadian identity, Sankeralli urged that "we need to turn to the Caribs" (1997:31). Kamal Persad, one of Trinidad's more militant Indocentric newspaper columnists, similarly wrote,

> December 1 [the anniversary of the 1699 Amerindian uprising] must be built as an important occasion when the entire country can reflect on the first nation of Kairi, their origins, way of life, their conquest and genocide

at the hands of Spanish and Catholic imperialists, and a clear agenda for
the future. Hindus and Indians and Africans can share the perspectives of
the Amerindian, and identify with their causes, especially so since our experiences were so similar. Clearly, the initiatives must originate from the
Amerindians. (Persad 1999)

Persad repeatedly refers to the Amerindians as the "first nation" and argues in
support of renaming Trinidad "Kairi" and of building a monument to commemorate the insurgents of 1699 (a monument erected by the church commemorates only the Spanish victims).

Besides serving as a figure for grounding modern Trinidadians within a local
history, the Amerindian can also be used either as a symbol of unity, as expressed
in the words of Sankeralli, or as a tool in ethnic contestation as when local
Africanist activists embrace and absorb the Caribs within a paradigm of those
who suffered slavery as opposed to the allegedly more privileged descendants of
indentured workers, the East Indians in Trinidad. However, this is not a strategy
reserved for Afrocentric activists alone, as Kamal Persad argues: "The Amerindian experience is very similar to the Hindu and Indian experience. Indian children who were orphans during indentureship and were placed in Catholic institutions were immediately converted and given Spanish names. This is the origin
of the 40,000 Indian Catholics in Trinidad" (Persad 1999).

Most prominent, however, is the symbolic role of the Amerindians, now referred to as First Nations by some prominent figures in Trinidad, in developing
a longer-term view of national history. "The Amerindians were key to defining
the foundation of the Republic," as John Donaldson, the vice-chairman of the
People's National Movement, stated in a speech on Republic Day in 1998 for the
opening of the PNM's "exhibition to commemorate *our First Peoples*." Indeed,
Donaldson also devoted some time to explaining that "First Nations" was the
most appropriate way of talking about the Amerindians, and he mentioned how
the term is in frequent and regular use in Canada, which presumably adds further
legitimacy to the term.

From a nationalist perspective, positing Amerindian history as being of foundational importance to the creation of the modern nation-state also serves to
bolster the construction of a national history that dates back not just to European
conquest, or the transplantation of workers from other continents, but even several thousand years further back. The Amerindian thus bestows on the new nation a sense of antiquity and a sense of continuity of occupation of the territory
that is Trinidad. Given some Caribbean nationalists' often invidious compari-
sons between themselves and their former European masters, the new antiquity
of a national history that appropriates the Amerindian renders Caribbean states
as ancient as any in Europe.

Cultural brokers—who specialize in excavating, disseminating, and promoting the past and the concept of an Amerindian heritage—cater to, perhaps even

nurture, such perspectives. The role of museums and archaeologists thus comes to the forefront. The National Museum of Trinidad and Tobago plays an important role in graphically inculcating the notion of Amerindian culture as the starting point of the nation's history. Archaeologists themselves, despite often being nonnationals, have also worked to foster local pride in Amerindian heritage. Dutch archaeologist Arie Boomert wrote in a 1982 article titled "Our Amerindian Heritage" in the *Trinidad Naturalist* that because of Trinidad's being "one of the world's most cosmopolitan populations . . . it is often forgotten that a few of the people now living in Trinidad are descended or partly descended from the original inhabitants of the island, the Amerindians." He also declared: "Trinidad can boast of the fact that it is the oldest settled site of the West Indies," the remains of "Banwari Man" having been dated to 7,200 BP (1982:27, 28). The cover of the magazine showed a picture of a well-known monument in Trinidad, the Amerindian warrior atop a pedestal at the remains of La Venezuela estate, with a bold caption: "The First Trinidadians."

Boomert's research is also featured prominently on laminated boards within the Cleaver Woods Museum located at the western entrance to Arima, with its reconstruction of an Amerindian dwelling and various archaeological remains and current arts and crafts of Arima's Carib Community. The museum was the result of an initiative taken by the National Parks Section of the Forestry Department of the Ministry of Agriculture, Fisheries, and Food Production in 1982. Their aim to construct an Amerindian house (*ajoupa*) in the Cleaver Woods Reserve, west of Arima, was "as a tribute to the original inhabitants of Trinidad and Tobago" (Boomert 1982:60). The museum "commemorates the Amerindian past of Trinidad and Tobago," and as Boomert added, "The Arima *ajoupa* is meant to keep *our Amerindian heritage alive* and, judging from the reactions of the *several thousands of interested people* who already have visited Cleaver Woods National Park since its official opening in March of this year [1982], it serves its purpose well!" (1982:60, emphasis added).

Peter Harris, an archaeologist, was instrumental in securing the state's official recognition of, and financial support for, the SRCC. Prior to obtaining this recognition and support, Harris told a newspaper reporter: "The Amerindian story goes back 8,000 years and the *Santa Rosa Community is the only surviving one*, but society as a whole has never really given them the *normal recognition* that is *due* to these *unique* survivors of *our Amerindian past*" (quoted in Kassie 1989, emphasis added). Following the Cabinet's 1990 decision, Harris wrote a letter to the editor of the *Trinidad Guardian* stating, "I must congratulate Cabinet on their acceptance that the cultural survival of the Amerindian Community is a traditional problem. For too long the Santa Rosa Caribs and perhaps other groups have had to struggle on their own" (Harris 1990a). In placing emphasis on the need for Trinidad to secure an identity as a nation-state in the modern world, Ahee urged: "As a society, Trinidad and Tobago must not be so caught up in the race to be part of the developed world that we neglect to place emphasis on the *values and traditions* that *distinguish* us from other societies" (1992:35, emphasis added).

Other archaeologists and local champions of archaeology have also publicly pushed for the preservation of Amerindian archaeological remains and the establishment of heritage tourism. Recently, writers such as de Verteuil have lamented that, although Trinidad's "rich and important Amerindian heritage" has attracted interest from foreign researchers "far afield," not enough is being done by Trinidadians to properly research their "Amerindian past" (de Verteuil 1999:40, 43). De Verteuil notes that Grenada, in contrast, "is now beginning to pay serious attention to its own Amerindian legacy," and Jamaica, Barbados, Antigua, and the French and Dutch Antilles have all shown an "active interest in preserving Amerindian sites." Moreover, he argues that they have all worked at "developing the economic benefits to be realized through heritage tourism" and they "enjoy the consequent pay-back, including opportunities for education and a fostering of civic pride" (de Verteuil 1999:45–46).

Popularized and Sponsored Indigeneity

The news media have played a key role in endorsing depictions of Amerindian cultural survival, seizing upon rituals or performances of the Carib Community as being necessarily ancient and authentic. The news media have also played a key role in disseminating the concept of "our Amerindian heritage" and of the Amerindians as "the First Trinidadians" (see Chouthi 1998a, 1998b). Contemporary school texts have rehabilitated the previously "savage" and "extinct" Carib, transforming the Carib into a surviving entity, further recast as the First Trinidadian (as in Brereton's *Introduction to the History of Trinidad and Tobago* [1996]). Also at the level of educational institutions, one finds growing interest in the Carib Community on the part of students of the University of the West Indies, with at least two Caribbean Studies theses having been produced in the last decade (Ahee 1992; Almarales 1994), whereas none was written before the 1990s.

In terms of popular literature, I have already cited Hosein's play on the Arima Caribs. Recently, books of poems, tales, and historical novels have been published that feature Trinidad's Amerindians. Examples include Norma McCartney's (1989) *Tales of the Immortelles,* which has two fairy tales centered on the Caribs of Arima. Knolly La Fortune's (1999) *Manzanilla,* a collection of poems, begins with a poem in memory of Chief Hyarima, part of a renewed contemporary interest in this chief, dubbed the first national hero of Trinidad in the plaque adjoining his recently erected monument at the entrance to Arima. Arthur de Lima's (1993) *Don José* is a novel devoted to the life of the popularized last Spanish governor of Trinidad, a possible expression of increased local interest in the Spanish and aboriginal history of Trinidad. Other recent, locally published texts on select aspects of Trinidad's colonial Amerindian history have also appeared (see de Verteuil 1995; Johnson 1997), as well as those that pay special attention to the "Amerindian background" (see Besson and Brereton 1991; Brereton 1981). Locally published books on the histories of Trinidad's towns almost invariably begin their entries for Arima with discussion of the Caribs, the Amerindian mission, and the Santa Rosa Festival (see, for example, Anthony 1988).

Popularized, mediated, and institutionalized depictions of the Carib or Amerindian presence (whether conceived in historical, symbolic, or demographic terms), while often not overtly nationalist in content or tenor, serve to bolster the nationalist articulation of the Carib insofar as they furnish the material that permits such articulation, while also framing the Carib as a fixture of local history, an object of local pride, or a landmark of Trinidad's local cultural landscape. What we witness is a purposive dissemination of what Rogers (1990) calls the "corpus of images" utilized in the definition and articulation of indigeneity.

An example of these popular images in the visual arts is the once-prominent mural, painted by the celebrated Trinidadian artist Carlisle Chang (see Raymond 2000), that greeted those arriving at Piarco International Airport. At the left of the mural was the figure of an Amerindian man, and below, an Amerindian woman, almost as if at the dawn of humanity, the dawn of time, or the dawn of the Trinidadian nation in particular—or perhaps it was meant to convey an impression of all of these simultaneously.

In the realm of commercial advertising one sees a few select cases of the perpetuation of important indigenous labels such as Carib and Arawak, as well as more veiled references to the Caribs of Arima. Mpule Kwelagobe, the winner of the 1999 Miss Universe pageant hosted in Trinidad, posed for Carib Beer under a sentence with obvious double meaning—"there's a bit of Carib in everyone"— an obvious reference to claims increasingly voiced by Trinidadian individuals as to possessing some degree of Carib ancestry. The Carib label was adopted in 1950 by the Caribbean Development Company, a Trinidadian corporation that has achieved transnational corporate status (see Carib 2000). Arawak Chicken prominently displays its advertising in newspapers and on billboards. A phone card produced by the Telecommunications Services of Trinidad and Tobago showed women making cassava *farine*, an item that writers and school texts identify as a Carib tradition. The Unit Trust Corporation has erected a billboard at the western entrance to Arima, with an apparent illustration of an elderly Amerindian woman, presumably depicting the essence of wisdom: "old age" plus "the native Indian." The banner heading on the billboard read: "Wisdom runs deep in Arima."

The performing arts and festivals have been another arena for the expression of interest in, and the dissemination of, symbols of indigeneity, whether this be in the form of professional dance troupes creatively enacting imagined Carib dances, such as that of Julia Edwards, a noted local choreographer who conducted some of her research with SRCC members, or in the much broader field of

Carnival with its categories of Fancy Indians, Red and Wild Indians, and Plains Indians (see Bellour and Kinser 1998). A recent Children's Carnival parade, spotlighted by the Tourism and Industrial Development Corporation, included a band of children masquerading under the banner of the "Arima Caribs" (TIDCO 2001). In addition, the National Carnival Commission (Trinidad's main organizational body for all Carnival activities) feels the need to even locate Carnival within an Amerindian historical heritage: "The evolution of Carnival in Trinidad and Tobago could be said to have started through the encounter of the Europeans with the earlier settlers (the Amerindians)—on Kairi—the former name of Trinidad" (NCC 2001). In the past, Carnival was noted for its resistance themes and the image of the Amerindian as a figure symbolizing resistance via motifs of savagery (see Bellour and Kinser 1998). One such figure was the "Midnight Robber," a bandit figure that gave eloquent speeches in public about his fearsome feats of treachery. "Benbow the Brave," played by Rupert Archibald, featured the Amerindian in this following sample of "robber talk":

> I am the incredible master Benbow
> Descendant of the Amerindian
> Amalgamated with Carib and Arawaks
> I arrive here by hurricane, storms and volcano
> Having to be shaking, shattering and plundering this earth
> For the avenge of my ancestors.
> I am the jaws of death and the ruler of mankind.[6]

As the late Daniel Crowley observed in Trinidad's Carnival in the early 1950s, among the robber characters there was one type, referred to as the "Blanket Robbers," that used to wear "Indian Blankets" from the United States, based on American Indian weavings (Crowley 1956:263).

The National Parang Association of Trinidad and Tobago (NPATT) maintains a small museum and archives that routinely highlight what NPATT directors see as the Carib heritage and basis of *parang*, with boards on display that feature the "Carib Legacy" in local knowledge of medicinal plants, religious rituals, and the "*sebucán* festival." Sylvia Moodie-Kublalsingh, Trinidad's leading researcher on *parang*, observed that Trinidad's *parang* came to be increasingly reinterpreted as symbolizing the rural folk roots of the nation: "At present, there is a growing interest in this culture and particularly in the Christmas parang. . . . It is part of the search for a 'national identity,' an obsession which has characterized the post-Independence period" (Moodie 1983:22). The location of the figure of the Carib within *parang* is thus significant.

Amerindian motifs and practices are also the subject of increased interest on the part of those in the performing arts more generally in Trinidad. The Centre for Performing Arts at the University of the West Indies regularly sends students to interview leading members of the Carib Community about Carib rituals, traditions, and styles of dress, in addition to hosting lectures by spokespersons such as the Carib president. The interest in Amerindian aesthetics and the development of Amerindian-derived styles in furniture design and interior decoration is also exemplified by the emergence of Manzanare Design Solutions,[7] which has recently held exhibitions of some of its Amerindian-inspired furniture pieces and decorative items. Basketry and other arts and crafts shaped or imaginatively inspired by Amerindian designs, or simply imported from Guyana, are also receiving commercial and media attention (John 2000; Mitchell 1998; Small 1998; *Trinidad Express* 1998e, 1998f, 1999c; *Trinidad Guardian* 1998d).

The Internet has seen the emergence of websites on Trinidad's Amerindian heritage, with some noteworthy feedback that suggests not simply widened interest but broader identification with Carib ancestry among Trinidadians (see Bermúdez Negrón 2000 2001, Johnson 2000, and PanTrinbago 2000a, 2000b). Judging from the feedback received by sites featuring Trinidad's Caribs—in the form of e-mail, postings on message boards, and entries in guest books—these sites seem to have acted as a magnet for expressions of national pride and local interest by Trinidadians at home and especially abroad.[8] While as much as half of all the messages are genealogy-related, with numerous individuals either asserting their Carib ancestry ("my paternal grandmother belonged to the Carib tribe") or wishing to research it further, another large proportion of visitors consists of Arimians residing abroad, and the dominant thrust in the majority of those messages is that of local and national pride in the Amerindians. Indeed, the number of such visitors claiming a Carib ancestry or expressing pride in the Carib heritage easily outnumbers the membership of the SRCC, pointing to the wider spread of this phenomenon of Carib identification. The following are just a few examples of these expressions: (1) "It is about time that the Caribs are recognized for their contribution to the island." (2) "Hi, I am a Trinidadian, also a Carib descendent living in Oakland, California, U.S.A. I was surfing through the different sites and stumbled upon yours. Seeing the artifacts brought back a lot of memories." (3) "Born and grew [up] there in Calvary, Arima: Keep doing what you're doing in enlightening people of the Carib history in Trinidad." (4) "I've been away from home for over 12 years now. I grew up in Sangre Grande, Toco, and Tunapuna. I am very, very proud to see that after all these years Trinidad, as a nation is coming to form and that the people who gave us the names of those homes we know so well are still there and that another generation will know that there is a Carib nation." (5) "This site not only took me back to my youth but also made me a bit homesick. I grew up with the Santa Rosa festival, it is part of who I am. Arima and the Carib Community are not mutually exclusive. You cannot separate one from the other. I am from a family of Parranderos and so proud to call Trinidad and in particular Arima . . . home!" (6) "My grandmother's grandmother was Carib and I have cousins in Arima who are married to pure Carib Indians. We do have to keep our culture alive and there's no better way to doing it than thru [sic] this medium. Although I now reside in the U.S. I know I can always browse home and my American friends/children can visit and experience what a diverse environment I was raised in." (7) "I am a Trinidadian and lived in Arima. I attended Arima Girls RC School. I always attended the Santa Rosa Festival. Now that I am living in USA (Westchester), I miss the *parang* and the whole spirit of the festival. I am quite happy to see that the Caribs, natives of the island, is [*sic*] making headway i.e. in making other people see what they have to offer." (8) "May the ancestors guide and protect all the descendants of the indigenous peoples in Trinidad & Tobago."

The tourist industry is increasingly seizing on the image of the Carib/Amerindian in Trinidad and Tobago in promoting another element of Trinidad's "uniqueness" as a locale. The Trinidad Tourist Board advertised the Santa Rosa Festival in Arima as a celebration of the town's first peoples.[9] A tour package offering "six days of birding in Trinidad and Tobago" features "visits to Amerindian communities" in its itinerary.[10] Other tourist sites, especially those located on the Internet, feature Arima and its Carib Community as an attraction in various tour packages.[11] Once again, the news media have promoted the Carib Community and loci of Amerindian heritage as tourist attractions (see Chouthi 1998c, 1998d; Herrera 1998; Mandol 1998; McLeod 1998b; Roberts-Griffith 1999; Rostant 1998), as has the state's Tourism and Industrial Development Corporation (TIDCO).[12] The objectification of culture in the context of tourism, via heritage display, is an increasingly important component of the complex of reengineering processes marking the production and valuation of the Carib presence in Trinidad.

Articulating and Valuing the Carib

The appropriation of the Amerindian in nationalist discourse has occurred through a variety of means, each of which has helped to add to the emergent conceptualization of the Amerindian past as the foundational bedrock of the modern nation. This has served to establish a link between the "first nations" and contemporary Trinidadians, via an implicit notion of territorial ancestry, a link that allows Trinidadians to refer to and speak collectively about "our Amerindian heritage." While the symbolism of Amerindian indigeneity has been increasingly utilized by intellectuals, politicians, and the media as a device for creating a sense of local primordiality and continuity with ancient times, the Carib in particular has also been reinterpreted in an anticolonialist light. The European attribution of savage and warlike qualities to the Caribs has been reinterpreted by nationalist elites as a sign that Caribs resisted colonialism, recasting them as primordial heroes in the struggle against slavery and for independence (in a broad sense of the term). Nevertheless, the corpus of assumptions and ascribed traits used to characterize the Carib during the colonial era (as outlined in earlier chapters) has also served to provide the basic parameters by which Carib identity and heritage have been defined and articulated in the present. The outcome of both SRCC and nationalist brokers' representations—separated here only for analytical purposes, as the two sets of brokers can often be one and the same—has been to fold the Carib into the nationalist canon of Creole culture that, in emic terms, encompasses yet transcends various ethnicities (compare Williams 1989).

The dual articulation of national and Carib indigeneity, the former utilizing the trope of the Amerindian and the latter defined and constructed out of the national setting, serves to enforce and add value to the presence of the Carib. Within the postcolonial political economy of tradition, aboriginality has become a national commodity, or at least a commodity of nationalist narratives. Indigeneity is not ontologically absolute, permanent, or inflexible in content, form, and meaning. Instead, indigeneity is thus elaborated and interpreted within specific political, economic, and historical conjunctures. In addition, at ground level, a number of agents and institutions have vested interests in the dissemination, promotion, and articulation of indigeneity, for various and often divergent reasons: nation building, ethnic consciousness, tourism, education, local self-reliance, and so forth.

The dissemination of images, symbols, and references to Caribs and the Amerindian heritage also helps to inseminate the idea of the Carib as a legitimate and recognized category, a category that can now be reinhabited. "Carib" has become an authoritative label, a loaded category that has had tremendous staying power for half a millennium, despite the many changes in the contexts and ways in which it has been used. Its authority is established and reproduced via repetition, reenactment, and ritual displays, especially when sanctioned or authored by powerful institutions and agents. The contemporary reengineering of this indigeneity occurs along external and internal boundaries where the SRCC is concerned, the national and the local, the social and the personal. Not only has the SRCC achieved considerable success in obtaining recognition and support, but also the valuation of the Carib continues to gain momentum. No longer suppressed as a vile identification appropriate only for savages, aboriginal ancestry seems to be in the process of being reclaimed by a groundswell of individuals across Trinidad and even Tobago.

5

Reproducing the Carib Locally

The Social Organization of Indigenous Representation in Contemporary Trinidad and Tobago

Ricardo is confident that with the perseverance and assistance from influential people outside of the SRCC, the community will achieve its aims and the nation will be proud to acknowledge their existence.

Beryl Almarales, SRCC researcher (1994:?5)

Over time the SRCC has had numerous prospective patrons offering some form of assistance but in return for some form of transformation within the SRCC. "You know," B.B., an Arimian businessman, told Ricardo, "You should go into that church and reclaim it with one of your bows and arrows"—urging Ricardo to be more confrontational in pressing the Santa Rosa Roman Catholic Church to let the SRCC have free use of its parkland for the Santa Rosa Festival. "Like you want to send me back to the Orinoco,"[1] Ricardo said and laughed uncomfortably. "All right, that aside, what music will you have at the center on the night of the festival?" asked B.B. Ricardo replied, "Well, we would have our *parang,* of course." "Parang!?"—B.B. seemed astonished: "What, you mean you still play that in August?"[2] Ricardo turned to B.B. and explained, "No, you see, after the church stripped us of our cultural traditions, they left us with nothing, except things like *parang.* We always play that music."

Another prospective patron was Arthur Sanderson, head of Communities United to Fight Underdevelopment (CUFU). He sought the alliance of the SRCC in pressing wealthy local conglomerates to donate funds to community projects. In meeting with the active SRCC members, Sanderson wished to begin with prayers. As if dismayed, he noted later in his speech to the SRCC, "I see you say Christian prayers." He asked, "You don't have your own prayers in your own language? You believe in your own god or gods, have your own religious ceremonies?" Ricardo explained, "Well, probably not like you're thinking. We believe in the Great Spirit, who is God, and we do perform a smoke ritual every now and again, but basically most members are Catholic." Sanderson then said, "Well, I know that in Dominica, where they have *much more* of the traditions, these things survive." The comparison, it struck me, cast the SRCC in a lesser light, as less authentically Amerindian.

At another event, Pearl Entou Springer, director of the National Heritage Library, asserted to a public gathering at the SRCC Centre that "there is the need to change the perception that the Caribs only exist to make cassava bread and coulev[r]es [cassava strainers]" (quoted in Almarales 1994:50).

These are three disparate instances involving different interests, different agendas, and different contexts of interaction, yet all possess one basic element in common: outsiders loudly voicing their expectations of what the Caribs ought to be, in line with some dominant convention for representing Carib identity. What they expect the Carib presence to be is often contrasted with the actual Caribs that are presented.

Carib self-representations are made visible and audible thanks to an organized body. To the extent that wider social institutions, agents, and social processes are enmeshed in the (re)production and valuation of the Caribs as an organized entity, one can speak in terms of the social organization of Carib tradition, to adapt the concept from Antoun (1989). The theoretical argument here is that "identity cannot be seen as divorced from the network of social relations" (Yelvington 1995b:22). The (re)production of indigeneity in Trinidad does not involve a group reviving or reinventing itself, by itself, for itself. Instead, mutuality and multilaterality are paramount, that is, as a vesting of interests and as a joint venture between various brokers and institutions. The multiplicity of cultural brokers and institutions connected to the SRCC bring their own interpretations of indigeneity to bear (see Jackson 1989:138).

Neither my argument nor the ethnography is about trying to prove that brokers are forced into constructing indigeneity to meet the demands of prospective patrons, even when they seem to be prisoners of the perception of others. To argue that would mean forgetting the myriad ways in which "Carib" has been conditioned and structured so that while both brokers and patrons operate within a common cultural field, different signifiers of indigeneity are at play attracting different interests and agendas. Both brokers and patrons operate within a particular field of preconfigured assumptions and multiple accepted truths—themes and notions familiar to most of the actors but in sufficient number to allow diversity and choice in representational angles. In part, this is what I have endeavored to detail in the previous chapters: there are conventions for representing the Caribs, but these have been refracted through the prisms of divergent interests and institutions over time, resulting therefore in an array of standard and routine representations that are not always consistent with one another.

In this chapter the political economy of tradition is not as bluntly cast as before. Perhaps in more abstract and symbolic terms, the commodity circulated within a national political economy of tradition is that of national history itself, where those of Amerindian descent are virtually inscribed as National Caribs, primordial contributors to the national foundation. In this sense, custom and ritual are more salient than commerce and politics. The emphasis on the political economy of tradition in the contemporary period is based on a view of traditions (especially those that are performed for a public audience) not as passive, routine reenactments but as deliberate, creative displays that can be reinterpreted for an audience, with hoped-for benefits in material, symbolic, and affective terms.

Refracted Representations, Contrasting Conventions

The Network and Its Burdens

Let me sketch the overall network of interests involved with the SRCC. First of all, the network consists of the group in question (the SRCC), offshoot organizations of the SRCC (two *parang* music groups, Los Niños del Mundo[3] and Los Niños de Santa Rosa; and two revivalist groups, Kairi Tukuienyo Karinya and Katayrana), allied organizations, local and national government and various ministries (the Arima Borough Council, the Ministry of Culture and Gender Affairs, the Ministry of Community Development, and so on), political parties, small business interests (a development bank, a supermarket chain owner, a photo studio owner, and the like), the church, and the media. Together, these patrons, brokers, and the relations among them form the network. This is also the primary reason that my field research took me to various circles surrounding the SRCC, with informants in and among these various quarters. To the extent that the network as a whole is involved in the overall reproduction, perpetuation, and representation of indigeneity in Trinidad, one could argue that the network itself is the medium for the reproduction of indigeneity as a social phenomenon in Trinidad.

Brokers involved with the Carib Community (and this includes myself) work to point to the presence of the Caribs in Trinidad and, in differing ways, seek to add value to the fact of their presence (that is, investing intellectual, symbolic, political, and even financial resources). The representational work of brokers is not restricted to definitional and propositional aims alone but also extends to debates over how to organize the Caribs.

The diverse brokers themselves often disagree over the substance and purpose of representations of the Caribs. The representations they produce or endorse are multiple and often contradictory. Some might argue that the more authentic representations are those that are spoken by the native voice. The problem that this poses lies in the fact that there is no single native voice. As may be the case in a kitchen crowded with individuals working on the same dish, there will be as many opinions as there are chefs, and not a few contending recipes.

The reality is that the Caribs have come to mean many different things to different brokers, both those who are formal members of the SRCC and those associated with select members. The SRCC has, in conjunction with diverse and divergent interests, developed multiple orientations, speaking with different voices and emphasizing different and even divergent organizational forms in particular contexts (that is, as a lineage, a religious group, an ethnic group, a business, an arm of the People's National Movement). In many ways, then, the SRCC is still in search of a stable, all-purpose mode of self-definition.[4]

Developing Locality: The Arima Borough Council

Several local politicians in Arima emphasize the Carib presence as a defining part of the Gens d'Arime (or "Arima folk") and of Arima's "unique Spanish heritage." Melan Garcia, the PNM's Arima borough councillor for Calvary Hill from 1987 until 1999, had a significant presence as an ally of SRCC brokers such as Cristo Adonis. Following in the tradition of some previous Arima politicians with interests in Arima's Carib heritage, Melan compiled a series of recorded oral history interviews with now-deceased elders of the Carib Community. Melan has also taken a leading role in the borough council in transforming Calvary Hill View Park into a potential tourist attraction designed according to Amerindian themes. He received the backing of the council and of the mayor, Elvin Edwards, who indicated that over $100,000 TT had been invested in the project, which began in August 1997 (McLeod 1998b). The park occupies a somewhat strategic location, not just for overlooking Arima but as the base of the cannon used to signal the start of the month of Santa Rosa on August 1 each year, a cannon that Mayor F. E. M. Hosein had succeeded in having returned to Arima by Governor Sir Claude Hollis as a donation, reportedly, to the Carib Community (Garcia 1991:9). With the aid of his friends in the regiment (he once served in the military), Melan secured a regular presence of the regiment to "blast" the nonfunctional cannon on the first of August and three times during the Festival Day. Melan once explained to me that the cannon "belonged to the Carib Community"; however, he added, "you know how politics is," saying that as the councillor for the area he had the cannon moved, so "I took it upon myself to act in the [Carib] Community's interest." Indeed, he argued that he was responsible for "reviving the tradition of the blasting of the cannon for Santa Rosa." On every August 1, it is Melan who acts as the master of ceremonies for the event, and not Ricardo.

An officer of the Second Battalion, whom I interviewed, explained that because many of the officers had families in Arima and were friends with members of the Arima Borough Council (ABC), the officers sought to do some "community work" in Arima. The regiment was motivated to aid the SRCC since the officers were told that "the Carib Community was dying, . . . Arima was losing its history, . . . the Carib Community lacked land, a communal spirit, few youths were getting involved, and there was little historical awareness" of the Caribs. The regiment can act autonomously in these matters, not relying on directives from Cabinet, and can also access its own resources, putting it in the position of patron.

Mayor Edwards indicated in an interview with me that "the Council feels very much for the Carib Community." He stated that this was due to many if not most Arimians having "some measure of Carib in them," adding, "I am sure that I have a bit of Carib in myself." In fact Mayor Edwards spoke in a manner echoing Ricardo's statements of his ties to the Carib Community as going back to his childhood and his memories of the Santa Rosa Festival: "I grew up very close to the Carib Queen, in fact in the very same block. I remember from my early childhood, from the age of four or five, I remember the Festival of the Caribs, . . . the Carib King, . . . the actual view of that procession through the streets." From his point of view, the Santa Rosa Festival serves to bridge the borough council and the SRCC: his perception is that during the annual ArimaFest celebrations in August, of which the "Carib Santa Rosa Festival" is a part, "you will find there is much togetherness between the [Arima Borough] Council and the [Carib] Community." There is also a political return on this investment: on one occasion, during a electoral campaign the mayor publicly boasted on television that Ricardo was running as a PNM candidate in Arima.

Edwards stressed his intentions regarding the Caribs: "I want to . . . make sure that Arima is always looked upon as the main site where the Caribs descended and that there is still that Carib presence here in Arima." Noting that during his tenure as mayor the annual council grant to the SRCC had increased from $500 TT to $5,000 TT, Edwards said, "the council has looked at that Carib situation very closely. We have committed ourselves, annually, to a grant . . . to develop their festival . . . which is of great benefit to the people of Arima."

The ABC, under various mayors over the years, has also formally awarded and recognized members of the SRCC for their community development work; these honorees include Elma Reyes; Norma Stephens (daughter of the late Queen Edith Martínez), who in 1988 received a certificate of recognition from the ABC for community service; and SRCC elder Julie Calderon, honored with a plaque from ABC on August 5, 1994, for her "dedication to the preservation of our Indigenous cultural traditions."

The ABC has also been active in the articulation of ways of defining the identity and heritage of Arima. As Mayor Edwards stated in a public address on December 4, 1998, the ABC is "not just about digging ditches and repairing drains . . . it is also about contributing to the cultural life of the Borough" (see also Price 1987:19). Primary-school students are instructed in the history of Arima and are asked more than a dozen questions related to the contemporary SRCC and Arima's Amerindian history in the annual "Know Arima" quiz sponsored and managed by the ABC. In order to answer these questions, students consult the Arima Public Library and visit the SRCC in organized groups, thus moving within a formal network of brokers and institutions engaged in disseminating and defining the Carib presence in Arima. In addition to this, the ABC also produces an annual Cultural Heritage Day, which begins by featuring the "Amerindian element" of Arima and "its" Caribs.

Developing Nationalism: Carib Presence and National Political Economy

Caribs have achieved sponsorship within what we might call the national system
of rewards for groups that embody some main facet of the nationalist ethos. We
have already encountered the way that the Trinidadian firm that produces Carib
Beer utilizes pride in Carib identification in some of its advertising. In 2000, the
company went a step further and actually sponsored the Santa Rosa Carib Community, in return succeeding in its demand that the SRCC Centre be repainted in
the gold and blue colors of the Carib Beer label. While not making note of this
fact in its own official publications, the brewery posted the following explanation
of its sponsorship in its newsletter:

As Carib Beer celebrates its 50th anniversary, Carib Brewery continues to
demonstrate its commitment to corporate sponsorship and its tradition of
giving to the community. When the International Indigenous Gathering of
the Carib Community opened in August . . . the delegates were hosted in a
new Visitors Resource Centre courtesy Carib Brewery. . . . The Centre will
host visitors, students and any other groups or persons interested in learning about the Indigenous Peoples of Trinidad and the Caribbean. (Carib
Brewery 2000)

The Carib presence in the national political system is exercised by very direct
and personal means. After all, Ricardo is himself tied to the state as an elected
civil servant in the Arima Borough Council. He has held the post of chair of the
Culture Committee, so that in addition to organizing and preparing the Carib
part of the Santa Rosa Festival, he has to organize the public ceremonies held in
Arima for Muslim holidays such as Eid, Hindu holidays such as Divali, Christian
holidays, and civic parades of various sorts. Ricardo became deputy mayor in
2003.

The state is the source of the greatest degree of rewards and the most important forms of recognition, especially as seen from the viewpoint of SRCC leaders.
Brokers internal to and affiliated with the SRCC have indeed achieved a fair
amount of success in obtaining official recognition and financial support from
the state and from all the political parties that have held government. As Ricardo
explained to me, "all the parties, when in power, have done something good for
the Carib Community." Two of the most striking of these forms of state recognition and support came in 1990 and 2000, with a formal Cabinet decision to
recognize the SRCC in the former year and with Prime Minister Panday's decision to establish an annual "Day of Recognition" for Trinidad's Amerindians in
the latter year. In both cases, the language of multiculturalism is present, along
with formalized recognition of the representative role of the SRCC.

With respect to the annual day of recognition,[5] long a major goal of the SRCC,
Senator Daphne Phillips, then the United National Congress's Minister for Cul-

ture and Gender Affairs, rose in the senate and made the statement of which parts
are reproduced below. I reproduce large segments of her speech since it is another
epitomizing statement that contains many of the nationalist ingredients in dominant contemporary valuations of the Carib presence. In addition, it is also one
way for the reader to hear the voice of one of the key patrons of the Caribs.

> This day of recognition, which is to be commemorated on October 14
> annually, is based on the acknowledgement of the contribution and signifi-
> cance of the Carib Community and to the uniqueness of our culture and
> national life in Trinidad and Tobago. The Santa Rosa community in its
> efforts to lift national awareness of the culture and history of the indig-
> enous people of Trinidad and Tobago had requested that a day of recogni-
> tion to be known as the Amerindian Heritage Day be designated to all our
> people of Amerindian origin who have, of course, contributed to the over-
> all development of Trinidad and Tobago. The Government of Trinidad and
> Tobago is of the view that installing an Amerindian Heritage Day into the
> national calendar would serve to highlight, educate and instill a sense of
> pride and recognition of the history, presence and cultural contribution of
> the first peoples of Trinidad and Tobago. (Hansard 2000:337–338)

Dr. Phillips explained that the significance of October 14 arises from its being the
date in 1637 when Chief Hyarima led a thousand warriors in the successful
destruction of the seat of Spanish power in Trinidad, the capital of the colony at
that time having been St. Joseph. As she added: "Hyarima is considered to be one
of the earliest national heroes of Trinidad who devoted his entire life to the
protection of his homeland from Spanish invaders" (Hansard 2000:338). What
I also found striking was the way that both race and presence were worked into
the address, qualifying the Carib presence yet reaffirming it as well. In this regard, the senator quoted Ricardo Bharath directly: "Although we have no more
pure Amerindians in Trinidad or Tobago, we do have descendants of the original
inhabitants, who can be found all over this country. Arima is, however, the only
place where we can still find an organized community, called the Santa Rosa
Carib Community" (Hansard 2000:338–339).

The prime minister made several striking statements according the Carib presence an importance that had previously not been so sharply underlined. In a
speech of June 29, 2000, Prime Minister Panday opened the "Third International
Gathering of Indigenous Peoples" at the SRCC Centre in Arima by saying, "we
stand on land that was the land of the ancestors of our hosts, the members of the
Santa Rosa Carib Community. This land was their land. Then came the colonizers from Europe. The indigenous peoples of the Americas were the first victims of
Europe's colonizers. The first nations were the first to be colonized in the Americas." Moreover, he stated, "We must recognize that this place was their space
long before the other people who came before Columbus, as well as those who

came after, those who came from India, from Africa, and from Europe included."
Panday went on to say, "it was inevitable that in these times of rising consciousness, the Caribs of the Caribbean would call for recognition and respect," adding, "it is our obligation to work to ensure that our aspiration, our commitment,
our belief that every creed and race should find an equal place should embrace
those whose ancestors came before Columbus, as well as those who have come
since." The prime minister concluded by saying: "it will be fitting that Trinidad
and Tobago concedes to its Carib citizens the position that should never be denied them, that they are our nation's first people" (Panday 2000).

The Cabinet decision of 1990 and the full text of Panday's speech in 2000
condense and epitomize the outcomes of brokered promotion and careful representation of the SRCC and indigenous identity and traditions, reflecting not only
the ideational foundations of Carib indigeneity laid during the colonial period,
but also nationalist, multiculturalist, and more contemporary discourses on identity and indigeneity.

More recently, with the grant of state lands to the SRCC (Forte 2002a) and
$19,000 TT to develop its new Resource Centre (Forte 2002b), state officials
have spoken in terms of "paying compensation" to the Caribs, phrasing that is
striking for the fact that the governments of independent Trinidad were not the
ones to have despoiled and alienated Carib lands. Almost each time that the state
grants the SRCC any kind of substantial support, there are also public ceremonies held to highlight the fact (for example, see Forte 2002b), where government
ministers not only have the chance to reaffirm the ethos of the development of
national pride and preservation of local culture, but can also speak as representatives of a particular political party, thus proving that they have, as Ricardo put
it, "the interests of the indigenous peoples at heart."

One of the outcomes of these various phases of support and recognition has
been the transformation of the SRCC into a public asset, both nationalized and
memorialized, one increasingly dependent on state support and yet with a de-
creasing capacity to build on internal sources of material self-generation.
Almarales noted that "as most of the members of the Community are either
pensioners, unemployed or recipients of low wages, financial contributions are
not collected at the meetings" (1994:12). Financial support from the state and its
various arms at the local and national level have also served to increase the value
of the SRCC: "for years the SRCC has had the unenviable lot of belonging to the
lowest rung of the social ladder and to the lowest income bracket" (Almarales
1994:55). Indeed, in comparison with state funding for other groups and festivals
in Trinidad, the SRCC's $30,000 annual subvention is substantial. Like the Santa
Rosa Festival, the Hosay festival also received $30,000 (Baptiste 1999)—except
that Hosay occurs over several days, in a busy and popular district in Port of
Spain, involving dozens of bands each constructing a series of mosque replicas,
involving the work of dozens of families and thousands of spectators. In other

words, the same amount of funding is provided for a festival that is, on all fronts, several times larger and more centrally located and thus more publicly visible than the Santa Rosa Festival.

It is also true that this degree of incorporation and reliance on state funding carries a burden as well, especially in recent times where the state has domesticated the policies of the International Monetary Fund and World Bank and sought to apply corporate managerial models to the making of social and cultural policy. The SRCC has come under the weight of what some call the new "audit culture" and the "political technology of neoliberalism" (see Shore and Wright 1999:558–561, 564), with maximum emphasis on state surveillance, accountability, budgeting, efficacy, and profitability. Indeed, from my own reading of correspondence between the Ministry of Culture and the SRCC, I noted the ministry's emphasis that the SRCC should lessen its "dependency" by seeking alternative sources of funding and by developing commercial ventures (see Bharath and Khan 1998, 1997a, 1997b; Gomez 1998; Rose Foundation 1997; SRCC 1998a, 1997). Having led the SRCC toward formal incorporation as a company, the state decisively proceeded to act once more to shape and recast the role and character of the SRCC, pushing the organization more into profit-gaining activities and heightening its degree of formalization and internal bureaucratization by requiring annual reports and audited statements.

This outcome of state support, resulting in incorporation into the state's system for regulating and monitoring registered entities, has placed constraints on the SRCC and certainly led it into directions it did not originally anticipate. Ricardo stressed to me once that little of what I saw of the current SRCC was the product of his original intentions. It was not until he sought a formal hold on property that the SRCC was to be organized as a company. While the corporate formalization may not have been part of his original design, and the current SRCC does not function as a regular commercial concern, many of the rules, regulations, and organizational format of a corporation have nonetheless been maintained voluntarily, even after the SRCC's status as a registered company lapsed in 1995. Formal incorporation was not, in the end, necessary to gain the church lands that Ricardo already occupied.[6] What the act of incorporation did supply was an organizational framework that some SRCC brokers favored. The title of president itself emerged from this process.

Ricardo's attachment to modern and corporate forms of organization continues into the present, as evidenced by the care he takes at the opening of a meeting in announcing "this is a general meeting" or "this is a special meeting," a distinction that may be lost on most members but nonetheless utilizing the terms extracted from the Companies Ordinance under which the SRCC was incorporated and which sets out the procedures and structures for company meetings. Ricardo's preference has been for establishing a professional management team to represent the SRCC. Thus while many of the state's requirements have been imposed, not for that reason were they entirely rejected, and in Ricardo's case

these external regulations could be internalized and adapted in ways that ratio-
nalized and legitimated his ascendancy in what, from the vantage point of the
previously existing Carib Community (pre-1973), would be considered a nontra-
ditional office. That his office should then be translated as one of chieftaincy, in
a postmission community whose sole figurehead of authority had previously
been the Queen, simply testifies to the successful adaptation of a state imposition
for internal purposes. Indeed, while agents of the state are very keen to underscore their commitment to facilitating the preservation of Carib traditions, their
own impositions have in fact served to marginalize and undermine one of the
most basic traditions of this Carib Community, the office of the Queen of the
Caribs.

Developing Awareness: The Carib Presence in the Media and Schools

The diffusion of what Goffman would call "the sign equipment" of Carib indigeneity, propagated via the media and schools, involves particular agents disseminating images, ideas, and information about the Caribs. Indeed, they do
not just inculcate an awareness of the Caribs; rather, they also work to construct
and reproduce the Caribs' presence. Within the educational sector, the work of
certain researchers has been almost critical to building the public prominence of
the Carib Community. For several academics, from Trinidad and abroad, the
SRCC represents the beleaguered survival of Trinidad's Amerindian heritage.
Peter Harris, a British archaeologist with extensive experience in Trinidad, and
who worked in the Department of History at the University of the West Indies,
played a fundamental role in obtaining official state recognition of the SRCC and
annual funding from the Ministry of Culture to aid in the maintenance of the
Santa Rosa Festival. Harris also authored a series of ethnohistoric monographs
on the Amerindian history of both precolonial and colonial Trinidad, along with
some hypotheses on the likely lifeways of Trinidad's Amerindians derived from
modern-day ethnographies of Amerindians in the Orinoco delta and the Guyanas
(see Harris 1989a, 1989b). These have become a firm part of the SRCC's knowledge base, meaning that SRCC documents continue to reproduce passages or
even entire pieces of Harris' work. Along with Elma Reyes, he helped to broadcast and promote the SRCC farther afield, at an international conference organized by the Organization of American States (Harris and Reyes 1990). Harris
also authored a few short pieces published in local newspapers, aimed at encouraging wider interest in the preservation of Carib traditions and recognition of
Trinidad's Amerindian heritage (for example, Harris 1990a).

Schools and youth groups have a continuing and strong interest in the Carib
Community as well. For the leaders of Girl Guide troops, the Caribs are a source
of valuable weaving and cooking knowledge. Performing arts classes from the
university are interested in the aesthetic styles of the Amerindians, their dress and
music. Practices marked as cornerstone traditions of the Caribs are being diffused

to others in the wider society and thus made a part of their own education, socialization, and cultural repertoire. In this manner those who are young, and presumably impressionable, no longer simply observe but directly participate. The SRCC has thus had limited success in reproducing Carib culture in the wider society, by getting some non-Caribs to "do Carib things."

The news media have played a central role in disseminating images and ideas concerning the Carib presence to the wider society, at least for the past four decades, and with especial intensity in the past fifteen years as the SRCC's cultural revival efforts reached a zenith. Rather than conduct a wide-ranging survey of media coverage of the Caribs, a project I would like to leave for another time, I will instead focus on the role of select brokers in line with the aims of this chapter. I have introduced one such broker, the late Elma Reyes, a journalist, who in fact became an active representative of the SRCC for at least two decades.[7] Almarales, another of the SRCC's own researchers, summed up Elma's contribution thusly: "[She] devotes a lot of her time to helping the SRCC discover and preserve their culture and oral traditions and to carve a niche among the [indigenous peoples] of the world" (1994:30).

Elma entered journalism in the 1960s. In that decade she lived twice in the United States, for two-year periods, living in the Bronx and Brooklyn, New York, where she wrote for the *New York Courier*. Back in Trinidad, Elma became, as she explained, a tabloid writer covering local beauty pageants. She was also an avid aficionado of *parang* music. From the late 1970s until the mid 1990s, Ricardo and Elma worked in close partnership, in a way that blurs distinctions between insiders and outsiders. The two first met when Ricardo approached various newspapers to post an advertisement, and she became interested in the SRCC then, added to the interest she had in Arima given her family connections, as she explained to me. As a researcher for the SRCC, Elma was criticized on occasion, either directly or in veiled comments, for being an "outsider" speaking for the Caribs—these episodes occurred before my time in Trinidad, and the details are rather unclear, apart from these general outlines. Both Ricardo and Elma recounted these criticisms. The closest I got to this debate was in a 1995 oped article by Elma in the *Trinidad Guardian*, where she wrote:

> I want to publicly inform that I have never promoted myself as a member of the Santa Rosa Caribs although I do have some Amerindian branches on my family tree. I became involved with their representative body AT THEIR REQUEST [capitalized in the original] due to the fact that I am related directly or indirectly to several of the families of the community, and was at that time a member of the working press. My role has been that of research and public relations representative, and it is an insult to the intelligence and retained knowledge of the Santa Rosa Caribs and other indigenous people of the region for anyone to insinuate that the information I have been able to share did not emerge from them. (Reyes 1995)[8]

A great deal of the framing and reinterpretation of the SRCC in terms of the Amerindian contribution to the national foundation, Amerindians as the bedrock of the national heritage, and Amerindians as possessing valuable ecological wisdom and special knowledge of alternative lifeways owes its origins to the promotional media work done by Elma. She zealously promoted Trinidad's Amerindians as the cultural cradle of an authentic, local, Trinidadian nationhood: "The only 'roots' of this nation are those planted by the first nations, for all other aspects of our culture and survival systems are transplants, branches which were successfully 'budded' to the main tree which existed long before their arrival. The denial of indigenous systems and the contribution of the 'first nations' in present day Trinidad and Tobago can only be described as base ingratitude" (Reyes 1998).

Elma also founded the Carib Fiesta Queen pageant, which was held on some occasions in the early 1980s and which produced the SRCC's long standing youth representative, Susan Campo. According to Elma, she realized that "we had to glamorize Carib culture in order to attract youths to the Carib Community," hence the adoption of the pageant. The Fiesta Queen, as in the case of Susan Campo, the SRCC youth representative and former Fiesta Queen, won a prize that consisted of two airline tickets to Miami, sponsored by British West Indian Airways (BWIA), Trinidad's international airline, so that she could meet with youth groups in Miami and visit a Seminole Indian reservation near Miami.

Elma frequently argued that the Caribs were discriminated against, scorned, and ridiculed because of the alleged cannibalism of their ancestors; furthermore, she argued that because they were at the bottom of the economic ladder and had no financial clout, they could be ignored safely by the powers that be. Given this perspective, Elma inevitably compared the SRCC to other ethnic groups in Trinidad, especially in terms of the SRCC's lacking state funding and support. As a result of highlighting this state of comparative disadvantage, Elma militated to remedy this situation on a number of fronts. She was instrumental in establishing various connections and designing a variety of key projects for the SRCC. One of the first strategies envisioned by Elma was to co-opt the services of the University of the West Indies and the Ministry of Culture and Community Development (Almarales 1994:15) for the purposes of, in the first case, research support for the SRCC, and in the second case, funding for the maintenance of Carib traditions as well as aiding its institutional development. As Almarales observed, she was successful in obtaining the support of the Ministry of Culture and Women's Affairs, which "has turned the spotlight not only on the local Carib Community but also on those of the other areas of the Caribbean by hosting two gatherings of [indigenous peoples]" (1994:30). Elma secured the interest and support of the Unit Trust Corporation and the Organization of American States for sponsoring a 1993 indigenous gathering in Arima. She worked with Ricardo on the proposed Amerindian model village with the objective of making it a viable economic activity.

We see through Elma a medley of internationalized discourses in the naming of the SRCC as "First Nations," the alignment of the organization with international institutions, which also serves to render it more legitimate and respectable as a means of making up for its lack of financial clout, and the association of the indigene with the environment. In telling language, Elma drew on the international validation of the SRCC in the following manner: "For the benefit of the general public, and media persons who regard the community as objects for the butt of their bigoted remarks, the Santa Rosa Caribs are part of the Caribbean Organisation of Indigenous People (COIP) which has membership in Dominica, St Vincent, Guyana, Belize, and is in constant contact with representative organizations of the First Nations of the Western Hemisphere, and the World Council of Indigenous People" (Reyes 1995). She was possibly one of the first brokers to seriously inject these internationalized discourses into the reinterpreted self-definition of the SRCC, a fact that has helped to attract further interest from like-minded brokers in subsequent years. Elma helped to foster the association between the Caribs and the internationalized discourse of environmental preservation. As she explained to newspaper readers, Amerindians "had formulated systems which allowed their usage of the assets nature provided without bringing about their destruction, and this is now acknowledged by every one of the major [environmentalist] organizations of what we are told is the 'First World'" (Reyes 1998). Moreover, she argued that while "within recent years there has been a growing number of bodies which all claim concern for the problems caused by misuse and abuse of the land and waters of Trinidad and Tobago," she lamented that "not one of them has ever publicly acknowledged the wisdom of the people met by the colonists" (Reyes 1998).

Elma was also responsible for putting the SRCC in contact with the now largely defunct World Council of Indigenous Peoples (WCIP), as well as establishing contact with, and eventual membership in, the Caribbean Organisation of Indigenous Peoples (COIP), established in 1988. Elma was instrumental in contacting the Saskatchewan Indian Federated College on the campus of the University of Regina, Canada, and getting a scholarship awarded to Susan Campo for the 1992–1993 academic year so that Susan could study administration and management of Amerindian communities (Almarales 1994:29).

One of Elma's latest efforts, starting in 1998, was to militate on behalf of the SRCC in urging Prime Minister Basdeo Panday to visit the SRCC in an official capacity and to grant an Amerindian Heritage Week, or Day at least—as she explained, again speaking in interethnic comparative terms, "everybody has one." As Elma further propounded on this issue: "Each time a new holiday is proclaimed, some national or visitor asks the representative body of the Santa Rosa Carib Community about the possibility of their having a public holiday proclaimed as well. The answer is always no. What the organization wants, and has been requesting of every government in power during the 20-plus years I have been associated with them is: Official proclamation of Amerindian Heritage Week" (Reyes 1998).

Elma Reyes' view of the Carib presence, in broad terms, was contrary to the notion that Caribs had ever become extinct. Instead, as she often argued, the Carib had been amalgamated into the foundational basis of the Trinidadian national heritage. Moreover, almost all Trinidadians could claim to be Carib—she summed up her views thus: "The original inhabitants did not disappear without a trace, nor were they 'wiped out' by the superior fighting skills of Spanish colonists. What really happened is that succeeding groups of arrived people interbred with them so that if all persons with Amerindian ancestry within our nation were to raise a hand to be counted, the number would not only be formidable, but would be inclusive of people who 'look' white, African, Chinese, East Indian, and 'ethnically mixed'" (Reyes 1995). Carib identity, for Reyes, consisted of some ancestral linkage to the precolonial population, added to knowledge of sustainable and ecologically sound lifeways. She was an avid proponent of the use of the label "Carib" as a valid generic term, as well as the adoption of the designation "First Nations."

While Elma Reyes was active in constructing what she deemed the proper representation of the Carib presence via the media, Carib brokers such as Ricardo "Kapaupana" Cruz[9] have in turn been constructed by the media as emblematic of that presence, thus constituting a self-reinforcing bidirectional process. Cruz is frequently seized upon by the media as an authentic, genuine, and pure Amerindian. What observers see in his straight hair, aquiline nose, and light brown complexion and hear in his manner of speaking with a soft voice in the somewhat staccato manner often associated with American Indian speakers of English—added to his fluent discussions of issues of Amerindian cosmology and culture history—serve to maximize this perception, possibly like no other member of the SRCC. When Cruz appeared on CCN/TV6's *Morning Edition* on November 5, 1999, the host, Paolo Kernahan, said to him, "I may be a little town-centric,[10] but I have to say you are the first genuine Amerindian person I have seen in Trinidad." In a newspaper interview, held at the Cleaver Woods Amerindian museum outside Arima, journalist Laura Ann Phillips reported the following: "A small group of students had just begun a tour there, and the forest officer who was conducting the tour spotted us. 'Ricardo! Ricardo!' he called. Gesturing to Cruz, the officer said to the students, 'This is one of them.' They peered at Cruz in the dim light. 'This is what they used to look like. See the kind of hair?' He raised Cruz's cap. 'So, you have a real, live Amerindian in front of you,' the officer declared. Cruz quietly excused himself" (Phillips 2000). Phillips describes Cruz as "an Amerindian shaman: a healer and holy man—a role found in most first nation tribes," thus repeating some of the contemporary stock characterizations of native indigeneity in Trinidad: shaman, healer, First Nations.

Cruz is one of the few members of the SRCC who will formally describe

164 / Ruins of Absence, Presence of Caribs

himself as an Amerindian, to the exclusion of any other ethnic designation. He is particularly sensitive to the issue of correct labels:

> The terms indigenous peoples and first nations, Cruz said, were preferable to "Amerindian" or "Carib" as names by which to describe his people. "[The names don't] define what tribe you're from or where you're from, but they reflect more respect for indigenous peoples, for first peoples," said Cruz. The term "Carib" is a derogatory term, he said, introduced by the Spanish conquerors. "Carib means 'cannibal,'" he explained. "That term was used to refer to people who fought back. That is the name which kind of stuck. . . . Our goal is to eventually phase that out." (quoted in Phillips 2000)

Once more we see Carib brokers actively referring to the textual distillates of colonial history in defining themselves. However, some elements of the self-definition owe their origins to more recent developments on the world stage, such as the growth of environmental movements and the tribute that is often paid to indigenous peoples as guardians of nature.

From the perspective of reengineered indigeneity, it is also important to note that brokers such as Cruz are very conscious of their media image, aware from experience of what journalists want to hear and see, and often actively play to the gallery in producing precisely the signs of an iconic indigenous authenticity that journalists are often keen to consume and reproduce. The problem with this tendency has been a growing standardization or even essentialization of what is to be considered truly Amerindian by the media, a fact not lost on brokers such as Ricardo, who has tried to resist these pressures.

Developing Commerce: Marketing the Carib

The commercial exploitation of the figure of the Carib, or the SRCC itself, is still in its infancy, though one can already perceive certain emergent tendencies. Local business interests maintain an eye on the potential tourist angle of Carib activities, in part given Arima's strategic location on a tourism route leading to the Asa Wright Nature Centre, an eco-resort that has won international awards—and, as we might expect, certain interests immediately perceive indigenous people as going hand-in-hand with flora and fauna, a representation that some have termed "the ecologically noble savage" (see Buege 1996). Local ecotourist entrepreneurs see some members of the SRCC as being valuable tourist guides for foreign visitors interested in bush walks and bird-watching. History texts containing Amerindian legends are sifted through for possible use in narrating certain elements of the landscape or wildlife for clients on a hike. Courtenay Rooks, the director of Rooks Nature Tours and co-owner of Paria Springs Eco-Community, Ltd., works closely with Cristo Adonis. Through Rooks, Cristo has attended a series of conferences and seminars oriented toward the budding ecotourist industry in Trinidad. This has opened up a new field of contacts and opportunities for Cristo, also aiding him in his attempts to link the SRCC with environmental entrepreneurs and activists. Cristo now owns his own ecotours company.

John Stollmeyer, somewhat of a renegade member of one of Trinidad's elite families, has cultivated a close relationship with all the main brokers internal to the SRCC. He specializes in the design and sale of artwork and jewelry inspired by indigenous motifs and utilizing native materials such as the calabash, coconut, and various seeds, crystals, and feathers (see Alfonzo-Sierra 2002). Moreover, Stollmeyer—via his business, John-John Enterprises, and his foundation, *Turtle Island Children* (Stollmeyer 1998b)—has a formal platform for regularly promoting the environmental and communal ethos of the Carib presence as he reinterprets it for the national audience. In the official brochure of *Turtle Island Children*, founded in December 1998, Stollmeyer aims to promote a "bioregional vision" combining an emphasis on renovating community fused with ecological sustainability, a vision that frames his approach to valuing and promoting the SRCC. He explains that bioregionalism "recognizes, nurtures, sustains and celebrates our local connections with: Land, Plants and Animals, Air, Springs, Rivers, . . . Families, Friends and Neighbors, Community, *Native Traditions, Indigenous Systems of Production and Trade*" (emphasis added). Stollmeyer hails indigenous knowledge and traditional lifeways as the only alternatives to "a crashing Western civilization." He tithes sales of his products to the SRCC so as to "further the process of educating the public to the important contributions made by indigenous peoples to our present knowledge and the necessary wisdom and understanding they offer to our future peace and well-being." His work, he says, "completely satisfies the environmentally conscious *new age* consumer interested in intentional ceremonial accessories" (emphasis added).

Local ethnobotanists have also literally set up shop, in part, on the basis of medicinal knowledge of herbal remedies derived from some of the elderly members of the SRCC (see Rickwood 2000). Francis Morean is the director of Herbal, Educational, Recreational, Biological Services (HERBS) and works closely with a number of SRCC members, especially Cruz, and a few of the elders, including Benedicta Perreira and Ian Capriata. Morean owns a large store in the center of Arima specializing in herbal remedies, or "bush medicine" as it is referred to in Trinidad. He has a manuscript ready for publication that begins with a section on the Amerindian heritage and its contribution to traditional herbal medical practice in Trinidad. A magazine feature on Morean was appropriately headlined: "Herbalist Francis Morean goes back to Trinidad's Spanish and Carib past to retrieve the remedies of old" (Rickwood 2000)—once more stressing, in folkloric and bucolic terms, the Trinidadian association between Spanish and Carib.

Ricardo Bharath has also developed what appears to be, at least on occasion, a thriving trade in marketing the products of his weaving skills to local boutiques, tourist resorts, diplomatic missions, and private homes. His skills in producing cassava bread and in catering also afford outlets for culinary items that are marketed, and sought, as representative of indigenous cuisine. Cristo innovated a unique style of platting coconut palms into the shape of human figures, a product that is increasingly sought for adorning public functions or even music pubs in Arima. Moreover, Cristo has also developed a reputation as an accomplished builder of *ajoupa*s, which in lean times has furnished him with lucrative contracts. This knowledge has been refined and enhanced through cultural exchange visits from Guyanese Amerindians. However, apart from relatively small-scale ventures in food, medicine, handicrafts, and ecotourism, capitalization of the cultural value of the Carib has not been rampant or entirely out of the hands of members of the SRCC. What these small industries perhaps have done, somewhat parallel to the work of the media, is to reduce the Carib presence, by subtle and unspoken means, down to a few emblematic products and practices.

Contesting Mores: Sacred Caribs, Profane Caribs

Stalwarts of the Roman Catholic Church in Arima attempt to maximize the historical devotion of the Caribs to the Catholic Church, as symbolized by the Santa Rosa Festival and Arima's mission history and may, at times, pay token respect to the revivalist side of the SRCC by insisting that the Santa Rosa Festival has "Amerindian elements" to it, with these usually left unspecified. In masses around the time of the Santa Rosa Festival, and of course the high mass for the festival itself, prelates are keen to underscore the Catholicity of Carib adhesion to church ceremonials and keen to downplay that which is in fact feared: that the Santa Rosa Festival is being appropriated by ethnic politicians such as Ricardo, state tourism authorities, and local business and political organizations that are equally keen to reframe the festival as a Carib tradition. (Recall the comments of B.B. at the outset of this chapter.)

At the 1998 Santa Rosa Festival, Bishop John Mendes condemned ethnic and religious divisions within the society as a whole, sidelining his own Portuguese ancestry and stating, "Some may say I am a '*Portugee*' . . . but I say, 'I is a *Trini*!'" Having denounced the dangers of particularistic affinities, he then turned to the Caribs, quite literally as they were off to his left in the front pews: "And here are these blessed Caribs, *dwindling* though they may be, still loyal to the Catholic Church after 500 years, the longest standing parishioners of Arima." In effect, the bishop was firing a warning shot: best that you adhere to *this* way of defining your presence in the festival, or else. Priests have often acted as if they carried the responsibility of screening and vetting SRCC representations of the Carib role in the Santa Rosa Festival, often endorsing a particular local researcher, Patricia Elie, dubbed the "parish historian," as the only reliable "authority on the Caribs" (sometimes even saying this in the presence of key SRCC spokespersons). Unlike Father Daudier and his "little Indians" in the 1870s, the current relationship between the church and the SRCC is often fraught with tension and mutual suspicion, especially over the reframing of the Santa Rosa Festival as, in some senses, a Carib festival; this perspective is gaining currency in the local media and with local politicians. At the same time, and given this interest and support by politicians and the media, the church has had to be very cautious in its attempts to circumscribe the ethnification and secularization of the festival.

Speaking in private, one former parish priest accused the SRCC of "making up traditions as they go along," alarming me to some degree when he scornfully referred to Ricardo as "a Hindu, who just wants to be mayor," adding that SRCC members are "not real Caribs, some of them don't even have a drop of Carib blood in them." Another priest who formerly served in the area said, "We had to be suspicious of these characters: they struck us as people out to get something." A third priest concurred:

> You won't see any of them in the church except maybe for baptisms and funerals, hardly even at Christmas or Easter. Then comes Santa Rosa, and lo and behold they file in, insisting on sitting in pews at the front that have to be specially reserved for them on this occasion. Only they can touch that statue of Saint Rose, they would cuss down anyone trying to touch it, and what's worse, they painted it all wrong: the colors of her habit were white and black, not pink and black! They themselves don't even know the tradition, and they want to call this the "Carib Santa Rosa Festival." Utter rubbish.

On the one hand, this latter speaker has evidence in his favor when he points to the rare appearances of SRCC members in the church. Here I would hazard to say that this may owe to their historical amalgamation with Venezuelan Panyols, who were very well known, both in Venezuela and in Trinidad, for their rejection of the often elitist and urban-based ecclesiastical hierarchy yet retention of spiritual loyalty to Catholic beliefs and practicing in a rural setting what some might call a folk Catholicism (Allard 2000:51; Moodie-Kublalsingh 1994:10). Similarly, one of the leading SRCC members made comments about their scarce attendance in church in terms almost identical to those of the priest above, referring to Caribs as Panyols on this occasion, saying: "Never would you see a damn Panyol in church." On the other hand, the Catholic Church in Trinidad has its own particularities that distinguish it from its counterparts in other countries. While Pope John Paul II has expressed sorrow for the church's role in the Spanish conquest of the Americas, and Catholic hierarchies in countries such as Canada and Australia have issued official apologies for their abuses of indigenous peoples, the Catholic Church in Trinidad has never come close to this position, instead reveling in the fact that Columbus "appropriately named this land after the Holy Trinity, bringing its native peoples into the light of Christ," words spoken by Bishop Mendes during the 1998 Santa Rosa Festival. Rather than formalized apologies, select priests have instead chosen to cultivate personal friendships with select SRCC members as an informal and less public means of building bridges.

The particularization of Santa Rosa as a Carib figure has alarmed certain clergymen. We have already seen one priest's reaction to the SRCC painting the habit of the statue of Saint Rose partly in pink, which Ricardo once explained is "a way for us to imprint our seal of ownership on that statue." On another occasion, a parish priest invited the SRCC to mount a display inside the church to highlight Carib traditions. They created a board that related that Saint Rose was born in Arima, which is factually wrong as she was born in Lima, Peru. The priest of the time said, "I told them to get that thing out of here!" At least one member of the SRCC still insists on this view of the life of Rose, continuing to relate this as a fact to visiting students and researchers. That official tourist brochures produced by the state tourism authority have repeatedly referred to the "Carib Santa Rosa Festival" and have explained it as a festival in which the Caribs honor an "Amerindian saint" and have indicated to interested visitors that they should telephone Ricardo Bharath rather than the church have only added fuel to the fire.

Apart from the mores of an established ecclesiastical body, disparate private individuals have warmed to the Caribs as soon as they have started seeing them in nostalgic and bucolic terms as symbolizing a diminished or lost rural past of affective communality, hospitality, and the simple, traditional life. As one Trinidadian explained it to me, "those rural people have values." Queen Justa Werges, who would never allow me to leave her home without first saying a prayer for me, making the sign of the cross on my forehead, and then proceeding to empty her entire pantry into bags to give me, would seem shocked at my attempt to be modest and refuse. An elderly gentleman who accompanied me to her home in rural Mundo Nuevo explained to me on the drive back to Arima: "Nah, you can't refuse. You see, these old time people have values. They know about treating guests from when they were small. She may even live in a dirt hut, but she will not for a moment lose that refinement that is their way, she will give you whatever she has, and you have to take it. End of story." Whether sacred or profane, the Carib presence is itself valued as embodying values of communality (whether secular or spiritual), and where the SRCC may lose ground in one domain, it gains in another.

Broker Overload

While SRCC leaders may quietly revel in the attention, the fact is that when a leader such as Ricardo attempts to maximize benefits and increase recognition and promotion of the Caribs by trying to cater to these various interests, he falls victim to what I call broker overload, that is, becoming unable to satisfy different, competing, and even contradictory interests, all to the same extent.[11] In addition there is overload in terms of the volume of visitors, many of whom ask him the same questions, over and over. Constraint and fatigue, these are prominent themes in the daily life of Ricardo: daily meetings, interviews, visiting school groups, orders of cassava or woven products to fill, and on the list goes. In the worst of times, I recall Ricardo saying, "I just cannot sleep. I get up at 2:00 a.m., and I start listing everything I need to do during the day, and then I can't fall asleep so I just start preparing. And no time for any nap during the day. Just rushing, rushing, until night." The development of the Resource Centre mentioned previously was in fact precisely one means of lessening the representational burden, and it was actively presented as satisfying the information needs of the many visitors who go to the SRCC Centre. Like the representations of actual actors, the Resource Centre has something for everyone: from a reconstructed *benab*, to samples of weaving, to boards on the history of the Amerindians of the Caribbean, to photo displays of the SRCC during the Santa Rosa Festival, to materials on the Queen, archaeological artifacts, many items presented as gifts from visiting indigenous delegations from abroad, letters of awards to the SRCC from the government, and so forth.

Cristo Adonis, though unfortunately unemployed for most of my first fieldwork period, was not much better off in terms of free time on any given day. Cristo has launched himself on a variety of platforms to promote the SRCC to a wider audience. He has been active in building *ajoupa*s for a range of parties. His brokerage network extends to music, as the lead vocalist of Los Niños del Mundo (and, later, Rebuscar), performing in the National Parang Festival as well as appearing on television and radio, and making himself available for newspaper articles stressing the Carib and shamanic qualities of his music (Burnett 1998a; Calliste 1998). In addition, Cristo has been actively engaged as a nature tour guide. He regularly receives groups of visiting schoolchildren, students from the University of the West Indies interested in what I call his Amerindian aesthetics and performances, and job applicants for the Tourism and Industrial Development Corporation (TIDCO), who are required to write essays on Trinidad's cultural heritage as part of their job applications. Last but not least, Cristo has been an energetic campaigner for the PNM in Arima, in alliance with his friend, the councillor for Calvary Hill, Melan Garcia. Moreover, he maintains an active presence on the local village council and the local PNM party cell.

Broker overload also comes in the form of representational strain caused by too many representations to cater to and too many brokers acting simultaneously to uphold these interests. Conflicts must, and do, result, especially when the external representatives of these various interests do not all interact with one another directly but instead compete with each other via proxies in the person of different SRCC brokers. There are differential rewards associated with each type of representation and the leading internal broker of that representation, a fact that can cause some friction between brokers. Thus far, those facets of SRCC representations that are most highly rewarded are those centering on the Santa Rosa Festival, *parang*, and weaving, whereas the more recent New Age aspects are the most lightly rewarded at the time of writing. By rewards I mean actual material rewards plus greater notoriety and enhanced prestige that leads to further networking.

Broker overload can arise when a given actor tries to personally convey diverse, sometimes divergent, representations of the Caribs. Archer (1988:xx) argued that situational logics are imposed when actors confront, realize, or are made to acknowledge that the propositions they endorse are "enmeshed in some inconsistency," thus actors can choose either to be dogmatic, or to reject the original belief altogether, or to simply seek to repair the inconsistency. In the case of the SRCC the practice seems to be that of wearing different hats in different settings. SRCC brokers are aware of the various apparent inconsistencies in their own representations but do not seem sure about how to go about repairing these inconsistencies, especially when a contradictory representation happens to be the favorite representation of one broker over that of another, or when one representation seems more suitable at one moment more than another. Some of the inconsistencies are maintained because there is a pragmatic logic that unifies them, a tactical approach that guides them to say one thing for one audience and another thing for a different audience, and this can apply, for example, to which ethnic label they choose in announcing themselves.

The main actors seem to be aware of the limits of credulity that constrain multiple self-representations, especially in one particular case of an SRCC broker who took things to an extreme, in the views of the other dominant SRCC brokers. This individual, whom I will call D.D., was chastised for "telling one journalist in the morning that he is a Carib, and then when another journalist came in the evening he said he was Taíno." Another of the Carib leaders, referring to D.D., stated at a meeting, "He himself doesn't know what he is. He says his mother is an Amerindian from a town in Venezuela—she was born here in Trinidad! She is no Amerindian either. He says his father was a Taíno, not that any of his brothers would ever back him up on that. His own mother once told me, 'Please tell D.D. to stop this; he is really embarrassing me with the things he's saying.'" While all of the brokers respond to various expectations and diverse representational interests, sometimes modifying their own self-presentation in the process, transparent and overly fluid forms of reengineering are actively resisted in most cases. Potential chaos has to be met with actual control through internal sanctions and perhaps with indirect reference to the representational stretches that the society will bear.

Pater, Patria, Patron

Patronage processes have been a relatively enduring part of local social organization and continue to shape relationships within the SRCC and between the SRCC and institutions and agents in the wider society. Etched into the oral history of the elders of the SRCC are anecdotes dealing with celebrated acts of laudable patronage. Queen Werges recalled how it came to be that the Caribs would receive a small annual stipend for the Santa Rosa Festival, a stipend that was given to the Queen. Governor Sir Claude Hollis, who held office in the 1930s and who had also donated a cannon to the Caribs for the celebration of the Santa Rosa Festival, was on close terms with her mother-in-law, the late Queen Maria Werges. On the day of the Grand Festival he would usually visit Maria Werges' home accompanied by his party. In order for the Queen to prepare a "proper" reception, "suited to his position" and that of his party, Governor Hollis would pay her $200 in advance. Following the procession of the statue of Saint Rose and the close of the high mass, the governor and his party would then join Maria Werges in her home and enjoy some refreshments, while the almost invisible members of the Carib Community would be received under a tent in her backyard. The Queen regularly undertook to host such dignitaries as the governor and then later the president of the republic or the prime minister.

Patronage shapes the vision some SRCC members have on the question of how the SRCC ought to be internally organized. A couple of members complained of the SRCC's lack of a material welfare dimension that would benefit its members. However, the notion of operating the SRCC as a cooperative—with communal sharing and reciprocity—is, ironically, not very popular. One informant who argued for a welfarist thrust for the SRCC scoffed at the idea of members getting together to work on joint business ventures that they would own, saying: "partnership is leaky ship." Thus, even some of the most persistent internal critics of the SRCC have often sought to reinforce a top-down structuring of patronage and dependency in the SRCC.

It seems to be true too that the position of patrons and brokers necessarily and logically presupposes the existence of those in a structurally lower position. I am referring here to the virtually invisible Caribs of this study: the elderly members of the SRCC who do much of the manual work, always quietly, never issuing opinions on how the group ought to be restructured, individuals who generally do not boast of their Caribness. They are invisible in the sense that at public functions they do not put themselves forward unless they are pushed forward, they do not speak out at private SRCC meetings, and they reside in the background, where one has to go seek them out. When filming and photographing preparations for the 1998 Santa Rosa Festival I missed documenting one or two of the preparations as a result of some of the members withdrawing from the limelight that individuals such as Ricardo and Cristo were expert at handling. They are also largely invisible in this study, given its deliberate focus on brokers. Even though I interviewed all members of the SRCC, the elderly ones were always the most reserved, almost shy, rarely wishing to offer a critical opinion for fear that it could be reported to others and cause trouble. When an argument breaks out during a lime gone wrong, or when someone simply says something he or she thinks is "a lot of mess," rather than argue, it is the tendency for some of them to quietly get up and filter out of the group with some quiet excuse. Even when speaking, as a companion noted, "their voices are as soft as mosquitoes.'"

Cristo, who grew up in a rural and remote setting in the Northern Range around the villages of Paria and Brasso Seco, explained that socialization was governed by what he called "blessings and beatings" designed to keep people in check and respectful of authority:

> You go on your way to school in the morning, and every little old lady you see on the way, whether she is related to you or not, holds up her hand and says "blessings on your child." Then at school maybe you got into a scrap with other boys and tear your pants. So you don't go back to class 'cause you know the priest will beat you. Walking back home on this mountain road, every single man you meet, whether he is related to you or not, says, "Oh ho, is so you does behave? You been fighting? You mess your uni form? And then you try to pass me straight?" and down come licks, licks like peas [so many]. Then you finally get home, and you get another set of licks from your Ma, and then your father when he reach back home. Blessings in the morning, beatings in the evening.

Queen Maria Werges, whose tenure lasted until the 1960s, was known for expecting absolute subordination from all members. At a meeting, I have been told by a few current members, an adult male questioned one of her instructions. Without speaking, she simply raised her stout body off the chair, made her way over to him, and slapped him sharply across the face. The man remained silent. Even her reigning daughter-in-law, Justa Werges, while residing at one time in a room at the SRCC Centre, apparently shouted to a member not to dare enter through the front door of the center when she was in residence, that he must always enter from the side. Only formally invited guests were to be received at the front door. I was well aware of how Justa Werges carried herself, and I too showed the necessary deference; interviews with her consisted of her talking usually without any questions from me, and when I was allowed any question, it was best that I kept it brief.

In terms of the structural position of those who do the manual work in the SRCC, issues of obedience, loyalty, and trust are paramount. At least three of the elders indicated that it was a matter of courtesy and decency for them to perform personal service for the president, regardless of whether or not it was "community business." Elder members also informed me that at one time, prior to the state's funding of the Santa Rosa Festival, it was the established practice that SRCC members would set up vending stalls around the church during the festival, and all moneys earned were passed on to Ricardo to help meet the costs of the festival. Most of the few younger SRCC members today view such a practice with suspicion and balk at the idea of turning over profits to someone else. If the invisible Caribs remain invisible in my text, then let us say that is also in part owing to the successful maintenance of internal relations of order and authority where patrons and brokers on the front stage function partly on the basis of keeping the rest backstage.

The Broker-Patron Network

Each individual broker injects certain inputs into the representation of the SRCC and reflects certain tendencies present within the wider local and global settings. Various interests, institutional affiliations, and representational tendencies can be embodied even in single individuals. Each leading SRCC member has at least one important and respectable ally from outside the SRCC. Moreover, a great deal of effort and time is spent by each SRCC broker in either working with his or her extra-SRCC colleagues or in cultivating relationships with extra-SRCC brokers.

The range of interests, even more than the range of brokers, tends to be quite complex and ever growing. These interests range among the New Age consumption of indigenous spirituality, ecotourism and ethnobotany, the construction of Caribs as central to the making of the Gens d'Arime, Caribs as the devout subjects of the Roman Catholic Church in Arima, Caribs as symbolic of the bedrock of nationhood, Caribs as part of the history of resistance against white domination, Caribs as a folkloric cornerstone of Trinidad's national heritage, Caribs as a fount of different artistic aesthetics. This wide range of symbols is available and offers diverse opportunities for attracting the interest and investment of a range of potential patrons, each acting with different (yet established) assumptions of the value of Carib indigeneity in Trinidad. I am inclined to believe that without this multiplicity of interests vested in reinterpreting and valorizing the Carib, there would not have been a viable Carib revival in Trinidad.

The predominant interests represented by brokers center on the church and the state. At least two of the leading SRCC brokers have a strong attachment to the church. The conduct of the Santa Rosa Festival and the work of representing Caribs as a cornerstone of Arima's history—both being vital projects of the SRCC and Ricardo—demand a close working relationship with the Catholic Church in Arima. The SRCC has also had at least three PNM politicians directly and immediately involved with it: Ricardo Bharath, Melan Garcia, and Rose Janeire. Ties to the state are fundamental, given that the Ministry of Culture and the Arima Borough Council provide most of the SRCC's annually renewed funding.

The focus on patron-client networks, mediation, and the organization of a matrix of multiple interests in the promotion, reinterpretation, and recognition of indigeneity in Trinidad has been the center of this chapter's attempt to substantiate the social organization of Carib tradition that underlies the reproduction of the Carib in Trinidad, and the multiple directions in which the Carib revival is pulled. The sedimentation of ideas generated in previous contexts and by previous actors—from the colonial canonization of "Carib" to its localization in Arima, its nationalization as a symbol of the ancestry of the modern nation, and its memorialization as a ceremonial product that can be put on display—has varyingly been seized upon by an array of brokers in the present, each of the brokers working in a joint venture of sorts with the SRCC. The complexity of the network of brokers and competing interests is the result not just of the number of brokers but also of the many different social fields that they occupy.

The impact of these multiple processes, interests, and brokers engaged in what I have termed the reengineering of indigeneity in Trinidad has resulted in two critical outcomes, at least from the perspective of both SRCC brokers and myself. One of these is that one cannot speak of the SRCC as an isolated, possibly patho-logical group, comically or perhaps tragically insisting on an identity and a his-tory that are dismissed by the wider society. The second critical outcome has been consistent state support and recognition for the SRCC. Both of these outcomes reflect patrons' and brokers' legitimating, valuing, and disseminating the Carib. Both of these outcomes thus underline the presence of the indigenous in the modern cultural development of Trinidad.

6

Representing the Carib

Brokers, Events, and Traditions

"How does one tell that a person is Carib?" In response to my question, various SRCC brokers listed a number of factors that entitle individuals to say they are Carib or are to be identified as such by others. Carib self-representations can be rather fluid, even while being broadly circumscribed by social conventions of race. Some emphasize their genealogical ties to Amerindian ancestors and explain that certain families in Arima are known to be of Amerindian ancestry (citing the surnames of families making up the Hernandez-Calderon lineage). Others explained to me that it was an emotion of "feeling at home" in Trinidad, that it was a state of mind more than a physical appearance or the things one does. Self-identification is critical, within the socially prescribed limits of plausibility. One should be of Carib descent, but not even that is sufficient, as Ricardo explained: "Up on Calvary you will see all sorts of people with Amerindian faces, but they don't want to call themselves Carib even though it is as plain as the light of day. Sometimes you get people who don't look much like any Amerindian, and yet are proud to say they are Carib. Having the blood matters, of course, but it's not everything."

Carib Self-Representations

Who Is a Carib?

If they are to self-identify, then which label do they use for that identity? Within the SRCC there is some debate over the most appropriate label. One elderly member, the daughter of the late Queen Edith Martínez, said they "were always called Caribs." A middle-aged member rejected the name as an offensive European imposition. Another accepted the stereotypes associated with the early colonial Carib-Arawak dichotomy, saying that Caribs were "invaders who killed Arawaks." The use of the Carib label by the leading SRCC brokers, while fitting adherents within a recognized category, has in the past also caused some to question the identification. In an official document[1] the SRCC claims that in Trinidad the "principal tribal groups were the Arawaks," and those people who were most successful at "resisting the 'toys and other trinkets' displayed by Columbus, and in defending themselves against attacks by the newcomers, were renamed *Caribales* or 'consumers of human flesh' by Columbus and other Spanish colonizers." Elma Reyes (1995) added that they accepted the Carib designation "for the same reason descendants of enslaved Africans accepted (until recently) being called 'negroes' and 'coloreds.'" In the same document, Elma argued that "it is therefore unrealistic to assume, as has been done by some supposed experts, after failure to discover evidence that the First Nations were indeed 'consumers of human flesh,' that the island's people were 'only peaceful Arawaks.'" In this instance, Elma was playing both sides of the debate: they are to be called Caribs simply because it is a conventional generic label, first imposed and later accepted, *and* they are to be called Caribs because that is what they really are. This type of dualist statement is in fact typical of most of the explanations offered by SRCC brokers at different times, in different contexts and with different audiences in mind, especially as their own articulations of Carib identity continue to develop and undergo reworking. I attended one SRCC meeting where a considerable amount of time was spent by members discussing the name they should use to refer to an event the SRCC was planning, a public dinner for which people would buy tickets, with suggestions ranging from Carib Indian to Carib Amerindian, Amerindian, Indigenous, First Peoples, and Native Indian. Their dilemma stemmed from uncertainty over what would be readily understood by the wider public.

In the last seven years SRCC brokers have begun to publicly assert that they ought to be referred to as First Nations, claiming that this is a designation accepted by various international bodies (see Almarales 1994:55; *Sunday Express* 1995). "Carib" connotes locally specific indigenous history, a label now heavily marked and almost synonymous with a character of being few in number, almost extinct, descendants of proud warriors. This can attract sympathy and interest. "First Nations," by contrast, has a global resonance and connotes connections with large and well-organized North American indigenous bodies; while aboriginal, it underlines a global and metropolitan position of importance.

SRCC members' synonymous usage of "Spanish" and "Carib" adds a complicating dimension to current articulations of indigenous identity in Trinidad. A membership form produced by the SRCC clearly invites people of "Spanish and Carib ancestry" to join "the Carib tribe." One of my elder SRCC informants explained that her parents would never have said, "I am proud to be a Carib," and they did "not know the difference between a Spanish and a Carib." Another two, one more than sixty-five years old and the other more than eighty-five years old, asserted, "Spanish and Carib makes no difference." Yet another surmised that his father must have been a "proud Carib" since "it was only Spanish, and a little [French] Patois he spoke, not English." Queen Justa Werges also stated that "long ago people only called themselves Spanish.[2] . . . they did not know enough to say they were Carib." There is a process at work here that I found quite challenging: it appears that "Carib" was preserved as a higher-order category, one that was known and referred to by educated elements in the wider society but not used as an individual's personal self-ascription until the recent post-1973 revitalization effort led by individuals such as Ricardo, Cristo, and Elma. Indeed, even during my fieldwork, while I found SRCC members saying that they would not personally call themselves Carib, in SRCC meetings I heard the same individuals make the comment "we are the Caribs," as if Caribness is more a property of groups and institutions and not individuals. An elderly Arima expatriate residing in London, who left Arima in 1957, stated in an e-mail interview, "I have never met anyone, either in Trinidad or in England, who describes himself as Carib, though they were known as Caribs," which once again presents this peculiar tension. One elderly resident of Calvary Hill of Venezuelan parentage seemed to resolve this tension for himself in the following manner: "'Carib' is a thing of the ancestors. . . . We are just the descendants." This explanation posits the principle of disjuncture between ancestor and descendant, where the ancestor is the pure and original substance while the descendant is a somewhat diluted derivative.

The overlap in practice between usages of the labels "Spanish," "Cocoa Panyol," and "Carib" adds a further facet of representational complication. While SRCC brokers such as Ricardo and some elder members say that those Venezuelan descendants referred to as Cocoa Panyols are "different people" and that "one should never confuse them with Caribs since they are Spanish people, from elsewhere, who settled here and grew cocoa," others such as Elma assert their Venezuelan ancestry precisely as a means of validating their ties to the Arima Caribs, thus conflating "Cocoa Panyol" and "Carib" (see Almarales 1994:29). Some SRCC members simply referred to themselves as "Carib Panyols."

Given these different emphases for defining oneself as Carib or of Amerindian ancestry, we can begin to perceive certain boundaries that demarcate indigeneity on a personal level in Trinidad. One may identify with an indigenous heritage via either membership in the SRCC or by virtue of the fact that one is a relative of SRCC members in Arima, even while not personally belonging to the SRCC. Other Arimians may claim Amerindian ancestry without kinship ties to current SRCC members and also lacking any interest in belonging to the SRCC. Then there are those I have met who say they know of their specifically Arima Carib descent but no longer live in Arima and prefer the designation of "Spanish" or just "Trinidadian." At a broader level, I encountered non-Arimians who may proudly proclaim their aboriginal ancestry without identifying themselves necessarily as Carib.

Costume and Custom

The representational challenges faced by SRCC brokers largely lie in the three following areas. First, there is the challenge of articulating an identity that some members of the national audience believe refers to an extinct or assimilated people. Second, demonstrating the "cultural stuff" that validates an ethnic identity (especially when racial appearance occasions uncertainty) is another Trinidadian social convention that informs the representational practice of the SRCC, and this is at least one of the reasons why the SRCC has developed a clear program for the development and display of traditional practices through the production of various public-oriented events and rituals. Third, given the problem that SRCC members do not look Amerindian to many visitors and observers (though it is equally unclear what they *do* look like), SRCC brokers have felt pressured to find ways of graphically demarcating the difference of the SRCC. Using the surface of the body as a tableau for demonstrating both difference and community, the SRCC has struggled over the years with the issue of developing a uniform or public costume. As Beth Conklin explains, writing of the Amazonian context, in "contemporary indigenous identity politics, exotic body images carry a . . . strategic weight in asserting symbolic claims to authenticity" (Conklin 1997:711). The objective of SRCC brokers has been to visibly display themselves as "the Carib Community" when in public. As one of the elderly ladies exclaimed at a meeting, "We are the Caribs, when we go places together, people should see that." Another complained that whenever they see documentaries of gatherings in Guyana, the Amerindian hosts all have a "traditional dress" so that "you can see they are Amerindian."

So how was the SRCC to address this problem? That has been an issue of contention. Previously, and usually only for the purpose of the Santa Rosa Festival, all ladies would wear pink dresses, and all men would wear black pants, white shirts, and a bright red *rosetta* on the chest, some wearing a red sash around the waist. As far back as one looks into archives of photographs, this has indeed been one of their traditions. However, this dress is limited to the festival, and to many outside commentators, it does not appear distinctively Amerindian. Some figures, such as Cristo, tended to opt for the predictable answer: a loincloth, bare back, and feathered headpiece. Visiting delegations of Taíno revivalists from New York also encouraged that type of dress. Asked if he wouldn't go bare-chested and wear a loincloth, one SRCC leader reportedly said quite bluntly, "I'm not getting caught dead in that." Members frequently argued for a uniform approach, not individual solutions. I attended one meeting where one of the members presented samples of dress items she had fashioned, mostly white and featuring hand-painted versions of the SRCC logo. This particular set of clothing was not chosen in the end. However, by the time of my return at the end of 2001, the SRCC had clearly opted for a new uniform, not necessarily one that is boldly indigenous in appearance—indeed, it is a variation on the previous festival outfits—but certainly one that is striking and attracts attention. On all public occasions, women wear either bright yellow or bright pink blouses (and you never find a mixture of the two, clearly indicating that they coordinate and decide in advance which color they will all wear in unison) and deep red skirts, while men wear blood-red shirts and black pants. This compromise maintains some aspects of the old formality yet responds to internal demands for an all-purpose uniformity and public expectations of a different community.

The National Indigene

In ethnic terms, it is in the asserted authenticity that is constructed around a body of traditions through which brokers tie the SRCC to an ancestral heritage. Given that Ricardo describes SRCC members as the "mixed-race descendants of an extinct tribe," he stresses that it is with the maintenance of certain traditional practices that they mark the Amerindian heritage, since race (as in physical appearance) is unavailable as a clear marker of Carib ethnicity in Trinidad. Yet, in proclaiming themselves as mixed and Trinidadian, even above Carib, this only helps to reinforce their own sense of belonging to the nation and of being perceived as such by the wider national audience. In being mixed, they belong to all Trinidadians—true Trinis, a truly national indigene—insofar as "they are a bit of all of us." Some non-SRCC participants in key Carib ceremonies remarked at the extent to which SRCC rituals resemble Hindu, Orisha, Baptist, and Catholic practices—quite unsurprising, given that the key SRCC brokers themselves experienced and were exposed to these various bodies of ritual. Cristo was a member of a Spiritual Baptist congregation and went to a Hindu primary school, and though ostensibly a Roman Catholic, he can fluently recite prayers in Hindi. Ricardo said he followed a swami while living in Detroit, and he has personal friendships with Hindus that also invite him to take part in the occasional *puja* (prayer ritual). The smoke ceremony exhibits elements common to both Orishas and Hindus (two religious bodies that in any case have shared a great deal in Trinidad; see Houk 1993 and Simpson 1980), especially in participants waving smoke onto themselves and in the use of food items offered as sacrifices to the fire. Onlookers at a Santa Rosa Festival commented on how the SRCC planted bamboo flags around Lord Harris Square, one saying that "everybody in this country has a flag like this now: Hindus have their *puja* flags, Baptists have flags, Orisha have flags."

As the indigene finds himself or herself in the nation, the converse of this process is the nation finding itself in the indigene. Sometimes even this can be expressed in ethnic terms, as in Ricardo's statement, "everybody claims to have a little Carib in them," a perspective that was echoed by Elma's public arguments (Reyes 1995) that "Carib blood" may run "in the veins" of most Trinidadians, a notion also picked up by Carib Brewery. This dual articulation of both a generic national sense of indigeneity and a specific Carib indigeneity is not without its share of tensions. On the one hand, creole nationalists attempt to define the nation in supraethnic terms; on the other hand, creole nationalism masks an inherent multiculturalism of embracing and putatively uniting all infranational or ethnic components of the creole nation. The tensions that can result can be glimpsed in the placement of ethnic holidays within the calendar of national events. The timing of events of recognition has impacted on the SRCC in various ways. The first of August has been recently highlighted at the Arima level as the start of the "month of Santa Rosa"; however, it is also the same day as African

Emancipation Day, the anniversary of the Royal Charter of the Borough of Arima, and the commencement of ArimaFest. This can lead to a certain "crowding," which some SRCC leaders resent. However, two more days have been set aside that spotlight the SRCC—the annual Santa Rosa feast day on August 23 and the new national day of recognition of Trinidad's Amerindian heritage to be observed every October 14, starting from 2000. On August 1, the SRCC shares the stage with Africanist organizations and the Arima Borough Council. August 23 is a feast day for all of (Catholic) Arima, where the SRCC shares the stage with the Catholic Church. Only on October 14 does the SRCC have the stage to itself, yet under the auspices of a "national day."

Ariman Aboriginality

An important part of the SRCC's work at self representation hinges on the specialness of Arima, the "place in which the Caribs fit" and through which they were articulated within the wider national setting in the period from the ending of the mission to the establishment of national independence. The figure of the Amerindian has been an important marker of the distinctiveness of Arima within the wider national setting. Simply put, Arima is a site of aboriginality. Arima is regularly cited as "perhaps the only district in Trinidad where remnants of the native Amerindians can still be found" (Anthony 1988:2). Echoing J. N. Lewis' appreciation of the Amerindian motif in Trinidad's cultural infrastructure, a local researcher has written that Arima "was a town developed through the adaptation of Amerindian influence" and noted that "out of a total of 1,909 dwellings in 1946 . . . 1,528 were built with tapia walls" and "thatched roofs, the *typical Amerindian practice*" (Garcia 1991:50, iii, emphasis added). Garcia also argues that in "many Arima homes" one can find Amerindian cooking implements (corn and cassava graters), adding that "many persons report that food prepared with the Carib implements have [*sic*] a much better flavor" (1991:50–51).

The twin themes of the presence of the Amerindian in Arima are those of persistence and miscegenation: "although *even here* [in Arima] it is difficult to find anyone of *pure* Amerindian stock. . . . they have *always* been *concentrated* here, long after they *disappeared* from the other villages and towns, and Arima has *always* been regarded as *their special home*" (Anthony 1988:2, emphasis added). Still another researcher has written, "the mixed descendants of the local Amerindians were still to be found in El Calvario, a village on a hill overlooking the town of Arima" (Moodie-Kublalsingh 1994:90). The "always here," "always their home," and persistence as a collectivity despite mixture/assimilation are emphases that serve to underline the place of Arima in defining the Caribs' indigeneity.

The Amerindians constitute "anchors and memories" of what Arima was, even with modernization (Ahee 1992:20–21; Anthony 1988:9). Arima as "the home of the Caribs" remains a common theme in popular and official narratives, as does the proclamation of Arima as "the seat of the Carib chief Hyarima" (Williams 1988:10, 11). Indeed, the Ministry of Local Government explicitly refers to Arima as "the home of the Caribs, the indigenous people of Arima" (Ministry of Local Government 1999:9). Referring to the SRCC, one of the dailies claimed that the "cultural practices of these people have become woven into the fabric of the Arima society" and hailed Arima as "one of the cultural centers of the country" (*Sunday Express* 1995).

Caribs and Their Concepts of Tradition

Identification with Carib heritage, as articulated by SRCC brokers, occurs through the medium of tradition. The emphasis on tradition is motivated by three main concerns: (1) the desire to demonstrate actual practices that mark Carib difference and Carib history; (2) the need to promote the inventory of Carib contributions to the national cultural foundation; and (3) the need to define their personal ties to Amerindian ancestry, other than through race, since the questions of "being mixed" and "not appearing like Caribs" are problematic issues for some SRCC brokers.

SRCC brokers have openly listed and defined their main concepts and goals where tradition is concerned. The first, to use their words, involves the *maintenance* of certain *retained traditions* (which they identify as the Santa Rosa Festival, weaving, cassava processing, herbal knowledge, hunting, and house construction). The second involves the *revival* or *retrieval* of traditions, which explicitly refers to acquiring "lost traditions" that they no longer practice but that are practiced by indigenous groups elsewhere (and can thus be borrowed through a process SRCC leaders describe as "cultural interchange"), or reviving those that are described in historical and ethnographic texts (that is, the smoke ceremony, traditional wear, language, and shamanic practices). The third consists of the *reclamation* of traditions, which does not always involve practicing certain traditions as much as formally *claiming*, in the mode of intellectual and cultural property, that certain traditions extant in the wider society are in fact of Amerindian origin. This can also involve claiming as Amerindian many practices that have not been marked as the property of any ethnic group, such as the bathing of dogs with special herbs by a river to enhance their hunting prowess, or the presence of stylized Amerindian figures in Carnival. The fourth concept regarding tradition used by SRCC brokers entails a process of *translation*, whereby current practices of the SRCC that are not obviously Amerindian in origin are depicted as a modern translation of an earlier practice (for example, the blasting of the cannon on the first day of August is formally described by SRCC spokespersons as "the voice of Hyarima calling forth his people"). SRCC representations thus highlight loss and change, yet project origins, survivals, and translations.

The reclamation and maintenance of particular traditions on the part of SRCC brokers are effected in order to underscore the cultural content of the articulations of Carib identity. Often the traditions identified as having been retained—and thus in need of preservation and maintenance—are those that have been symbolically reclaimed from the wider society. They are reclaimed on two accounts: (1) for being of Amerindian origin, even if no longer practiced by people of Amerindian descent alone, or even if not practiced by any people of Amerindian descent;[3] and (2) for being a form of property, a possession of the SRCC, given the labor the SRCC has invested in the particular tradition (whether or not it is perceived as a creole or Amerindian tradition) and the extent of time it has been associated with a particular ritual or practice. Examples of the latter case include *parang*,[4] the *sebucán* dance (or the Maypole dance), and the Santa Rosa Festival. It is in this vein that I believe we can speak of one's indigeneity being discovered and acquired in and through the wider society (the nonindigenous society, according to the conventional terminology). It is the boundary that is drawn around a body of practice, more than the body itself, that is used to articulate Carib identity and heritage. The production of the cultural material intended to signify Carib indigeneity is forged from a multicultural milieu reflective of the nation. That is, Carib indigeneity embodies, embeds, and enacts a creole culture that has been symbolically indigenized as Amerindian and is communicated back to creole society as being indigenous. We thus run into the duality of national and ethnic indigeneity once more.

Ceremonials of Carib Commemoration: The Santa Rosa Festival

An Introduction to the Performance of the Santa Rosa Festival

August, the month of the festival, starts with a ceremonial cannon blasting atop Calvary Hill. Depending on who one asks, the cannon blasting replaced the firing of a rocket, which itself replaced the blowing of a conch shell. SRCC brokers such as Ricardo and Jacqueline Khan explain that this ritual involves a translation: all of these practices stand for the "voice of Hyarima calling his people together," for the purpose of beginning preparations for the festival. (This connection between Hyarima and Saint Rose was mythologized in the play by F. E. M. Hosein, *Hyarima and the Saints*.) The cannon is blasted three times during the day of the Santa Rosa Festival, at 6:00 a.m., at midday, and again at 6:00 p.m.

Certain procedures are followed prior to the actual mass for the festival. One of the most important of these is what SRCC members call "the dressing of the statue." The statue of Saint Rose is cleaned (some of the elderly members believe that the water running off of the statue has medicinal properties), and the smaller statue of the Infant Jesus is tied into its hands. The "throne" or "canopy" that houses the statue, and is used to lift it, is carefully decorated from top to bottom in garlands of yellow, pink, white, and red roses made by female members of the SRCC.

Another decorative process consists of cleaning Lord Harris Square and planting tall bamboo poles at regular intervals around the circumference (the poles used to secure the Caribs' flags). Each flag is either red and white, or pink and white, or yellow and white. Immediately opposite the entrance to the church, an iron cross is laid down on the pavement. At the cardinal points of the cross are metal cups, into which short bamboo poles are inserted, much like candles on a cake. The tops of the poles are filled with coconut oil, and wicks are inserted. On the eve of the festival, following the termination of nine days of praying the Novena of Santa Rosa, the wicks are lit. This is officially called the "wake" (colloquially, "the lighting of the park"). During the wake, members of the SRCC (usually) perform *parang* songs as the mass inside the church ends and the parishioners exit. The Santa Rosa Festival is not a celebration of the birth of Saint Rose, it is meant to be a somber commemoration of her death, and the rituals that constitute the festival are funerary in nature.

Public processions form a large part of the public performance of the festival, and in 1998 I took part in no less than seven, though there can be as many as nine. There is always the main procession through the streets of Arima on the Grand Festival Day, during the high mass. If August 23 falls on a Sunday, then there is only the one procession for the mass. However, most times the holiday will fall on a weekday. On that day, a smaller mass is held, with a shorter procession around Lord Harris Square, and the following Sunday the high mass and grand procession occur. Moreover, there are exclusively SRCC processions for each step of the decoration of the church and the square: one to deliver materials used for the decorations, another to deliver the Infant Jesus, another for the "undressing" of the statue and the church, and so forth. For the grand procession, in 1998 the SRCC came as a unit behind the Arima Borough Council, which marched behind the acolytes and the parish priest at the head of the procession. The remainder of the congregation follows the SRCC, so that the procession is divided into four sections. By 2002, this had changed slightly, with the SRCC having been moved to the front of the procession almost in unison with the acolytes bearing the cross and incense burners that are swung to and fro as the parishioners slowly march through the streets reciting the rosary or singing the hymn "O Santa Rosa."

The Structure of the Festival as a Cultural History of Revival

The degree to which the Santa Rosa Festival is a reflection of the late-nineteenth-century processes of Venezuelan immigration may help to account for the Santa Rosa Festival and the Carib connection to it as a phenomenon of resurgence, of presence reasserted through institutional vehicles of the wider society. Let us start by examining a relatively simple practice, that of firing a blast within defined ceremonial procedures. The testimony of Pedro Valerio (a self-described Carib descendant of the late nineteenth century, who wrote of his upbringing in a peasant family) indicates that gun blasts were an established part of rituals such as baptisms (1991:323). Also writing in the late 1800s, one traveler noted with respect to Christmas and New Year's celebrations that "all classes" celebrated the holidays by letting off "any amount of gunpowder and superfluous steam in the form of fireworks" (Collens 1886:48). With respect to the public ceremoniality encouraged by Governor Woodford in the 1820s, we have this description of events during a high mass he attended: "At the Elevation of the Host the troops presented arms and a salute of twenty-one guns was fired from the Sea Fort Battery" (Fraser 1971 [1896]:11). I note these disparate items only because they seem to provide shreds of evidence that serve as a possible explanation for the presence of this practice within the Santa Rosa Festival.

Another relatively unexceptional practice, which nevertheless we should not take for granted, is that of a standard or staff bearer at the head of a public procession on festival days. This also has a wider history behind it, some of it predating the mission of Arima, and some of it from the same period as the mission. In San Francisco de los Arenales, destroyed in the Amerindian rebellion of 1699, records speak of a Spanish layman acting as the standard bearer: "He carried the banner to and in the church on the great feast days for the processions, and particularly on the patronal feast of the parish, that of St. Francis of Assisi" (de Verteuil 1995:100). In the 1820s, during the time of Governor Sir Ralph Woodford, a local observer wrote that on "grand occasions" such as New Year's Day or the Festival of Corpus Christi, Woodford would attend the celebration of high mass "accompanied by a brilliant staff," followed by members of the council for the colony (Fraser 1971 [1896]:11).

More striking is the presence of festivals and ritual procedures almost entirely identical to today's Santa Rosa Festival and rooted in the traditions of the Venezuelan Panyols. The Santa Rosa Festival as practiced in the mission of Arima was not itself unique in Spanish colonial times: since at least the 1750s, there are records of the festivals of Saint Augustine and Saint Paul in the missions named after those saints, under the governance of the "*corregidor* of the Nepuyos," Gabriel Infante (Noel 1972:36–37). I asked previously: What accounted for the resurgence of the elaborate festival, which, according to local observers and clerics, had either been severely diminished or grossly secularized? I suggested that the explanation was to be found in the renewed Hispano-Amerindianization of the festival from the late 1800s, resulting from Venezuelan immigration.

Let us take one documented example. Writing in the late 1800s, Father Cothonay spoke of the community of Tumpuna, now San Rafael, about a twenty-minute drive south of Arima. The parish priest, according to Cothonay, was a Venezuelan exiled from the mainland. This part of the interior, Cothonay noted, was a favorite location for Spanish families that had left the coastal area to the new British conquerors (Cothonay 1893:242, 243). This locale, therefore, was to some degree a combination of earlier Spanish Trinidadian families and later Venezuelan immigrants.

His detailed description of the Tumpuna festival was written on January 18, 1885 (Cothonay 1893:243–246). Cothonay came to Tumpuna to preach at the "Feast of the Holy Name of Jesus and of the Sacred Infant." On Saturday evening, the eve of the feast, he observed a group of children preparing for "the illumination of the night" (recall the "wake" or "the lighting of the park" on the Saturday eve of the Santa Rosa Festival). The priest was the one to have assigned all of the work tasks for the festival to individual persons (in this case serving the same role as the Queen of the Caribs or the contemporary SRCC president). Some individuals were assigned to cut bamboo (like current SRCC members), others to form them into "lamps," still others to procure coconut oil for the bamboo torches. Cothonay described youths taking these four- to five-foot-long pieces of bamboo (the same dimensions as those cut by SRCC members) and planting them around the church and presbytery and along the streets of the village (similar to what the SRCC does today). At night, the villagers exploded firecrackers and other fireworks, an event repeated at 5:00 in the morning (much like the SRCC's cannon blasting). Cothonay also wrote of a parish group called the "associates of the Sacred Infant," observing that within the church on this day they occupied "a place of honor," and described them as wearing a red sash and "beautiful silver medal around the neck." (The red sash calls to mind the now-outdated dress of SRCC members during the Santa Rosa Festival. As for the reference to the "associates," obviously a parish body or sodality, this reminds me of the position of the Carib Community within the postmission history of the Church of Santa Rosa.) In fact, Cothonay later described the Association of the Sacred Infancy (Sainte-Enfance) as taking care of "burials, marriages, praying and chanting of members for the happiness of their newlywed young ones, an association for all the inhabitants," indicating that the association also had a life outside of the festival period. What struck me especially was Cothonay's description of the procession following the mass:

> But the most beautiful part of the festival was the procession that followed the mass. They carried in triumph *el Santo Niño*, sitting on his throne, enthroned in flowers and candles. From the eve, they decorated his throne with excellent taste. . . . Around him [the statue], were vases of flowers and chandeliers which were artistically placed on three grades. This throne was carried by four associates of the *Sacred Infancy*; a choir boy carried the incense burner in front. A young girl carried the pretty banner of the Infant Jesus, and four other young girls carried its cordons. The procession passed through the whole village. (Cothonay 1893:245)

Returning to my suggestion that Venezuelan Cocoa Panyols actively participated in festivals such as those described at Tumpuna, I argue that such rituals mirror and amplify in public what is a private, home-based religious ritual that oral historians such as Moodie-Kublalsingh (1994) have identified as a favorite among the Panyols who came to Trinidad at the end of the 1800s. This is known as the *velorio de la Cruz*, or the Cross Wake, which can be held at different times of the year, the most popular for the SRCC having been for the feast of Saint Raphael in October. In my view, the *velorio de la Cruz* provides the structural, procedural, and symbolic foundation behind what we know today as the Santa Rosa Festival.

At the center of the *velorio* is the cross, which like the statue of Saint Rose is "dressed": usually with lilies and roses, a cloth draped around the arms of the cross, candles lining its base or even placed on the horizontal sides of the cross, thus forming an altar of sorts. The cross itself is under the care of a caretaker, the so-called *ama de la Cruz*, usually the principal female figure of a household, *ama* being the Spanish word for housewife. Like the keeper of the statue of Saint Rose in the period before Ricardo, the *ama* has the same responsibilities and position as the Queen of the Caribs. Like the Queen of the Caribs, who supervises a queen and king of the Festival Day, the *ama* also relies on a *madrina* and a *padrino* (godmother and godfather). Juanita Rodriguez, an elderly *ama* who was one of Moodie-Kublalsingh's informants, explained, "To prepare the *velorio de cruz* [*sic*] I had people cut down bamboo and scrape it well" in order to make torches that were installed around the perimeter of the house and then lit. Juanita also explained that one must "dress" the cross, "like a Queen" (Moodie-Kublalsingh 1994:113). Moodie-Kublalsingh also describes some of the proceedings of a *velorio*: "On the evening of the *velorio*, the cross was ceremoniously raised step by step on the altar. A loud noise, *un cañonazo*, the retort of exploding bamboo, marked each one of the three steps on which the cross was placed. There would be a similar *cañonazo* at the end of the service when the cross was being lowered early next morning" (1994:113). A procession also takes place around the perimeter of the house (Moodie 1983:25–27).

Apparently this was a popular folk ritual practiced by Venezuelan immigrants, who often avoided formal church proceedings and prelates, often distrusting the latter. The church hierarchy is not involved in these rituals, nor does it officially sanction them. I am therefore suggesting that, in large part, the resurgence of the Santa Rosa Festival as a religious event of prominence in Arima, prepared by the Caribs, stems from the influx of people precisely like Juanita Rodriguez: it has become a public assertion of a household ritual form.

The Legend of Santa Rosa

The legend surrounding Santa Rosa's apparition—a legend enshrined in the oral history of SRCC members, recounted with frequency, and sung in a *parang* song by Cristo Adonis—raises important historical questions surrounding issues of the development and current proprietary claims to the meanings and performance of the Santa Rosa Festival. In the most frequently spoken versions of the legend, three male Carib hunters by the unusual names of Ramon, Puyon, and Punya (the latter two appearing to be neither Spanish nor Amerindian names) ventured into the forest around what is today known as Santa Rosa Heights. By a natural spring (some say at the entrance to a cave), the hunters found a young Spanish girl, alone, seemingly lost (some members say they found a statue). They brought this girl back to the mission. The next morning she had disappeared. A second time they ventured into the forest, found her again, and once more brought her back to the mission. However, the little girl disappeared once again the next morning. These events transpired a third time. After her third disappearance (of course the symbolism of the holy trinity repeats itself in this story), all they found at the spring was a corona of roses. They went to the priest and related these mysterious events to him. Pondering the matter, he told the Carib hunters, "That was no ordinary girl, that was Saint Rose herself, and now you must carve a statue by which to remember and honor her, and keep her feast day." Carib informants quickly add to this seemingly short and simple story that she appeared to the hunters in order to exhort them to convert to Christianity. However, this detail seems to have been extracted from the play *Hyarima and the Saints,* where Santa Rosa appears in Anacaona's dream. One may assume that the hunters, residing in a mission, had already converted to Catholicism, and so the exhortation would be redundant. The church itself does not endorse the notion that the missionary priest ever said such words or that the event ever even happened. Once again, we see a divide between ecclesiastical and folk approaches, in this case with reference to the saint, the church celebrating her life and her deeds as patron saint of the New World and the Philippines, the Caribs celebrating their unique and personal relationship with her within the confines of Arima itself.

Saint Rose herself seems to have an especially inclusive if not amorphous value as a convergence of various key symbols of the Catholic faith and its particular Marian orientations. Representations of Saint Rose show her wearing a crown of roses, one that resembles the crown of thorns worn by Christ on the cross, and one quite appropriate for Rose, who practiced mortification of the flesh in sympathy with Christ's suffering. The roses are rich in symbolism referring to Mary, the Holy Mother and Blessed Virgin. Rose was not so named at birth; this is a name that had later been ascribed to the young girl who sold roses in the streets of Lima, Peru, to support her parents or to make donations to the poor Amerindians and Africans of the city (see Windeatt 1993). In fact, her reputation is of having been especially close to Amerindians and Africans and of having been a friend of the Afro-Peruvian saint, Martin de Porres.

Rose, who sold roses, wore a crown of roses. Roses have long been symbolically associated with the Virgin Mary, especially if one thinks of the rosary itself, traditionally made of rose petals compressed into small beads, and with fifty repetitions of the Hail Mary said during a rosary. Reported apparitions of the Virgin speak of witnesses being showered by rose petals falling from the sky just before the appearance of the Mother of Christ. As if to echo the image of Christ's mother, Saint Rose is shown carrying the Infant Jesus during the Santa Rosa Festival. A Muslim companion at the 2002 Santa Rosa Festival kept asking me about "the statue of Mary," which is how he saw the statue of Saint Rose, and I would suspect that many other onlookers, perhaps even a few Catholics, might be swayed into seeing the statue as one of the Blessed Virgin.

Saint Rose's Marian associations in Trinidad may extend farther afield, to other parts of Trinidad and to Spain itself, as part of a regional and indeed global network of associations. Moodie-Kublalsingh (1994:138–139) explains the origins of another Virgin present in Trinidad, the Virgin of Montserrat, patron of the area by the same name in south-central Trinidad. The origin of her presence in Trinidad dates to 1687, with the arrival of the first Capuchins, who were to set up the first missions for the Amerindians. Moodie-Kublalsingh describes the legend surrounding this Virgin: "In 717, when Spain was under occupation by the Arabs, according to an old legend, the Christians in Catalonia hid a statue of the Virgin Mary in a cave in the most craggy part of the mountain known as Montserrat. . . . In 880 . . . the statue was discovered by three shepherds who saw a rain of stars illuminating the mountain and signaling the spot where the image of Mary was hidden" (1994:139). Three shepherds (like the three wise men of the Nativity)—like the three Carib hunters, a possible indigenization and localization of the legend—discover a statue by a cave (like Christ in the manger), much like the alternative version of the legend of Santa Rosa that I described.

Santa Rosa and the Virgin of Montserrat were not the only such figures introduced to Trinidad. The Capuchin monks also introduced La Divina Pastora (the Divine Shepherdess) as the patron of Siparia, a former mission. La Divina Pastora is surrounded by two legends, one relating to how she came to be in Trinidad and the other about how she came to be in Spain: "Tradition has it that in Seville in 1703, Our Blessed Lady appeared to a Capuchin known as the Venerable Isidore and instructed him to spread devotion to her under the title of Our Lady Mother of the Good Shepherd. The Capuchin Order made this devotion its own, spreading it throughout the world. In 1795 Pope Pius VI named the Divina Pastora the special patroness of the Capuchin missions" (Rétout 1976:55). Like the legend of Santa Rosa, where the saint exhorts the Caribs to convert to Christianity, here the Venerable Isidore is charged with the role. The fact that the Pope had entrenched La Divina Pastora in the missions of Trinidad suggests another possible twist: far from not sanctioning the legend of Santa Rosa, past prelates or perhaps overzealous lay members (possibly Amerindians themselves) used "templates" circulated within the church itself in order to construct and develop the legend of Santa Rosa. Santa Rosa, as an intercessor or broker between the earthly and the heavenly, thus comes to be inscribed with multiple meanings: Spanish, Catholic, universal, particular, Carib, Christlike, Marylike, guardian and protector of indigenous peoples.

The Caribs had become embroiled in several intertwined histories, and the need to establish the Carib interpretation is never satiated or rendered redundant, at least not as long as other actors read different interpretations into the life of Rose and propose alternative representations. The historicity of the festival forms an acute part of Carib self-representations: "This is the longest running, oldest and most continuous festival in Trinidad and Tobago," Ricardo repeats to visitors and audiences. The statue of a snow-white Rosa, delicately and expertly carved like no other statues produced in Trinidad today, is one I have seen in photographs dating back almost a century, and I have no evidence from any source to suggest that the statue's presence has not been continuous for at least over a century.

Santa Rosa's Earthly Broker: The Queen of the Caribs

> Unlike the other tribes, instead of a King they [the Caribs] had a Queen
> Now the Queen of this tribe was a gentle old Carib woman. Her hair was
> quite grey but her dark eyes were full of laughter. She was simply called
> Mama, the Queen, and everyone loved her.
> From "The Caribs and the Birds," in Norma McCartney, Tales of the Immortelles
> (1989:15–16)

The persona of the Queen of the Caribs almost possesses a legendary quality within Trinidad, grist for the mill of fairy-tale writers. No source, written or otherwise, is able to provide an adequate or convincing account for the emergence of this figure, who exists in no other Island Carib community today and who leaves Carib visitors from places such as Dominica and St. Vincent a little mystified. And yet the "Queen of the Caribs" is one of the oldest recorded offices of the preformalized Carib Community, one that has been subject to various transformations reflective of a history of brokerage and patronage, the subject of shifting representations by both SRCC brokers and the Trinidadian media (Andrews 2000b; Assing 2000; Burnett 2000; De Coteau 2000; Elie 2000). The Queen of the Caribs' primary functions consisted of overseeing preparations for the festival and acting as the representative and spokesperson for the Carib Community. She is Santa Rosa's own earthly broker. As the late Queen Justa Werges once exclaimed to me, eyes bright with fervor, "I am the Ambassador of Santa Rosa."

My impression is that the contemporary Queen of the Caribs represents a convergence of cultural influences and fossilized elements of practices pertaining to different moments in the history of Arima's Amerindians, from various declines and revivals, obtaining from periods of neglect and interest and shaped by in-migrations of diverse peoples into Arima, and all shrouded by incomplete historical research based on fragments of knowledge and passing mentions in old texts. For example, local historical writings of the mid 1800s make reference to a king and queen of the Santa Rosa Festival, who were selected from the Amerindian population of the Arima mission. As De Verteuil wrote, "The village of Arima was formerly, and for a long time, celebrated for its festival of Santa Rosa, the patron saint of the mission. On that day the Indians elected their king and queen—in general, *a young man and young girl—and all appeared in their best apparel and most gawdy [sic] ornaments*" (1858:301, emphasis added). There is no indication whether these figures carried any responsibilities of any kind. De Verteuil further explained, "Once every year, they elected, with the sanction of the corregidor, a king and queen to preside over their festivities, and to act as their principals on solemn occasions" (1858:300). For this period, the early to mid 1800s, there is no mention of a paramount King or Queen ruling over the young king and queen of the festival day. Indeed, the institution of an elderly lady as Queen, who remained in place for years, may well have started in the late 1800s and may have emerged out of this previous and temporary institution.

The SRCC's official list of Carib Queens reaches back only to the 1880s (see Almarales 1994:19). Lists kept by the SRCC, along with notes (Reyes n.d.h), state that Dolores MacDavid, née Medrano (also known as "Ma Gopal"), was Queen from 1875 until 1908. She was born in 1824 and passed away in 1908. There is some confusion surrounding this person, not so much for being called by an East Indian name (her husband was reportedly East Indian), as much as for the statement that she was born under a different name, Yldefonsa de los Dolores. The following Queen was Maria Fuentes Werges Ojea ("Ma Werges"), who reigned from 1908 until 1962, when she died at the age of 113. Her daughter, Edith Martínez, née Werges, served as Queen, in the first instance from 1962 until 1974, when she was temporarily dethroned. Reinstated as Queen in June of 1975, she continued in that office until her death on August 6, 1987. She died at the age of 95. Adolphine Werges, sister of Edith, temporarily served as Queen for seven months between 1974 and 1975. Following the death of the reinstated Queen Edith Martínez, in 1988 Justa May Werges, daughter-in-law of Queen Maria Werges and sister-in-law of Edith, was crowned. Queen Justa Werges' tenure lasted from May 1, 1988, until her death on January 16, 2000. She was born on May 1, 1915. Valentina Medina, née Assing (also known as "Mavis"), is the current Queen of the Caribs, having been chosen in March of 2000.

After Ricardo instituted the position of president in the 1970s, as a result of ordinances that required this office for registered companies, the limited authority and representational responsibilities of the Queen were gradually supplanted by the president, thus reducing her to a figurehead whose office was subsequently retitled "Titular Queen," as if to make the point even clearer. While "it has always been customary for the reigning 'Queen' to nominate her successor when she feels that she is no longer able to continue her reign," according to Almarales (1994:19), the position of Queen since the 1980s and the ascent of Ricardo ceased to be hereditary, and contemporary leaders of the Carib Community now claim that it was always an elected position. This claim is made even though Queen Maria Werges passed her position on to her daughters, Adolphine Werges and Edith Martínez, the latter having selected her daughter, Norma Stephens, as her successor, which Ricardo opposed (see Almarales 1994:19–20).

Queen Justa Werges interpreted herself as an instrument of divine intervention, and her fervent religiosity dominated the several visits I had with her (blessings, prayers in Spanish, prayers before entering her home, sprinklings of holy water, and so forth). "I am here doing the work of Jesus Christ!" she exclaimed on occasion. She recounted a time she had died from stroke: "When I passed away, Jesus Christ sent me back. He told me: 'You have work to finish. You must return.'" As an expert in *oraciones*, prayers much dreaded by some non-Hispanic Trinidadians for their allegedly malignant magical powers, Queen Justa Werges pointed out, "When Queen and Government after you, you cannot escape." "The Queen works for Church and State," she would add. Queen Justa Werges would proudly point to a framed certificate on the wall of her tapia-walled home, indicating Pope John Paul II's blessings for her ascent to office, and she recalled with stout pride the mass said on the day of her coronation, presided over by the admiring parish priest of Arima, Father Malcolm Galt. "The Queen," she emphasized, "is Saint Rose's representative": "When the members elected me, it was God working through them. Only God can remove me," she added. The current secretary of the SRCC, Jacqueline Khan, stated that regardless of any "troubles" with the Queen, "there must always be a Queen of the Caribs: when people come to the [Santa Rosa] Carib Community they expect to see the Queen. The Queen is what dignifies the community."

Consuming the Labor of Caribs

Ricardo emphasizes that Caribs have invested labor into the building of the church in Arima and the Santa Rosa Festival and that any act of universalizing the meanings of these phenomena without any reference to the Caribs is an act of expropriation. Ricardo has often declared, "Our ancestors built that church stone by stone; they carried the stones on their head from the river."[5] This assertion, added to the array of work duties SRCC members have performed in cleaning and maintaining the church (especially during the festival), is cast as an indication of an actual investment of labor, the fruits of which are now being reclaimed by the SRCC. SRCC brokers are thus affirming a mutual obligation with the local parish. In addition, the SRCC has drafted a formal set of "do's and don'ts" on how clerics should conduct and observe the Santa Rosa Festival.[6] Ricardo has stressed to SRCC members that "we need the church's recognition— if we don't first get the church's recognition we cannot succeed."

It is not so much a case then of the SRCC seeking a divorce from the church, but quite the contrary: the aim is to ensure that the church does not forget its mutual obligations with the Caribs, obligations that are rooted in written histories of the mission of Arima. Already there seems to be too much distance. The church has no role whatsoever, and no apparent interest, in ensuring that those individuals selected to be queen and king of the Festival Day are morally upright, baptized and confirmed Catholics, married in the church, without a reputation as adulterers, gamblers, or drinkers. In this instance, Ricardo serves as an unofficial cleric internal to the SRCC. Ricardo also leads the novena for Saint Rose in the church itself, leading up to the festival. Within the SRCC Centre, he calls members forward to kiss the statue of the Infant Jesus.

The church does not inform itself of the actual preparations undertaken by the SRCC for the festival. In 1998, when the SRCC insisted that it was the SRCC's job to clean the church for the festival, "according to tradition," members of the SRCC arrived to find that a professional cleaning crew using power floor-polishers was busy on the scene. Ricardo explained to me that it was the tradition for a row of Caribs with cloths to go down on their knees and polish the floor of the church, from the front down to the back—an act of devotion and sacrifice, as he put it, and certainly a claim on reciprocity as well.

Labor integrates the SRCC into the established institutions of the wider society. At a more fundamental level, the fruits of Carib labor are meant to integrate the parish into the Carib Community. One of the fruits of their labor, one that occasions tremendous amounts of work in the weeks leading up to the festival, is cassava bread. In my very first meeting with Ricardo in 1993, an elderly yet wiry and energetic medicine man, Ian Capriata Dickson, entered and began speaking with me on a torrent of issues. He asked Ricardo for cassava bread: "*dame una.*" He held this large round white cracker, something I had not seen before, and raised it to the light seeping in through gaps of the thatched hut Ricardo used as a kitchen. He was raising it as if it were a communion host. Firmly pressing the base with his forefingers, he gently sent a crack running up the middle of the cassava bread. He placed one half in my hand: "Have this. This is our Carib food."

Ritual, Ceremoniality, and Commemorated Caribs

The Santa Rosa Festival embodies and enacts Carib concepts of tradition, particularly those of maintenance (communal cohesion, cassava bread), reclamation (the history of Carib labor in the festival), and translation (the use of the cannon to stand in for the voice of Hyarima, plus the festival itself). The festival also provides a regular means by which the Caribs can appear in public as a separate body with local roots, through different dress and seating reserved for them as a group at the front of the church on the festival day, by marching as a group during the seven to nine street processions conducted during the festival period, and by planting flags atop tall bamboo poles along the route connecting the SRCC headquarters to the Church of Santa Rosa.

I tend to see the Santa Rosa Festival in terms set out by the late Erving Goffman, as the performance of a ceremony. As he explained, there is a tendency for performers to offer an idealized impression (Goffman 1990 [1959]:44), and in this case I see that idealized impression being one of a continuous and coherent Carib Community, retaining its traditions—not that this is a false representation, at least not beyond the degree that all representations involve selectivity. What is more important is sustaining the Santa Rosa Festival as a reproduced social phe-nomenon: "When an individual or performer plays the same part to the same audience on different occasions, a social relationship is likely to arise" (Goffman 1990 [1959]:27). Moreover, public performance "will tend to incorporate and exemplify the officially accredited values of the society" (Goffman 1990 [1959]: 45), which in the case of the Santa Rosa Festival we may list as those of adherence to one's faith, boundedness within one's ethnic community, and exemplification of one's historical contribution to the cultural foundation of the nation, the oldest festival in a nation proud of its very many festivals. Goffman explains that such performances can be defined as ceremonies and celebrations in the following terms: " Io the degree that a performance highlights the common official values of the society in which it occurs, we may look upon it, in the manner of Durkheim and Radcliffe-Brown, as a ceremony—as an expressive rejuvenation and reaffir-mation of the moral values of the community. Furthermore, in so far as the expressive bias of performances comes to be accepted as reality, then that which is accepted at the moment as reality will have some of the characteristics of a celebration" (Goffman 1990 [1959]:45). The duality of the Santa Rosa Festival as a social ceremony is that certain actors can perceive it as a celebration of the pious self-sacrifice of the saint or by others as a celebration of the survival of the Caribs against all odds.

Performances are meant to communicate select aspects of a reality, not to catalogue and disgorge all known facts to an audience. This control over an audience's room for perception is also control over the form of contact and com-munion between audience and performers (Goffman 1990 [1959]:74). One way in which such control is exercised is though control of the setting of the perfor-mance: in this case, the interior of the church as it is being cleaned by Caribs; Lord Harris Square, which the SRCC has pleaded to use for its harvest festivities; the SRCC Centre itself, with its graphic manifestations of indigeneity; and the SRCC Centre's alternate religious symbolism, such as the hanging of a bunch of corn-stalks from the ceiling, positioned over the head of the priest where he sat as a guest of honor for lunch after the Santa Rosa Festival, and placed immediately behind him a bowl of water, tobacco, and cassava, materials from the shamanic smoke ceremony. Control over setting is control over information that the audi-ence is able to acquire (Goffman 1990 [1959]:98).

Also, in controlling both the setting and the performance, there is a need for a "director," which Goffman sees as possessing a like-mindedness everywhere: "Whether it is a funeral, a wedding, a bridge party, a one-day sale, a hanging, or a picnic, the director may tend to see the performance in terms of whether or not it went 'smoothly,' 'effectively,' and 'without a hitch,' and whether or not all possible disruptive contingencies were prepared for in advance" (Goffman 1990 [1959]:102). Indeed, this is much like the expected role of a film or stage director. I recall Ricardo huddled with a group of ladies in the SRCC in the days leading up to the 1998 festival: "Ladies, remember last year? You remember the positions you took in the procession? You remember how you all marched together? Yes, that! That's how I want to see it this year, please! That was just perfect!"

Rituals can be used, as the SRCC uses them, to show a certain commonality "or even to create it" (Moore and Myerhoff 1977:6). As Ricardo explained to me on different occasions, "The festival is what keeps us together as a community. . . . People who have not been in Arima for years will come from all over to be together again with friends and family for the festival." Carib participation in, and preparation of, the Santa Rosa Festival helps to cement, legitimate, and disseminate the definition of social reality the SRCC wishes to convey: continuity and survival through adaptation and what they call cultural translation.

SRCC brokers propound the view that the Caribs have been instrumental in maintaining Trinidad's "oldest and most continuous festival," emphasizing the national value of the Santa Rosa Festival in comparison with other, and more recent, festivals such as Carnival, Hosay, and so forth. Indigeneity in the form of the precedence principle is thus extended to the festival arts. With these arguments SRCC brokers are catering to the nationalist desire for a long temporal background while also engaging in the comparative politics of organized bodies seeking recognition and funding. The Santa Rosa Festival is thus inserted into the inventory of the national cultural foundation. However, the festival, and its Carib history, in the words of SRCC brokers, is also enshrined as a defining element of Arimian history, in a way that is designed not to undermine nationalist narratives as much as it is intended to supplement them.

Rituals of Retrieval: The Shaman's Smoke

The smoke ceremony, as it is formally called, is largely part of the development "on the ground" of ritual practices defined as tradition by SRCC brokers and exemplifying cultural retrieval and cultural interchange; these practices also embody the outcomes of international networks of indigenous organization and representation. Cristo most often performed the ceremony during the period of my fieldwork, with the participation of Ricardo. In developing this ritual, Cristo has drawn sustenance from what some might call a New Age, generic American Indian culture that is reshaped and presented in Trinidad as indigenous yet, as Cristo states, "not necessarily Carib."

Whenever Ricardo is asked about whether or not today's Caribs have any religious practices or beliefs stemming from precolonial times, it is usually the smoke ceremony that is foregrounded in an otherwise negative reply. Unlike the situation faced in the Santa Rosa Festival, the SRCC controls both the time and the space and all of the elements of the setting in performing the smoke ceremony. It is the only ritual that is regularly and routinely performed at SRCC public events and gatherings. The smoke ceremony, like the many approaches to tradition enumerated by the SRCC and like its many brokers and divergent interests, is another face that the SRCC can present to the public, to satisfy the more essentialist expectations of certain audiences and some members. As if to cover all possible representational bases, the smoke ceremony is also performed on the first of August each year, at least for the last six years, as a way of celebrating and marking the start of the month of Santa Rosa.

The expression of an internationalized indigeneity, drawing heavily on metropolitan influences, characterizes much of Cristo's practice of reinterpreting, articulating, and representing indigeneity for the wider national and even international audiences. Cristo has an especial interest in popularized North American Indian rituals (smudging, vision quests) and motifs (dream catchers, medicine wheels, totem poles, and so forth), with especial input from a co-broker, Vincent La Croix, who had lived with the Sun Bear Tribe in the United States.[7] A number of Sun Bear books have been published, copies of which Cristo possesses and consults (see Sun Bear and associates 1988).

To an even greater degree than Ricardo, Cristo shies away from race-based definitions of indigeneity, preferring to define indigenous people as "Earth People." Cristo explains in his statements that, from his perspective, indigenous identity is rooted in "feeling indigenous," feeling at home in the forests and by rivers—and not by purity of blood. Cristo has cultivated close associations with New York–based Taíno revivalists who, in some cases, have also been confronted with hostile incredulity over their "black" appearance. Cristo is not embarrassed to explain that his paternal side derives from Martinique and his maternal side comes from Maturín, Venezuela. Cristo's identification is with what he describes as an ecological and globalized sense of aboriginality that is not necessarily rooted in any one location or culture; to highlight this, his adopted middle name, Atékosang, means "The Traveler," as he explained, and his favorite logo (as represented by his *parang* band, Los Niños del Mundo, or "The Children of the Earth") is the globe. The New Age dimension of the ritual, drawing on indigenous sources yet developed and articulated by people outside of a given tribe, is a vehicle that has allowed Cristo to navigate his way between essentialist depictions of the true spiritual core of aboriginality, and his own background as a miscegenated person in a society that stresses racial purity when speaking of privileged categories such as white or Carib.

One of Cristo's primary endeavors within the SRCC, in line with the stated project of cultural retrieval, has been the cultivation of shamanic rituals and his own development as a shaman. This process apparently took definite shape in the 1990s, when he built on an array of local personal experience and his exposure to international influences. Cristo's emergence into the SRCC's formally enunciated position of shaman stemmed, he argues, from his exposure to his great-aunts and godmother in the village of Paria in the hills of northern Trinidad, where he spent many of his childhood years; these women, whom he recalls served as *curanderas* (healers) or *parteras* (midwives), also possessed a repertoire of special prayers referred to locally as *oraciones*. He explained to me that he additionally developed a personal acquaintance with Spiritual Baptist and Orisha practices, rituals, and meanings. As a youth, he was a pupil at an Arima Hindu junior secondary school. Cristo describes himself as an ardent student of all religious knowledge, and he joined a variety of different religious groups at different times. He often describes this in terms of subversion and infiltration, relishing that he learned their practices and meanings "better than their priests." His donning of what SRCC leaders call "traditional wear" began sometime after 1992, as did his public performances of the smoke ceremony. Much of Cristo's public persona as a member of the SRCC literally embodies various currents of internationalized indigeneity, as well as reflecting diverse currents of transculturation within Trinidad.

As Cristo has plugged himself into the world of internationalized indigeneity and the globally heightened attention to shamanic practices—what some refer to as the process of globalized "shamanic transfers" (see Chalifoux 1999; Guedon 1999)—he adopted the originally Tungusian word *shaman,* routinely used by anthropologists for all such practitioners everywhere, rather than the Mainland Carib word *piache* or the Island Carib word *behique,* which refer to the medicine men of Amerindian communities in those regions. It is only lately, and under the influence of a broker outside of this study who became prominent during my absence from 1999 to 2001, that he began to publicly introduce himself as the "piai man or medicine man of the Carib Community."

His personal image and his pronouncements have served to impress an array of outside interests, students and researchers, and especially the local news media, which appears to be infatuated with him (as examples, see Burnett 1998a; Calliste 1998; Chouthi 1998a, 1998b), seizing upon his every ritual as "authentic" and "ancient." Indeed, as if to lament the apparent solemnity and rigidity of the 1999 Santa Rosa Festival he was observing, a local journalist said to me, "Now, Adonis, that is the *real* thing! *That* is the Amerindian culture." One has to appreciate that having been raised on a North American diet of images of Indians that consisted of feathers, smoke signals, and whooping cries—as shown in countless Hollywood Westerns and American publications, and as reproduced in the local Carnival—many Trinidadians may indeed expect these images to be associated with anything indigenous and may be rather disappointed or confused by their absence.

The smoke ceremony began to be performed following Carifesta V in 1992 when the SRCC hosted various Amerindian delegations from across the Caribbean and South America. Cristo showed me the photo of the first such public ceremony in 1992. It was conducted in a manner visibly different from what I saw during my fieldwork: no ceremonial wear was donned (just jeans, jerseys, and plain hats), and a simple pile of sticks on the ground was burned as SRCC members stood around. Since then, as two of my informants stated (even complained), the ceremony "changes each time it is performed." At one time Cristo would spray participants with water. Then that practice was replaced by the puffing of a cigar. The pile of sticks was replaced by an incense pot, burning incense and tobacco leaves. Costume became more and more elaborate. Silence was replaced by maracas rattling, whooping cries, and the muttering of various sentences from the mainland Cariban language.

The smoke ceremony is designed as a series of offerings and invocations with the intent of praising the earth and protecting its spiritual and physical integrity, remembering the ancestors, blessing the families of the Caribs, and asking for the blessing and guidance of the "Great Spirit," whom the specialists explain is simply "God." Special offerings may also be made to Saint Rose if the ceremony is held on the first of August. Incense is burned. Corn, highlighted as an indigenous food crop, is offered to the fire. A feather is used to fan smoke onto the participants. Tobacco, long a favorite substance of Amerindian shamans, is burned, and a cigar is smoked by the shaman, who then puffs smoke onto the foreheads of the participants as a form of blessing and communion. Cassava bread (symbolic of the labor of the Caribs) and water (symbolizing purity) in a calabash are spatially and symbolically central features as well, in a ceremony that thus embraces the elements of earth, air, fire, and water. The Carib participants carry special spears. Feather headpieces are worn, chests are bare, and loincloths are donned. Maracas are periodically rattled during the ceremony. Necklaces made of seashells and Job's Tears beads, made by the shaman himself, are also worn by the Carib participants. Lastly, four stones are placed around the fire, symbolizing the guardians of the Four Corners of the universe, usually seen as taking the form of different wild animals native to Trinidad.

The material items that make up the "sign equipment" of the ceremony are, from a merely diffusionist standpoint, also indicative of wider processes of networking and representation of indigeneity. According to the relevant Carib specialists, some of the maracas are from Suriname and Mexico; the feather headpieces were gifts of visiting delegations of Amerindians from Suriname and Taínos from New York City. The use of the cigar, and the subsequent development of a cigar ceremony, is acknowledged as an adaptation of what they learned from a visiting delegation of Taínos. Sometimes, Christian elements seem to sneak in, such as beginning and ending the ceremony by making the sign of the cross. Cristo's larger repertoire of Amerindian and other indigenous cultural items includes *zemis* from Puerto Rico, dream catchers from North America, a bullroarer from Australia, and items of clothing from New York's resurgent Caribbean Amerindian groups. Cristo also reads heavily, especially books by or about modern-day American Indians provided by his close friend Vincent La Croix, as well as books on medicinal and shamanic traditions and rituals in South America and books on gemology, magic, and ritual (examples of these include

Cunningham 1997; Schultes and Raffauf 1992; Scott 1991). Those familiar with smudging and other smoke ceremonies in North America will note some similarities.

The adaptation of cultural items, emblems, and practices from abroad implies networking, brokers, and what Chalifoux (1999) calls "global neo-shamanic transfers." La Croix also makes key inputs into the structure of the ceremony. He has taken a leading role in designing the smoke ceremony, advising on its conduct, and adapting North American Indian practices and motifs of a somewhat generic nature, that is, dream catchers, medicine wheels, and other ideas and practices derived from what some call New Age tribes such as the Sun Bear Tribe. On one occasion I sat in on a session where La Croix took Cristo through several books on American Indian smudging ceremonies, descriptions of medicine wheels, and the way a smoke ceremony should be ordered (the number of gatekeepers, stones, and so forth). On another occasion, La Croix actively directed each step of the ceremony, instructing participants on where to stand, what to say, and what to do.

The accumulation of both recently introduced and Native American–inspired items has led to a certain representational stress. The irony is that while credulity on the part of many audiences has been enhanced, with reference to the "authentic indigenous cultural stuff" of the SRCC, Cristo's own personal qualms have been heightened as well. "What, you want me to do some Buffalo Dance next?" he snapped at one fellow broker during discussions about how to present the smoke ceremony. Comments by those who see his costume as similar to that of a Carnival Indian or who have told him that he is "too Negro" to appear dressed as an Indian may have stung a little. Given that the SRCC has been quite successful in obtaining formal recognition from the state, heightened visibility in the wider society, and support from indigenous groups abroad, some of the recent overcommunication of indigenous motifs spearheaded by projects of cultural retrieval may simply diminish as the social need for them declines.

7

Globalizing the Carib

Solidarity, Legitimacy, and Networked Indigeneity

We are ending the millennium in which these people were discovered by
Europeans, destroyed and decimated by Europeans, and now they are
coming out of that, recapturing themselves, their history, their culture and
becoming self sufficient again and moving forward. And they want to start
that right here.
Robert Sabga, high commissioner of Trinidad and Tobago to Canada, speaking
on the occasion of the visit of the Assembly of Manitoba Chiefs to Trinidad
and its Carib Community (quoted in Beharry 1999)

SRCC brokers associate their concept of cultural retrieval with that of cultural
interchange. They define cultural retrieval as the process of rediscovering, relearning, and practicing "the ancient ways," including language, religious practices, and traditional costume. While most SRCC brokers do not speak in terms
of a wholesale continuity of traditions, this does not mean that they abandon all
interest in acquiring or underscoring their authenticity as "indigenous" for the
wider audience and for prospective patrons whose recognition and funding they
seek. Cultural interchange, as a process of cultural retrieval, involves acquiring
indigenous traditions (that they have "lost," as Ricardo says) from other Amerindian communities that are seen as still practicing them. This involves considerable networking on the international front.

International exchange relationships have become a central part of the local
recovery of Amerindian traditions. The implicit premise here is that there was a
homogeneous Carib culture in the Caribbean,[1] mainland or island regardless,
and what other Caribs practice is a survival from ancient times. SRCC brokers
often speak of the founts of authentic Amerindian traditions as being located
either in other times or in other places. By associating themselves with indigenous
groups elsewhere in the Caribbean and the Americas, and in drawing on their
symbolic resources, SRCC members have been aided in enhancing their own
identity and legitimacy as indigenous at the local level (see also Mato 2000:352).
As one of the SRCC brokers wrote in telling terms: "While the members of the
SRCC are striving for recognition by the nationals of Trinidad and Tobago, they
are accepted by all *true Amerindians* from the Mohawk council of tribal people
of Canada and the United States, to the Carib Community of Dominica"

(Almarales 1994:34, emphasis added). How their identification as indigenous is developed and defined is, in part, in and through this internationalized network. The adoption of the "First Nations" designation is a trademark of this internationally networked sense of indigeneity. The concept of cultural interchange also implies, within reasonable limits, a network where local platforms are more or less interchangeable. The principle at work seems to be that what is indigenous *over there* can be indigenous *here* and maybe indigenous *everywhere*.

Owing to the SRCC's international connections, their resulting status is heightened especially in an outward-oriented society such as Trinidad's that values foreign appreciation, global exposure, and international connections as prestigious forms of validation.[2] This international exposure thus feeds back into the local politics of cultural value (Forte 1998f). Thus the dissemination within Trinidad of metropolitan (that is, European and North American) and wider international valorizations of the indigenous further bolsters the value of indigenicity at the national level. That a range of international organizations (such as the Organization of American States, the United Nations' World Intellectual Property Organization, UNESCO, and indigenous organizations such as Canada's Assembly of First Nations, the Assembly of Manitoba Chiefs, and the Federation of Saskatchewan Indian Nations) have all worked with the SRCC in some capacity at some time only serves to heighten the profile of the group within the national politics of cultural value and the cultural politics of national value.

Indigeneity and indigenization make no logical sense without at least implicit reference to a prior notion of "the global," with the active construction and representation of indigeneity implicitly relating, reading, responding, and reacting to processes of globalization (see Robertson 1992:46). The international network of indigenous organizations and communities works to heighten the SRCC's local value and legitimacy, while also helping to sustain the morale and internal cohesion of the SRCC. The SRCC's visible association with an array of international indigenous groups that frequently exercise a presence on the ground in Trinidad helps to offset potential Trinidadian sanctions against individuals who locally might otherwise be seen as primarily not pure or not real Amerindians.

Local-Global Dynamics

It is difficult to overstate the depth and range of powerful affirmations of the importance of indigenous peoples as promoted in various international media over the decades. There has been a growing visual association between celebrities, prominent world leaders, and Amerindian images as presented in international news reports that are usually recycled in Trinidadian media or presented directly via cable television, the Internet, and local televised news.

The question of globalized indigeneity, to the extent that one can meaningfully speak of this, represents an important paradox of indigeneity: seemingly free floating while emphasizing local rootedness. There are at least three main ways we can outline the globalization of indigeneity, and I tend to draw on all three at different points.

First, we can take a world-systemic perspective of how the category emerged in the context of the foundation of the modern world system. I spoke of this already in chapter 1.

Second, I suggest that the globalized spread of motifs, practices, products, ideologies, cosmologies, organizations, media, and support networks of indigeneity have led to the construction of indigeneity as a macro phenomenon, lifted from the confines of any one location and seemingly applicable to any other location. At this level, we are then speaking of an indigenous macrocommunity that is translocal and constitutes a virtual meta-indigencity. Only to the extent that this has an empirical grounding can one speak of interchangeable local platforms and adaptable globalized meanings, motifs, and so forth, ultimately leading to a situation where the network is the indigene. In this regard, it is important to underscore the extent to which the symbols and discourses of indigenous groups in one part of the world can and do impact the symbols and discourses of indigenous groups in another part of the world. Clifford speaks in roughly similar terms using a diaspora metaphor. Noting the second part of the paradox (rootedness), he observes that "tribal or 'Fourth World' assertions of sovereignty and 'first nationhood' do not feature histories of travel and settlement, though these may be part of the indigenous historical experience. They stress continuity of habitation, aboriginality, and often a 'natural' connection to the land" (Clifford 1994:308). Noting the first part of the paradox (transnationalism), he states that "the kinds of transnational alliances currently being forged by Fourth World peoples contain diasporic elements. United by similar claims to 'firstness' on the land and by common histories of decimation and marginality, these alliances often deploy diasporist visions of return to an original place—a land commonly articulated in visions of nature, divinity, mother earth, and the ancestors" (Clifford 1994:309). Thus, "in claiming both autochthony and a specific, transregional worldliness, new tribal forms bypass an opposition between rootedness and displacement" (Clifford 1994:309).

A third way to sketch the globalization of indigeneity is in terms of the international relations of diverse indigenous bodies and movements (Stephen Ryan 1990; Sanders 1997; van de Fliert 1994; Wilmer 1993a, 1993b). These can be witnessed in the popular, though sometimes contradictory, association of indigenous peoples with environmental struggles worldwide, the establishment of regional and international organizations such as the World Council of Indigenous Peoples, the capacity and ability of local indigenous movements to enter international fora and make their cases the subject of world media attention, the development and diffusion of indigenous media, and so forth. As Mato observes, globalizing factors "stimulated and enabled representatives of diverse indigenous peoples to meet each other and begin to develop regular relationships, representations of identity, organizational forms and associated sociopolitical agendas" (2000:351).

There is a further paradox to be considered along the lines of structure and agency. Groups such as the SRCC, when viewed primarily in a local context, appear to demonstrate considerable agency in pursuing and affirming their international connections with other indigenous bodies. Yet Caribbean Amerindian organizations are still largely peripheral to the development of the phenomena outlined above and continue to act as takers of metropolitan trends rather than makers of new global trends. For these organizations, the North American Indian-led international resurgence of indigenous politics and motifs acts as both an inspiration (a fund of materials that can be drawn upon) and the standard by which one's group is to be measured. I would argue that the United States, Canada, and Brazil are most likely the symbolic core of internationalized paradigms of indigeneity, providing perhaps a disproportionate amount of the motifs of indigeneity, the emblematic struggles, and the trademark representations of indigenous issues. To a great extent, Brazil aside, the dominant representations of indigenous issues and perspectives follow the broad contours of the center-periphery tension in the world system, with those indigenous groups that are active in the core countries (groups with financial resources and access to the international mass media) having a disproportionate prominence. Caribbean Amerindian organizations are acutely aware of this unequal structuring of representations of indigeneity at the international level and have largely accommodated themselves to this reality—not just out of necessity, but also by choice given precisely the influential and (in some quarters) prestigious value of associating with North American indigenous bodies.

From Caribs to First Nations

Why do leaders of the SRCC and its affiliated brokers see a need for inserting the SRCC within a globalized network of indigenous bodies? The answers go straight to the heart of the process of the reconstruction of indigeneity in Trinidad. From interviews I conducted with my key informants and specialists in the SRCC, I have gathered a corpus of important statements that explain why leaders and brokers in the SRCC desire these contacts, relations, and exchange visits.

The SRCC's principle of cultural interchange has been a leading force motivating SRCC brokers toward engagement with the wider network of indigenous revivals and political organization. Beyond that, the reason of "greater strength," as my informants have put it, is another major consideration. By this they mean that locally, in Trinidad, they cannot be easily dismissed by the authorities or by commentators when they appear wrapped in the validating presence of visiting Amerindians. Their wish is to put potentially hostile agents in the wider society on alert by showing that they have friends abroad and interested foreign observers concerned for the welfare and progress of Trinidad's Caribs. International recognition is another critical reason that my informants outlined. The active presence and collaboration of outside Amerindian representatives serves to demonstrate that the Arima Caribs are in fact being supported and recognized as Caribs by other recognized Caribs and Amerindians. Moreover, some of my informants have testified that relations with indigenous groups abroad have been a real source of encouragement and moral support, serving as a form of inspiration. Lastly, there is the issue of future promise: always at work among my key informants are visions of possible futures that involve a broader merger between themselves and their Amerindian friends in neighboring territories, such as promoting intermarriage between groups. In addition, there are more mundane reasons that attract SRCC members to the fruits of international association developed by SRCC brokers. As one of my survey respondents indicated, "I like all these Amerindian visitors who come just to visit us, and stay with us, and all the events that happen around them. It cheers us up!"

There are several modes, stages, and partnerships by which the SRCC has inserted itself within larger networks of international indigeneity. The impetus toward greater and more formal contact between the SRCC and other indigenous bodies got under way starting in 1991, when Caribs from across the Caribbean met—along with hundreds of Amerindian organizations from across the Americas—in Ottawa, Canada, for a congress hosted by the Assembly of First Nations of Canada and sponsored in part by the World Council of Indigenous Peoples. Ricardo Bharath and Susan Campo attended; there they met for the first time with their Dominica Carib counterparts, Chief Irvince Auguiste and Sylvanie Burton, as well as their Vincentian counterparts. It was a "Caribbean homecoming," yet staged in Canada. The congress was held November 10–14, 1991, and was titled "Strengthening the Spirit, Beyond 500 Years" (AFN 1991a, 1991b, 1991c).[3] Many of Susan Campo's subsequent contacts and experiences stemmed from this event, as she later spent a year in Saskatchewan, Canada, at the Federated Indian College along with other Caribbean Amerindian scholarship recipients, among whom were students from Dominica. Susan subsequently visited the Dominica Carib Territory. As Ricardo explained, he is often tempted to give up, but events such as these help to renew his resolve "to continue developing and strengthening the Carib Community." The knowledge of being part of a global network of friends in the "indigenous struggle," as he put it, is a key source of "inspiration and motivation."

Ricardo also found that he could place the SRCC within a wider perspective, noting that "many indigenous peoples around the Americas face many of the same problems that we do: the loss of language and religion, the passing of traditions, the lack of interest of youths, and the lack of lands." In establishing these linkages, SRCC brokers also introduce a certain degree of transference, that is, the substitutability of indigenous histories and experiences across locales. Fitting the SRCC within this wider framework also served to diminish Ricardo's anxiety over proving Amerindian-ness, lessening his personal desire to dress up to rigid expectations of continuity and notions of authenticity as frozen culture, while also spurring him to analytically reframe indigeneity not so much as a static sense of being but as a problem. This may be one reason for Ricardo's repeated statements to the press, and researchers like myself, focusing on themes of cultural loss and disinterest in traditions. In addition, these statements might also help to evoke sympathy and support, deriving from a "last of the Mohicans" effect—not that I know this to be done deliberately for that reason. Perhaps Ricardo would be diminishing his own role as a leader seeking to raise the Caribs from oblivion if he did not see the situation he faces as one of potential extinction.

Another critical venue has been the Caribbean Festival of the Arts (Carifesta), a regional inter-state platform for the performing arts, that the government of Trinidad hosted in 1992 and 1995, the former occasion combining with celebrations of the Columbian Quincentenary and with a strong focus on the region's Amerindian peoples. The event in 1992 came to be known as the First Gathering of the region's indigenous peoples; it was held in Arima and hosted by the Santa Rosa Carib Community. In that same period the SRCC joined the Caribbean Organisation of Indigenous People (COIP). The year 1992, in which both Carifesta V (August 22–28) and the Columbian Quincentenary occurred, was in many ways a watershed for Caribbean Amerindian revivalism, combined as it was with a number of complementary currents. Officials in the states of the Commonwealth Caribbean had certainly decided that Carifesta V would "focus on indigenous art and culture," with Arima acting as the locus of what was intended to be a newly created permanent site, "a village of indigenous peoples" (*Caricom Perspective* 1992:26). Planners for Caricom's Caribbean Events Committee stressed the global value of its chosen themes for 1992: "The world will only watch, listen and take us seriously, if we lock into international themes which are of interest and value almost everywhere to almost everyone in the global village.... Moreover we will only be able to make an impact on the power centers of the world if we can link our thrust to dominant international concerns, ... [hence] the strategy to use 1992 as a platform for making a meaningful and lasting impact on the world community" (*Caricom Perspective* 1991b:48). As a means of achieving these goals, the Caricom planners highlighted, among others, the "Encounter between Worlds Programme" and Carifesta V itself. The Trinidadian government had also committed itself to showcasing the Arima Caribs, as indicated in its 1990 instrument of recognition of the SRCC, where it explicitly stated that support for the SRCC came "into higher relief and sharper focus as the country prepares to celebrate Columbus' Quincentennial in October 1992." Activists in various Caribbean Amerindian bodies and territories also were conscious of how "renewed interest in the fate of the Carib people had coincided with the quincentennial of Christopher Columbus'... voyage to the Caribbean," providing an "opportune moment in modern Carib history to reiterate decisively the collective commitment to preserve their cultural traditions" (Gregoire and associates 1996:108). Hulme also argued that the Columbian "quincentenary and its associated events may well have raised . . . [the Caribs'] own consciousness of their place in history" (1992:214).

In 1993, for the United Nations' International Year of the World's Indigenous People, the Trinidadian government's newly formed Amerindian Project Committee helped the Santa Rosa Carib Community to host the so-called Second Gathering in Arima. The third was recently held in 2000, still with the sponsorship of the Trinidad government. In this swirl of events and international exposure, by 1995 SRCC leaders began to publicly state that the proper way to refer to them was as "First Nations." Moreover, the expectation within the SRCC was that visits from indigenous bodies abroad would strengthen the group internally. Queen Justa Werges stated at the Second Gathering that Amerindian visitors from across the Caribbean should establish "a strong and lasting bond" to help the younger generations to be "proud of their ancestors whom Columbus met here" (Almandoo 1993:1).

In June 1997, the Arima Caribs hosted a visiting delegation from the Dominica Carib Territory, arriving as a result of the landmark "Gli-Gli Carib Canoe Project" that involved the building of a large Carib canoe that was then sailed down the Caribbean islands and into the Orinoco River in an attempt to symbolically relink the region's Amerindian communities by a replication of traditional Carib means. This voyage was the subject of a recent BBC documentary[4] that also featured Arima's Caribs; it was also featured in reports in the international media (Freeman 1999; Neggers 1997). In the film the leader of the Dominica Carib crew, Jacob Frederick, said of his encounter with the SRCC, "We are meeting our own flesh and blood . . . they are just like us . . . this trip shows that blood is thicker than water . . . blood is calling." When I met Jacob Frederick in Dominica he and others reiterated this theme that the SRCC members "are like family." Former chief Faustilus Frederick, who traveled to Trinidad in 1995 for Carifesta VI, also told me, "They're just like us—they look like us." Jacob Frederick's constant emphasis during the Gli-Gli visit was on "reviving the culture," "reviving the language," renewing connections, and "going back to the source," which ultimately meant the Orinoco region of Guyana and Venezuela. In the documentary the SRCC was featured as a proud, large, thriving community; the leaders appeared forceful in how they spoke on camera; the Dominicans were greeted under the statue of Hyarima, with Cristo Adonis appearing in his feather headdress with maracas, bead necklaces, and loincloth.

I attended two screenings of the film in Arima, one held in my apartment in late July 1999 and another held under Cristo's *ajoupa* shortly thereafter. On the latter occasion I filmed the members of the SRCC watching themselves as they appeared on screen. They seemed engrossed and studied themselves seriously. Afterwards, as the film ended, one of the ladies exclaimed, "When people come we have nothing to show. You see like in Guyana, they have dances and dresses and music. But when people come to see us, we just look like everyone else." It was at that point that Cristo asserted, "Don't worry—by this time next year we will have traditional clothing," which is a telling statement about creating something in the future and yet classing it as traditional, and doing so as encouraged by wider contacts.

The media response to the Gli-Gli in Trinidad was very instructive in terms of explicitly endorsing Carib cultural revitalization. An editorial in the *Trinidad Guardian* (online edition, 1997), while restating some of the older tropes of dwindling Caribs, apparently saw these renewed linkages as encouraging:

> Hopefully . . . the journey will spark a resurgence of interest in Carib culture. . . . We expect that during the next five days, the visiting Caribs of Dominica, where a 3,000 strong community exists, will spend some time with members of the local Carib community at Arima where the aboriginal culture survives but their numbers have dwindled to a few dozen persons with "some Carib blood in their veins." The visit   may well stimulate the local Carib community to renew their appeal to the Government for a parcel of land on the Blanchisseuse Road where they would like to establish a permanent settlement.

The media presence was critical in publicizing if not creating the significance of the event for the wider national audience. Rostant (1997) in fact observed that the Gli-Gli canoe was met by a crowd that consisted mostly of members of the local Trinidadian media.

The Dominica Caribs hold a special attraction for the SRCC, in large part for being another island community that has faced many of the same problems of cultural loss and, if I can put it this way, overexposure to the modern world. My research in Dominica, centered on Dominica Carib connections with Trinidad, revealed that overall no fewer than thirty-seven Dominica Caribs visited Trinidad, on at least ten separate visits from 1992 to 1997. One broad suggestion of the impact of these visits is the fact that more Dominica Caribs visited Arima than there are people in the active core of the Santa Rosa Carib Community. Apart from the Gli-Gli project, in October 1997 a five-member team of Dominica Caribs, funded by the British Development Division and the Caribbean Association of Local Government Authorities, spent two weeks in Arima. The interests of this group included canoe making, weaving, women, and politics. What I also discovered in Dominica during my research trip in September of 1998 is that those who had visited Trinidad retained strong affective ties to the Arima Caribs. It was in Dominica that I first encountered the strong view that the two communities should merge, that intermarriage should be promoted, and that population exchange should occur.

The Venezuela-Guyana region of the Orinoco is a key source of cultural and historical interest for SRCC brokers. As an example, in a proposal submitted to the embassy of Venezuela in Trinidad in 1990 (Harris 1990b), the SRCC's researchers suggested "renewing our Amerindian links with Venezuela," with a visit to a Cariña community to "strengthen . . . traditional skills in food and drink preparation and handicraft" and to "restart the custom" of having Warao Indians visit south Trinidad for trade and to renew rituals they practiced in Trinidad. The idea was that the Warao "may be interested in establishing a sales outlet for their traditional hammocks and basketry in south Trinidad. . . . In this way persons of partial Warao descent, and the Trinidad public at large, could build a living relationship with Warao culture." In line with this theme, delegations of Amerindians from Guyana have stayed at the SRCC headquarters on several occasions (in 1988, 1992, 1993, 1995, and again in August 2002; see Forte 2002d), sometimes for weeks at a time, to teach the Lokono language and traditional weaving skills, and to produce handicraft items that have since been incorporated into the SRCC's own repertoire of items for public display of their traditions.[5] As Guyana represents an important source of "original Amerindian culture" to some people in the Arima Carib Community, Ricardo visited the Carib settlements of the Pomeroon River area of northwestern Guyana. Ricardo is the main specialist in relations with the Guyanese Amerindians, and he is kept abreast of indigenous issues in Guyana via regular receipt of the newsletter of the Guyanese Organization of Indigenous Peoples.

Apart from the SRCC and state institutions, other local private actors got in on the regionalized Amerindian revivalist scene. In November 1997, a private Baha'i organization in Trinidad, Harmony in Diversity,[6] sponsored a much-publicized international gathering of indigenous representatives in the SRCC Centre in Arima, with a delegate from as far away as Australia, and with representatives of newly established self-described "restorationist" Puerto Rican Taíno groups based in New York. Once more, this event achieved prominence in the press and served to widen SRCC international contacts and legitimacy as a representative body. The relationship between the SRCC and Taíno revivalist organizations based in the United States is still a relatively novel one, having emerged only with the staging of this November 1997 conference.

Harmony in Diversity invited two Taíno representatives to Trinidad: Daniel Waconax Rivera and Kacique René Çibánakan, of the Taíno Nation of the Antilles (see Kearns 1999–2000a, 1999–2000b). Çibánakan has immersed himself in learning shamanic knowledge and traditions and shared these with his like-minded Arima counterpart, Cristo Adonis. There were two platforms for the interchange of cultural ideas and the forging of personal ties between the revivalist side of the SRCC and such neo-Taíno groups. One was the performance of the smoke ceremony. This is a ritual that Çibánakan was apparently keen about. In the process both Çibánakan and Cristo adopted some of each other's practices. For example, the cigar and tobacco leaves have now become a central feature of Cristo's smoke ceremony, and he attributes this to Çibánakan's influence. Also, Cristo has incorporated Taíno *zemis* in his personal repertoire of shamanic items. Moreover, both men have an interest in promoting the revival of Amerindian ceremonial aesthetics, such as traditional wear and body adornments, and in reclaiming Amerindian names. The second platform was more abstract and concerned the issue of the "race of indigeneity." Both Çibánakan and Cristo have felt some of the suspicion that comes from feeling and claiming an indigenous heritage and identity while appearing in the eyes of others as black. Both have rejected the racial purity approach to indigeneity, noting how "many of the racially pure actually care little for their culture," in Cristo's words.

One of the more momentous events to have occurred during my fieldwork was the arrival in November 1999 of a delegation from the Assembly of Manitoba Chiefs (AMC), led by Grand Chief Rod Bushie, who spent a week in Trinidad proposing a wide array of economic investments, as well as developing working ties with the SRCC under the rubric of establishing a proposed World Indigenous Assembly in Trinidad (Beharry 1999; Gooding 1999; Jarette 1999; Milne 1999).[7] This delegation had a tremendous impact in the local media, and the delegation ended up visiting with almost every prominent businessman and politician in Trinidad (Beharry 1999) Grand Chief Bushie indicated that Trinidad was chosen as a destination given the historic links between Canada and Trinidad and his own exposure to Trinidadian teachers in Catholic mission schools, and not specifically because of the presence of the SRCC in Trinidad. Indeed, the primary aims of the Manitoba chiefs' visit to Trinidad during November 19–26, 1999, seem to have been political and economic, that is, establishing ties with Third World states and seeking investment opportunities. The Trinidadian press reported that the Assembly of Manitoba Chiefs was interested in investing in steel mills, petrochemicals, the oil industry, soft drinks, hotels, and casinos. The meetings between the Manitoba chiefs and the Arima Caribs served to provide some excitement within the community and a further impetus for organization and promotion of Carib traditions in Trinidad, heightening local attention to and respect for the SRCC, and encouraging if not galvanizing leaders of the SRCC in their revival efforts. Indeed, the year following the visit ushered in an intense series of activities and projects in the SRCC such as hosting the Third Gathering of Indigenous Peoples and the successful dialogue with the prime minister on the questions of lands, funds, and a national commemorative day.

For the visit of the Manitoba chiefs, when the presentation of maximum numbers and the papering over of internal differences was paramount within the SRCC, one could see an unusual mélange of the various representational faces of the SRCC in one place at the same time: the president (Ricardo) in his crisp white shirt and black pants; the shaman (Cristo) in street clothes and wearing a straw hat with a feather; elderly ladies dressed in the pink dresses they would wear for the Santa Rosa Festival; men wearing Amerindian-styled decorative items; the singing of *parang*; the performance of a smoke ceremony; and a long-standing rival of the Carib Queen acting as her representative. Around the SRCC and within the SRCC Centre, the combination of elements made for an almost dizzying atmosphere, electrified by the ceaseless flashing of cameras: the presence of local PNM stalwarts at a time when the SRCC was being courted by the ruling UNC; the various local speakers' applause for the "reuniting" of Canadian First

Nations and Carib "First Peoples"; and the pride expressed by some local speakers and artists in listing "Carib" in their inventory of mixed ancestry. Events such as these tend to heighten the public value and legitimacy of the SRCC. The way the SRCC manifests these connections on the walls of its community center tells a similar story.

Upon entering the SRCC Centre, one is faced with walls and a small stage adorned with various Amerindian artifacts. Some of these pertain to Trinidad's Caribs. Others, however, serve as traces of encounters and exchanges between the Arima Caribs and their counterparts in the Dominica Carib Territory, friends in Guyana, and even an Australian connection. One sees photographs of Chief Irvince Auguiste visiting in Arima, engraved calabashes from Dominica, baskets from Dominica and their local replicas made as a result of classes held by one of the Dominica Carib visitors in Arima, small replicas of canoes, and a number of other items. These photos and objects are graphic traces of a network of SRCC associations and are of interest by either being incorporated into religious ceremonies or serving as a symbolic and material reservoir surrounding members whenever they meet in the SRCC Centre, encasing them quite literally in a regionalized Amerindian identity.

The Regional and International Articulation of Caribbean Indigeneity

The foundation of the Caribbean Organisation of Indigenous People (COIP) weaves together Caribbeanwide and North American indigenous activism in important ways. COIP was formed in 1988 and included the indigenous communities of Belize, Dominica, St. Vincent, and Guyana (*Caricom Perspective* 1991a; Palacio 1989:49; Wilk and Chapin 1989:44). It was led by a Belizean Garifuna anthropologist, Dr. Joseph Palacio.

In 1984 two leaders of Canada's Federation of Saskatchewan Indian Nations (FSIN) traveled to the eastern Caribbean and Belize to "initiate dialogue with indigenous peoples"; upon their return to Canada they encouraged the Canadian University Services Overseas (CUSO)—which Palacio says then acted as "the prime mover"—and Oxfam Canada, USA and U.K. to sponsor a conference held August 13–17, 1987, titled "Caribbean Indigenous Revival: Towards Greater Recognition and Development," which led to the founding of COIP (Palacio 1992:68, 69). Endorsement of the conference by various international organizations was seen by the participants as part of "the overall emphasis that the world community has given to the struggle of the indigenous peoples throughout the Americas within the past few years," according to Palacio (1992:68). A local awareness of the globalized valorization of indigenous struggles appears to be at work here.

One of COIP's objectives was to "seek out" all Caribbean Amerindian communities and to have each of them recognize each other (Barreiro 1992:352). Among COIP's proposals was the plan for "exchange visits during which indigenous peoples would learn skills from each other that would broaden their own self-discovery" (Palacio 1992:70, emphasis added)—this is another way of stating the cultural interchange concept. COIP's role also involved producing an "inventory of information on cultural aspects of indigenous groups of the region" while also seeking to "mobilize groups at the local level through projects, preferably income-generating activities" and to "establish a communication network among the various indigenous groups, as well as nonindigenous solidarity groups" (Wilk and Chapin 1989:44). COIP was the first international indigenous body with which the SRCC became actively involved.

Where the Arima Caribs are concerned, the work of the FSIN also had a direct impact, as the SRCC's youth representative was awarded a one-year scholarship to study administration and management of Amerindian communities at the Indian Federated College (SIFC) in Regina, Saskatchewan. Susan Campo was one of several Caribbean Amerindian students to study there for the Columbian Quincentenary, the 1992–1993 academic year. According to Susan, this scholarship was a rare opportunity for foreign Amerindian students insofar as the SIFC faces financial constraints. The increased funding was made available due to the fact that 1992 was the quincentenary year, followed by 1993, which the United Nations declared the International Year for the World's Indigenous People. The program of Amerindian studies, a one-year diploma course, focused on the administration and management of Amerindian communities, with courses in computer science, marketing, and history, among other subjects.

Academics have played a leading role in connecting and promoting Amerindian communities at the regional level. In addition, academics have played a role in fostering identification with an indigenous heritage and in identifying certain heritages as indigenous. Internationally trained academics such as Joseph Palacio have played key roles in the regionalized revival, and the list includes Dr. José Barreiro at Cornell University (and his work with Taínos in Cuba) and Dr. George Norton in Guyana (who also headed COIP). Perhaps unsurprisingly, formal venues such as conferences have been one of the primary vehicles chosen by academics in organizing regional connections. Barreiro (1997a:5) describes his own attempts at encouraging families in eastern Cuba to gather in a conference of people with Indian backgrounds in order to exchange knowledge.

The United Nations has played a central role in the global dissemination and valorization of indigenous issues and causes, and the 1990s witnessed a proliferation of indigenous-related public events mounted by the United Nations internationally. The United Nations' International Year of the World's Indigenous People (1993) was promoted as a "landmark event" for indigenous peoples' struggles and was designed as a "major public awareness campaign" on an international level.[9] "Perhaps most important," United Nations announcements stated, "indigenous peoples themselves will be given a platform to convey their message and to promote an understanding of their cultures and way of life." The year was officially cited as the beginning of a "new partnership," encouraging the development of new relationships between states, indigenous peoples, and the international community. The United Nations declared its intention to "establish networks of indigenous organizations and communities for the sharing of information and experience" (again, resembling the SRCC's and COIP's view of cultural interchange), as well as stating that it would promote "an international trade fair for indigenous products." In the Trinidadian case, the government's Amerindian Project Committee was formed partly as a response to the United Nations urging member states to establish such committees to commemorate the international year, encouraging even states without a defined indigenous population to do so (see UN 1992). United Nations agencies have thus sought to play a role in the process of cultural preservation: "strengthening cultural identity" of indigenous peoples is an established goal, setting up networks of indigenous communities and organizations is another established goal; and the "right to be different," the "right to development," and the "right to revitalize" of indigenous people were made into matters of international concern and responsibility. The United Nations' declarations of the international year and decade, as Mato observes, were not only important "symbolic advancements," but they also provided "further opportunities for representatives of these [indigenous] peoples to meet and develop their representations of a shared identity and to organize and promote their agendas at national and transnational levels" (2000:351).

These trends at the wider regional and international levels have a generative cultural impact on the ground. In Guyana, involvement with COIP inspired the formation of the Guyanese Organisation of Indigenous Peoples (GOIP) (Fox 1996:88). This in turn fed back into the wider Caribbean arena, with GOIP developing its own connections beyond COIP. Another example of the locally transformative and even creative impact of the regionally organized Amerindian revival is provided by St. Vincent. There has been an increase in pride in Amerindian heritage since the visits by Belizean Garifunas began in the 1980s (Roberts 1996:17). The Council for the Development of the Carib Community (CDCC) also emerged from the August 1987 conference in St. Vincent that led to the founding of COIP, with the CDCC being created in 1988 (Roberts 1996:18). Visiting delegations found St. Vincent wanting in terms of Carib cultural distinctiveness. Sebastian Cayetano, a Garifuna who visited in the 1980s, spoke of the "cultural drought" in St. Vincent: "here were my people of the same kin, blood and ancestry. Biologically, they were true Garinagu, but culturally they had lost everything. It was a sad, mournful experience . . . that such a situation could have befallen our people" (quoted in Roberts 1996:31). While visits helped to revitalize identification among the so-called Yellow Caribs of northern St. Vincent, delegations of Belizeans also helped to revive Black Carib identification in places such as Greggs in southern St. Vincent. As affirmed by one researcher, "until about a decade ago most Vincentians did not regard residents of Greggs as

Caribs. It was not until . . . the 1980s when the Garifuna from Belize visited St. Vincent that many Vincentians became aware of the Black Caribs living in Greggs" (Roberts 1996:34).

These wider processes of international networking, regionally organized revivals of indigenous identification, and their impacts on the ground in each territory are still subject to certain limitations. Among these limitations the two primary ones appear to be metropolitan orientations, on the one hand, and preoccupations with race on the other.[10] In terms of the first, there are some tendencies to favor alliances with North American Indians more than with Caribbean Amerindian groups. A chief of the Dominica Carib Territory told me in an interview that he was more interested in cultivating ties, exchange, and even trade relations with wealthy American Indian groups in the United States (mentioning specifically the Mashantucket Pequots, owners of the Foxwoods Casino). Indeed, he wondered aloud as to what could be gained, financially and in terms of economic development, from deepening ties with Trinidad's SRCC compared to deepening ties with U.S. Indian organizations.

Race has emerged as another critical barrier in regional Amerindian organization. In the Gli-Gli documentary mentioned previously, we see Jacob Frederick arriving in Guyana and declaring, "We meet as Caribs . . . to share our one-ness." The Gli-Gli's Guyanese hosts insist on calling the Dominican Caribs "Black Caribs." Frederick, in an aside with the camera, states, "It's true, we are a mixed race, a mixed breed of people." In a short space of time (in the film), Frederick is thus forced to go from saying "we're exactly the same" to privately wondering "they might or might not accept us as Carib." There is no gainsaying the fact that many Amerindians involved in both national and regional organizations harbor decidedly racialized notions of identity and culture. There is an enduring legacy of defining a true or pure Amerindian in racial terms, that is, in terms of phenotype. What is feared by some Dominica Carib leaders is the possibility that wider regional interconnections may validate and strengthen the position of the blacker members of the Dominica Carib Territory. The result of these stances is that regional organization can become fractured along racial lines as well.

The increased diffusion of North American emphases on blood quanta in the measurement of authentic indigenous identity and the increasing friction within American Indian bodies along the lines of race and around the question of barring black Indians from federal entitlements (see Glaberson 2001; Sturm 1998) finds resonance with certain Caribbean Amerindian leaders who are exposed to such discourses. Indeed, as Sturm (1998) points out, indigeneity runs up against the issue of blackness almost everywhere in the Americas where the plantation economy left its cultural mark. While debates rage around whether an Amerindian mixed with black should be considered indigenous, one rarely hears any such debate about those who are offspring of European and Amerindian unions.

With respect to the network of relationships between Caribbean and North American indigenous bodies, we have seen that there is a differential in terms of influence in the shaping of indigenous representations at the global level. While I have witnessed the adaptation of items imported from North American Indian groups into the Caribbean, I cannot say that I have seen the reverse happen. Furthermore, while North American Indian organizations include those that own casinos or are seen as important or internationally prominent in political terms, such as Canada's Assembly of First Nations, and others that have tertiary educational institutions attached to them and have the ability to periodically offer international scholarships, I do not see Caribbean Amerindian groups having anywhere near as prominent a voice or "muscle" as their North American friends have. In other words, the so-called development gap and center-periphery relations pertaining to the inter-state system are echoed just as much in the distinction between indigenous people in the North American core and the Caribbean periphery.

Conclusion

Reengineering Indigeneity

The time of becoming the same is also the time of claiming to be different. The time of modernizing is also the time of inventing tradition as well as traditionalizing innovations; of revaluing old categories and recategorizing new values
Stanley J. Tambiah (1994:440)

Indigeneity in Trinidad and Tobago as a question that involves the problem of presence lies at the heart of this work. The question of indigeneity as a presence is one that I have endeavored to treat cautiously, not in terms of strict continuities of a cultural kind but as part of that "repertory set down by colonial experience" and later refurbished by nationalist historiography, the media, the educational system, the SRCC, and a wide variety of other actors and institutions situated in Trinidad and abroad. This repertory consists of a set of discourses, labels, objects, and practices that at different points in time, for different reasons, and in the hands of different interests have been marked as indigenous traditions. The data referred to in this work underline the presence of the Amerindian in both colonialist and nationalist projects. Yet indigeneity poses a problem in the anthropology of the Caribbean, for even while continuities and survivals of the transplanted cultures of Africa and Asia have been accepted by some, virtually no one in the social sciences (until very recently) applied the same notions to Caribbean Amerindians. After all, the truism is that the reason for importing vast numbers of African slaves and Asian indentured laborers was that Amerindians were either wiped out (thus not present) or so severely diminished as to be a negligible entity. The supposed continuity of the transplanted was thus a function of the discontinuity of the indigenous. The anthropological uniqueness of the Caribbean was, in part, a function of this perceived discontinuity of the indigenous. Even among anthropologists studying indigenous peoples, only a handful have ever conducted research in Caribbean island territories, possibly reflecting what Field observed as "anthropologists' preference for describing the 'most Indian' sociocultural areas" (1994:234). Indigeneity in Caribbean territories such as Trinidad and Tobago thus poses theoretical problems on top of significant ethnographic and historiographic challenges.

At the outset I asked: Why does "Carib" still exist as a category and as an acceptable identification in Trinidad? I then broke that question down into four subquestions: (1) What were, and what are, the conditions that make possible the reproduction of Carib as a history and an identity? (2) When, how, and why did Carib emerge and come to be canonized as a key label in the Caribbean? (3) Who was responsible for the ascription of this label, what were the responses, and how did the results of these interactions (codified as texts, reproduced as doxic interpretations) shape subsequent interactions? (4) What value does Caribness hold, and to whom, when, and why?

In addressing these questions I have argued that we could characterize the processes and conditions involved as a reengineering of indigeneity, focusing on the multiple and divergent ideas, interests, institutions, and actors involved in establishing, altering, and promoting key conceptions of the indigenous presence in Trinidad and its value. Of critical importance is the recognition that neither one process (whether reinvention, articulation, reinterpretation, and so forth), nor just one set of actors and institutions, nor one historical characterization (continuity, discontinuity, survival, revival) suffices in explaining this phenomenon. Actors within this framework include a wide array of cultural brokers acting on behalf of diverse material and ideational interests and engaged in reinterpreting, objectifying, and articulating traditions, within a wider social organization of tradition defined through and shaped by various political economic contexts. Moreover, indigeneity is a problematic concern at the intersection of colonialism, nationalism, and contemporary globalization, exhibiting the following tendencies: (1) colonialist conceptions and ascriptions in relation to native reformulations, and vice versa; (2) constructions of a national sense of indigeneity as being the truly local (residence principle), in relation to an ethnic sense of indigeneity as being those who were here first (precedence principle); and (3) the reinvention of the Carib as Trinidad's "First Nations." Tradition, lying conceptually at the crossroads of culture and history (Field 1994:232), while spotlighting identity and ritual as practice (Ortner 1994:398), provides a key conceptual entry point even while posing a problem that needs to be explained. The SRCC was perhaps the most obvious ethnographic entry point for my study, although with the variety of actors and institutions with interests vested in promoting Carib history and heritage, perhaps the media, schools, the church, or state bodies could have served just as well as entry points.

Reengineering is not advanced as a new theory; rather, I present it as affording one way (compare Sissons 1993) of undertaking an overdue consolidation of certain established concepts, while emphasizing particular facets that seem most suitable for bringing to light many of the key features of a challenging ethnographic case. One way that I describe reengineering is as comprising multiple processes making a certain identity possible—meaning how an identity is made to seem valid and valuable—and the wider ways in which an identity is communicated (or made communicable) and understood. This is another way of seeing the indigenous as not just, or even primarily, self-defining, self-constructing, or self-inventing. I often align myself with what Rogers refers to as the "dialogic coproduction of 'indigenous' rhetoric," involving a selective interaction with national and global contexts (1996:79), although I stress that this is rarely a coproduction between equals in terms of power. I prefer "reengineering" as a term since it suggests structure, design, and purpose in response to a problem, while also implying prior action and thus history.

For analytical purposes, I have suggested that reengineering could be seen as comprising three axes: (1) structure-agency—processes of social interaction within a certain social organization, the impact of these processes on the cultural system, and vice versa, and the role of brokers in these processes; (2) past-present—cultural processes referring to history and its perceived distillates (texts, rituals, and so forth) and shaped by historical processes; and (3) local-global—the stretch of social processes and organizational and representational practice.

Starting with the first axis, structure agency, I have outlined how the concept of the Carib achieved and maintains a canonical status that ultimately serves as the wider framework of ideas and symbols with which groups such as the SRCC have had to work—this forming a part of what Archer (1988) has called the "cultural system" that is used and produced by material and ideational interests in the process of sociocultural interaction. My emphasis is thus on interests always having been vested in the creation, dissemination, perpetuation, or even elimination of particular representations. Furthermore, I wish to underline the fact that no one group or individual was, or is, capable of inventing the Carib in isolation from a wide array of institutions, social interactions, and various interests. I further locate the development of the multiple meanings and symbolic values of the Carib within the history of colonial power relations in the Caribbean. What I call the political economy of tradition is a means of referring to the way representations are structured and valued.

The point here is to emphasize the ways in which representations are articulated within the specific social contexts that produce them (compare Rogers 1996:78), contexts that are significantly determined by political economic forces above and beyond any one set of human actors. Like Rogers (1996:108), I have sought to outline the "corpus of raw materials" from which indigenous identity is constructed, that "wide vocabulary of imagery" from which actors choose in order to make different statements in different contexts. I have demonstrated in previous chapters how the institutional context imposed certain values on particular types and combinations of these images of the Carib, making certain choices appealing and viable and regularizing the patterning of such choices along institutional lines (compare Rogers 1996:109). This emphasis serves to foreground the wider social institutions and social processes enmeshed in the (re)production and valuation of Carib indigeneity, by teaching, mediating, publicizing, politicizing, rewarding, and funding its representation. There is a complex interplay between forces of ascription and choice, involving social power and cultural legitimacy.

Looking at just two bodies as an example, the state and the SRCC, we can see this interplay at work in the regulation of Carib indigeneity. Agents working at the state level take the SRCC's embeddedness in Arima, its international legitimation, and the utility of history in nation building as parameters for recognizing and rewarding the SRCC, as the state began to do in earnest from 1990 onward. SRCC leaders regulate Carib indigeneity in similar and different ways, grounding legitimate membership in the group (ideally) in terms of the kinship ties and residential location of prospective members, or in terms of commitment to the Santa Rosa Festival, while representing the group externally by wrapping it within international indigenous recognition, documentary support, and the place of the Caribs within constructions of Arimian identity and history. Tradition is also at the focus of SRCC brokers' representations, because dominant conceptions of racial purity in place especially since British colonialism cannot be used to validate Carib identity as continuous. The key agents at the center of this project, the various cultural brokers and patrons, are those especially knowledgeable specialists and intermediaries or individuals with material and political power. It is agency at this level especially that has been responsible for the Carib revival as a phenomenon registered in the wider society.

The dialogue between past and present constitutes the second axis of reengineering; it is an especially vital one since SRCC brokers ground Carib indigeneity within a concept of tradition that perforce refers to and is conditioned by history and the writing of history. The SRCC's main platforms—maintenance, reclamation, translation, revival/retrieval, and cultural interchange—are all rooted in a historical framework used to talk about the origins and development of Carib traditions. Multiple practices are put forth by SRCC brokers as embodying Carib indigeneity. Each of these operates within a particular perception of history. Ricardo's representation of indigeneity goes back not so much to a precolonial Arima as to the mission and is based on what he presents as long-established rituals and practices (that is, the Santa Rosa Festival). Cristo is keen to represent an indigeneity that goes back to precolonial times, yet he does so via innovative ceremonies (that is, the smoke ceremony). Ricardo defines his practice as that of maintenance; Cristo defines his practice as that of revival or retrieval. The two involve different historical moves. Maintenance (added to what SRCC brokers call reclamation) consists of a set of practices, rituals, and so forth, around which a boundary is then drawn or reaffirmed, a boundary that is labeled "Carib" or another suitable cognate of "indigenous." In the case of retrieval and revival, the boundary is first drawn, and then there begins a search for materials to fill in the contents.

"Carib" predates the SRCC, a temporality that should not be sidelined in social theory, as Archer (1988) has stressed. Above and prior to the SRCC, we have to recall how colonial elites in their interactions with Caribbean natives set about establishing a field of signification that would condition the deployment of the label "Carib." Carib thus became an authoritative label, a loaded category that has endured and acquired new meanings, thereby effecting a transition from invention to convention. Its authority is established and reproduced via repetition, reenactment, and ritual displays, especially when sanctioned or authored by powerful institutions and patrons. Carib ascription is a European reinvention that was institutionalized, especially during colonialism, and later reinterpreted in the wake of nationalism and current processes of cultural globalization. Therefore, I agree with Field (1994:231) that when discussing particular indigenous groups we need to foreground the way groups are named and the way certain markers are historically constituted and deployed. In broader terms, we can argue that "'Indians' did not live in the Americas until Europeans invented the term and its social positioning" (Field 1994:231), and indeed, "the idea of indigeneity took its present form from Europe's colonial project in the New World. . . . its source is to be found in the pivotal moment of European arrival" (Beckett 1996:5).

Taking a large view of the historical contexts of the political economy of tradition, we can sketch the Carib presence along a particular path, as shown in figure 4. This illustration is intended only to demonstrate some of the key historical landmarks and political economic processes within which one can locate the ways in which the Carib presence has been interpreted, articulated, disseminated, asserted, and organized. At the same time, the sketch does not show a linear continuity, as marked by the intersection of the two trajectories, since I am not equating or conflating Carib military and political power or the demographic presence of Caribs with subsequent symbolic representations of Caribness. The vertical cutoff line is meant to emphasize the fact that from the late 1700s onward, Amerindians in Trinidad became marginalized, by and large, in social, political, and economic terms, especially outside of Arima, even while representations of the symbolic centrality of the Amerindian historical presence (especially within Arima) began to take off through the 1800s. In other words, while the apparent numbers and power of Amerindians in Trinidad declined in gross terms, the power of symbolic references to, and political reinterpretations of, Amerindians as an image underwent an upsurge—the loop shown is thus actually an overlap of the sociopolitical and the symbolic,[1] the latter waxing where the former is waning. In the case of the SRCC, these developments have been of critical significance in providing them with what Rogers calls that wide vocabulary of images and the corpus of raw materials from which they select in defining and representing Carib heritage. Of course, as with some of my other diagrams, this one also creates an illusion of symmetry, by squeezing three hundred years of history (left half) into the same space as thirty years (right half).

The third axis of reengineering consists of the local-global continuum. Like those writing in the world systems school, I also prefer to see globalization as a process that has been occurring at least for the past five hundred years, hence colonialism can be subsumed under that term (see Forte 1998e; Wallerstein 1998). As argued elsewhere, it is out of the emergent world system that indigeneity as a concept and concern has come to life (compare Geschiere and Meyer 1998:604). The interesting consequence of this is that the label "Carib,"

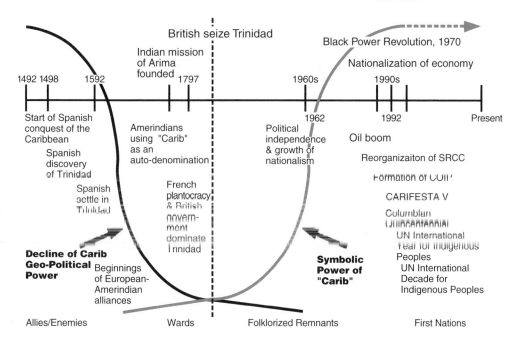

Figure 4. An overview of the political economy of Carib presence.

denoting an indigenous identity presumably located in a particular place, was first created through early colonial processes and was only subsequently localized in Trinidad, and later in Arima. Indeed, in the process of the early European search for the Carib, the Carib was repeatedly localized and delocalized, as witnessed by the sometimes intense disagreement in imperial and ecclesiastic circles over whether or not Caribs really were in Trinidad. Subsequently, the figure of the Amerindian, later reinterpreted as Carib, was emplaced in Arima in particular, so much so that the notion of "Arima, home of the Caribs" has achieved doxic status.

This type of interplay between locality and globality creates the kind of tension addressed by Robotham (1998:308) when he argued that identities in the Caribbean have not successfully taken the form of "autochthonous, primordial fundamentalisms" as much as they have formulated themselves "in the guise of some form of transnationalism." Olwig makes a similar point with reference to ways of defining Caribbean societies as creole, in the sense that "their culture cannot be seen to be the product of an indigenous culture which has evolved *in situ* without significant external interference or of one culture brought to the area from the outside" (1993b:10–11). Put differently by Rogers (1996:110), the effect of globalization is to make ethnicity "not a local, nor even a regional or national, but a global force." By contrast, Cohen (1989:76) sees the "aggressive assertion of locality and ethnicity" as occurring "*against* the homogenizing logic

of the national and international political economies," thus marking the "renaissance of community" in the 1970s and 1980s.

The view that I take differs in varying degrees from these perspectives. I see
locality/community/ethnicity as being forged in and through rather than against
these global processes, which do not necessarily imply total homogenization. In
addition, while respecting Robotham's and Olwig's arguments, what they say
does not preclude the quest for indigeneity in the Caribbean. Indeed, globalization processes have provided some of the raw materials, conditioning processes,
and impetus for developing indigeneity in the Caribbean and for developing it
along particular lines, though not necessarily in an overdetermined manner—as
Rogers states, "identity is neither a strictly local phenomenon, nor an instance of
untrammeled global cultural flows" (1996:110).

SRCC leaders' work of deliberately engaging and associating with international indigenous bodies helps to maximize the SRCC's authenticity within the
Trinidadian context. The revivalist facets of SRCC brokers' practice especially
involve reading and sifting through various globalized ideas, images, and symbolic resources in order to define their indigeneity as "First Nations," which is
itself a North American trope of indigeneity, as Beckett (1996) argues. Several
authors have also posited the existence of a "transnational constituency" of
indigeneity that some describe as a "worldwide community of indigenous
peoples" (Murumbi 1994:52) or what Chief George Manuel called the "Fourth
World" (see Corntassel and Primeau 1998:139). As Beckett observes, there is
also pressure on groups to present themselves "in such a way as to appear 'indigenous' to a constituency that, while sympathetic, may have inappropriate expectations of indigenous alterity" (1996:10; see also Conklin 1997). This is one
dimension of what Mato recognizes as the processes whereby indigenous organizations develop "their practices and discourses in interaction with a significant
number of transnational and international agents" (1996:68, 69). However,
there is nothing to say that the interaction proceeds as a dialogue among equals.

Throughout the course of this volume I have maintained certain assumptions
about the significance of this study. I found the fact of the ethnographic case itself
significant insofar as the notion of an existing Carib community in Arima was
unheard of in the anthropological literature on Trinidad—thus my first research
question was: "Who are the Caribs of Arima?" This case necessarily raises issues
of how we think of modern Caribbean cultural development, cultural processes
of globalization, the construction of indigeneity, and the impact of mediated
representations. How indigeneity is situated has therefore been treated here as a
problem, one that is increasingly receiving the attention of scholars and that
necessitates an analysis of the conditions that make discourses of indigeneity
possible (see Scott 1992:384). I thus have stressed that indigeneity is not
ontologically absolute, permanent, or inflexible in content, form, and meaning.
The significance of this lies in treating indigeneity as elaborated and interpreted
within specific political, economic, and historical conjunctures.

The ways in which we may theorize indigeneity are thus one of the important dimensions of this research. One of the problems we encounter is that the term "indigenous" homogenizes, suggesting that varying groups acting in different contexts and arenas (even if interacting at a transnational level) can all be analyzed as members of the same set and that they are also internally undifferentiated—"identity talk homogenizes," caution Handler and Segal (1993:6). Moreover, reference to "the indigenous" can act to trigger various assumptions that may evoke an array of standardized expectations, obviating discussion of specifics. The concept of indigenous is itself not originally a rooted indigenous concept. It emerged as an ascriptive way for Europeans to talk about the others they had colonized, into whose lands they had moved, a concept and a way of categorizing people that can take shape and meaning only in the context of the expansion of the modern world system. Another problem that we are forced to grapple with is posed by the fact that when "indigenes speak," what one hears should not be essentialized as "the indigenous voice."

However, antiessentialism has attracted certain criticisms for its own part, especially on political grounds. Friedman wrote critically of positions such as the one that I just enunciated: "I am quite astonished at the attitude . . . that seems to have a rather wide following among anthropologists today and which seems to pit itself against indigenous groups that have dared to take their identity into their own hands" (1996:127). He argues that "anti-essentialism when applied to . . . social identities . . . is an attack on the collectivity itself, a concerted effort to falsify the genuineness of such identities" (Friedman 1996:128). My argument is that we do not need to pose these issues in this manner. First, along with Rogers (1996:77) I agree that the advocacy position "runs the risk of reifying a single, unitary indigenous perspective and in the process downplaying the internal diversity of indigenous populations" (Rogers 1996:77). When the divergent interests and perspectives of members of indigenous bodies are ignored, sidelined, or quietly folded into a larger whole that the anthropologist has constructed, then it is also possible that such an approach may antagonize and even harm such people. Second, again like Rogers (1996:76), I agree that constructionist analyses have been useful for challenging "Western positivism, essentialism, and Orientalism" and that we ought to be careful not to reintroduce these perspectives through the back door, so to speak. Third, I note that there are three further problems with the politics of critiques of constructionism, to the extent that they assume that indigenous groups and advocates are all always essentialists, that indigenous groups are always engaged in oppositional politics and resistance, and that indigenous spokespersons object to the notion of invention. None of these conditions is fully met by the SRCC case. Indeed, this is one of the reasons that I found the ethnography significant: for bringing certain theories down to earth.

The leading SRCC brokers are not as fixated on the politics of authenticity as are indigenous groups elsewhere, not having been locally opposed as much as groups elsewhere have been—they have not gone through a Mashpeelike experience (compare Clifford 1988). For a variety of reasons, there is not as much contestation and conflict over indigenous identification in Trinidad as there is in other areas of the world, and thus SRCC brokers tend to be more transparent and less defensive than their counterparts abroad. Moreover, the SRCC is still a relatively young organization, one without radical aims, not seeking to be separate, and not challenging the nation-state. Even those brokers who may be sensitive to the charge of invention often turn it around—"All cultures are invented everywhere," said one of my informants in a discussion on this issue—sometimes proudly claiming to be "the inventor" of a particular practice that has now "caught on," and in other cases speaking about other SRCC brokers' or other indigenous groups' invention of traditions.

I do not argue that there are outcomes of construction that are fake—all outcomes of construction are equally constructed, and all human representations are constructed. We therefore need to discuss the ways in which representations are produced and constructed—the strategies of representing—without getting caught up in an unnecessarily overwrought angst over the human fall from the Edenic garden of authenticity. Otherwise, we risk indulging in what Alcida Ramos calls the construction of the "hyperreal Indian": "a tendency that has been around for a while in the indigenist circuit, namely the fabrication of the perfect Indian whose virtues, sufferings and untiring stoicism have won for him the right to be defended by the professionals of indigenous rights. That Indian is more than the real Indian. He is the hyperreal Indian" (1994:161). Examples of this type of approach result, in some cases, in the framing of the "ecologically noble savage" (see Buege 1996 and Sackett 1991; compare IUCN 1997; Durning 1992), assimilating the indigene to the flora and fauna of a particular habitat and thereby also effecting what Fabian (1983) referred to as the "denial of coevalness" that results in distancing "the native" from "our" contemporary society. What ought to be at the focus of critiques is the fact that indigenous groups are put under pressure to conform to these images to begin with—or they lose out on resources that are desperately needed—and not divert our energies into deciding "good" versus "bad" essentialism. In other words, the focus of critiques ought to be states and other powerful institutions that prescribe and impose notions of cultural authenticity as a benchmark for awarding funds and other assistance to indigenous groups, forcing these groups to play an essentialist game in order to claim rewards from state institutions that have defined the legitimacy of particular indigenous bodies largely according to essentialist definitions concerning the retention of their character as traditional communities (contra Lattas 1993).

In the course of writing this book I sought to bring into focus the observation that the production, valuation, and perpetuation of categories and symbolic power of indigeneity can be the work of powerful elites, embodied in the formation of reservations and missions, the promulgation of laws, the production and distribution of texts, state financial support, and so forth. Elite representations of the indigenous, historically constituting the range of authorized opinions and

perspectives, were incorporated into this ethnography because they have structured the reality that I studied in the field. I also emphasize in these pages the role
of cultural brokers, not just as a means of bringing to light the key actors one
encounters in the field, but also as a means of adjusting some of the structure-
agency discussions of the knowledgeable agent. The diverse work of multiple
brokers, each oriented toward particular interests and perspectives on indigeneity, creates tensions in the representations of the Caribs in Trinidad, a fact that
I have chosen to address in terms of admission of change and loss, as well as
attempts by some to overcompensate, engaging in aesthetic hypercorrection by
dressing according to expectations of what a real Indian should look like. In
other words, this book is an attempt to debunk the idea of a single representational strategy adopted by the indigenous, especially since control over what
constitutes the form and content of indigeneity is not in the hands of one particular group alone. The study of indigeneity can never be just the study of indigenous
peoples.

This project also leaves certain questions unresolved and other areas unex-
plored. Every work must necessarily be limited; moreover, each is shaped by the
time and circumstances in which it was conducted. Gender, class, and genera-
tional issues remain to be further explored and explained at greater length with
respect to the SRCC, given that the majority of members are lower-income fe-
males over the age of fifty, and given the fact that historically the leader of the
association was the elder Queen. Indeed, if I had adopted a perspective focused
on gender or class, I might have arrived at different conclusions, raised different
questions, and afforded a greater purchase on select aspects of social organization and cultural construction than are covered here. Gender issues are starting to
receive the attention of those who entered the field after I had left.[2] Future research of the SRCC may focus on those members not in the limelight, the
nonbrokers, a project that by necessity would involve posing different questions
than I did and which could well take research into different directions from those
outlined herein. Such projects may also benefit from not having to cover the
ground that I have covered here in describing and analyzing the presence of the
Carib. In a broader write-up of my fieldwork I would also have liked to present
much more of the personal interactions among members of the SRCC, the play of
personalities, the everyday issues of concern to members, and what united and
divided them—far more than I have done here. A parallel study would thus focus
on the question of "What is community?" and how it is developed and articulated in this case.

Just as by necessity any research project leaves certain gaps uncovered, so are
there a number of fruitful areas for further research. In addition to those gaps
that I mention above, processes of internationalization and especially the role of
the Internet in developing, promoting, and articulating the Caribbean Amerindian revival deserve more sustained attention, and I have largely devoted myself
to that both during and since completing the earliest version of this text. From a

literary perspective, there is room for far greater analysis of key colonial texts relating specifically to Trinidad and its Amerindians, perhaps along the lines of the work done by Peter Hulme at the wider regional level and with reference to Dominica and St. Vincent. As the SRCC continues to develop, especially with its much-anticipated move to a large estate where a re-created Amerindian village is to be established, there will be room for restudies of the organization and its changing patterns of association and representation. Last but not least, it would be useful for students and advanced researchers alike to have at their disposal a large, comprehensive, empirical and historical overview of the Amerindians of Trinidad, in order to consolidate and hopefully improve on the many disparate sources referred to in the bibliography.

Imagining the future trajectories of the SRCC is a complex affair beyond the usual difficulties encountered with any speculative analysis. On the one hand, the SRCC could be seen as having achieved its immediate goals (funds, land, recognition) and thus being able to take off in developmental terms, attaining a broader membership and greater social prominence. On the other hand, having achieved its immediate goals, the group could just as easily find itself on a pla-teau, stagnating, without an answer to the question "What next?" Internal divisions have been problematic and sometimes acute in the recent history of the SRCC, especially in the jockeying for prominence among its main spokespersons. The SRCC that I studied was fragmented, with two offshoot organizations formed while I was there. Recruitment efforts remain the group's major handicap with respect to future growth and internal reproduction.

The SRCC is still not a group that orients itself to popular culture, at least not as much as it is oriented to officialdom. I have said that thus far neither is the SRCC's presence posed or received as a threat to the nationalist elaboration of a sense of Trinidadian indigeneity that submerges the African–East Indian dichotomy while rooting all citizens in that particular territory, nor is it perceived as a threat to the identity politics and claims of key ethnic spokespersons and organizations in Trinidad. Indeed, Afrocentrics such as Selwyn Cudjoe and Indocentrics such as Kamal Persad both embrace the SRCC. One must wonder if it could happen that Carib identification in Trinidad would become widespread and radical enough to achieve a degree of opposition to the state and the other foreign ethnicities that seems to mark the development of Caribism in Dominica. While I personally doubt that this will occur in the foreseeable future, we should be mindful of the fact that, until recent years, we as scholars were not even speaking of Caribs in Trinidad, nor were we conscious of the Jama'at al Mus-limeen. On one issue I am more or less certain: the success of processes of re-engineering can be gauged by the fact that—regardless of the presence or absence of an actual group such as the SRCC in Trinidad—for a long time to come, "Carib" will remain a central part of Trinidadian reflections on national history and personal identity.

Glossary

Ajoupa
This was a common Amerindian architectural style of dwelling, often with four to six hardwood posts and a slanted roof thatched using fronds from either the *timite* or the *carat* palm.

Behique
This term is often translated as "shaman" and refers to priestly healers in the Greater Antilles, among the Taíno especially.

Cacique
This term has been loosely translated to mean "chief."

Cemi or Zemi
Commonly found in the Greater Antilles in settlements now characterized as dominated by the Taíno, this is an object that was sculpted from either stone or bone, or made out of cloth, usually depicting a skeletal figure with exaggerated features and said to possess spirits. It was an object commonly associated with shamans—in some cases depicting a shamanic figure—and chiefs.

Coulevre
From the French word for snake; see *sebucán* and *matapí*.

Lime, Liming
To lime in Trinidad refers, in a broad sense, to casually getting together with people and spending time engaged in recreational conversation, or when a group engages in a prearranged get-together for the purpose of some enjoyable activity or for idle chatter.

Manare
This is a square-shaped utensil, woven from the *terite* reed, used for sifting grated and strained cassava.

Matapí
An Island Carib term for *coulevre*; see *sebucán*.

Parang
From the Spanish *parranda* (to spree). In Trinidad it refers to a particular type of music, now folkloric, of Hispanic American origins, especially popular on a na-

tional level during the Christmas season. Though normally sung in Spanish, *parang* songs in English are also becoming common. *Parang* is no longer the reserve of any one ethnic group, though the dominant theories are that *parang* in Trinidad originated with either the immigrants from Venezuela or the Hispanized Amerindians of the mission villages of Trinidad, or both. The music often consists of religious songs devoted to the birth, crucifixion, and resurrection of Jesus Christ, as well as a variety of nonreligious songs about animals, rivers, or other themes. *Parang* bands often consisted of four to six singers accompanied by guitar, cuatro, mandolin, box bass, and maracas. They would move from house to house during festive seasons, singing in the homes of families and being greeted with drinks and food; there were specific steps or rituals that accompanied the entry into a home, the dedication of songs to a host, the eating and drinking, and the departure.

Piai, Piacho, Piai Man

Much like *behique,* this term is often translated as "shaman" and is prevalent among mainland Cariban-speaking groups.

Sebucán

This is the Mainland Carib word for the long, flexible cassava strainer woven from the *terite* reed; see also *coulevre* and *matapí.*

Tapia

A mixture of mud, grass, and pebbles, this is packed onto a wood or bamboo frame, left to dry, and then possibly coated with plaster in order to make walls for a home.

Trapiche

This is the Spanish word for a sugarcane press. It consists of a tree trunk with a hole in its middle, through which a wooden platter is inserted along with a long pole. Sugar cane is placed on the platter and then squeezed using the long pole. The juice runs off the end of the platter and into a container.

Zemi

Same as *cemi.*

Notes

Introduction. Reviving Caribs

1. The abbreviation stands for the Caribbean Festival of the Arts, an event involving the participation of most states in the Caribbean Basin by sending delegations of artists. Carifesta V was held in Trinidad while I was still living there in 1992, which was also the quincentenary of Columbus' entry into the Caribbean: the "Encounter of Two Worlds," as it was officially referred to. Because the year was 1992, and on the eve of 1993—the United Nations' International Year for the World's Indigenous People (with the International Decade for the World's Indigenous Peoples beginning in 1994)—Caribbean governments made a concerted effort to showcase their indigenous populations—"marketing the cultural product," as former prime minister Robinson put it in a television interview.

2. WIPO 1999.

3. Harris does not reveal the means by which he came to this estimate. That number may be conservative, given the influx of a large number of Venezuelans, many of whom were *mestizos* and *indios* (Indians), who arrived throughout the 1800s.

4. Ricardo Bharath explains that those who wish to join must go through the following process: "they would register by giving their name, their address, a little history about their family and . . . we monitor . . . the actions of the person, if they [are] really willing to work to preserve the traditions and so on. After a while, well . . . we consider you part of the Community. . . . traditionally in Arima there are families . . . the Lopez family, the Calderons, the Hernandez, the Guerreros. There are certain people that can easily be identified as belonging to the Community" (Bharath 1995).

5. Companies Registry 1976.

6. By estranged I mean that the Queen at that time, Justa Werges, had largely disassociated herself from Ricardo Bharath, the two often acting as rivals, with the main points of division being who should wield authority within the group and who should handle funds and external contacts. My dedication of this book to Queen Justa Werges is not an act of taking sides on my part but simply a reflection of my own personal affection and respect for the late Queen.

7. The estimated population figures of Port of Spain and San Fernando are approximately 46,800 and 28,600 respectively, and they are the two largest cities in Trinidad (UNDP 2001a). However, these figures appear to be based on the strictest definition of the boundaries of these urban areas, seemingly excluding their surrounding suburbs.

8. See also the *Trinidad and Tobago Country Review* 2000.

9. See World Bank Group 2001a.

10. World Bank Group 2001b.

11. It is not clear to me whether the ethnic terms are chosen by respondents or ascribed by census takers.

12. For related anthropological coverage of the "artificial societies" created through colonial processes, using examples from Africa and Southeast Asia, see Tambiah 1994:

434. The references made by Tambiah could also be used to dispute the convention of marking the Caribbean as unique for being a zone of colonial artifice.

13. Indeed, while speaking of the Amerindians of the Caribbean, Knight says that "these island peoples have been especially vulnerable to influences from the outside, and their society has been more of a reflection of eclectic adaptation than original creation" (1978:21).

14. For example, one historian has noted that "those West Indians who are not yet mixed will be effectively mixed in a few generations, the conclusion is unavoidable that miscegenation is not only the biological base of the society but must also assuredly become its operative ideal" (Lewis 1968:20).

15. As Yelvington explains, the creationists "emphasise cultural creativity, cultural blending and borrowing, cultural adaptations to local circumstances, and ethnogenetic processes" (2001:42).

16. I rely upon Hulme's work to a significant extent in framing the historical interpretation in this study.

17. In this regard, current theses on Caribbean Amerindian revivals include the doctoral dissertation by Lynne Guitar (1998a; see also Guitar 2000) and the doctoral dissertation of Peter J. Ferbel (1995). See also Arévalo 1990 and McComie 1990.

18. I use this term in line with the French origin of the word, of putting a little of this and that together to "make do." The notion of patching things together in an ad hoc on-the-spot fashion also has a counterpart in Trinidadian parlance, often transcribed as "vikey vie" (although I believe this derives from the Italian *vai che vai*, which has identical connotations), meaning a type of approach in which "as you go, you put things together."

19. I borrow this phrase from Basdeo Panday, prime minister of Trinidad and Tobago, who outlined in a 1999 speech in Arima the need for the state to "manage diversity" in order to prevent the country from "becoming another Kosovo or Rwanda."

20. Erving Goffman also argues that while all representations to some extent involve misrepresentation, as a matter of course, it is not that the "facts" that would embarrass these representations are necessarily any more the "real reality" (Goffman 1990 [1959]:72).

21. The notion that recently formed traditions, borrowing elements from a wider repertory than was previously available locally, are somehow unreal or inauthentic is sharply disputed by Sahlins, who argues: "The *a priori* conceit that authenticity means self-fashioning and is lost by reliance on others seems only a legacy of bourgeois self-consciousness. Indeed, this self-centered determination of authenticity is contrary to the normal human social condition. Most peoples find critical means of their own reproduction in beings and powers existing beyond their normal borders and their customary controls" (Sahlins 1999:411).

22. This document is also available at <http://www.kacike.org/srcc/project.htm>, accessed April 26, 2004.

23. This was an essay competition that failed to materialize—see *The Independent* 1998 and *Newsday* 1998.

Chapter 1. Canonizing the Carib

1. Hulme has been at the forefront of contemporary critical reinterpretations of the historical literature, and his work has been indispensable in my interpretations of the

literature, and history, that is specific to Trinidad. The works of both Hulme and Whitehead provided me with the basic framework for allowing to me to apply, elaborate, and
further substantiate their work (in this case, applied to Trinidad and Tobago).

2. When Archer speaks of the "cultural system" (which she capitalizes), she restricts
this to the "register of propositions existing in any given social unit at a particular time,"
noting that while the propositional is not exhaustive of the meaningful, it "constitutes the
corpus of truths and falsehoods cherished in society at any given time" (1988:277). Archer
calls this a system because items in society's "propositional register" have to be intelligible
and stand in some logical relationship to one another, whether that relationship is one of
consistency or contradiction (1988:105). She also speaks of the cultural "intelligibilia," by
which she means "any item which has the dispositional capacity of being understood by
someone," even if not everyone (1988:xvi). Within the cultural intelligibilia she distin-
guishes a subset of items that are the propositions mentioned above, that is, statements that
assert truth or falsity and that can be discerned as being consistent or in contradiction with
one another. Archer thus restricts the cultural system to "the propositional register of
society at any given time" (1988:xvi). I also find Victor Turner's concept of social fields to
be useful insofar as it includes a notion of the propositional register in terms of concepts
and beliefs, noting that each field provides people "with opportunities, resources, concepts, beliefs; yet each [imposes] certain limitations" (1974:132).

3. As Archer explains, "subsequent interaction will be different from earlier action
precisely because it is now conditioned by the elaborated consequences of that prior action" (Archer 1988:xxvii). Cultural conditioning is defined by Archer (1988:xxiv) as "the
prior development of ideas (from earlier interaction) [that] conditions the current context
of action, confronting agents with both problem-free and problem-ridden clusters of beliefs, theories and ideas."

4. In the mid 1600s, well after these denominations had already come into play, one
missionary in St. Vincent wrote, "The Caribs themselves never liked to be called Carib, but
insisted that their original and right appellation was Callinago. The name Caraibes,
Caribs, Galibis, etc., they claim were appellations given to them by their enemies. The
Arrawaks used to call them Caribs, and subsequently the Europeans too called them
Caribs, so much so that one author says: 'Elle semble été consacrée par l'usage et elle est
commode.' The missionaries apparently avoided this injurious appellation and were careful enough to call them Callinagos" (van der Plas 1954:13). Writing roughly fifty years
later, a French missionary among the Caribs of St. Vincent added, "The Caribs called
themselves *Kalinas* but they had no written language. The world today therefore has to live
with the result of a complicated evolution of the spellings and misspellings of the Spanish,
French and English, as they recorded in their respective languages the words and names of
the *Kalinas* that they heard or thought they heard" (Le Breton 1998 [1702]:40).

5. One observer wrote, "Each Arrawak [*sic*] called himself a *Luku*, and spoke of the
tribe and language as those of the *Lukus*, 'The People'" (van der Plas 1954:3). "Luku" is
almost certainly a cognate of the Hispanized word for the mainland Arawak, the
"Lokono."

6. As Axtell summarizes, Europeans saw Indians "through a glass darkly; at worst, they
never saw them at all but only tawny reflections of their own self-projections and neuroses,
as in a mirror," and that in any event "the Europeans' 'ethnocentrism,' their monolithic
concept of 'savagism,' whether noble or ignoble, so clouded their vision that the human

and cultural reality of native life was almost never recognized and less seldom acknowledged" (1988:126).

7. Jiménez Román (1999:82–83) adds that there were no Taínos before 1492: "expeditiously [Columbus] designated the indigenous people whom he encountered 'Taínos' because he assumed that in greeting him with the word 'Taíno' they were naming themselves. In fact, they were offering assurances of their harmlessness (the word, the Spanish would soon learn, actually meant 'noble' or 'good'), and were trying to distinguish themselves from their more aggressive neighbors, the 'Caribs,' who inhabited the islands to the southeast."

8. As when we read, for example, that in 1531 Diego de Ordas came upon a large Arawak village that he called Aruacay, containing two hundred houses and nine chiefs, led by a chief priest (Whitehead 1988:12).

9. Other such edicts granting similar actions against the Caribs were announced in 1508 and 1512 (Beckles 1992:1). These edicts justified the exception for Caribs on the basis that they manifested hostility toward Christians and threatened the captured native labor force, used by the Spaniards, by allegedly eating them, as the dogma of the time urged (see Honychurch 2002:11).

10. The "C" indicated either their destination—Cubagua or Castille—or their origin as Caribs. A poetic verse was written about this fact: "Castille, Cubagua or Caribe, what might be the effect of this initial, left forever on the body of a free man, as a mark of opprobrium and death?" (quoted in Whitehead 1988:76).

11. "There are islands much nearer [to Hispaniola] from which they can be brought, and, moreover, as it is an island of some size and it is said to have gold and that it is at peace and that trade is carried on with the Indians for pearls, and, that by offending the Indians of the island [of Trinidad] we should lose the pearl trade because there are not at present any other Indians along the whole coast of Tierra Firme at peace, and, that, it is well to maintain peace in these islands, as the pearl trade is so profitable. . . . Therefore I do order you that from now on you shall not allow nor permit anyone to take Indians from this said island [Trinidad], and, that these said Indians shall always be well treated and preserved" (decree quoted in Ottley 1955:3).

12. "And I do hereby and I therefore give licence and permission to all those who are so ordered by me both in the island [and] in Tierra Firme of the Mar Oceana that up to now are discovered—in the future—that they may wage war against the Caribs of the island of Trinidad, of Vari, of Domynica, of Concepcion, Martinico, Santa Lucia, San [. . .] Vicente, Barbados, Cubaco and Mayo, and also that these Carib Indians may be captured and taken to such ports and islands wheresoever, and that these Indians may be sold for profit without punishment or penalty for so doing, and, without paying any duty provided they are not taken or sold outside the Indies" (decree quoted in Ottley 1955:4; see also Harricharan 1983:8).

13. Of course, while this may have been an actual Amerindian tactic in the 1530s, we must also be mindful of the possibility that this episode could have been entirely the concoction of Oviedo or his informants, designed to produce the requisite shock-effect back home.

14. Dominica is often portrayed as the center of the Carib regional domain, the base from where they launched attacks on the isolated plantations of Spanish settlers as far away as Puerto Rico, even capturing Spanish ships and occupants as they passed Dominica. Hulme and Whitehead note that "although European adult males were often

killed outright during such attacks, many other individuals were simply taken into captivity as wives [and] servants" (1992:38). Moreover, there were common estimates of "there being up to 300 European and African captives on Dominica" (Hulme and Whitehead 1992:38). Bernáldez de Quiroz, the procurator general of Puerto Rico, speaking of attacks from Dominica against Puerto Rico, wrote, "they have carried away a great quantity of negroes and left some in Dominica and distributed the rest amongst the Indians of these islands, which they take to their lands in order to serve them" (quoted in Hulme and Whitehead 1992:40). Reportedly they also captured Spanish infants as well as "important" Spanish women from passing ships. Some assimilation is remarked to have occurred by eyewitness accounts offered by escapees, who spoke of captives that "go about naked by day and night, and they paint them like themselves, making them sleep on the ground" (de Quiroz quoted in Hulme and Whitehead 1992:40). These accounts speak of Spanish men and women in Dominica "who were already as much *caribes* as the rest of them, and the women say that they no longer remember God. . . . and they do just as the Indians do (witnesses quoted by de Quiroz in Hulme and Whitehead 1992:42).

15. Father Raymond Le Breton, who lived among the Dominica Caribs for most of the twenty years that he spent in the Caribbean from 1635 to 1654, wrote, "I have finally learned from captains [chiefs] on the island of Dominica that the words Galíbi and Carib were names that the Europeans had given them. Their true name was Callínago although they designated themselves only with the words oubaobanum and baloüébonum: that is to say either 'from the islands' and 'from the continent'" (Breton 1929:1).

16. The Warao dominated in the northeastern portion of Venezuela.

17. The Warao are not classified as either Carib or Arawak, nor is their language classed within the linguistic stocks of either of those groups. The Warao long exercised a presence in Trinidad, well into the 1950s.

18. They "had been encouraged in days of slavery by the Dutch to restore, dead or alive, those escaped slaves who ventured as far inland along the great rivers of Guiana. The Amerindians were sometimes extolled by the Europeans as the simple and unspoilt children of nature, but they could not be regarded in the same light by the Negroes, for even after emancipation their reputation as slave-catchers remained" (Wood 1968:6).

19. "You on your part should hold these fathers in every possible way, assisting them to obtain their objects which are so important and aid them to reduce the Indians, and bring them, and, incorporate them, into the missions, so that they may learn to live a quiet and civilized life. This is a matter in which you must help, as it is important to bring all the Indians possible under the influence of these missionary fathers" (quoted in Ottley 1955:23–24).

Chapter 2. Placing the Carib

1. There is no consensus on any specific meaning of the term "resurgence." I am using it as a short form for referring to ways in which Amerindians became more visible, garnered new material or symbolic resources, attracted wider attention, or became more prominent. "Resurgence" can also be an expression of the agency of the Caribs themselves, in redefining and reasserting their identity and cultural practices, in making themselves heard and seen by the wider society.

2. De Verteuil confirmed the specifics of this move: "Soon after the [1783] settlement of the colony, these Indians had been formed into two missions at Tacarigua and Arima. But

as the formation of *ingenios,* or sugar estates, was proceeding eastward, they were removed to the quarter of Arima, where a village was formed, and houses built by them, on about one thousand acres which has been granted for the formation of a mission, along the right bank of the river, and as the full and unalienable property of the inhabitants" (De Verteuil 1858:299–300).

3. A mission in Arima had been founded during a first attempt around 1757, according to one author (Rétout 1976:45), but had apparently been dissolved shortly thereafter for reasons unexplained.

4. I use this term here to indicate that these families had a paternal if not proprietary relationship with the mission Indians, as representatives of upstanding Spanish Catholic families who owned lands in the area.

5. This is according to a letter by Father Louis Daudier, parish priest of Arima, dated April 27, 1881. Here Father Daudier quoted "the oldest surviving Indians" of the area in establishing an oral history of the Indian mission.

6. Testimony by Martin Sorzano, Friday, July 16, 1841, at Port of Spain, quoted in Burnley 1842:103.

7. Daudier, letter of February 4, 1869.

8. To this day, the street running along the east side of Lord Harris Square (named after a subsequent governor) and passing the door of the church is named after Woodford.

9. How long Wright actually served as the *corregidor* is unclear, given that, while still under the Woodford administration, one de Verteuil signs as the *corregidor de Arima* at the start of a new year of entries in the baptismal register for 1827 and 1828.

10. An anonymous cocoa planter from Arima wrote on Harris' plans for territorial regulation and taxation: "Should this law of indirect confiscation be passed, these planters will see their lands taken from them every year—those lands which many families have held long before the Conquest [the British takeover of 1797], and which were respected even by Sir Ralph Woodford as being in the *Libro Becero.* Little did the poor cocoa and coffee planters, and the small proprietors of every description, expect that, under a show of even-handed justice, the enormous [tax] burden would be laid on those least able to bear it.... The *Sturdy Beggars* of Arima will employ every legal means to avert the destructive blow." *Port of Spain Gazette,* Friday, March 19, 1847.

11. Daudier, letter to M. Mitchel, April 16, 1873.

12. Daudier, letter to the Monsignor, October 4, 1871.

13. See, for example, *Trinidad Standard and West Indian Journal,* Friday, December 14, 1838.

14. Father François Esteva, letter dated August 18, 1868.

15. See also *Trinidad Standard and West Indian Journal,* Friday, July 13, 1838: "As to any demand existing or likely to be created on the part of our Cocoa and Coffee planters, there is little to be feared on that score. The prices of these two articles of Produce, give no encouragement to extend the cultivations."

16. Notes from displays at the National Museum of Trinidad and Tobago.

17. See *Trinidad Standard and West Indian Journal,* Tuesday, November 13, 1838.

18. Notes from displays at the National Museum of Trinidad and Tobago.

19. In his search for the remains of the Mission of San Francisco de los Arenales, Father Cothonay detailed his encounter with a "pure blood Indian" in a house in the forest, occupied by a dozen people, noting that the family of the Indian came from Venezuela after the wars of independence (1810–1820); when his grandmother came to settle in this re-

gion, Cothonay related, there existed a good number of Indians of "this country" (Trinidad) who either died or went to settle elsewhere (Cothonay 1893:361–362).

20. "I love the Spanish ladies to my heart; after my own dear and beautiful countrywomen I think a señorita would be my choice. Their dress is so gay yet modest, their walk so noble, their manners so quiet, so gentle and so collected. . . . A Spanish woman, whether her education have been finished or not, is in her nature a superior being. Her majestic forehead, her dark and thoughtful eye assure you that she hath communed with herself" (Coleridge 1826:73).

21. *Port of Spain Gazette*, Tuesday, March 23, 1847.

22. Racial designations were entered in the registers only when the designation carried a real legal status, hence, black slave, Indian, apprentice, indentured—native of Africa, and coolie (the term "Indian" was never applied to East Indian indentured laborers in nineteenth-century Trinidad). As these legal statuses came to an end, so did the designations. Individuals of African descent, ex-slaves, ex-apprentices, and all those who were non-voluntary migrants from Africa, for example, were in excess identified by the final and available resort of "black" after this category lost any special legal status in the colonial labor scheme.

23. See, for example, "History of the Indian Tribes of North America," *Trinidad Standard and West Indian Journal*, Tuesday, July 17, 1838, and "Humboldt on El Dorado," *Trinidad Standard and West Indian Journal*, Tuesday, June 19, 1838.

24. My father-in-law, a customs officer, recalls inspecting Warao canoes at the harbor in Port of Spain in the 1960s, laden with trade items such as bows and arrows, birds, hammocks, and other items.

25. Scheult and Scheult, letter to the Monsignor, November 14, 1867.

26. Rouger, letter to the Monsignor, May 2, 1871.

27. Rouger, letter to the Monsignor, July 19, 1871.

28. Daudier, letter to the Monsignor, March 10, 1873. Indeed, I too have seen this designation in scattered remnants of the first baptismal register, on file at the Archbishop's Residence.

29. Daudier, letter to the Monsignor, March 10, 1873.

30. Daudier, letter to the Monsignor, August 20, 1873.

31. Daudier, letter to the Monsignor, April 27, 1881.

32. Daudier, letter to the Monsignor, April 27, 1881.

33. Burke, *Abstract of Grant of Lands in the Village of Arima.*

34. Wilson, letter to the archbishop of Port of Spain, March 5, 1881.

35. Daudier, letter to the Monsignor, March 22, 1881.

36. Daudier, letter to the Monsignor, April 27, 1881.

37. Daudier, letter to the Monsignor, April 27, 1881.

38. Daudier, letter to the Monsignor, April 27, 1881.

39. Daudier, letter to the Monsignor, April 27, 1881.

40. Daudier, letter to the Monsignor, April 27, 1881.

41. Daudier, letter to the Monsignor, April 27, 1881.

42. Daudier, letter to the Monsignor, April 27, 1881.

43. Daudier, letter to M. Mitchel, April 16, 1873.

44. Daudier, letter to M. Mitchel, April 16, 1873.

45. Daudier, letter to the Monsignor, June 2, 1881.

46. Daudier, letter to M. Mitchel, April 16, 1873.

47. Parishioners of Arima, letter to the archbishop of Port of Spain, December 12, 1909.

48. Today the Bermudez family owns one of Trinidad's largest manufacturing concerns, the Bermudez Biscuit Company.

49. *Port of Spain Gazette,* Tuesday, April 20, 1847.

50. *Port of Spain Gazette,* Thursday, October 18, 1892.

51. *Port of Spain Gazette,* Wednesday, August 3, 1938, p. 11.

52. *Port of Spain Gazette,* "Trinidad Celebrates Its Discovery," Wednesday, August 3, 1938, p. 12.

Chapter 3. Writing the Carib

1. Cristo never knew at that time that I was working on this concept of reengineering—the fact that he chose to use the term "engineering" struck me as a startling coincidence.

2. As surprising as it may seem, given that Trinidad, after all, is a relatively small island, regional differences in word usage do differ: what is defined as a Spanish in, say, a Arima or Toco differs wildly from what Trinidadians of East Indian descent in places like Chaguanas take this term to mean.

3. My thanks to Peter Hulme for making this suggestion.

4. By educational I mean that these sources are part of the education industry, not that they are inherently valuable as such. It is one way of distinguishing these sources from the news media, advertising, and popular culture, which are the concern of following chapters.

5. I must thank Gary Ribeiro, a Caribbean history and social studies teacher at St. Mary's Roman Catholic College in Port of Spain, for giving me an overview of materials that are taught, along with the actual texts from which I quote here.

Chapter 4. Nationalizing the Carib

1. See, for example, Blood 2001; *Trinidad Guardian (Online)* 2001a, 2001b; Pierre 2001.

2. For further insight as to how these processes impacted on and spurred the development of local pride and ethnic consciousness, see Henry 1983 on the Yoruba Orisha revival in the 1970s and its growing appeal to the middle-class youths.

3. This was one of the main platforms of the NAR government under Prime Minister Robinson (1986–1991).

4. These are the words of Prime Minister Robinson, speaking in a television interview in 1991 on the upcoming Seville World Expo and Carifesta V, hosted in Trinidad in 1992.

5. There are multiple ways of interpreting "red" in this context: (1) "Red Indian"; (2) the Trinidadian notion of "red," which can be synonymous with "Spanish" or a person who is "mixed with white"; and (3) in some instances "red" might also connote being of no race as a result of being the product of all races.

6. *Trinidad (Internet) Express* 1998g.

7. See <http://community.wow.net/manzanare/manznewstuff.htm>, accessed January 12, 2000.

8. These observations and surveys are based on my research of the following Internet projects: see Forte 1998a, 1998b, 1998d, 1998g, 1998h, and 1998i.

9. See BWIA Caribbean on the Internet at <http://www.bwiacaribbean.com/events/

trinidad.htm> and <http://www.caribbean-beat.com/archive/trinadventure.html>; see also "Festive Islands: Trinidad and Tobago" by Paris Permenter and John Bigley <http://www.travellady.com/ARTICLES/article-festiveislands.html>, all accessed November 18, 1999.

10. See Earthfoot at <http://earthfoot.org/places/tt001.htm>, accessed November 17, 1999.

11. As examples, see Exploring Trinidad at <http://www.discovertobago.com/trinexplore.html> and Elder Hostel International at <http://www.elderhostel.org/catalog/int/FAJ/sumI06D01000.html>, both accessed November 18, 1999.

12. A TIDCO documentary aired on TTT on December 26, 1998, titled "Dis Place Nice," spoke of Cocoa Panyols as "descended from Caribs"; the Cocoa Panyol was described as the main inhabitant of the Northern Range, one who can be characterized as a "hunter, herbalist, French Patois speaking, religious, Parrandero." A TTT documentary shown on Sunday, February 21, 1999, titled "Trails and Traditions," focused on the ecotourist angle of the Northern Range, on "rustic traditions" and "pristine ecology," and showed local museums featuring Amerindian artifacts and Carib crafts.

Chapter 5. Reproducing the Carib Locally

1. Here Ricardo is making a reference to the Orinoco River Basin, which is viewed by some SRCC members as a repository of authentic and continuous Carib traditions.

2. In the wider society, *parang* is viewed as a seasonal musical form, played mostly during Christmas. Among the Panyols, however, *parang* can be both secular and religious, played at any festivity and present at most of the major annual events on the Catholic calendar.

3. This group was disbanded circa early 2000, after my fieldwork period.

4. This brought to mind Goffman's quote of Flournoy: "We may practically say that he has as many different social selves as there are distinct *groups* of persons about whose opinion he cares. He generally shows a different side of himself to each of these different groups" (Goffman 1990 [1959]:57).

5. See also Wanser 2000b.

6. The SRCC actually already possessed church property when it submitted its application for registration as a limited liability company in 1976, as evidenced by the fact that Ricardo's home address then is listed on the application as being in the same location it is today, that is, on lands donated by the church (see Companies Registry 1976).

7. Elma Reyes authored at least dozen newspaper articles on the SRCC, coauthored a chapter with British archaeologist Peter Harris (Harris and Reyes 1990), and self-published a booklet on the SRCC (Reyes 1978), as well as a booklet that highlighted Carib cultural inputs into Trinidadian Christmas traditions (Reyes 1996). Elma also prepared many of the SRCC documents cited in this work.

8. Rising to Elma's defense, Almarales stated, "she is in fact qualified to be a member of the community. Her ancestors were 'peones' from Venezuela" (1994:29). This explanation by Almarales reaffirms the assimilation of Venezuelan immigrants into the Carib history of Trinidad and, more importantly, emphasizes SRCC brokers' own desire to blur the dividing lines between themselves and important "outside" brokers.

9. Like Cristo, Cruz founded an organization separate from the SRCC, Kairi Tukuienyo Karinya ("Hummingbird People of Trinidad and Tobago," or KTK), in October 1998,

along with environmentalist/artist John Stollmeyer and others. KTK formally described itself as an "offshoot of the Carib Community," motivated by the "need to teach the younger generation" and to "pass on the history, language and traditions of the Karinya (. . . the name the people, who the Europeans called Carib, called themselves)." KTK's founders stressed the need for "young ones to participate as equals with their elders in community events." Moreover, KTK called on the society "to recognize the extremely important contributions made by the Amerindian peoples to our present knowledge and the necessary wisdom and understanding they offer to our future peace and well-being" (Kairi Tukuienyo Karinya 1999).

10. In Trinidad, "town" refers to Port of Spain.

11. Broker overload may be seen as a form of what Ortner (1994:395) calls strain theory, outlined as a counterbalance to interest theory: "actors in strain theory are seen as experiencing the complexities of their situations and attempting to solve problems posed by those situations. . . . the strain perspective places greater emphasis on the analysis of the system itself, the forces in play upon actors, as a way of understanding where actors, as we say, are coming from. In particular, a system is analyzed with the aim of revealing the sorts of binds it creates for actors, the sorts of burdens it places upon them, and so on."

Chapter 6. Representing the Carib

1. "The Santa Rosa Carib Community of Arima, Trinidad, West Indies," given to the author by Elma Reyes (n.d.e).

2. "Spanish," at least in northeastern Trinidad, has distinct qualities in the view of my informants, friends, and even my own in-laws who self-identify as Spanish. A "Spanish" need not be unmistakably Iberian in appearance but is usually expected to be somewhere between light brown in skin color to nearly white. In addition, a Spanish surname is often expected, and at one time even some knowledge of the Spanish language or at least French patois was expected. In northeastern Trinidad self-identified "Spanish" people often are those who can trace their ancestry to Venezuela; indeed, many of those that I encountered were only first- or second-generation Trinidadians and still only in their forties. The defining features of "Spanish" are far less ambiguous than those encountered by Aisha Khan (1993) among her informants of East Indian descent, in part due to what I suspect are important regional and ethnic variations in the use of this term. In fact, Trinidadians of East Indian descent are viewed by northeastern self-identified "Spanish" people as having a notoriously peculiar notion of "Spanish" that can be as extreme as saying that "any Negro with soft [straight] hair is a Spanish."

3. One example that comes to mind is the manufacture of hammocks in Trinidad. This has come to be an industry dominated by Trinidadians of East Indian descent, which is interesting given that their knowledge of hammock production was acquired entirely in Trinidad.

4. Moodie-Kublalsingh discusses how Amerindians may have acquired the *parang* music form: "We know that missionaries paid special attention to music in the catechization of the native populations of America. So the Capuchin missionaries in Trinidad must have taught sacred songs to the Trinidad aborigines" (1994:68).

5. This is a comment that is supported by De Verteuil (1858:300), author of one of a number of historical texts that inform current SRCC reinterpretations.

6. This document (Bharath et al. n.d.) is also available at <http://www.kacike.org/srcc/santarosa.htm>, accessed March 10, 2002.

7. The Sun Bear Tribe is a self-described "tribe in-progress," composed of "people who are constantly learning better ways of serving the sacred web of life" and whose "cross-cultural teachings are based on many sources of Earth Wisdom." In addition, it is "not a tribe bounded by geography or ethnicity, but rather by belief and action" and consists of Chippewa and non–native Americans living on a sixty-acre farm, originally created by the Ojibwa-descended Chief Sun Bear (founder of the Bear Tribe Medicine Society of Spokane, Washington). For more information on this, see <http://members.aol.com/InfoBT/home.html>; Sun Bear's Unofficial Home Page <http://www.liteweb.org/wildfire/>; Star Spider Dancing, Dedicated to the Bear Tribe <http://eweb.tribe.com/BearTribe/>; and Internet Public Library, Native American Authors Project: Sun Bear (Gheezis Mokwa) 1929–1992 <http://www.ipl.org/cgi/ref/native/browse.pl/A136>, all accessed January 3, 2000.

Chapter 7. Globalizing the Carib

1. Implicitly, the emic concept of culture with which SRCC brokers are working involves an agglomeration of practices and rituals, along with language, religious belief, and a whole range of lifeways.

2. Numerous authors and commentators, in both the social sciences and the humanities, have remarked extensively on this feature of what many see as either a colonial legacy (where real value was located in the metropole—the mother country was always superior to the colony) or a symptom of Caribbean islands' small size and peripheral positioning in the world system.

3. In addition to the SRCC, the other six organizations representing indigenous peoples of the Caribbean that attended this conference include the "Black Carib Community" (St. Vincent), Carib Indian Cultural Group (Dominica), Caribbean Organisation of Indigenous Peoples (COIP), Council for the Development of the Carib Community (St. Vincent), Dominica Carib Council, and National Garifuna Council (Belize). Dominica Carib chief Irvince Auguiste was also one of the keynote speakers opening the conference. See also Indigenous 500 Committee 1991a, 1991b, 1991c, 1991d; World Council of Indigenous Peoples 1991; and Mercredi 1991b.

4. "Quest of the Carib Canoe," directed by Eugene Jarecki (documentary, 50 minutes, 2000). See also Auguiste 2000.

5. Also, in November 1993, a weeklong workshop and exhibition of Guyanese handicraft was held at the SRCC Centre, featuring a team of Arawaks and Caribs from Guyana whose trip had been funded by the Guyana Tourist Board (Almarales 1994:50).

6. This is a local Baha'i foundation headed by Pat McLeod and oriented toward emphasizing multiculturalism, tolerance, and interethnic unity in Trinidad and Tobago, as stated in its promotional literature and on its website at <http://www.trinidad.net/hdiversity/index.html>, accessed April 21, 2000.

7. Further information was available from the report of Anne-Marie Ganase, aired on *Panorama,* the evening news of Trinidad and Tobago Television, on November 22, 1999.

8. "Acting upon the recommendation of the Federation of Saskatchewan Indian Nations, the SIFC opened an Office of International Affairs in June of 1983. It began the process of facilitating ties in the Third World and co-ordinating FSIN's role in international

Indigenous political front. . . . The office's early efforts focused on working with the Indigenous peoples in Central America, South America and the Caribbean." The Saskatchewan Indian Federated College, International Indigenous Connections, and the Caribbean—A History of the Early Years of the SIFC <http://142.3.161.11/icid/overearly.htm>, accessed May 13, 2001.

9. The United Nations also established the International Decade for the World's Indigenous People (1995–2004) (see UN 1994).

10. These limitations, of course, are added to the expectable ones such as funding and communication.

Conclusion. Reengineering Indigeneity

1. This is not to deny that the symbolic can and does have very powerful sociopolitical effects. What I mean, instead, is that the sociopolitical power of native societies, understood as a geopolitical and demographic force, began to decline, while symbolic representations of natives and their descendants began to rise, in number and value.

2. I am referring here to the ethnographic research of Genevieve Bicknell, conducted for the M.A. in anthropology at the University of Edinburgh in 2000.

Bibliography

Primary Sources

Arima Borough Council (ABC). 2000. *Arimafest: Arima Borough 112th Anniversary Celebration.* Brochure. Arima: Arima Borough Corporation. 3 pages.

———. 1998. *110th Anniversary, The Royal Chartered Borough of Arima, 1888 to 1998.* Arima: Arima Borough Corporation.

———. 1997. *Arima Borough Corporation: The Only Royal Chartered Borough in the Caribbean, 17th–20th April 1997.* Brochure published on the occasion of the Antilles Eucharistic Congress. Arima: Arima Borough Corporation. 3 pages.

Assembly of First Nations (AFN). 1992. *Interim Report: 'Strengthening the Spirit' Conference, November 10–14, 1991, Ottawa-Hull, Canada.*

———. 1991a. "Declaration of the First Nations of the Americas." November 14.

———. 1991b. *Strengthening the Spirit/Beyond 500 Years: Indigenous Nations of the Americas International Conference (November 10–14, 1991, Ottawa-Hull, Canada).* Ottawa: Indigenous 500 Committee/Assembly of First Nations.

———. 1991c. "Indigenous Nations of the Americas 1991 International Conference, 'Strengthening the Spirit': Vision Statement."

Baptismal Register of the Church of Santa Rosa, Arima. 1910–1916. Book No. 10.

———. 1906–1910. Book No. 9.

———. 1900–1906. Book No. 8.

———. 1892–1899. Book No. 7.

———. 1887–1892. Book No. 6.

———. 1877–1887. Book No. 5.

———. 1866–1876. Book No. 4.

———. 1840–1852. Book No. 3.

Baptismal Register of the Mission of Santa Rosa, Arima. 1835–1840. Book No. 2.

———. 1820–1835. Book No. 1.

———. 1809.

———. 1792–1794.

Baptiste, Peter A. (communications manager, Ministry of Culture and Gender Affairs). 1999. "Ministry of Culture Responds." *Trinidad Guardian,* Tuesday, August 24:8.

Bharath, Ricardo. 1995. Interview with Maximilian Forte. Arima, Trinidad and Tobago. June 10.

Bharath, Ricardo, and Jacqueline Khan. 1998. Letter to Dr. Hollis Liverpool (director of culture, Ministry of Culture and Gender Affairs). June 24.

———. 1997a. Letter to The Hon. Senator Dr. Daphne Phillips (minister of community development, culture and women's affairs). June 23.

———. 1997b. Letter to Dr. Hollis Liverpool (director of culture, Ministry of Community Development, Culture and Women's Affairs). June 23.

Bharath, Ricardo Hernandez, Jacqueline Khan, and Elma Reyes. N.d. *The Preserved Historical Traditions of Santa Rosa de Arima as Practiced by the Carib Community.*

Burke, J. S. (administrator). "Abstract of Grant of Lands in the Village of Arima," grant dated July 17, 1874, registered June 27, 1878, No. 1023 (1878, Protocol of Deeds).

Cabinet Secretariat Office of the Prime Minister. 1990. Letter from K. Boswell Junin (permanent secretary, Office of the Prime Minister and Secretary to Cabinet) to Jacqueline Khan (secretary, Santa Rosa Carib Community). May 23.

Campo, Susan. 1993. Survey questionnaire form.

Companies Registry, Registrar General's Office, Ministry of Legal Affairs. 1976. "Draft Copy of Declaration of Compliance of the Santa Rosa Carib Company Limited," Form 41, T-544. September 22.

———. 1976. "Draft Copy of Memorandum and Articles of Association of the Santa Rosa Carib Company Limited," T-544. September 22.

Daniel, Edward W. (Department of Education). Letter to the archbishop of Port of Spain. November 5, 1951.

Daudier, Father Louis, O.P. (parish priest of Arima). Letter. March 31, 1886.

———. Letter to M. L. Guppy. March 24, 1886.

———. Letter to the Monsignor. June 2, 1881.

———. Letter to the Monsignor. April 27, 1881.

———. Letter to the Monsignor. March 22, 1881.

———. Letter to the Monsignor. February 18, 1876.

———. Letter to the Monsignor. August 20, 1873.

———. Letter to the Monsignor. April 16, 1873.

———. Letter to M. Mitchel. April 16, 1873.

———. Letter to the Monsignor. March 10, 1873.

———. Letter to the Monsignor. February 19, 1872.

———. Letter to the Monsignor. February 12, 1872.

———. Letter to the Monsignor. October 4, 1871.

———. Letter. February 4, 1869.

———. Letter. N.d.

Dumelie, Roger (director, International NGO Division, Canadian International Development Agency). 1991. Letter to Donald Rojas (president, World Council of Indigenous Peoples). October 29.

ECLAC. 1999. Economic Profiles of Caribbean Countries. General LC/CAR/G.572. October 18. Port of Spain: United Nations Economic Commission for Latin America and the Caribbean. <http://www.eclacpos.org/>, accessed December 9, 1999.

Eleggua Project. 1997. Indigenous Legacies of the Caribbean—Interdisciplinary Conference and Field Study, Baracoa, Cuba, 16–23 November. Toronto: Eleggua Project. A brochure.

Esteva, Father François (parish priest of Arima). Letter. March 28, 1869.

———. Letter. March 17, 1869.

———. Letter. March 12, 1869.

———. Letter. August 18, 1868.

Gomez, Garnet. 1998. "Income and Expenditure Report of the Arima Santa Rosa Carib Community for the Financial Year 1997." Arima: Garnet Gomez Accounting Services.

Hansard. 2000. "Carib Community: Day of Recognition." Transcript of the Sitting of the Senate of Trinidad and Tobago on Tuesday, July 18, pp. 329–382. Port of Spain: Government Printing Office. <http://www.ttparliament.org/hansard/senate/2000/hs20000718.pdf>, accessed September 9, 2000.

IBRD. 2000. *Trinidad and Tobago at a Glance.* August 25.

Indigenous 500 Committee. 1991a. Draft news release on the "Strengthening the Spirit" Conference. October 31.

———. 1991b. Conference agendas for "Strengthening the Spirit" Indigenous Nations of the Americas Conference. October 16.

———. 1991c. Cultural activities for "Strengthening the Spirit" Indigenous Nations of the Americas Conference. October 16.

———. 1991d. *Background Plan for the Indigenous Nations of the Americas 1991 International Conference.* September 4.

Information Division, Office of the Prime Minister. 1990. News Release No. 360: "Recognition of Santa Rosa Carib Community." May 8.

International Labour Organisation (ILO). Convention No. 169.

Jiménez, Antonio Nuñez (president, Fundación de la Naturaleza y el Hombre, Havana, Cuba). 1997. Letter to Jonathan Watts (executive director, Eleggua Project). June 2.

Kairi Inkruienyo Karinya. 1999. "Urgent Press Release: Press Invitation to Attend Events—Commemoration of Our Amerindian Heritage." November.

Labrie, Louise (coordinator, International Relations, AFN). 1992. Letter to Konrad Sioui (executive director, International Relations, AFN). May 6.

———. 1992. Memorandum to all Indigenous 500 Committee members. February 21.

Lands and Surveys Division. 1983. Map of the Northern Range North of the Borough of Arima. Sheet 14F. 1st ed. Trinidad and Tobago Government: Lands and Surveys Division. January.

———. 1980. Map of the Borough of Arima. Sheet 24C. 1st ed. Trinidad and Tobago Government: Lands and Surveys Division. May.

Louis, P. Joachin (archbishop, Port of Spain). Letter to David Wilson (sub-intendant of the colony). April 17, 1887.

———. Letter to David Wilson (sub-intendant of the colony). April 12, 1881.

Mercredi, Ovide (chairman and national chief of the AFN, and Indigenous 500 Committee chairman). 1992. Letter to Donald Rojas (president, World Council of Indigenous Peoples). April 1.

———. 1992. Letter to Adele Wessel. March 2.

———. 1992. Letter to Hon. Monique Landry (minister for external affairs and international development, and minister of state for Indian affairs and northern development. February 25.

———. 1991. Letter to Marcel Masse (president, Canadian International Development Agency). December 3.

———. 1991. Letter to Donald Rojas (president, World Council of Indigenous Peoples). December 3.

———. 1991a. Opening statement for the "Strengthening the Spirit" Conference. November 10.

———. 1991b. "Speech for the Opening Ceremony of the 'Strengthening the Spirit' Conference." November 10.

Ministry of Local Government. 1999. *Local Government for All,* vol. 1. Port of Spain: Ministry of Local Government.

Ministry of Youth, Sport, Culture and Creative Arts. 1990. Letter from Mervyn R. Williams (acting director of culture) to Jacqueline Khan (secretary, Santa Rosa Carib Community). July 5.

National Parang Association of Trinidad and Tobago (NPATT). 1997. "Recounting Traditions and Preparing the Future." Program brochure. Arima: NPATT and the Ministry of Community Development, Culture and Women's Affairs.

Owens, Richard (director, Global Intellectual Property Issues Division, World Intellectual Property Organization). 1999. Letter to Cristo Adonis. July 20.

Panday, Basdeo (prime minister of the Republic of Trinidad and Tobago). 2000. "Remarks at the Launching of the International Indigenous Gathering, Santa Rosa Carib Community Centre," June 29. Port of Spain: The Official Website of the Government of the Republic of Trinidad and Tobago. <http://www.gov.tt/speeches/speeches/indigenous_0gather.html>, accessed September 9, 2000.

Paria Publishing. N.d. [1797] Plan for the Isle of Trinidad made from actual surveys in the year 1797. Survey map

Parishioners of Arima. Letter to the archbishop of Port of Spain. December 12, 1909.

———. Petition to the Rev. Monsignor De Martini. March 4, 1902.

Parish of Arima. Handwritten list of prominent parishioners, circa 1872

Research Unit of the Santa Rosa Carib Community. N.d. "Proposal: Establishment of Phase One: Center for Amerindian Studies." Arima: Santa Rosa Carib Community.

Reyes, Elma (research officer, Santa Rosa Carib Community). N.d.a. "The Amerindian People of Trinidad before 1970." 2 pages.

———. N.d.b. "Historical Notes on Arima." 3 pages.

———. N.d.c. "The Santa Rosa Festival and the Carib Community." Photo essay.

———. N.d.e. "The Santa Rosa Carib Community of Arima, Trinidad, West Indies." Parts 1 and 2. 4 pages.

———. N.d.f. "The Santa Rosa Carib Community of the Late 20th Century." 4 pages.

———. N.d.g. Untitled introduction to the history of the Caribs of Trinidad. 7 pages.

———. N.d.h. "The Titular Queens of the Santa Rosa Carib Community of Arima." 1 page.

Rose Foundation. 1997. Santa Rosa Carib Community: Proposal for Financial Assistance, Presented to The Hon. Senator Dr. Daphne Phillips, Minister of Community Development, Culture and Women's Affairs. Arima: Santa Rosa Carib Community.

Rouger, Father M. (parish priest of Arima). Letter to the Monsignor, July 19, 1871.

———. Letter to the Monsignor, May 2, 1871.

Saint-Martin, Jean-Guy (Canadian International Development Agency). 1992. Letter to Ovide Mercredi (national chief, Assembly of First Nations). January 28.

Santa Rosa Carib Community (SRCC). 1998a. Santa Rosa Carib Community: Annual Report to the Ministry of Culture for 1997–1998, Including Activity Report, Audited Account Statement, Income and Expenditure Overview, Schedule of Activities for 1998. June 24.

———. 1998b. "In Observation of the United Nations' International Day for the World's Indigenous People, 09 August, 1998, The Santa Rosa Carib Community Announces the Opening of a Permanent Amerindian Research Centre at the Santa Rosa Carib Community Centre." Cost proposal.

———. 1998c. "A Project Proposal for the Development of an Amerindian Heritage Complex."

———. 1997. "Santa Rosa Carib Community: Report for the Period July 1996–June 1997, for the Ministry of Community Development, Culture, and Women's Affairs." June 23.

———. 1996a. "Public Lecture: The Spanish and Indigenous Influence from Venezuela to Trinidad, Town Hall, Sorzano Street, Arima." Program brochure. Arima: The Rose Foundation.

———. 1996b. Schedule of activities for the 237th Annual Santa Rosa de Arima Festival hosted by the Santa Rosa Carib Community of Arima.

———. 1993a. *Amerindian Art, Craft and Way of Life Exhibition from Guyana*. Brochure. November 11.

———. 1993b. Membership application form.

———. 1990. "Amerindian Heritage Week, Saturday, 28 October–Saturday, 03 November." Pamphlet of events.

———. N.d.a. "Advisors to the Planning Committee (Official Profile of Key Members of the Santa Rosa Carib Community)."

———. N.d.b. "Membership Form for the Santa Rosa Carib Community."

Santa Rosa Roman Catholic Church of Arima. 1989. *Bicentenary of Worship on the present site 1789–1989, Pontifical Mass, celebrated by Archbishop Anthony Pantin, O. D., on Sunday, 30 April, 1989*. Arima: Santa Rosa RC Church.

Scheult, Ch., and D. A. Scheult (owners of Santa Rosa Estate). Letter to the Monsignor. November 14, 1867.

Singh, Chandradath (consul general for the Republic of Trinidad and Tobago, Miami, USA). 1998. Fax to Ricardo Bharath Re: "Real Colours: A Trinidad and Tobago Extravaganza." April 8.

Sioui, Konrad (chairman, FNCC). 1992. Letter to Donald Rojas (president, World Council of Indigenous Peoples). April 7.

Stollmeyer, John. 1999. *Turtle Island Children—The Autochthonous Voices of Amerikua*. Port of Spain: Turtle Island Children. A brochure.

Tourism and Industrial Development Corporation (TIDCO). 1998. "Community Tourism Awareness Program: Community Awareness Facility—Eligibility Criteria and Guidelines." Port of Spain: Coordinator, Community Tourism Awareness Program, TIDCO. (E-mail attachment from TIDCO, July 15, 1998.)

———. 1998. "TIDCO's Mission." Port of Spain: TIDCO.

Trinidad and Tobago Country Review. 2000. <http://www.countrywatch.com>, accessed May 1, 2001.

Trinidad and Tobago Gazette. 1995. "Legal Supplement Part A: The Companies Act (Act No. 35 of 1995)." 34 (227) November 2.

United Nations Conference on Environment and Development (UNCED). 1992. Agenda 21, Chapter 26: "Recognizing and Strengthening the Role of Indigenous People and their Communities." Rio de Janeiro, Brazil.

United Nations Development Program (UNDP). 2001a. *Report on Living Conditions in Trinidad and Tobago*. Port of Spain: United Nations Development Program. <http://www.undp.org.tt/tt/ttcont.htm>, accessed April 15, 2001.

———. 2001b. *Trinidad and Tobago: Facts and Figures*. Port of Spain: United Nations Development Program. <http://www.undp.org.tt/tt/ttfacts.htm>, accessed April 15, 2001.

United Nations Organisation (UN). 1994. *United Nations International Decade of the World's Indigenous People 1995–2004*. DPI/1608/HR—December. New York: United Nations Department of Public Information.

———. 1992. "Indigenous People: A New Partnership—International Year 1993." DPI/

1249—927109—July—30M. New York: United Nations Department of Public Information.

———. 1986. *Study of the Problem of Discrimination against Indigenous Populations.* E/ CN. 4/ Sub. 2/1986/7 and Add. 1–4.

United Nations Technical Conference on Indigenous Peoples and the Environment. 1992. E/CN. 4/ Sub. 2/1992/31. Santiago, Chile, May 18–22.

United Nations Working Group on Indigenous Populations. 1993. "Draft of Universal Declaration on the Rights of Indigenous Peoples," 11th session. <http://www. pantribalconfederacy.com/confederacy/un_dec.htm>, accessed March 12, 2001.

United States, Department of State (USDoS). 1998. *Background Notes: Trinidad and Tobago, March.* Released by the Bureau of Inter-American Affairs. <http://www.state. gov/www/background_notes/trinidad_tobago_0398_bgn.html>, accessed February 12, 2001.

Valiente, Jorge (vice-president of the World Council of Indigenous Peoples). 1991. Letter to Ovide Mercredi (chairman, Indigenous 500 Committee), November 26.

Vignale, Ralph P. (mayor of Arima). Letter to the archbishop of Port of Spain, August 11, 1939.

Wessel, Adele. 1992. Letter to Assembly of First Nations. January 28.

Wilson, David (sub-intendant of the Commissioners Office). Letter to the archbishop of Port of Spain. March 5, 1881.

World Bank Group. 2001a. *Countries: Trinidad and Tobago.* <http://www.worldbank. org/html/extdr/offrep/lac/tt2.htm>, accessed May 1, 2001.

———. 2001b. *Country-Competitiveness Indicators, Trinidad & Tobago.* <http:// wbln0018.worldbank.org/psd/compete.nsf/1f2245620075540d85256490005fb73a/ b2204a92c9209bf5852564e40068dc61?OpenDocument>, accessed May 1, 2001.

World Council of Indigenous Peoples. 1991. "Supplementary Information on the International Conference on Aboriginal Culture in the Americas." Project No. 02073–S41692.

World Intellectual Property Organization. 1999. *Interim Mission Report: Fact Finding Mission on Traditional Knowledge, Innovations and Culture of Indigenous Peoples, Local Communities and Other Holders of Traditional Knowledge and Culture—Caribbean Region.* Geneva: United Nations, WIPO.

Secondary Sources

Addo, Herb, et al. 1985. *Development as Social Transformation: Reflections on the Global Problematique.* London: Hodder and Stoughton.

Addo, Herb, ed. 1984. *Transforming the World-Economy: Nine Critical Essays on the New International Economic Order.* London: Hodder and Stoughton.

Agostini, Lisa-Allen. 1999. "Revising the Arena Affair." *Trinidad Guardian,* November 30:21.

Ahee, Cecil B. 1992. "The Carib Community of Arima, Five Hundred Years after Columbus." Bachelor's thesis, University of the West Indies, St. Augustine, Trinidad.

Akong, Al. 1999. "How about an Amerindian Heritage Day . . . The Indigenous Caribbean People Gave Us the Sturdy Pirogue." *The Independent,* October 1:23.

Alexander, Gail. 2000a. "Fracas in PNM Camp." *Sunday Guardian (Online),* April 30.

———. 2000b. "A Shamanic Journey in T&T." *Trinidad Guardian (Online),* April 12.

Alfonzo-Sierra, Edgar. 2002. "Susan Dayal y John Stollmeyer están comprometidos con su cultura: Telas, alambres y taparas de Trinidad procrean obras utilitarias y contem-poráneas." *El Nacional,* August 11. <http://www.el-nacional.com/l&f/ediciones/2002/08/11/pC15s1.htm>, accessed September 9, 2002.

Allard, Francisca Carol. 2000. "The Evolution of Parang (Music and Text) in Trinidad from 1900–1997." Masters thesis, University of the West Indies, St. Augustine, Trinidad.

Almarales, Beryl. 2002. *The Santa Rosa Carib Community, 1974–1998.* Arima.

———. 1998. "Help Needed for Carib Research Centre." *Trinidad Guardian,* June 27:8.

———. 1994. "The Santa Rosa Carib Community from 1974–1993." Bachelor's thesis, University of the West Indies, St. Augustine, Trinidad.

Amit, Vered. 2000. "Introduction: Constructing the Field." In *Constructing the Field: Ethnographic Fieldwork in the Contemporary World,* ed. Vered Amit, pp. 1–18. London: Routledge.

Anderson, Benedict. 1991. *Imagined Communities: Reflections on the Origins and Spread of Nationalism.* Rev. ed. London: Verso.

Andrews, Marlise. 2000a. "Ministry Proposes Housing Facility for Vagrants in Arima." *Trinidad Guardian (Online),* June 13.

———. 2000b. "Medina Is New Carib Queen." *Trinidad Guardian,* March 28:6.

Anthony, Michael. 1998. "Columbus Spots 'The Galley.'" *Sunday Guardian,* April 26:42.

———. 1988. *Towns and Villages of Trinidad and Tobago.* St. James, Port of Spain: Circle Press.

Antoun, Richard T. 1989. *Muslim Preacher in the Modern World.* Princeton: Princeton University Press.

Appadurai, Arjun. 1996. *Modernity at Large: Cultural Dimensions of Globalization.* Minneapolis: University of Minnesota Press.

———. 1994. "Disjuncture and Difference in the Global Cultural Economy." In *Colonial Discourse and Post-Colonial Theory,* ed. Patrick Williams and Laura Chrisman, pp. 324–339. New York: Columbia University Press.

———. 1991. "Global Ethnoscapes: Notes and Queries for a Transnational Anthropology." In *Recapturing Anthropology: Working in the Present,* ed. Richard G. Fox, pp. 191–210. Santa Fe, N.Mex.: School of American Research Press.

———. 1986. "Introduction: Commodities and the Politics of Value." In *The Social Life of Things: Commodities in Cultural Perspective,* ed. Arjun Appadurai, pp. 3–63. Cambridge: Cambridge University Press.

"Arawak." 2000. *The Columbia Encyclopedia,* 6th ed. <http://www.bartleby.com/65/ar/Arawak.html>, accessed January 3, 2000.

"Arawak." 1997–2000. *MSN Encarta Online Encyclopedia 2000.* <http://encarta.msn.com/find/Concise.asp?z=1&pg=2&ti=03CE3000>, accessed January 3, 2000.

Archer, Margaret S. 1988. *Culture and Agency: The Place of Culture in Social Theory.* Cambridge: Cambridge University Press.

Arévalo, Manuel A. García. 1990. "El indigenismo dominicano." In *Pueblos y políticas en el Caribe Amerindio,* pp. 37–42. México, D.F.: Instituto Indigenista Interamericano.

Ashcroft, Bill, Gareth Griffiths, and Helen Tiffin. 1995. "Introduction: Ethnicity and Indigeneity." In *The Post-Colonial Studies Reader,* ed. Bill Ashcroft et al., pp. 213–214. London: Routledge.

Assing, Tracy Kim. 2000. "Carib Politics 500 Years Later." *Sunday Guardian,* January 30:12.

Auguiste, Myriam. 2000. "Documentary on Carib Canoe Expedition." *Chronicle [Dominica]*, July 28.

Austin, Diane J. 1983. "Culture and Ideology in the English-Speaking Caribbean: A View from Jamaica." *American Ethnologist* 10(2) May:223–240.

Axtell, James. 1988. *After Columbus: Essays in the Ethnohistory of Colonial North America*. Oxford, U.K.: Oxford University Press.

Bandelier, Adolph F. 1999a. "Arawaks." *The Catholic Encyclopedia*, vol. 3. <http://www.newadvent.org/cathen/01680c.htm>, accessed January 3, 2000.

———. 1999b. "Caribs." *The Catholic Encyclopedia*, vol. 3. <http://www.newadvent.org/cathen/03348a.htm>, accessed January 3, 2000.

Banks, E. P. 1956. "A Carib Village in Dominica." *Social and Economic Studies* 5:74–86.

———. 1955. "Island Carib Folk Tales." *Caribbean Quarterly* 4:32–39.

Baker, Patrick. 1988. "Ethnogenesis. The Case of the Dominica Caribs." *América Indígena* 48(2):377–401.

Barbon, Keith. 1999. "Paktoha Ethnicity and Indigeneity." *Social Analysis* 43(2) July: 33–40.

Barome, Joseph. 1966. "Spain and Dominica, 1549–1647." *Caribbean Quarterly* 12(4) December.

Barreiro, José. 1997a. "Taíno Ascendant: Extinction, Continuities, and Reassertions." Mimeograph.

———. 1997b. "Taíno Voices: Indigenous Legacies." *Eleggua Project Newsletter* 1(4) September:4.

———. 1996. "Taíno Journal: The Cacique's Prayer." *Native Americas* Spring:38–47.

———. 1992. "Carib Gallery." In *Wild Majesty: Encounters with Caribs from Columbus to the Present Day*, ed. Peter Hulme and Neil L. Whitehead, pp. 345–353. Oxford: Clarendon Press.

———. 1990. "A Note on Taínos: Whither Progress?" *Northeast Indian Quarterly* Fall:66–77.

———. 1989. "Indians in Cuba." *Cultural Survival Quarterly* 13(3):56–60.

Barreiro, José, and Marie-Helene Laraque. 1998. "Canada First Nations Back Taíno Treaty." *Native Americas Magazine*, Hemispheric Digest, Winter.

Barth, Fredrik, ed. 1969. *Ethnic Groups and Boundaries: The Social Organization of Culture Difference*. London: George Allen and Unwin.

Basch, Linda, et al. 1994. *Nations Unbound: Transnational Projects, Postcolonial Predicaments, and Deterritorialized Nation-States*. Langhorne, Penn.: Gordon and Breach.

Bear Tribe Publishing. 1999. "The Bear Tribe Medicine Society." Canandaigua, N.Y.: Bear Tribe Publishing.

Beckett, Jeremy. 1996. "Contested Images: Perspectives on the Indigenous Terrain in the Late 20th Century." *Identities* 3(1–2):1–13.

Beckford, George L. 1983. *Persistent Poverty: Underdevelopment in Plantation Economies of the Third World*. London: Zed Books.

———, ed. 1975. *Caribbean Economy: Dependence and Backwardness*. Kingston, Jamaica: Institute of Social and Economic Research.

Beckles, Hilary McD. 1992. "Kalinago (Carib) Resistance to European Colonisation of the Caribbean." *Caribbean Quarterly* 38(2–3) June–September:1–15.

Beharry, Prior. 1999. "Put Aboriginal Centre in Trinidad says Chief." *Trinidad Guardian,* November 25:14.

Bell, Avril. 1999. "Authenticity and the Project of Settler Identity in New Zealand." *Social Analysis* 43(3) November:122–143.

Bell, Henry Hesketh. 1992 [1899]. "Glimpses of a Governor's Life." In *Wild Majesty: Encounters with Caribs from Columbus to the Present Day—An Anthology,* ed. Peter Hulme and Neil L. Whitehead, pp. 265–270. Oxford: Clarendon Press.

———. 1902. *Report on the Caribs of Dominica.* Colonial Report No. 219. Dominica, July 29.

Bellour, Helene, and Samuel Kinser. 1998. "Amerindian Masking in Trinidad's Carnival: The House of Black Elk in San Fernando." *Drama Review* 42(2) Fall:1–23 (page numbers corresponding to the electronic version).

Bennett, Herman L. 1989. "The Challenge to the Post Colonial State: A Case Study of the February Revolution in Trinidad." In *The Modern Caribbean,* ed. Franklin Knight and Colin Palmer, pp. 126–146. Chapel Hill: University of North Carolina Press.

Bentley, G. Carter. 1991. "Response to Yelvington." *Comparative Studies in Society and History* 33(1):169–175.

———. 1987. "Ethnicity and Practice." *Comparative Studies in Society and History* 29(1):24–55.

Berdichewsky, Bernardo. 1989. "Del indigenismo a la indianidad y el surgimiento de una ideología indígena en Andinoamérica." *Canadian Journal of Latin American and Caribbean Studies* 12(24):25–43.

Beriss, David. 1993. "High Folklore: Challenges to the French Cultural World Order." *Social Analysis* 33 September:105–129.

Bermúdez Negrón, René. 2000–2001. *300 Years of Spanish Presence in Trinidad.* Port of Spain. <http://community.wow.net/300history/toc.html>, accessed March 10, 2001.

Besson, Gerard, and Bridget Brereton, eds. 1991. *The Book of Trinidad.* Port of Spain: Paria Publishing.

Beyer, Peter. 1994. *Religion and Globalization.* London: Sage.

Bhabha, Homi K. 1995. "Cultural Diversity and Cultural Differences." In *The Post-Colonial Studies Reader,* ed. Bill Ashcroft et al., pp. 206–209. London: Routledge.

Birge, William S. 1900. *In Old Roseau. Reminiscences of Life as I Found it in the Island of Dominica, and Among the Carib Indians.* New York: Isaac H. Blanchard.

Birth, Kevin K. 1994. "Bakrnal: Coup, Carnival, and Calypso in Trinidad." *Ethnology* 33(2) Spring:165–178.

Bisnauth, Dale. 1996. *History of Religions in the Caribbean.* Trenton, N.J.: Africa World Press.

Blain, Jenny. 1999. "On Shamans, Stones, and Appropriation: Contestations of Invention and Meaning." Paper presented at the 25th Annual Conference of the Canadian Anthropology Society (CASCA), May 12–16, Université Laval, Québec, Canada.

Blood, Peter Ray. 2001. "A Season of Consciousness." *Trinidad Guardian (Online),* April 21.

Bodley, John H. 1990. *Victims of Progress,* 3rd ed. Mountain View, Calif.: Mayfield.

Bollinger, William, and Daniel Manny Lund. 1982. "Minority Oppression: Toward Analyses that Clarify and Strategies that Liberate." *Latin American Perspectives* 9(2) Spring:2–28.

Boomert, Arie. 1996. *The Prehistoric Sites of Tobago: A Catalogue and Evaluation.* Alkmaar, The Netherlands.

———. 1986. "The Cayo Complex of St. Vincent: Ethnohistorical and Archaeological Aspects of the Island Carib Problem." *Antropologica* 66:3–68.

———. 1982. "Our Amerindian Heritage." *Trinidad Naturalist* 4(4) July–August:26–38, 60.

Borde, Pierre-Gustave-Louis. 1883. *The History of the Island of Trinidad under the Spanish Government, Second Part (1622–1797).* Paris: Maisonneuve et Cie, Libraires-Editeurs.

———. 1876. *The History of the Island of Trinidad under the Spanish Government, Second Part (1498–1622).* Paris: Maisonneuve et Cie, Libraires-Editeurs.

Borofsky, Robert. 1994. "On the Knowledge and Knowing of Cultural Activities." In *Assessing Cultural Anthropology,* ed. Robert Borofsky, pp. 331–348. New York: McGraw-Hill.

Boucher, Philip P. 1992. *Cannibal Encounters: Europeans and Island Caribs, 1492–1763.* Baltimore: Johns Hopkins University Press.

Bourdieu, Pierre. 1994. "Structures, Habitus, Power: Basis for a Theory of Symbolic Power." In *Culture/Power/History,* ed. Nicholas B. Dirks et al., pp. 155–199. Princeton, N.J.: Princeton University Press.

———. 1992. *The Logic of Practice,* trans. Richard Nice. Cambridge, U.K.: Polity Press.

———. 1977. *Outline of a Theory of Practice.* Cambridge: Cambridge University Press.

Braithwaite, Lloyd. 1973. "The Problem of Cultural Integration in Trinidad (1954)." In *Consequences of Class and Colour: West Indian Perspectives,* ed. David Lowenthal and Lambros Comitas, pp. 241–260. Garden City, N.Y.: Anchor Books.

———. 1953. "Social Stratification in Trinidad." *Social and Economic Studies* 2:5–175.

Brathwaite, Edward Kamau. 1995. "Creolization in Jamaica." In *The Post-Colonial Studies Reader,* ed. Bill Ashcroft et al., pp. 202–205. London: Routledge.

Brecht, Fatima, Estrellita Brodsky, and John Alan Farmer, eds. 1997. *Taíno: Pre-Columbian Art and Culture from the Caribbean.* New York: Monacelli Press, El Museo del Barrio.

Brereton, Bridget. 1996. *An Introduction to the History of Trinidad and Tobago.* Oxford: Heinemann.

———. 1991a. "Cocoa, the Golden Bean: Cocoa and the Second Frontier (1870–1920)." In *The Book of Trinidad,* ed. Gerard Besson and Bridget Brereton, pp. 317–322. Port of Spain: Paria Publishing.

———. 1991b. "Trinidad: 1592 to the 1770s." In *The Book of Trinidad,* ed. Gerard Besson and Bridget Brereton, pp. 36. Port of Spain: Paria Publishing.

———. 1989. "Society and Culture in the Caribbean: The British and French West Indies, 1870–1980." In *The Modern Caribbean,* ed. Franklin Knight and Colin Palmer, pp. 85–110. Chapel Hill: University of North Carolina Press.

———. 1981. *A History of Modern Trinidad, 1783–1962.* London: Heinemann.

———. 1979. *Race Relations in Colonial Trinidad, 1870–1900.* Cambridge: Cambridge University Press.

Breton, Raymend P. 1929. *Les Caraibes, la Guadeloupe, 1635–1656.* Paris: Librairie Générale et Internationale G. Ficker.

———. 2001. [1665]. *Carib-Spanish Dictionary.* Trans. Duna Troiani. Paris: CELIA-CNRS. <http://www.sup-infor.com/ultimes/breton/dico_gari.htm>.

Bridenbaugh, Carl, and Roberta Bridenbaugh. 1972. *No Peace beyond the Line: The English in the Caribbean, 1624–1690.* New York: Oxford University Press.

Browman, David L. 1974. "Cariban." *Encyclopedia of Indians of the Americas,* vol. 4, pp. 58–59. St. Clair Shores, Mich.: Scholarly Press.

Buege, Douglas J. 1996. "The Ecologically Noble Savage Revisited." *Environmental Ethics* 18(1) Spring:71–88.

Bullbrook, John A. 1962. "Trade and Tragedy of a Thinly Cultured People. An Entrepot too for the Aborigines." *Sunday Guardian,* August 26:10, 12.

———. 1960. *The Aborigines of Trinidad.* Royal Victoria Institute Museum, Occasional Papers No. 2. Port of Spain: Royal Victoria Institute Museum.

———. 1953. *On the Excavation of a Shell Mound at Palo Seco, Trinidad, B.W.I.* New Haven: Yale University Press.

———. 1949a. "The Aboriginal Remains of Trinidad and the West Indies." *Caribbean Quarterly* 1(1) April–May:16–20.

———. 1949b. "The Aboriginal Remains of Trinidad and the West Indies—II." *Caribbean Quarterly* 2(2) July–September:10–15.

———. 1940. "The Ierian Race." (A lecture delivered at the meeting of the Historical Society of Trinidad and Tobago held in the hall of the Victoria Institute on Friday Evening 8:30 o'clock 3rd March, 1939.) Port of Spain: Historical Society of Trinidad and Tobago.

Burnett, Trevor. 2000. "Carib Queen Dies at 84." *Trinidad (Internet) Express,* January 19, General News.

———. 1999. "Santa Rosa Celebrations Starts with a Bang." *Trinidad Express,* September 2:27.

———. 1998a. "Shaman Unveils Carib-Parang Music." *Trinidad Express,* November 11, Sec. 2:4–5.

———. 1998b. "Caribs Feel Slighted by PM Panday." *Trinidad Express,* September 22:11.

———. 1998c. "Caribs Celebrate Santa Rosa Festival." *Trinidad Express,* August 24:11.

Burnley, William Hardin. 1842. *Observations on the Present Condition of the Island of Trinidad, and the Actual State of the Experiment of Negro Emancipation.* London: Longman, Brown, Green, and Longmans.

Butler, Afiya. 2000. "Mystery of the Pitch Lake." *Trinidad Express,* April 10. <http://209.94.197.2/apr00/apr10/features.htm>, accessed May 5, 2000.

Calliste, Gillian. 1998. "Galeron Singer Revives Parang." *Sunday Guardian,* November 8:2.

Campbell, Susan. 2001. "Defending Aboriginal Sovereignty: The 1930 'Carib War' in Waitukubuli (Dominica)." Paper presented at the University of the West Indies' Dominica Country Conference. <http://www.uwichill.edu.bb/bnccde/dominica/conference/paperdex.html>, accessed June 2, 2002.

"Cannibalism." 2000. *The Columbia Encyclopedia,* 6th ed. <http://www.bartleby.com/65/ca/cannibal.html>, accessed January 3, 2000.

Caputo, Virginia. 2000. "At 'Home' and 'Away': Reconfiguring the Field for Late Twentieth-Century Anthropology." In *Constructing the Field: Ethnographic Fieldwork in the Contemporary World,* ed. Vered Amit, pp. 19–31. London: Routledge.

Carib. 2000. "Brand Profiles: Carib Lager Beer." Port of Spain: Carib Brewery. <http://www.caribbeer.com/brands/carib.htm>, accessed February 2, 2000.

"Carib." 1997–2000. *MSN Encarta Online Encyclopedia 2000.* <http://encarta.msn.com/find/Concise.asp?z=1&pg=2&ti=02BFA000>, accessed January 3, 2000.

"Carib." 1993. *Dictionary of Indian Tribes of the Americas,* 2nd ed., vol. 1, pp. 224–229. Newport Beach, Calif.: American Indian Publishers.

Carib Brewery. 2000. "Carib Builds Visitor Resource Centre for Carib Community." *Carib Brews Newsletter* July–September. <http://www.caribbeer.com/brews/brews9.htm>, accessed February 2, 2000.

"Caribs." 2000. *The Columbia Encyclopedia,* 6th ed. <http://www.bartleby.com/65/ca/CaribInd.html>, accessed January 3, 2000.

Caricom Perspective. 1992. "Carifesta V." January–June:26–27.

———. 1991a. "COIP." 50/51, January–June:11

———. 1991b. "Encounter of Worlds—A Conceptual Framework for Caribbean Events 1992." 50/51, January–June:48–49.

———. 1991c. "The Umana Yana." 50/51, January–June:10–11.

———. 1990. "The Santa Rosa Community Trinidad and Tobago." July–December: 16–17.

"Carina." 1994. In *Encyclopedia of World Cultures,* vol. 7: *South America,* ed. Johannes Wilbert, pp. 102–103. Boston: G.K. Hall.

Catholic News. 1999. "Caribs Seen in a Different Light." January 24:12.

Catholic News Online. 2000. "Fr. Pereira: Santa Rosa Feast Important to Whole Country." Sunday, September 3, Front Page, Parish News.

Chalifoux, Jean-Jacques. 1999. "Shamanism and Insignificant Innovations." Paper presented at the 25th Annual Conference of the Canadian Anthropology Society (CASCA), May 12–16, Université Laval, Québec, Canada.

———. 1998. "Chamanisme et couvades chez les Galibi de la Guyane Française." *Anthropologie et Sociétés* 22(2):99–122.

Chapin, Mac. 1989a. "Introduction." *Cultural Survival Quarterly* 13(3):1–2.

———. 1989b. "The 500,000 Invisible Indians of El Salvador." *Cultural Survival Quarterly* 13(3):11–16.

Charan, Richard. 1998. "Moruga to Mark the 500th Anniversary of Columbus' Discovery." *Newsday,* July 20:7.

Chin, David J. 1999. "Letter to the Editor: All Lands belong to the Caribs." *Sunday Mirror,* June 6:24.

Chouthi, Sandra. 1998a. "Celebrate Our Carib Heritage." *Trinidad Express,* June 29, Sec. 2:1.

———. 1998b. "21st Century Carib." *Caribbean Beat Magazine* September–October: 20–22.

———. 1998c. "T&T Goes after Billion-Dollar Travel Trade: Rustic Resort to Lure Eco-Tourists." *Trinidad Express (Online),* February 4. <http://209.94.197.2/feb/feb4/features.htm>, accessed March 5, 1998.

———. 1998d. "More to Tourism than Sea and Sand." *Trinidad Express,* April 23:33.

Clarke, Colin. 1993. "Spatial Pattern and Social Interaction among Creoles and Indians in Trinidad and Tobago." In *Trinidad Ethnicity,* ed. Kelvin A. Yelvington, pp. 116–135. Knoxville: University of Tennessee Press.

Clarke, Le Roy. 1998. "Hard on the Humour of Hard." *Trinidad Guardian,* February 21:11.

Clifford, James. 1994. "Diasporas." *Cultural Anthropology* 9(3) August:302–338.

———. 1988. *The Predicament of Culture: Twentieth Century Ethnography, Literature, and Art.* Cambridge, Mass.: Harvard University Press.

CMR. 1999. "Letter to the Editor: Historical Tragedy of Errors." *Trinidad Guardian,* April 21:11.

Cohen, Abner. 1980. "Drama and Politics in the Development of a London Carnival." *Man* 15:65–87.

———. 1974. "The Lesson of Ethnicity." In *Urban Ethnicity,* ed. Abner Cohen, pp. ix–xxiii. London: Tavistock.

———. 1969. *Custom and Politics in Urban Africa.* Berkeley: University of California Press.

Cohen, Anthony P. 1989. *The Symbolic Construction of Community.* London: Routledge.

Cohen, Colleen Ballerino, and Frances E. Mascia-Lees. 1993. "The British Virgin Islands as Nation and Desti-nation: Representing and Siting Identity in a Post-Colonial Carib-bean." *Social Analysis* 33 September:130–131.

Coke, Thomas, 1971 [1810]. *A History of the West Indies Containing the Natural, Civil, and Ecclesiastical History of Each Island.* London: Frank Cass.

Coleridge, Henry Nelson. 1991 [1826]. "Six Months in the West Indies." In *The Book of Trinidad,* ed. Gerard Besson and Bridget Brereton, pp. 117–126. Port of Spain: Paria Publishing.

———. 1826. *Six Months in the West Indies.* London: John Murray.

Collens, James Henry. 1912. *Handbook of Trinidad and Tobago for the Use of Settlers.* Prepared by a Committee of the Board of Agriculture. Port of Spain: Government Printing Office.

———. 1896. *Centenary of Trinidad, 1797–1897. The Trinidad and Tobago Year Book, 1897, Compiled from Official Records.* Port of Spain: Government Printing Office.

———. 1886. *Guide to Trinidad: A Handbook for the Use of Tourists and Visitors.* Port of Spain.

Collier, George A. 1999. Review of *Indigenous Movements and Their Critics: Pan-Maya Activism in Guatemala* by Kay B. Warren. *American Ethnologist* 26(4) November:1009–1010.

Colson, Elizabeth. 1968. "Contemporary Tribes and the Development of Nationalism." In *Essays on the Problem of Tribe,* ed. June Helm, pp. 201–208. Seattle: American Ethnological Society, University of Washington Press.

Columbus, Christopher. 1992 [1493]. "The Letter of Columbus." In *Wild Majesty: Encounters with Caribs from Columbus to the Present Day—An Anthology,* ed. Peter Hulme and Neil L. Whitehead, pp. 9–16. Oxford: Clarendon Press.

Comaroff, Jean, and John L. Comaroff. 1999. "Occult Economies and the Violence of Abstraction: Notes from the South African Postcolony." *American Ethnologist* 26(2):279–303.

Conklin, Beth A. 1997. "Body Paint, Feathers, and VCRs: Aesthetics and Authenticity in Amazonian Activism." *American Ethnologist* 24(4) November:711–737.

Connelly, Corey. 1998. "Arima Honours 24 of Its Own." *Trinidad Guardian,* August 17:6.

Corntassel, Jeff J., and Thomas Hopkins Primeau. 1998. "The Paradox of Indigenous Identity: A Levels-of-Analysis Approach." *Global Governance* 4(2) April–June:139–156.

Cothonay, R. P. Marie-Bertrand, O.P. 1893. *Trinidad: Journal d'un Missionaire*

Dominicain des Antilles Anglaises. Preface by R.P. Ch.–Anatole Joyau, O.P., editor. Paris: Victor Retaux et Fils, Libraires-Éditeurs.

Craton, Michael. 1986. "From Caribs to Black Caribs: The Amerindian Roots of Servile Resistance in the Caribbean." In *Resistance: Studies in African, Caribbean, and AfroAmerican History,* ed. Gary Y. Okihiro, pp. 96–116. Amherst: University of Massachusetts Press.

Crowley, Daniel J. 1957. "Plural and Differential Acculturation in Trinidad." *American Anthropologist* 59:817–824.

———. 1956. "The Midnight Robbers." *Caribbean Quarterly* 4(3–4) March–June:263–294.

Cudjoe, Selwyn R. 2000. *Selwyn Cudjoe Archives.* Port of Spain: TriniCenter.com.

——— 1995 *Tacarigua: A Village in Trinidad.* Wellesley, Mass.: Calaloux Publications.

Cunningham, Hilary. 1999. "The Ethnography of Transnational Social Activism: Understanding the Global as Local Practice." *American Ethnologist* 26(3) August:583–604.

Cunningham, Scott. 1997. *Cunningham's Encyclopaedia of Crystal, Gem and Metal Magic.* St. Paul, Minn.: Llewellyn Publications.

Cupid, John. 1971. "There's More to Parang." *Trinidad Guardian,* December 26:17.

Danns, George K. 1997. "Race and Development in Plural Societies: The Case of Guyana." *Caribbean Dialogue* 3(2) June:32–41.

Dávila, Arlene. 1999. "Local/Diasporic Tainos: Towards a Cultural Politics of Memory, Reality and Imagery." In *Taíno Revival: Critical Perspectives on Puerto Rican Identity and Cultural Politics,* ed. Gabriel Haslip-Viera, pp. 11–29. New York: Centro de Estudios Puertorriqueños, Hunter College, City University of New York.

Davis, Dave D. 1992. "Rumor of Cannibals: Columbus Hears Stories of Carib Ferocity." *Archaeology* 45(1) January–February:49.

Davis, Dave D., and R. Christopher Goodwin. 1990. "Island Carib Origins: Evidence and Non-evidence." *American Antiquity* 55(1):37–48.

Deagan, Kathleen. 1985. "Spanish-Indian Interactions in Sixteenth Century Florida and the Caribbean." In *Cultures in Contact,* ed. W. Fitzhugh, pp. 281–318. Washington, D.C.: Smithsonian Institution Press.

De Coteau, Alvin. 2000. "Walking in Columbus' Footsteps." *Trinidad (Internet) Express,* August 3, Features Page.

de Lima, Arthur. 1993. *Don José.* Devon: Arthur H. Stockwell.

De Mallie, Raymond J. 1993. "'These Have No Ears.' Narrative and the Ethnohistorical Method." *Ethnohistory* 40:515–530.

Denzin, Norman K. 1994. "The Art and Politics of Interpretation." In *Handbook of Qualitative Research,* ed. Norman K. Denzin and Yvonna S. Lincoln, pp. 500–515. Thousand Oaks, Calif.: Sage.

de Verteuil, Alex. 1999. "Spirit of the Americas." *Caribbean Beat* 40 November–December:40–47.

de Verteuil, Anthony, C. S. Sp. 1995. *Martyrs and Murderers: Trinidad, 1699.* Port of Spain: St. Mary's College.

De Verteuil, L. A. A. 1858. *Trinidad: Its Geography, Natural Resources, Administration, Present Condition, and Prospects.* London: Ward and Lock.

Díaz-Polanco, Héctor. 1982. "Indigenismo, Populism, and Marxism." *Latin American Perspectives* (Issue 33) 9(2) Spring:42–61.

Dirks, Nicholas B., Geof Eley, and Sherry B. Ortner. 1994. "Introduction: Culture/Power/

History." In *Culture/Power/History*, ed. Nicholas B. Dirks et al., pp. 3–46. Princeton, N.J.: Princeton University Press.

Douglas, Tricia N. F. 1999. "Gens d'Arime: The Original French Settlers of Arima." Bachelor's thesis, University of the West Indies, St. Augustine, Trinidad.

Drummond, Lee. 1977. "On Being Carib." In *Carib-Speaking Indians: Culture, Society, and Language*, ed. Ellen B. Basso, pp. 76–88. Tucson: University of Arizona Press.

Duany, Jorge. 1999. "Making Indians Out of Blacks: The Revitalization of Taíno Identity in Contemporary Puerto Rico." In *Taíno Revival: Critical Perspectives on Puerto Rican Identity and Cultural Politics*, ed. Gabriel Haslip-Viera, pp. 31–56. New York: Centro de Estudios Puertorriqueños, Hunter College, City University of New York.

Durning, A. T. 1992. *Guardians of the Land: Indigenous Peoples and the Health of the Earth*. Worldwatch Paper No. 112. Washington, D.C.: The Worldwatch Institute.

Du Tertre, Jean-Baptiste. 1958 [1667]. *Histoire générale des isles de S. Christophe, de la Guadeloupe, de la Martinique et autre dans L'amerique*, trans. Marshall McKusick and Pierre Verin. Human Resources Area Files: ST 13 Callinago.

Ebron, Paulla A. 2000. Review of *Mestizo Logics: Anthropology of Identity in Africa and Elsewhere* by Jean-Loup Amselle. *American Anthropologist* 102(1) March:178–179.

Edwards, Bryan. 1966 [1819]. *The History, Civil and Commercial, of the British West Indies*. New York: AMS Press.

Eguchi, Nobukiyo. 1997. "Ethnic Tourism and Reconstruction of the Caribs' Ethnic Identity." In *Ethnicity, Race, and Nationality in the Caribbean*, ed. Juan Manuel Carrión, pp. 364–380. San Juan: Institute of Caribbean Studies, University of Puerto Rico.

Einhorn, Arthur C. 2002. "Out of Pandora's Closet," *CAC Review* 3(5) June. <http://www.centrelink.org/June2002.html>, accessed July 10, 2002.

Elie, Jean Patricia. 2000. "The Carib Queens of Arima." *Catholic News Online*, March 5, Features.

———. 1990. *A Short History of Santa Rosa de Arima*. Arima: J. P. Elie.

Eriksen, Thomas Hylland. 1993a. "Do Cultural Islands Exist?" *Social Anthropology* 1. <http://www.uio.no/~geirthe/Culturalislands.html>, accessed February 2, 2000.

———. 1993b. "The Epistemological Status of the Concept of Ethnicity." Paper presented at the Anthropology of Ethnicity Conference, December, Amsterdam. <http://www.uio.no/~geirthe/Status_of_ethnicity.html>, accessed February 2, 2000.

———. 1992. "Multiple Traditions and the Question of Cultural Integration." *Ethnos* 3–4. <http://www.sv.uio.no/~geirthe/Multiple.html>, accessed February 2, 2000.

Espinosa, Antonio Vázquez de. 1968. *Description of the Indies (c. 1620)*, trans. Charles Upson Clark. Smithsonian Miscellaneous Collections Vol. 102. Washington, D.C.: Smithsonian Institution Press.

Fabian, Johannes. 1991. "Dilemmas of Critical Anthropology." In *Constructing Knowledge: Authority and Critique in Social Science*, ed. N. Lorraine and P. Pels, pp. 184–211. London: Sage.

———. 1983. *Time and the Other: How Anthropology Makes Its Object*. New York: Columbia University Press.

Ferbel, Peter J. 1998. "The Taino Heritage of Casabe in the Dominican Republic." Paper presented at the Indigenous Legacies of the Caribbean Interdisciplinary Conference and Field Study, January 3–11, Baracoa, Cuba.

———. 1997. "Taino Heritage in the Dominican Republic." Paper presented at the Indigenous Legacies of the Caribbean Interdisciplinary Conference and Field Study, November 16–23, Baracoa, Cuba.

———. 1995. "The Politics of Taíno Indian Heritage in the Post-Quincentennial Dominican Republic: 'When a Canoe Means More than a Water Trough.'" Ph.D. diss., University of Minnesota.

Fermor, Patrick Leigh. 1950. "The Caribs of Dominica." *Geographical Magazine* 26(6): 256–264.

Field, Les. 1994. "Who Are the Indians?" *Latin American Research Review* 29(3):227–238.

Figueredo, Alfredo E., and Stephen D. Glazier. 1991. "A Revised Aboriginal Ethnohistory of Trinidad (1978)." In *Earliest Hispanic/Native American Interactions in the Caribbean*, ed. William F. Keegan, pp. 237–240. New York: Garland Publishing.

Fogelson, Raymond D. 1989. "The Ethnohistory of Events and Nonevents." *Ethnohistory* 36(2):133–147.

Forte, Janette. 1996. *Thinking about Amerindians*. Georgetown, Guyana: Janette Forte.

Forte, Janette, and Ian Melville, eds. 1989. *Amerindian Testimonies*. Georgetown: Janette Forte.

Forte, Maximilian C. 2003. "Co-Construction and Field Creation: Website Development as both an Instrument and Relationship in Action Research." In *Virtual Research Ethics: Issues and Controversies,* ed. Elizabeth Buchanan, pp. 222–248. Hershey, Penn.: Idea Publishing Group.

———. 2002a. "Arima Caribs Win Lands after 30 Years." *CAC Review* 3(10) December. <http://www.centrelink.org/Dec2002.html>, accessed January 3, 2003.

———. 2002b. "The First Nations Resource Centre in Arima, Trinidad." *CAC Review* 3(7–8) August–September. <http://www.centrelink.org/Sept2002.html>, accessed January 3, 2003.

———. 2002c. "The 2002 Santa Rosa Festival of the Arima Caribs." *CAC Review* 3(7–8) August–September. <http://www.centrelink.org/Sept2002.html>, accessed January 3, 2003.

———. 2002d. "Guyanese Amerindian Contingent at the Carib Centre in Arima." *CAC Review* 3(7–8) August–September. <http://www.centrelink.org/Sept2002.html>, accessed January 3, 2003.

———. 2001. "'Our Amerindian Ancestors: The State, the Nation, and the Revaluing of Indigeneity in Trinidad and Tobago." *Issues in Caribbean Amerindian Studies* 3(1). <http://www.centrelink.org/Forte.html>, accessed February 6, 2002.

———. 2000. "The Contemporary Context of Carib 'Revival' in Trinidad and Tobago: Creolization, Developmentalism, and the State." *KACIKE: Journal of Caribbean Amerindian History and Anthropology* 1(1) January–June:18–33. <http://www.kacike.org/>, accessed May 14, 2004.

———. 1999a. "Arima: An Introduction to the History of the Gens d'Arime." *Los Niños del Mundo Trinidad Parang Website.* <http://trinidadtobagoparang.freeyellow.com/Arima.html>, accessed March 5, 2002.

———. 1999b. "Beyond the Boundary, Within the Domain: Ethnographic Partnerships with Caribbean Amerindians and the Transformative Projection of Anthropology." Paper presented at American Anthropological Association (AAA) meetings, November 17–21, Chicago, Illinois.

———. 1999c. "Ethnographer, Broker, Partner, Spy: Between Investigation and Intervention in Fieldwork among the Caribs of Trinidad." Canadian Sociology and Anthropology Association (CSAA) meetings, June 6–9, Bishop's University, Lennoxville, Québec, Canada.

———. 1999d. "Renewed Indigeneity in the Local-Global Continuum and the Political Economy of Tradition among Modern West Indian Caribs." In *Visioning the 21st Century: Globalization, Transformation and Opportunity. Proceedings of the 24th Annual Third World Conference*, ed. R. K. Oden, pp. 68–75. Chicago: TWCF/Governors State University.

———. 1999e. "Reviving Caribs: Recognition, Patronage, and Ceremonial Indigeneity in Trinidad and Tobago." *Cultural Survival Quarterly* 23(4) Winter:35–41.

———. 1999f. "Trinidad's Caribs and the Globalization of Caribbean Aboriginality." *Boletín Informativo de la Nación Taína de las Antillas* 7(2) March April:1 3.

———. 1998a. *Caribbean Amerindian Centrelink*. Arima. CAC. <http://www.centrelink. org>, accessed May 16, 2004.

——— 1998b *The First Nations of Trinidad and Tobago* <http://www.centrelink.org/ ma/maxforte/index.html>, accessed May 16, 2004. <http://www.centrelink.org/II.html>, accessed May 14, 2004.

———. 1998c. "From Smoke Ceremonies to Cyberspace: Globalized Indigeneity, Multi-Sited Research, and the Internet." *Issues in Caribbean Amerindian Studies* 1. <http:// www.centrelink.org/Internet.html>, accessed May 14, 2004.

———. 1998d. *Gateway to the Caribs of Trinidad and Tobago*. <http://members.tripod. com/Trinidad_TobagoCARIB/Carib.htm>, accessed January 4, 2001.

———. 1998e. "Globalization and World-Systems Analysis: Toward New Paradigms of a Geo-Historical Social Anthropology (A Research Review)." *Review* 21(1):29–99.

———. 1998f. "The International Indigene: Regional and Global Integration of Amerindian Communities in the Caribbean." *Issues in Caribbean Amerindian Studies* 1.

———. 1998g. *The Santa Rosa Carib Community of Arima, Trinidad*. <http://www. kacike.org/cac-ike/srcc/>, accessed May 14, 2004.

———. 1998h. "Trinidad and Tobago Parang Music." *Cristo Adonis' Los Niños del Mundo Sonified Website*. <http://www.freeyellow.com/members6/trinidadtobagoparang/index. html>, accessed March 5, 2002.

———. 1998i. *A University of Adelaide Anthropological Field Project on Trinidad's Self-Identified Amerindian Descendants and Their Organizations, 1998–1999*. <http:// members.theglobe.com/mcforte/default.html>, accessed January 4, 2001.

———. 1996a. *Against the Trinity: An Insurgent Imam Tells His Story (Religion, Politics, and Rebellion in Trinidad and Tobago)*. Binghamton, N.Y.: Ahead.

———. 1996b. "The Modern World-System and the Carib Community of Santa Rosa, Arima, Trinidad: Ethnohistory and Ethno-politics from Colonialism to Revitalization." Master's research paper. Department of Anthropology, State University of New York at Binghamton.

———. 1995. "The Crisis of Creolization in Trinidad and Tobago? Globalized Revitalizations, Systemic Ethno-Politics, and Alter-Nationalisms." *International Third World Studies Journal and Review* 7:41–54.

———. Forthcoming. "Amerindian@Caribbean: Internet Indigeneity in the Electronic Generation of Carib and Taino Identities." In *Going Native on the Net: Indigenous Cyber Activism on the World Wide Web*, ed. Kyra Marie Landzelius. London: Routledge.

Foster, Robert. 1991. "Making National Cultures in the Global Ecumene." *Annual Review in Anthropology* 20:235–290.

Fox, Desrey. 1996. "Continuity and Change among the Amerindians of Guyana." In *Ethnic Minorities in Caribbean Society,* ed. Rhoda Reddock, pp. 9–105. St. Augustine, Trinidad: ISER, University of the West Indies.

Fraser, Lionel Mordant. 1971 [1896]. *History of Trinidad (Second Period), from 1814 to 1839,* vol. 2. London: Frank Cass.

———. 1971 [1891]. *History of Trinidad (First Period), from 1781 to 1813,* vol. 1. London: Frank Cass.

Freeman, Miller. 1999. "In Brief [On the Gli-Gli Carib Canoe]." *Travel Trade Gazette (UK & Ireland).* August 16.

Fried, Morton. 1968. "On the Concepts of 'Tribe' and 'Tribal Society.'" In *Essays on the Problem of Tribe,* ed. June Helm, pp. 3–20. Seattle. American Ethnological Society, University of Washington Press.

Friedman, Jonathan. 2002. "From Roots to Routes. Tropes for Trippers." *Anthropological Theory* 2(1):21–36.

———. 1999. "Indigenous Struggles and the Discreet Charm of the Bourgeoisie." *Australian Journal of Anthropology* 10(1) April:1–14.

———. 1996. "The Politics of De-Authentification: Escaping from Identity, a Response to 'Beyond Authenticity' by Mark Rogers." *Identities* 3(1–2):127–136.

———. 1994. *Cultural Identity and Global Process.* London: Sage.

———. 1990. "Being in the World: Globalization and Localization." In *Global Culture: Nationalism, Globalization and Modernity,* ed. Mike Featherstone. London: Sage.

———. N.d. "Transnationalization, Socio-Political Disorder, and Ethnification as Expressions of Declining Global Hegemony." <http://www.soc.lu.se/san/papers/transnateth.html>, accessed March 5, 2002.

Fugelstad, Finn. 1992. "The Trevor-Roper Trap or the Imperialism of History: An Essay." *History in Africa* 19:309–326.

Gans, H. 1979. "Symbolic Ethnicity: The Future of Ethnic Groups and Cultures in America." *Ethnic and Racial Studies* 2:1–20.

Garbett, Kingsley. 1970. "The Analysis of Social Situations." *Man* 5(2):214–227.

Garcia, Beulah P. 1991. "The Borough of Arima: The War Years and beyond, 1938–1988." Master's thesis, University of the West Indies, St. Augustine, Trinidad.

Geertz, Clifford. 1994. "The Uses of Diversity." In *Assessing Cultural Anthropology,* ed. Robert Borofsky, pp. 454–467. New York: McGraw-Hill.

Gellner, Ernest. 1983. *Nations and Nationalism.* Oxford: Basil Blackwell.

Geschiere, Peter, and Birgit Meyer. 1998. "Globalization and Identity: Dialectics of Flow and Closure." *Development and Change* 29:601–615.

Giddens, Anthony. 1994. *Beyond Left and Right: The Future of Radical Politics.* Stanford: Stanford University Press.

———. 1991. *Modernity and Self-Identity.* Stanford: Stanford University Press.

———. 1990. *The Consequences of Modernity.* Stanford: Stanford University Press.

———. 1984. *The Constitution of Society: Outline of the Theory of Structuration.* Berkeley: University of California Press.

———. 1979. *Central Problems in Social Theory: Action, Structure, and Contradiction in Social Analysis.* Cambridge: Cambridge University Press.

Gilkes, A. Corey. 1998a. "Letter to the Editor: Unveiling the Myth of Columbus." *Newsday,* July 3:22.

———. 1998b. "Letter to the Editor: Discovering Columbus and His Story." *Trinidad Guardian,* July 13:08.

Girvan, Norman, and Owen Jefferson, eds. 1971. *Readings in the Political Economy of the Caribbean.* Kingston, Jamaica: Institute for Social and Economic Research.

Girwar, Peter. 1964. "Carib Customs Are Dying Out." *Evening News,* July 14:05.

Glaberson, William. 2001. "Who Is a Seminole, and Who Gets to Decide?" *New York Times* (Internet edition), January 29.

Glazier, Stephen D. 1983. *Marchin' the Pilgrims Home: A Study of the Spiritual Baptists of Trinidad.* Salem, Wisc.: Sheffield Publishing.

Glick, Leonard B. 1985. "Epilogue: The Meanings of Ethnicity in the Caribbean." In *Caribbean Ethnicity Revisited,* ed. Stephen D. Glazier, pp. 149–164. New York: Gordon and Breach.

Glissant, Edouard. 1989. *Caribbean Discourse.* Translated by Michael J. Dash. Charlottesville: University Press of Virginia.

Gobin, Crystal. 1998. "No Stopping Discovery Day in Moruga." *Trinidad Express,* August 1:13.

Godelier, Maurice. 1994. "'Mirror, Mirror on the Wall . . .' The Once and Future Role of Anthropology: A Tentative Assessment." In *Assessing Cultural Anthropology,* ed. Robert Borofsky, pp. 97–112. New York: McGraw-Hill.

Goffman, Erving. 1990 [1959]. *The Presentation of Self in Everyday Life.* London: Penguin.

Goldwasser, Michele. 1994/96. "Remembrances of the Warao: the Miraculous Statue of Siparia, Trinidad." *Antropologica* 843–862.

———. 1996. "The Rainbow Madonna of Trinidad: A Study in the Dynamics of Belief in Trinidadian Religious Life." (Ph.D. diss., University of California at Los Angeles.) Ann Arbor, Mich.: University Microfilms International.

Gonzalez, Nancie L. 1990. "From Cannibals to Mercenaries: Carib Militarism, 1600–1840." *Journal of Anthropological Research* 46(1) Spring:25–40.

———. 1988. *Sojourners of the Caribbean: Ethnogenesis and Ethnohistory of the Garifuna.* Chicago: University of Illinois Press.

———. 1983. "New Evidence on the Origin of the Black Carib, with Thoughts on the Meaning of Tradition." *New West Indian Guide* 57(3–4):143–172.

Gooding, Ian. 1999. "Trinidad to be World Indigenous Headquarters." *Newsday,* November 23:5.

Gordon, Shirley C. 1983. *Caribbean Generations: A CXC History Source Book.* Port of Spain: Longman Caribbean.

Gosine, Susan. 1998. "Trinis in Miami to Mark Independence." *Trinidad Express,* August 24:9.

Government of the Republic of Trinidad and Tobago. 2000. "About T&T: Historical Overview." *The Official Website of the Government of the Republic of Trinidad and Tobago.* <http://www.gov.tt/trinbago/history.html>, accessed February 2, 2000.

Gregoire, Crispin, Patrick Henderson, and Natalia Kanem. 1996. "Karifuna: The Caribs of Dominica." In *Ethnic Minorities in Caribbean Society,* ed. Rhoda Reddock, pp. 107–172. St. Augustine, Trinidad: ISER, University of the West Indies.

Gregoire, Crispin, and Natalia Kanem. 1989. "The Caribs of Dominica: Land Rights and Ethnic Consciousness." *Cultural Survival Quarterly* 13(3):52–55.

Guedon, Marie-Françoise. 1999. "Teaching Shamanism." Paper presented at the 25th Annual Conference of the Canadian Anthropology Society (CASCA), May 12–16, Université Laval, Québec, Canada.

Guitar, Lynne A. 2000. "Criollos—The Birth of a Dynamic New Indo-Afro-European People and Culture on Hispaniola." *KACIKE: Journal of Caribbean Amerindian History and Anthropology* 1(1) January–June:1–17. <http://www.kacike.org/LynneGuitar. pdf>, accessed May 14, 2004.

———. 1998a. "Cultural Genesis: Relationships among Indians, Africans and Spaniards in Rural Hispaniola, First Half of the Sixteenth Century." Ph.D. diss., Vanderbilt University.

———. 1998b. "Myth Management: An Historian Examines How and Why the Myth of Taino Extinction Began." Mimeograph.

———. 1998c. "La herencia Taina en la República Dominicana." Summary of a brief lesson for secondary students at the Book Festival. Mimeograph.

Gullick, Charles J.M.R. 1985. *Myths of a Minority: The Changing Traditions of the Vincentian Caribs.* Assen, The Netherlands: Van Gorcum.

Gupta, Akhil, and James Ferguson. 1992. "Beyond 'Culture': Space, Identity, and the Politics of Difference." *Cultural Anthropology* 7(1):6–23.

Hall, Stuart. 1994. "Cultural Identity and Diaspora." In *Colonial Discourse and Post-Colonial Theory,* ed. Patrick Williams and Laura Chrisman, pp. 392–403. New York: Columbia University Press.

———. 1991. "The Local and the Global: Globalization and Ethnicity." In *Culture, Globalization, and the World System: Contemporary Conditions for the Representation of Identity,* ed. Anthony D. King, pp. 19–39. London: Macmillan.

Handler, Jerome S. 1970. "Aspects of Amerindian Ethnography in 17th Century Barbados." *Caribbean Quarterly* 9(4) January:50–72.

Handler, Richard. 1988. *Nationalism and the Politics of Culture in Quebec.* Madison: University of Wisconsin Press.

———. 1985. "On Having a Culture: Nationalism and the Preservation of Quebec's *Patrimoine.*" In *Objects and Others,* ed. George Stocking, pp. 192–217. Madison: University of Wisconsin Press.

Handler, Richard, and Jocelyn Linnekin. 1984. "Tradition, Genuine or Spurious." *Journal of American Folklore* 97(385):273–290.

Handler, Richard, and Daniel A. Segal. 1993. "Introduction: Nations, Colonies, and Metropoles." *Social Analysis* 33 September:3–8.

Hannerz, Ulf. 1996. *Transnational Connections: Culture, People, Places.* London: Routledge.

———. 1992. *Cultural Complexity: Studies in the Social Organization of Meaning.* New York: Columbia University Press.

———. 1991. "Scenarios for Peripheral Cultures." In *Culture, Globalization, and the World-System,* ed. Anthony D. King, pp. 107–128. Binghamton: Department of Art and Art History, State University of New York at Binghamton.

———. 1990. "Cosmopolitans and Locals in World Culture." In *Global Culture: Nationalism, Globalization, and Modernity,* ed. Mike Featherstone, pp. 237–251. London: Sage.

———. 1987. "The World in Creolisation." *Africa* 57(4):546–559.

Hanson, Allan. 1989. "The Making of the Maori: Culture Invention and Its Logic." *American Anthropologist* 91(4):890–902.

Harricharan, Fr. John Thomas. 1985. Homily of the Catholic Indian Mass—140th anniversary of Indians' Arrival Day. Saturday, June 1:13–14.

———. 1983. *The Catholic Church in Trinidad, 1498–1852*, vol. 1. Port of Spain: Inprint Caribbean.

Harris, Peter. 1990a. "Letter to the Editor." *Trinidad Guardian*, May 29:8.

———. 1990b. Letter to Señora Olivia Hernandez, Embassy of Venezuela, re: Amerindian Linkages between Venezuelan Waraos and Trinidad Caribs. February 8.

———. 1989a. "Culture-Histories of Trinidad and Tobago—The Amerindian Community." St. Augustine, Trinidad. Archaeology Centre, University of the West Indies. September 5.

———. 1989b. "Notes on the Historic Heritage of the Santa Rosa Carib." St. Augustine, Trinidad: Unpublished mimeograph. April.

———. 1978. "A Revised Chronological Framework for Ceramic Trinidad and Tobago." In *Seventh International Congress for the Study of Pre-Colombian Cultures of the Lesser Antilles*, pp. 47–63. July 11–16. Caracas: Universidad Central de Caracas.

Harris, Peter, and Elma Reyes. 1990. "Supervivencias amerindias en Trinidad and Tobago." In *Pueblos y políticas en el Caribe Amerindio*, pp. 55–64. México, D.F.: Instituto Indigenista Interamericano.

———. N.d. "Amerindian Survival in Trinidad and Tobago." Mimeograph.

Harvey, David. 1990. *The Condition of Postmodernity*. Oxford: Basil Blackwell.

Haslip-Viera, Gabriel. 1999a. "Introduction." In *Taíno Revival: Critical Perspectives on Puerto Rican Identity and Cultural Politics*, ed. Gabriel Haslip-Viera, pp. 1–10. New York: Centro de Estudios Puertorriqueños, Hunter College, City University of New York.

———, ed. 1999b. *Taíno Revival: Critical Perspectives on Puerto Rican Identity and Cultural Politics*. New York: Centro de Estudios Puertorriqueños, Hunter College, City University of New York.

Heeralal, Darryl. 1998. "PM Embraces Manning." *Trinidad Express*, October 5:7.

Henry, Frances. 1983. "Religion and Ideology in Trinidad: The Resurgence of the Shango Religion." *Caribbean Quarterly* 29(3/4):63–69.

H.E.R.B.S. Star. 1999. Vol. 4, Independence Issue. *Trinidad Express*, August 27:15–16, 57–58.

H.E.R.B.S. 1998. "Another Herbal Workshop Next Weekend at Asa Wright." *Sunday Express*, November 14:17.

Herrera, Heather Dawn. 1998. "Riches of Gran Tacaribe Cave." *Trinidad Guardian*, September 28:20.

Herskovits, Melville J. 1941. *The Myth of the Negro Past*. New York: Harper and Brothers.

Herskovits, Melville J., and Frances S. Herskovits. 1947. *Trinidad Village*. New York: Knopf.

Hintzen, Percy C. 1985. "Ethnicity, Class, and International Capital Penetration." *Social and Economic Studies* 34(3):107–163.

Hobsbawm, Eric J. 1992. *Nations and Nationalism since 1780: Programme, Myth, Reality*. 2nd ed. Cambridge: Cambridge University Press.

———. 1983. "Introduction: Inventing Traditions." In *The Invention of Tradition,* ed. Eric Hobsbawm and Terence Ranger, pp. 1–13. Cambridge: Cambridge University Press.

Homer, Louis B. 1998a. "Councillor: Moruga in Dark Ages—Bad Roads, No Water . . ." *Trinidad Guardian,* August 3:1.

———. 1998b. "Heroes of the Post-Emancipation Era." *Trinidad Guardian,* August 1:43.

Honychurch, Lennox. 2002. "The Leap at Sauteurs: The Lost Cosmology of Indigenous Grenada." Paper presented at the Grenada Country Conference of the University of the West Indies. < http://www.uwichill.edu.bb/bnccde/grenada/conference/papers/LH.html>, accessed June 20, 2002.

Hosein, F. E. M. 1976 [1931]. *Hyarima and the Saints: A Miracle Play and Pageant of Santa Rosa.* Marabella, Trinidad: John S. Mowlah-Baksh.

Houk, James. 1993. "Afro-Trinidadian Identity and the Africanisation of the Orisha Religion." In *Trinidad Ethnicity,* ed. Kelvin A. Yelvington, pp. 161–179. Knoxville: University of Tennessee Press.

Hulme, Peter. 2000. "Yellow and Black in the Caribbean: Racial and Ethnic Classification on St Vincent during the Revolutionary Wars of the 1790s." Paper presented at a seminar in the Department of Anthropology at the University of Wisconsin-Madison, March.

———. 1999. *Remnants of Conquest: The Island Caribs and Their Visitors, 1877–1997.* Manuscript.

———. 1993. "Making Sense of the Native Caribbean." *New West Indian Guide* 67(3–4):189–200.

———. 1992. *Colonial Encounters: Europe and the Native Caribbean 1492–1797.* London: Routledge.

———. 1990. "The Rhetoric of Description: The Amerindians of the Caribbean within Modern European Discourse." *Caribbean Quarterly* 23(3–4):35–49.

Hulme, Peter, and Neil L. Whitehead, eds. 1992. *Wild Majesty: Encounters with Caribs from Columbus to the Present Day.* Oxford: Clarendon Press.

Humboldt, Alexander von. 1995. *Personal Narrative of a Journey to the Equinoctial Regions of the New Continent,* trans. Jason Wilson. London: Penguin.

The Independent. 1998. "Essay Contest for Arima's Anniversary." April 23:10.

Inter-Commission Task Force on Indigenous Peoples (IUCN). 1997. *Indigenous Peoples and Sustainability: Cases and Actions.* Utrecht: International Books.

IWGIA. 2001. "Indigenous Issues: Indigenous Peoples—Who are They?" International Working Group for Indigenous Affairs.

Jackson, Jean. 1989. "Is There a Way to Talk about Making Culture without Making Enemies?" *Dialectical Anthropology* 14(2):127–143.

James, C. L. R. 1980. *Spheres of Existence: Selected Writings.* Westport, Conn.: Lawrence Hill.

Jarette, Dionne. 1999. "Grand Chief Trying to Unite First Nation People." *Trinidad Express,* November 24:6.

Jesse, C. 1973. "The Caribs in St. Lucia after A.D. 1605." *Fourth International Congress for the Study of Pre-Colombian Cultures of the Lesser Antilles,* pp. 90–93. July 26–30. Castries, St. Lucia: St. Lucia Archaeological and Historical Society.

Jiménez Román, Miriam. 1999. "The Indians Are Coming! The Indians Are Coming!: The Taíno and Puerto Rican Identity." In *Taíno Revival: Critical Perspectives on Puerto*

Rican Identity and Cultural Politics, ed. Gabriel Haslip-Viera, pp. 75–109. New York: Centro de Estudios Puertorriqueños, Hunter College, City University of New York.

John, Deborah. 2000. "Out of the Woods: Former Copy Writer Applies Amerindian Ethics to Her Eco-Craft." *Sunday Express*, April 16. <http://209.94.197.2/apr00/apr16/features.htm>, accessed May 5, 2000.

Johnson, Kim. 2000. *The Story of the Caribs and the Arawaks, Parts 1–6*. Trinidad and Tobago: S.E.L.F. Education 2000 RaceAndHistory.com. <http://www.raceandhistory.com/Taino/>, accessed February 2, 2000.

———. 1999a. "British Feared 'Cocoa Panyols.'" *Sunday Express*, August 29. <http://209.94.197.2/aug99/aug29/opinion.htm>, accessed September 9, 1999.

———. 1999b. "Raleigh's Tall Tales." *Sunday Express*, July 4. <http://209.94.197.2/july99/july4/opinion.htm>, accessed August 8, 1999.

———. 1999c. "Trinidad's First Governor Confused El Dorado with Fountain of Youth." *Sunday Express*, June 27. <http://209.94.197.2/june99/june2//opinion.htm>, accessed July 9, 1999.

———. 1998a. "Kelshall: You Would Have Killed the Amerindians Too." *Sunday Express*, August 2:18.

———. 1998b. "Do You Remember? Celebrating the Abolition of Slavery." *Sunday Express*, Sec. 2, August 2:2–3.

———. 1997. *The Fragrance of Gold: Trinidad in the Age of Discovery*. St. Augustine, Trinidad: School of Continuing Studies, University of the West Indies.

Jones, Marlene. 1965. "She Reigns over a Dwindling Tribe but . . . Carib Queen in Her Glory." Newspaper clipping, Arima Branch Library. August 31:n.p.

Joseph, E. L. 1970 [1838]. *History of Trinidad*. London: Frank Cass.

Joseph, Terry. 1989. "Parang Forever!" *Sunday Guardian*, November 26:24.

Kahn, Joel. 1989. "Culture: Demise or Resurrection?" *Critique of Anthropology* 9(2) Fall:5–25.

Kassie, John. 1998. "Amerindian Discovery on Harris Promenade." *Trinidad Guardian*, June 27:11.

———. 1990a. "Amerindians under Threat—Carib Official." *Trinidad Guardian*, May 29:8.

———. 1990b. "Focus on Our Surviving Caribs." *Trinidad Guardian*, November 8:6.

———. 1989. "Carib Corner Example to Rest of TT." *Trinidad Guardian*, August 27:18.

Kearney, Michael. 1995. "The Local and the Global: The Anthropology of Globalization and Transnationalism." *Annual Review of Anthropology* 24:547–565.

———. 1986. "From the Invisible Hand to Visible Feet: Anthropological Studies of Migration and Development." *Annual Review of Anthropology* 15:331–361.

Kearns, Richard. 1999–2000a. "The Return of the Taínos, Our Own 'Lost Tribe.'" *Issues in Caribbean Amerindian Studies* 2(1). <http://www.centrelink.org/KearnsA.html>, accessed May 14, 2004.

———. 1999–2000b. "Nación Taína: Recovery and Restoration of the Culture." *Issues in Caribbean Amerindian Studies* 2(5). <http://www.centrelink.org/KearnsE.html>, accessed May 14, 2004.

Keegan, William F., ed. 1991. *Earliest Hispanic/Native American Interactions in the Caribbean*. New York: Garland.

Keesing, Roger M. 1987. "Anthropology as Interpretive Quest." *Current Anthropology* 28(2) April:161–176.

———. 1974. "Theories of Culture." *Annual Review of Anthropology* 3:73–97.

Khan, Aisha. 1993. "What Is 'a Spanish'?: Ambiguity and 'Mixed' Ethnicity in Trinidad." In *Trinidad Ethnicity*, ed. Kevin A. Yelvington, pp. 180–207. Knoxville: University of Tennessee Press.

King, Anthony. 1999. "Against Structure: A Critique of Morphogenetic Social Theory." *Sociological Review* 47(2) May:199–228. (Electronic version downloaded from Academic Search Elite, AN: 2178742.)

King, Anthony D. 1991. "Introduction: Spaces of Cultures, Spaces of Knowledge." In *Culture, Globalization, and the World System*, ed. Anthony D. King, pp. 1–18. Binghamton: Department of Art and Art History, State University of New York at Binghamton.

Kingsley, Charles. 1877. *At Last: A Christmas in the West Indies*. New edition. London: Macmillan.

Klass, Morton. 1991. *Singing with Sai Baba: The Politics of Revitalization in Trinidad*. Boulder, Colo.: Westview Press.

———. 1995. "Discussion, New Ethnicity, New Horizons." In *Caribbean Ethnicity Revisited*, ed. Stephen D. Glazier, pp. 139–148. New York: Gordon and Breach.

———. 1961. *East Indians in Trinidad*. New York: Columbia University Press.

Knight, Franklin W. 1978. *The Caribbean: The Genesis of a Fragmented Nationalism*. New York: Oxford University Press.

Knowles, Caroline. 2000. "Here and There: Doing Transnational Fieldwork." In *Constructing the Field: Ethnographic Fieldwork in the Contemporary World*, ed. Vered Amit, pp. 54–70. London: Routledge.

Kottak, Conrad, and Elizabeth Colson. 1994. "Multilevel Linkages: Longitudinal and Comparative Studies." In *Assessing Cultural Anthropology*, ed. Robert Borofsky, pp. 396–412. New York: McGraw-Hill.

Kowlessar, Geisha. 2000a. "Drugs, Prostitution Rage in Arima: Dealers, Residents, Confirm Mayor's Charge of Police Collusion." *Sunday Guardian (Online)*, July 9.

———. 2000b. "Arima on the Run: Pushers, Bandits Take Over, Mayor Edwards Laments." *Trinidad Guardian (Online)*, July 4.

———. 1998. "Feast of Santa Rosa Ends Borough Celebrations." *Trinidad Guardian*, August 29:35.

Kuper, Adam. 1994. "Anthropological Futures." In *Assessing Cultural Anthropology*, ed. Robert Borofsky, pp. 113–118. New York: McGraw-Hill.

Lafleur, Gerard. 1992. *Les Caraïbes des Petites Antilles*. Paris: Editions Karbala.

La Fortune, Knolly S. 1999. *Manzanilla: The Collected Poems of Knolly S. La Fortune*. London: Felix Press.

Landsman, Gail, and Sara Ciborski. 1992. "Representation and Politics: Contesting Histories of the Iroquois." *Cultural Anthropology* 7(4):425–447.

Lanternari, Vittorio. 1962. "Messianism: Its Historical Origin and Morphology." *History of Religions* 2(1):52–72.

Las Casas, Bartolomé de. 1992a. *The Devastation of the Indies: A Brief Account*, trans. Herma Briffault. Baltimore: Johns Hopkins University Press.

———. 1992b. "The Journal of Columbus." In *Wild Majesty: Encounters with Caribs from Columbus to the Present Day—An Anthology*, ed. Peter Hulme and Neil Whitehead, pp. 17–28. Oxford: Clarendon Press.

Lattas, Andrew. 1993. "Essentialism, Memory, and Resistance: Aboriginality and the Politics of Authenticity." *Oceania* 63:240–267.

Layng, Anthony. 1985. "The Caribs of Dominica: Prospects for Structural Assimilation of a Territorial Minority." *Ethnic Groups* 6:209–221.

———. 1983. *The Carib Reserve.* Lanham, Md.: University Press of America.

———. 1979–80. "Ethnic Identity on a West Indian Reservation." *Revista Interamericana* 9(4):577–584.

Leahy, Vincent. 1980. *Catholic Church in Trinidad, 1797–1820.* Arima: St. Dominic Press.

Le Breton, Adrien, Rev. Fr., S.J. 1998 [ca. 1702]. *Historic Account of Saint Vincent, the Indian Youroumayn, the Island of the Karaÿbes.* Reprint ed. Foreword and Preface by Fr. Mark da Silva. Introduction by Fr. Robert Divonne. The Mayreau Environmental Development Organization, Mayreau Island, Southern Grenadines, St. Vincent and The Grenadines.

Lee, Simon. 2000a. "140 Storms In Carifesta Teacup." *Sunday Guardian (Online),* September 3.

———. 2000b. "In the Spirit of the Gli Gli." *Sunday Guardian,* February 27:23.

———. 1998. "Dominica's World Creole Music Festival." *Trinidad Guardian,* July 29:11.

Levinson, David. 1994. "Cannibalism." In *Aggression and Conflict: A Cross-Cultural Encyclopedia,* pp. 27–28. Santa Barbara: ABC-CLIO.

Lewis, Gordon K. 1968. *The Growth of the Modern West Indies.* New York: Monthly Review Press.

Lewis, John Newel. 1983a. *Ajoupa.* Trinidad: J. Newel Lewis.

———. 1983b. *Architecture of the Caribbean and Its Amerindian Origins in Trinidad.* Washington, D.C.: American Institute of Architects Service Corp.

Lieber, Michael. 1981. *Street Life: Afro-American Culture in Urban Trinidad.* Cambridge, Mass.: Schenkman Publishing.

Linnekin, Jocelyn S. 1992. "On the Theory and Politics of Cultural Construction in the Pacific." *Oceania* 62(4):249–263.

———. 1983. "Defining Tradition: Variations on the Hawaiian Identity." *American Ethnologist* 10(2) May:241–252.

Linton, Ralph. 1943. "Nativistic Movements." *American Anthropologist* 45:230–241.

Loubon, Michelle. 2002a. "Flower of the Santa Rosa Festival." *Sunday Guardian (Online),* September 1.

———. 2002b. "Guyanese, Trinis, Rescue 'First Nation' Culture." *Sunday Guardian (Online),* September 1.

Lowenthal, David. 1972. *West Indian Societies.* New York: Oxford University Press.

Luke, Sir Harry. 1950. *Caribbean Circuit.* London: Nicholson and Watson.

Maharaj, Petal. 1998. "Historical Work Fails to Meet Potential." *Sunday Guardian,* November 1:18.

Mandol, Narrisa. 1998. "Wave of Change: Move Over Maracas, Get Ready Toco." *Trinidad Guardian,* September 28:19.

Mannah, Vidhisha. 1998. "Arawak Artifacts Found at Harris Promenade." *Trinidad Express,* January 3. <http://209.94.197.2/jan/jan3/features.htm>, accessed January 4, 1998.

Marcus, George E. 1995. "Ethnography in/of the World System: The Emergence of Multi-Sited Ethnography." *Annual Review of Anthropology* 24:95–117.

———. 1994. "After the Critique of Ethnography: Faith, Hope, and Charity, But the

Greatest of These Is Charity." In *Assessing Cultural Anthropology*, ed. Robert Borofsky, pp. 40–54. New York: McGraw-Hill.

———. 1986. "Contemporary Problems of Ethnography in the Modern World System." In *Writing Culture: The Poetics and Politics of Ethnography*, ed. James Clifford and George E. Marcus, pp. 165–193. Berkeley: University of California Press.

Marcus, George E., and Michael M. J. Fischer. 1986. *Anthropology as Cultural Critique: An Experimental Moment in the Human Sciences*. Chicago: University of Chicago Press.

Marquez, Abdelkader. 1989. "Parang, Parang, Parang." *Trinidad Guardian*, December 25:6.

———. 1979. *La Parranda Trinitaria/Trinidadian Parang*. Port of Spain: Embassy of Venezuela.

Marshall, Bernard. 1973. "The Black Caribs—Native Resistance to British Penetration into the Windward Side of St. Vincent—1763–1773." *Caribbean Quarterly* 19(4) December:4–19.

Massé, Armand. 1995. *De La Vendée aux Caraïbes: Le Journal (1878–1884) d'Armand Massé, Missionaire apostolique*. Paris, Éditions l'Harmattan.

———. 1988. *The Diaries of Abbé Armand Massé, 1878–1883*, vol. 2. Translated in four volumes from the original French by M. L. de Verteuil. Port-of-Spain, Trinidad.

Mato, Daniel. 2000. "Transnational Networking and the Social Production of Representations of Identities by Indigenous Peoples' Organizations of Latin America." *International Sociology* 15(2) June:343–360.

———. 1996. "On the Theory, Epistemology, and Politics of the Social Construction of 'Cultural Identities' in the Age of Globalization: Introductory Remarks to Ongoing Debates." *Identities* 3(1–2):61–72.

Matroo, Carol. 2000. "Arimians Block Road for Water." *Trinidad Guardian (Online)*, November 25.

McArdle, Rev. Fr. J., O.P. 1936/37. *The Dominicans in the West Indies, with Special Reference to Trinidad*. Port of Spain: Trinidad Historical Society.

McCartney, Norma. 1989. *Tales of the Immortelles: A Collection of Caribbean Fairy Tales*. London: Macmillan Education.

McComie, Val. 1990. "Descubrir la raíz amerindia." In *Pueblos y políticas en el Caribe Amerindio*, pp. 23–28. México, D.F.: Instituto Indigenista Interamericano.

McDonald, James. 1999. "Letter to the Editor: Billions for Land for All Tribes." *Sunday Guardian*, June 6:10.

McLeod, Michelle. 1998a. "Hope for a Dying People." *Trinidad Guardian*, March 27:43.

———. 1998b. "Plans to Transform Arima's Calvary Hill into Tourist Resort." *Trinidad Guardian*, March 6:11.

Mejias, Olivia. 1999. "John Stollmeyer Returns to the Earth." *Trinidad Express,* January 6:19.

Menezes, Sr. M. Noel (RSM). 1992. "Who is the Christianized Amerindian?" *Caricom Perspective* January–June:19–20.

———. 1982. *Amerindian Life in Guyana*. Georgetown, Guyana: Ministry of Education, Social Development and Culture.

Mentore, George P. 1988. *The Relevance of Myth*. Edgar Mittelholzer Memorial Lectures: Eleventh Series. Georgetown, Guyana: Department of Culture.

Millet, Trevor M. 1993. *The Chinese in Trinidad*. Port of Spain: Inprint Caribbean.

Milne, Anthony. 1999. "Indigenous Canadians Seek Ties with T&T Caribs." *Trinidad Express*, November 24:53.

———. 1998a. "The Real Columbus." *Trinidad Express*, July 18:9.

———. 1998b. "July 31 Marked 500th Anniversary of Columbus' Arrival." *Sunday Express*, Sec. 2, August 2:4–5.

Mintz, Sidney W. 1996. "Enduring Substances, Trying Theories: The Caribbean Region as Oikoumenê." *Journal of the Royal Anthropological Institute* 2(2) June:289–312.

———. 1994. "Global Echoes in the Caribbean Playground." *American Anthropologist* 96(3) September:689–692.

———. 1977. "The So-Called World System: Local Initiative and Local Response." *Dialectical Anthropology* 2(4):253–270.

Mintz, Sidney W., and Richard Price. 1992. *The Birth of Afro-American Culture: An Anthropological Perspective.* Boston: Beacon Press.

Mitchell, Sharlyn Tricia. 1998. "From Guyana with Love Seats Divine. *Sunday Guardian Magazine* November 29:17.

Moberg, Mark. 1992. "Continuity under Colonial Rule: The *Alcalde* System and the Garifuna in Belize, 1858–1969." *Ethnohistory* 39(1) Winter:1–19.

Moerman, Michael. 1968. "Being Lue: Uses and Abuses of Ethnic Identification." In *Essays on the Problem of Tribe*, ed. June Helm, pp. 153–169. Seattle: American Ethnological Society, University of Washington Press.

———. 1965. "Ethnic Identification in a Complex Civilization: Who are the Lue?" *American Anthropologist* 67:1215–1230.

Montique, George. 1987. "A History of Rio Claro since 1900." Master's thesis, University of the West Indies, St. Augustine, Trinidad.

Moodie, Sylvia Maria. 1992. "Parang: Revival of an Old Hispanic Tradition in Trinidad." Mimeograph.

———. 1983. "Survival of Hispanic Religious Songs in Trinidad Folklore." *Caribbean Quarterly* 29(1):1–31.

Moodie-Kublalsingh, Sylvia. 1994. *The Cocoa Panyols of Trinidad: An Oral Record.* London: British Academic Press.

Moore, Gillian. 1998. "An Equal Place." *Trinidad Express*, December 3:13.

Moore, Richard B. 1973. "Carib 'Cannibalism': A Study in Anthropological Stereotyping." *Caribbean Studies* 13:117–135.

Moore, Sally Falk. 1994. "The Ethnography of the Present and the Analysis of Process." In *Assessing Cultural Anthropology*, ed. Robert Borofsky, pp. 362–376. New York: McGraw-Hill.

Moore, Sally Falk, and Barbara Myerhoff. 1977. "Introduction: Secular Ritual: Forms and Meanings." In *Secular Ritual*, ed. Sally Falk Moore and Barbara Myerhoff, pp. 3–24. Assen, The Netherlands: Van Gorcum.

Munn, N. D. 1992. "The Cultural Anthropology of Time: A Critical Essay." *Annual Review of Anthropology* 21:93–123.

Murumbi, D. 1994. "The Concept of Indigenous Peoples in Africa." *Indigenous Affairs* 1 January–March:52–57.

Naipaul, V. S. 1981 [1962]. *The Middle Passage: Impressions of Five Societies—British, French, and Dutch—in the West Indies and South America.* London: Andre Deutsch.

———. 1969 [1967]. *The Mimic Men.* New York: Penguin.

Nandy, Ashis. 1983. *The Intimate Enemy: Loss and Recovery of Self under Colonialism.* New Delhi: Oxford University Press.

Nash, June. 1981. "Ethnographic Aspects of the World Capitalist System." *Annual Review of Anthropology* 10:393–423.

National Carnival Commission (NCC). 2001. "Introduction to Trinidad and Tobago Carnival." <http://www.trinbagocarnival.com/Misc/introduction_to_trinidad_carnival.htm>, accessed March 5, 2002.

National Library and Information System (NALIS). 2000a. *Biography of Pearl Entou Springer.* <http://www.nalis.gov.tt/Biography/bio_EintouSpringer.html#pearlspringer>, accessed March 5, 2002.

———. 2000b. *Biography of F. E. M. Hosein.* <http://www.nalis.gov.tt/Biography/bio_Alcazar&Hosein.html>, accessed March 5, 2002.

———. 2000c. *Biography of A. N. R. Robinson, President of Trinidad and Tobago.* <http://www.nalis.gov.tt/Biography/bio_ANR_ROBINSON.html>, accessed March 5, 2002.

——— 2000d. *Trinidad and Tobago Commemorative Days.* <http://www.nalis.gov.tt/Culture/COMMEMORATIVE_DAYS.html>, accessed March 5, 2002.

Neggers, Xavira. 1997. "Descendants Trace Indians' Sea Voyage." *Fort Worth Star-Telegram.* August 8.

Newsday. 2000. "Arima Mayor Hosts Indigenous Peoples." August 4:31.

———. 1998. "Arima Launches 110th Anniversary Essay Competition." April 20:4.

Newson, Linda. 1976. *Aboriginal and Spanish Colonial Trinidad: A Study in Culture Contact.* London: British Academic Press.

Noel, Jesse A. 1972. *Trinidad, Provincia de Venezuela: Historia de la administración española de Trinidad.* Caracas: Biblioteca de la Academia Nacional de la Historia.

Ober, N. 1894. "Aborigines of the West Indies." *Proceedings of the American Antiquarian Society* 9.

Ofosu, Natasha. 2000a. "Book on Amerindian History for Carifesta." *Trinidad Guardian (Online),* August 11.

———. 2000b. "Revival of African Spirit at Rain Fest." *Trinidad Guardian (Online),* June 13.

Olwig, Karen Fog. 1999. "The Burden of Heritage: Claiming a Place for a West Indian Culture." *American Ethnologist* 26(2):370–388.

———. 1993a. "Between Tradition and Modernity: National Development in the Caribbean." *Social Analysis* 33 September:89–104.

———. 1993b. *Global Culture, Island Identity: Continuity and Change in the Afro-Caribbean Community of Nevis.* Reading, U.K.: Harwood Academic Publishers.

Ortner, Sherry B. 1999. "Some Futures of Anthropology." *American Ethnologist* 26(4) November:984–991.

———. 1994. "Theory in Anthropology since the Sixties." In *Culture/Power/History,* ed. Nicholas B. Dirks et al., pp. 372–411. Princeton, N.J.: Princeton University Press.

Ottley, C. Robert. 1955. *An Account of Life in Spanish Trinidad (From 1498–1797).* 1st ed. Diego Martin, Trinidad: C. R. Ottley.

Overbeek, Henk. N.d. "Cycles of Hegemony and Leadership in the Core of the World System." International Political Economy Paper, Department of Political Science, University of Amsterdam. <http://dev.pscw.uva.nl/tnu/ipe/programme/library/henk1.htm>, accessed May 10, 2001.

Oviedo y Valdés, Gonzalo Fernandez de. 1959. Reprint ed. *Historia General y Natural de las Indians, II,* ed. Juan Perez de Tudela Bueso. Biblioteca de Autores Españoles, Colección Rivadeneira. Madrid: Real Academia Española.

Owen, Nancy H. 1974. "Carib." *Encyclopedia of Indians of the Americas,* vol. 4, pp. 54–58. St. Clair Shores, Mich.: Scholarly Press.

Oxaal, Ivar. 1968. *Black Intellectuals Come to Power: The Rise of Creole Nationalism in Trinidad and Tobago.* Cambridge, Mass.: Schenkman Publishing.

Palacio, Joseph. 1993. "Feature Address, Symposium in Connection with the Second Gathering of Indigenous Peoples of the Caribbean, August 29 to September 5, Arima, Trinidad and Tobago." <http://www.kacike.org/cac-ike/palacio.htm>, accessed May 14, 2004.

———. 1992. "The Sojourn toward Self-Discovery among Caribbean Indigenous Peoples." *Caribbean Quarterly* 38(2–3) June–September: 55–72.

———. 1989. "Caribbean Indigenous Peoples Journey toward Self Discovery. *Cultural Survival Quarterly* 13(3):49–51

Pantin, Manuel Adrian. 2000. "A Once Great Tribe Fights for Survival." *Sunday Guardian,* January 30:12.

PanTrinbago. 2000a. *The Amerindians of Trinidad and Tobago.* Port of Spain. <http://www.pantrinbago.com/Amerinidian1.htm>, accessed March 5, 2002.

———. 2000b. *The Missions.* Port of Spain. <http://www.pantrinbago.com/Landofbeginings3.html>, accessed March 5, 2002.

Peace, Ade. 1998. "Anthropology in the Postmodern Landscape: The Importance of Cultural Brokers and Their Trade." *Australian Journal of Anthropology* 9(3):274–284.

Pena, Donna-Lisa. 2002. "Caribs: All We Want Is Respect." *Catholic News (Online),* Sunday, August 18.

Persad, Kamal. 1999. "Remember the Amerindians." *Sunday Express,* December 4. <http://209.94.197.2/dec99/dec5/opinion.htm>, accessed December 5, 1999.

Phillips, Laura Ann. 2000. "Way of the Shaman." *Trinidad Express,* October 11:29.

Pierre, Donna. 2001. "Ethnic Fashion." *Trinidad Guardian (Online),* April 19.

Poncelet, Léo. 2001. "L'ethnographie et l'analyze des systèmes mondes." *Anthropologica* 43(1):43–70.

Port of Spain Gazette. 1938. "The Arena Massacre: Fr. Bussinck's Historical Contribution." November 6.

———. 1938. "Arima Council Wishes Governor's Speedy Recovery." September 17:7.

———. 1938. "Arima Borough Council Meets." September 2:6.

———. 1938. "Municipal Dinner at Arima, In Celebration of Borough's Jubilee; Governor Promises Electricity Soon; Borough Showered with Congratulations." August 5:6.

———. 1938. "Trinidad Celebrates Its Discovery: Popular Events in Town and Country; Thousands Witness Fireworks Display; Big Parade of School Children." August 3:12.

———. 1938. "Our Discovery Day." August 3:11.

———. 1938. "Arima Celebrates Golden Jubilee of Borough: Coadjutator Archbishop Officiates at Pontifical High Mass; His Grace Blesses Mayoral Chain; Red Letter Day in the History of Arima." August 3:6.

———. 1892. "The Arima Municipal Farce." November 5:4.

———. 1892. "The Fourth Centenary of the Discovery of America." October 18:4.

———. 1892. "The Santa Rosa Races." August 27:4.

———. 1892. "Santa Rosa Races: Friday and Saturday 26th and 27th Augt., '92. At the

Arima Savanna. Under the Patronage of His Excellency the Governor." July 29, supplement.

———. 1888. January 7.

———. 1847. October 29.

———. 1847. April 20.

———. 1847. "The Land Tax." March 23.

———. 1847. "Letter from 'A Cocoa Planter' in Arima." March 19.

———. 1847. "Minutes of the Council of Government." February 2.

———. 1847. Friday, January 22.

———. 1825. September 21.

Premdas, Ralph. 1997. "Public Policy and Ethnic Conflict: Evaluating the Strategy of Multiculturalism." *Caribbean Dialogue* 3(2) June:1–6.

———. 1999. "Ethnic Conflict in Trinidad & Tobago: Domination and Reconciliation." In *Trinidad Ethnicity,* ed. Kelvin A. Yelvington, pp. 136–160. Knoxville: University of Tennessee Press.

Price, Cornelius M. Kelvin. 1987. "The Arima Borough Council Its Organization and Operation (1962–1982)." Master's thesis, University of the West Indies, St. Augustine, Trinidad.

Rabess, Gregory. 1990. "Caribs Documenting History." *Caricom Perspective* July–December:47.

Raffles, Hugh. 1999. "'Local Theory': Nature and the Making of an Amazonian Place." *Cultural Anthropology* 14(3) August:323–360.

Ramcharitar, Roger. 1999a. "From Cacique to Cabildo to Whitehall: Public Administration Ministry Takes a Look at the History of T&T's Public Service." *Trinidad Guardian,* Tuesday, November 23:20.

———. 1999b. "Hats Off to the Ladies." *Trinidad Guardian,* September 6:13.

Ramirez, Gladys Nieves. 2001a. "Con herencia indígena 62% de los boricuas." *El Nuevo Día* (Puerto Rico), Friday, May 4. <http://www.endi.com/locales/html/p58c03m5.asp>, accessed May 9, 2001.

———. 2001b. "Misioneros de la cultura taína." *El Nuevo Día* (Puerto Rico), Friday, May 4. <http://www.endi.com/locales/html/p58b03m5.asp>, accessed May 9, 2001.

Ramlakhan, Rajnie. 1998. "Columbus Day Protests in Latin America." *Trinidad Express,* October 26:13.

Ramos, Alcida. 1994. "The Hyperreal Indian." *Critique of Anthropology* 14(2):153–171.

Ramos Perez, Demetrio. 1973. *El mito del Dorado: Su genesis y proceso.* Biblioteca de la Academia Nacional de la Historia, 16. Caracas: Academia Nacional de la Historia.

Rampersad, Kris. 1999. "Pearl Entou Springer: A Fire Raging." *Sunday Guardian,* November 21:4.

Ramsaran, Ramesh. 1989. *The Commonwealth Caribbean in the World Economy.* London: Macmillan Caribbean.

Rappaport, Joanne. 1988. "History and Everyday Life in the Colombian Andes." *Man* 23(4):718–739.

Raymond, Judy. 2000. "Chang." *Caribbean Beat.* <http://caribbean-beat.com/archive/chang.html>, accessed March 3, 2000.

Reddock, Rhoda E. 1996a. "Ethnic Minorities in Caribbean Creole Societies: Four Ethno-Historical Studies." In *Ethnic Minorities in Caribbean Society,* ed. Rhoda Reddock, pp. 1–7. St. Augustine, Trinidad: ISER, University of the West Indies.

———, ed. 1996b. *Ethnic Minorities in Caribbean Society.* St. Augustine, Trinidad: ISER, University of the West Indies.

Rétout, Sr. Marie Thérèse, O.P. 1990. "The Religious History of San Rafael (1687–1989) in Trinidad, West Indies." Pamphlet.

———. 1976. *Parish Beat.* Port of Spain: Inprint Caribbean.

Reyes, Elma. 1999a. "Letter to the Editor: We Did Not Export Our Culture." *Trinidad Guardian,* January 27:10.

———. 1999b. "Letter to the Editor: True Origin of 'Dougla.'" *Trinidad Guardian,* April 20:8.

———. 1999c. "Letter to the Editor: For Those Who Earned Freedom." *Trinidad Guardian,* July 29:8.

———. 1999d. "Letter to the Editor: Sat Seeking to Promote Conflict." *Trinidad Guardian,* June 8:6.

———. 1998. "We Must Acknowledge the 'Wisdom of Indigenous People.'" *Newsday,* June 10:9.

———. 1996. *The T&T Heritage at Christmas.* Port of Spain: A Trini and Toby Heritage Publication.

———. 1995. "Carib Blood May Run in Your Veins." *Trinidad Guardian,* May 31:8.

———. 1991. "The Amerindian Heritage." *Trinidad Express,* November 5.

———. 1989. "Give Caribs Their Place in T & T Culture." *Trinidad Express,* March 20:20.

———. 1988. "Reviving Traditions." *Trinidad Express,* January 20:29.

———. 1981. "We Are a Forgotten People Say Caribs." *Trinidad Express,* March 21:11.

———. 1978. *The Carib Community.* Arima: Santa Rosa Carib Community.

———. 1974. "Group Planning to Revive Carib Culture." Newspaper clipping. May 5:6.

Rickwood, Peter. 2000. "Medicine Man: Herbalist Francis Morean Goes Back to Trinidad's Spanish and Carib Past to Retrieve the Remedies of Old." *Caribbean Beat.* <http://caribbean-beat.com/archive/medicine.html>, accessed November 9, 2000.

Roberts, Peter. 1999. "What's in a Name, an Indian Name?" In *Taíno Revival: Critical Perspectives on Puerto Rican Identity and Cultural Politics,* ed. Gabriel Haslip-Viera, pp. 57–74. New York: Centro de Estudios Puertorriqueños, Hunter College, City University of New York.

Roberts, Shereline L. 1996. "The Integration of the Caribs into the Vincentian Society." Bachelor's thesis, University of the West Indies, St. Augustine, Trinidad.

Roberts-Griffith, Aneka. 1999. "Off the Beaten Track: In Search of Brazil." *Sunday Guardian Magazine,* June 13:8, 9, 10.

Robertson, Roland. 1992. *Globalization: Social Theory and Global Culture.* London: Sage.

Robotham, Don. 1998. "Transnationalism in the Caribbean: Formal and Informal." *American Ethnologist* 25(2) May:307–321.

Rogers, Mark. 1996. "Beyond Authenticity: Conservation, Tourism, and the Politics of Representation in the Ecuadorian Amazon." *Identities* 3(1–2):73–125.

Ross, Charlesworth. 1970. "Caribs and Arawaks." *Caribbean Quarterly* 16:52–59.

Rostant, Rory. 1998. "Asa Wright Nature Centre." *Trinidad Guardian,* November 8:5.

———. 1997. "Caribs to Meet 'Brothers.'" *Trinidad Guardian (Online),* June 12.

Rouse, Irving. 1992. *The Taínos: Rise and Decline of the People Who Greeted Columbus.* New Haven: Yale University Press.

———. 1991. "Whom Did Columbus Discover in the West Indies." In *Earliest Hispanic/ Native American Interactions in the Caribbean,* ed. William F. Keegan, pp. 89–96. New York: Garland.

———. 1953. "Indian Sites in Trinidad." In *On the Excavation of a Shell Mound at Palo Seco Trinidad, B.W.I.,* ed. J. A. Bullbrook. Yale University Publications in Anthropology, no. 50. New Haven, Conn.: Yale University Press.

———. 1948a. "The Arawak." In *Handbook of South American Indians,* vol. 4: *The Circum-Caribbean Tribes,* ed. Julian H. Steward, pp. 507–546. Washington, D.C.: Smithsonian Institution, Bureau of American Ethnology.

———. 1948b. "The Carib." In *Handbook of South American Indians,* vol. 4: *The Circum-Caribbean Tribes,* ed. Julian H. Steward, pp. 547–566. Washington, D.C.: Smithsonian Institution, Bureau of American Ethnology.

———. N.d. "Carib Indians." *The Encyclopedia Americana,* intl. ed., vol. 5, p. 654.

Ryan, Selwyn. 1997. "The Clash of Cultures in Post Creole Trinidad and Tobago." *Caribbean Dialogue* 3(2) June:7–28.

——— 1990 In *Trinidad under Siege: The Muslimeen Uprising 6 Days of Terror.* Port of Spain: Trinidad Express Newspapers.

Ryan, Stephen. 1990. *Ethnic Conflict and International Relations.* Aldershot: Dartmouth.

Sackett, Lee. 1991. "Promoting Primitivism: Conservationist Depictions of Aboriginal Australians." *Australian Journal of Anthropology* 2(2):233–246.

Sahlins, Marshall. 1999. "Two or Three Things that I Know about Culture." *Journal of the Royal Anthropological Institute* 5(3) September:399–421.

———. 1994. "Cosmologies of Capitalism: The Trans-Pacific Sector of 'The World System.'" In *Culture/Power/History,* ed. Nicholas B. Dirks et al., pp. 412–455. Princeton, N.J.: Princeton University Press.

———. 1993. "Goodbye to Tristes Tropiques: Ethnography and the Context of Modern World History." In *Assessing Anthropology,* ed. Robert Borofsky, pp. 377–394. New York: Macmillan.

———. 1987. *Islands of History.* London: Tavistock.

———. 1981. *Historical Metaphors and Mythical Realities.* Ann Arbor: University of Michigan Press.

Sanders, Andrew. 1987. *The Powerless People: An Analysis of the Amerindians of the Corentyne River.* London: Macmillan.

———. 1976. "American Indian or West Indian: The Case of the Coastal Amerindians of Guyana." *Caribbean Studies* 16(2):117–144.

———. 1972. "Amerindians in Guyana: A Minority Group in a Multi Ethnic Society." *Caribbean Studies* 12(2):31–51.

Sanders, Douglas E. 1977. *The Formation of the World Council of Indigenous Peoples.* IWGIA Document 29. Copenhagen: International Work Group for Indigenous Peoples.

Sankeralli, Burton. 1997. "Unity, Ethnic Contestation, and the Point Galera Possibility." *Caribbean Dialogue* 3(2) June:29–31.

Sauer, Carl Otwin. 1991. "Organization of the Indies, 1502–1509." In *Earliest Hispanic/ Native American Interactions in the Caribbean,* ed. William F. Keegan, pp. 315–328. New York: Garland.

Schultes, Richard Evans, and Robert F. Raffauf. 1992. *Vine of the Soul: Medicine Men, Their Plants and Rituals in the Colombian Amazonia.* Santa Fe, N.Mex.: Synergetic Press.

Scott, David. 1992. "Criticism and Culture: Theory and Post-Colonial Claims on Anthropological Disciplinarity." *Critique of Anthropology* 12(4):371–394.

Scott, Gini Graham. 1991. *Shamanism and Personal Mastery: Using Symbols, Rituals, and Talismans to Activate the Powers within You.* New York: Paragon House.

Segal, Daniel A. 1998. "A Response to Birth." *American Ethnologist* 25(3) August:498–499.

———. 1993. "Race and Colour in Pre-Independence Trinidad and Tobago." In *Trinidad Ethnicity,* ed. Kevin A. Yelvington, pp. 81–115. Knoxville: University of Tennessee Press.

Shephard, C. Y. 1936. *The Cacao Industry of Trinidad: Some Economic Aspects.* Port of Spain: Government Printing Office.

Shore, Chris, and Susan Wright. 1999. "Audit Culture and Anthropology: Neo-Liberalism in British Higher Education." *Journal of the Royal Anthropological Institute* 5(4) December:557–575.

Simpson, George Eaton. 1980. *Religious Cults of the Caribbean: Trinidad, Jamaica and Haiti.* 3rd ed. Rio Piedras: Institute of Caribbean Studies, University of Puerto Rico.

Sissons, Jeffrey. 1999. "Siteless Ethnography: Possibilities and Limits." *Social Analysis* 43(2) July:88–95.

———. 1993. "The Systematization of Tradition: Maori Culture as a Strategic Resource." *Oceania* 64(2) December:97–116.

Small, Essiba. 1998. "Furniture from the Rainforest: Trinidad Homes get a Taste of Guyanese Style." *Trinidad Express,* October 3:23.

Smith, Anthony D. 1993. "The Ethnic Sources of Nationalism." In *Ethnic Conflict and International Security,* ed. Michael E. Brown, pp. 27–41. Princeton, N.J.: Princeton University Press.

———. 1981. *The Ethnic Revival in the Modern World.* Cambridge: Cambridge University Press.

Smith, Michael G. 1965. *The Plural Society in the British West Indies.* Berkeley: University of California Press.

Solien, Nancie L. 1971. "West Indian Characteristics of the Black Carib." In *Peoples and Cultures of the Caribbean,* ed. Michael Horowitz, pp. 133–142. Garden City, N.Y.: Natural History Press.

Solomon, Norris. 2000a. "Arima Dial Back by Christmas." *Trinidad Guardian (Online),* October 6.

———. 2000b. "Holly Delivers Elma Eulogy." *Trinidad Guardian (Online),* August 30.

Sookram, Caldeo. 2002a. "Caribs Revive Ancient Ritual." *Trinidad Exress (Online),* August 6.

———. 2002b. "Reclaiming the Past." *Trinidad Express (Online),* September 5.

Sorillo, John. 1998. "The 500-year European Sham." *Sunday Guardian,* August 2:9.

Sprott, Julie E. 1994. "Symbolic Ethnicity and Alaska Natives of Mixed Ancestry Living in Anchorage: Enduring Group or Sign of Impending Assimilation." *Human Organization* 53(4):311–322.

Stephens, Cherryl. 1985. "Labour Supply and Labour Organization in the Cocoa Industry of Trinidad, 1870–1920." Master's thesis, University of the West Indies, St. Augustine, Trinidad.

Steward, Julian H. 1948a. "The Circum-Caribbean Tribes." In *Handbook of South*

American Indians, vol. 4: *The Circum-Caribbean Tribes,* ed. Julian H. Steward, pp. 24–27. Washington, D.C.: Smithsonian Institution, Bureau of American Ethnology.

———, ed. 1948b. *Handbook of South American Indians,* vol. 4: *The Circum-Caribbean Tribes.* Washington, D.C.: Smithsonian Institution, Bureau of American Ethnology.

Steward, Julian H., and Louis C. Faron. 1959. *Native Peoples of South America.* New York: McGraw-Hill.

Stewart, John O. 1989. *Drinkers, Drummers, and Decent Folk: Ethnographic Narratives of Village Trinidad.* Albany: State University of New York Press.

———. 1986. "Patronage and Control in the Trinidad Carnival." In *The Anthropology of Experience,* ed. Victor W. Turner and E. M. Bruner, pp. 289–315. Urbana: University of Illinois Press.

Stollmeyer, John. 2000. "Kairi Tukuienyo Karinya." Port of Spain: Turtle Island Children <http://www.angelfire.com/id/kairi/tukuienyo.html>, accessed March 5, 2002.

———. 1998a. "John John Enterprises, Eco-Art from the St. Ann's/East Dry River Watershed." Port of Spain: John John Enterprises. <http://www.angelfire.com/id/kairi/johnjohn.html>, accessed March 5, 2002.

———. 1998b. "Turtle Island Children, the Autochthonous Voices of Amerikua, Promoting the Bio-Regional Vision." Port of Spain: Turtle Island Children. <http://www.angelfire.com/id/kairi/turtle.html>, accessed March 5, 2002.

Strathern, Marilyn. 1994. "Parts and Wholes: Refiguring Relationships." In *Assessing Cultural Anthropology,* ed. Robert Borofsky, pp. 204–217. New York: McGraw-Hill.

Strong, Pauline Turner, and Barrik Van Winkle. 1993. "American Indians and American Nationalism." *Social Analysis* 33 September:9–26.

Sturm, Circe. 1998. "Blood Politics, Racial Classification, and Cherokee National Identity: The Trials and Tribulations of the Cherokee Freedmen." *American Indian Quarterly* 22(1–2) Winter/Spring:230–258.

Sued-Badillo, Jalil. 1992. "Christopher Columbus and the Enslavement of Amerindians in the Caribbean." *Monthly Review* 44 July–August:71–102.

Sun Bear, Wabun, and Nimimosha. 1988. *Bear Tribe's Self Reliance Book.* New York: Prentice Hall Press.

Sunday Express. 1998. "'The Fragrance of Gold,' An Amerindian Tale." September 13:24.

———. 1995. "The Carib Community of Arima." Arimafest Supplement, August 13:5.

Sunday Guardian. 2000. "Congratulations Arima! 112 Years as a Borough." July 30: 28, 29.

———. 1998. "Holding History in One's Hand." July 26:18.

———. 1988. *ArimaFest Supplement.* August 28.

Sunday Guardian Magazine. 1994. "Remains of the Caribs." August 7:8.

———. 1992. "Cover Story: COIP." January 5:2.

Syms, Raymond. 2002. "Santa Rosa, Our Guide: Arima Celebrates Patronal Feast." *Catholic News (Online),* September 1.

Tambiah, Stanley J. 1994. "The Politics of Ethnicity." In *Assessing Cultural Anthropology,* ed. Robert Borofsky, pp. 430–442. New York: McGraw-Hill.

Taylor, Daphne Pawan. 1977. *Parang of Trinidad.* Port of Spain: National Cultural Council of Trinidad and Tobago.

Taylor, Don. 1974. "Uneasy Lies the Neck of the Carib Queen." September 22:20.

Taylor, Douglas. 1992 [1941]. "Columbus Saw Them First." In *Wild Majesty: Encounters with Caribs from Columbus to the Present Day,* ed. Peter Hulme and Neil L. White-head, pp. 306–316. Oxford: Clarendon Press.

———. 1958a. "The Place of Island Carib within the Arawakan Family." *International Journal of American Linguistics* 24(2) April:153–156.

———. 1958b. "Carib, Caliban, Cannibal." *International Journal of American Linguistics* 24(2) April:156–157.

———. 1957. "On the Affiliation of 'Island Carib.'" *International Journal of American Linguistics* 23(4) October:297–302.

———. 1950. "The Meaning of Dietary and Occupational Restrictions among the Island Carib." *American Anthropologist* 52(3) July–September:343–349.

———. 1949. "The Interpretation of Some Documentary Evidence on Carib Culture." *Southwestern Journal of Anthropology* 5:379–385.

Thomas, J. Paul. 1991. "The Caribs of St. Vincent: A Study in Maladministration, 1763–1773." In *Caribbean Slave Society and Economy,* ed. Hilary Beckles and Verene Shepherd, pp. 78–35. New York: New Press.

Thomas, Nicholas. 1992. "The Inversion of Tradition." *American Ethnologist* 17(2) May:213–232.

Thompson, Alvin. 1991. "Amerindian-European Relations in Dutch Guyana." In *Caribbean Slave Society and Economy,* ed. Hilary Beckles and Verene Shepherd, pp. 13–27. New York: New Press.

TIDCO. 2001. "Downtown Kiddies Carnival 2001: Photo Gallery." Port of Spain: Tourism and Industrial Development Corporation. <http://www.visittnt.com/ToDo/Events/Carnival2001/Mas/kiddies/kiddies1.html>, accessed March 5, 2002.

Todorov, Tzvetan. 1992. *The Conquest of the Americas: The Question of the Other,* trans. Richard Howard. New York: Harper Perennial.

Trinidad Express. 1999b. "Parang Association Honours Pioneers." April 9, Sec. 2:8, 9.

———. 1999c. "$22,200 Home for Handicraft." August 27:23.

———. 1999d. "Amigos Meet in Brasso Seco." September 2:26.

———. 1999e. "Sat: Ministry Vague on Money Spent for Culture." August 26:10, 20.

———. 1998a. "Arima: The Rich History of an Exciting Town." March 26:48.

———. 1998b. "Early Basic Instincts . . . but Not Our Caribs!" March 12:44–45.

———. 1998c. "Fancy Indians on Parade." February 25:3.

———. 1998d. "Ruta Quetzal . . . In The Wake of Columbus." April 23:37.

———. 1998e. "Baskets . . . In the Best Tradition." October 10:39.

———. 1998f. "Hang on to Comfort!" October 10:28.

———. 1997. "Caribs Celebrate Diversity." September 16:1.

———. 1989. "It's Santa Rosa Time in Arima." August 24.

———. 1982a. Editorial, August 17.

———. 1982b. "Caribs at the Savannah." September 12:19.

———. 1973. "Make Life Easier for Carib Queen." May 23:1.

Trinidad (Internet) Express. 1999a. "First Nation Couple Weds in T&T." November 26, General News.

———. 1998g. "A Fancy Robber Remembers: 'I Kill Them with Talk.'" Tuesday, February 3, Features. <http://209.94.197.2/feb/feb3/features.htm>, accessed February 2, 2000.

Trinidad Guardian. 2000. "Our Spanish Heritage." January 1:4.

———. 1999a. "Hyarima." November 30:21.

———. 1999b. "Parang Goes on the Internet." August 30:12.

———. 1998a. "PM Will Visit Caribs Soon—Griffith." September 28:3.

———. 1998b. "All Roads Lead to Moruga Weekend." July 29:19.

———. 1998c. "102 and Still Battling On." July 15:3.

———. 1998d. "Carib Craft Display for Royal's Arima Customers." May 6:5.

———. 1992. "Historian Sees Change in Attitudes to Caribs." August 21:3, 14.

———. 1987. "Editorial: Vanishing Caribs." N.d, n.p.

———. 1975. "Caribs Get Second Queen in 7 Months." June 8:10.

Trinidad Guardian (Online). 2001a. Editorial: "Black Power Remembered." April 21.

———. 2001b. "Black Skins, White Masks: Women Using Chemicals to Look Lighter." April 18.

———. 2000a. "Caribs Honour Patron Saint." August 28.

———. 2000b. "ArimaFest Pays Tribute to Kitch." July 17.

———. 2000c. "Residents Celebrate Spanish Ancestry." April 28.

———. 2000d. "Amerindian Heritage at Kiskadee." April 7.

———. 1997. Editorial: "Caribs Are Coming!" June 10.

Trinidad Standard and West Indian Journal. 1838. "Humboldt on El Dorado." June 19.

———. 1838. July 13.

———. 1838. "History of the Indian Tribes of North America." July 17.

———. 1838. November 13.

———. 1838. "Agricultural Report for November." December 4.

———. 1838. December 14.

Trouillot, Michel-Rolph. 1992. "The Caribbean Region: An Open Frontier in Anthropological Theory." *Annual Review of Anthropology* 21:19–42.

Turner, Terence. 1999. "Indigenous and Culturalist Movements in the Contemporary Global Conjuncture." Paper presented at the VIII Congreso de Antropología de la Federación de Asociaciones de Antropología de España, Santiago de Compostela, España, September.

———. 1991. "Representing, Resisting, Rethinking: Historical Transformations of Kayapo Culture and Anthropological Consciousness." In *Colonial Situations: Essays on the Contextualization of Ethnographic Knowledge,* ed. George W. Stocking, Jr., pp. 285–313. History of Anthropology, vol. 7. Madison: University of Wisconsin Press.

Turner, Victor W. 1974. *Dramas, Fields, and Metaphors: Symbolic Action in Human Society.* Ithaca: Cornell University Press.

———. 1967. *The Forest of Symbols: Aspects of Ndembu Ritual.* Ithaca: Cornell University Press.

Valerio, Pedro. 1991. "Sieges and Fortunes of a Trinidadian in Search of a Doctor's Diploma: My Birth and Early Childhood." In *The Book of Trinidad,* ed. Gerard Besson and Bridget Brereton, pp. 322–327. Port of Spain: Paria Publishing.

van de Fliert, Lydia. 1994. *Indigenous Peoples and International Organisations.* Nottingham: Spokesman.

van der Plas, D. Gualbert, O.S.B., D.D. ca. 1954. *The History of the Massacre of Two Jesuit Missionaries in the Island of St. Vincent, 24th January, 1654.* Kingstown, St. Vincent: N.p.

Varese, Stefano. 1982. "Restoring Multiplicity: Indianities and the Civilizing Project in Latin America." *Latin American Perspectives* (Issue 33) 9(2) Spring:29–41.

Vayda, Andrew P. 1994. "Actions, Variations, and Change: The Emerging Anti-Essentialist View in Anthropology." In *Assessing Cultural Anthropology,* ed. Robert Borofsky, pp. 320–330. New York: McGraw-Hill.

Vespucci, Amerigo. 1963 [1500]. "Por el Mar Caribe." In *Cronistas de las culturas precolombinas,* ed. Luis Nicolau D'Olwer, pp. 43–47. México, D.F.: Fondo de Cultura Económica.

Walcott, Anna. 1992. "No True Caribs Left." *Sunday Guardian,* December 12:23.

Wallace, Anthony F. C. 1956. "Revitalization Movements: Some Theoretical Considerations for Their Comparative Study." *American Anthropologist* 58(2):264–281.

Wallerstein, Immanuel. 1998. "The Rise and Future Demise of World-Systems Analysis." *Review* 21(1):103–112.

———. 1992. "The West, Capitalism, and the Modern World-System." *Review* 15(4) Fall:561–619.

———. 1991a. *Geopolitics and Geoculture: Essays on the Changing World-System.* Cambridge. Cambridge University Press.

——— 1991b *Unthinking Social Science* Cambridge: Polity Press

———. 1990a. "Culture as the Ideological Battleground of the Modern World-System." In *Global Culture: Nationalism, Globalization, and Modernity,* ed. M. Featherstone, pp. 31–56. London: Sage.

———. 1990b. "Culture Is the World-System: A Reply to Boyne." In *Global Culture: Nationalism, Globalization, and Modernity,* ed. M. Featherstone, pp. 63–66. London: Sage.

———. 1984a. "Civilization and Modes of Production: Conflicts and Convergences." In *Culture, Ideology, and World Order,* ed. R. B. J. Walker, pp. 60–69. Boulder, Colo.: Westview Press.

———. 1984b. *The Politics of the World-Economy.* Cambridge: Cambridge University Press.

———. 1974. "Dependence in an Inter-Dependent World: The Limited Possibilities of Transformation within the Capitalist World Economy." *African Studies Review* 28(1) Winter:1–26.

———, et al. 1977. "Patterns of Development of the Modern World-System." *Review* 1(2) Fall:111–145.

Wanser, Debra. 2000a. "Masman, Blind Worker get Arima Awards." *Trinidad Guardian (Online),* August 11.

———. 2000b. "PM Supports Call for Amerindian Heritage Day." *Trinidad Guardian (Online),* April 3, Features.

———. 1999. "Caribs Demand Respect." *Trinidad Guardian,* August 2:3.

———. 1997. "Arima Celebrates Its 109th Anniversary." *Trinidad Guardian,* August 6:19.

———. 1994. "The Oldest Woman from Arima." *Sunday Guardian Magazine,* July 8:9.

Wardle, Huon. 1999. "Jamaican Adventures: Simmel, Subjectivity, and Extraterritoriality in the Caribbean." *Journal of the Royal Anthropological Institute* 5(4) December:523–539.

Warner-Lewis, Maureen. 1991. *Guinea's Other Sons: The African Dynamic in Trinidad Culture.* Dover, Mass.: Majority Press.

Washburn, Richard A. 1999. "The Honduras Report." *Oxcart* 157 December:116–117.

Waters, Malcolm. 1995. *Globalization.* London: Routledge.

Watson, Jack. 1982. *The West Indian Heritage: A History of the West Indies.* 2nd ed. London: John Murray Publishers.

Watson, M. S. 1999. "Letter to the Editor: Love Mother Trinidad and Tobago." *Trinidad Guardian,* May 28:8.

Webb, Yvonne. 2000. "Beggars Mob Siparia Samaritans." *Trinidad Guardian (Online),* April 22.

Webster, Steven. 1993. "Postmodernist Theory and the Sublimation of Maori Culture." *Oceania* 63:222–239.

White, Alison. 1998. "Why Do We Eat What We Eat?" *Trinidad Guardian,* March 6:24.

Whitehead, Neil L. 1990. "Carib Ethnic Soldiering in Venezuela, the Guianas, and the Antilles, 1492–1820." *Ethnohistory* 37(4) Fall:357–385.

———. 1988. *Lords of the Tiger Spirit: A History of the Caribs in Colonial Venezuela and Guyana, 1498–1820.* Koninklijk Instituut Caribbean Series 10. Dordrecht, Holland: Foris Publications.

Wilk, Richard, and May Chapin. 1992. "Belize, Land Tenure and Ethnicity." *Cultural Survival Quarterly* 13(3),41–47.

Williams, Brackette. 1989. "A Class Act: Anthropology and the Race to Nation across Ethnic Terrain." *Annual Review of Anthropology* 18:401–444.

Williams, Eric Eustace. 1970. *From Columbus to Castro: The History of the Caribbean, 1492–1969.* London: André Deutsch.

———. 1964. *Capitalism and Slavery.* London: André Deutsch.

———. 1962. *History of the People of Trinidad and Tobago.* London: André Deutsch.

Williams, Nyasha John. 1988. "Arima: A Historical Perspective from Indian Mission to Royal Borough (1888–1988)—Centennial Celebration of the Borough of Arima." Pamphlet.

Wilmer, Franke. 1993a. *The Indigenous Voice in World Politics.* London: Sage.

———. 1993b. "The International Political Activism of Indigenous Peoples and the World System." In *The Ethnic Dimension in International Relations,* ed. Bernard Schechterman and Martin Slann, pp. 141–166. Westport, Conn.: Praeger.

Windeatt, Mary Fabyan. 1993. *Saint Rose of Lima: The Story of the First Canonized Saint of the Americas.* Rockford, Ill.: Tan Books and Publishers.

Winford, Douglas. 1975. "'Creole' Culture and Language in Trinidad: A Socio-Historical Sketch." *Caribbean Studies* 15(3) October:31–56.

Wise, K. S. 1938a. *Historical Sketches of Trinidad and Tobago,* vol. 4. Port of Spain: Historical Society of Trinidad and Tobago.

———. 1938b. *Historical Sketches of Trinidad and Tobago,* vol. 3. Port of Spain: Historical Society of Trinidad and Tobago.

———. 1936. *Historical Sketches of Trinidad and Tobago,* vol. 2. Port of Spain: Historical Society of Trinidad and Tobago.

———. 1934. *Historical Sketches of Trinidad and Tobago,* vol. 1. Port of Spain: Historical Society of Trinidad and Tobago.

Wolf, Eric R. 1994. "Perilous Ideas: Race, Culture, People." *Current Anthropology* 35(1) Winter:1–7.

———. 1990. "Distinguished Lecture: Facing Power—Old Insights, New Questions." *American Anthropologist* 92(3) Summer:586–596.

———. 1984. "Culture: Panacea or Problem?" *American Antiquity* 49(2):393–400.

———. 1982. *Europe and the People without History*. Berkeley: University of California Press.

Wolff, Janet. 1991. "The Global and the Specific: Reconciling Conflicting Theories of Culture." In *Culture, Globalization, and the World System*, ed. Anthony D. King, pp. 161–173. Binghamton: Department of Art and Art History, State University of New York at Binghamton.

Wood, Donald. 1968. *Trinidad in Transition: The Years after Slavery*. London: Oxford University Press.

Wood, Raymond. 1990. "Ethnohistory and Historical Method." In *Archaeological Method and Theory*, vol. 2, ed. M. B. Schiffer, pp. 81–109. Tucson: University of Arizona Press.

Yelvington, Kevin A. 2001a. "The Anthropology of Afro-Latin America and the Caribbean: Diasporic Dimensions." *Annual Review of Anthropology* 30:227–260.

———. 2001b. "Trinidad and Tobago." In *Countries and Their Cultures*, vol. 4, ed. Melvin Ember and Carol R. Ember, pp. 2238–2247. New York: Macmillan Reference USA.

———. 1996. "Caribbean." In *Encyclopedia of Social and Cultural Anthropology*, ed. Alan Bernard and Jonathan Spencer, pp. 86–90. London: Routledge.

———. 1995a. "Cricket, Colonialism, and the Culture of Caribbean Politics." In *The Social Roles of Sport in Caribbean Societies*, ed. Michael A. Malec, pp. 13–51. London: Gordon and Breach.

———. 1995b. *Producing Power: Ethnicity, Gender and Class in a Caribbean Workplace*. Philadelphia: Temple University Press.

———. 1993. "Introduction: Trinidad Ethnicity." In *Trinidad Ethnicity*, ed. Kevin A. Yelvington, pp. 1–32. Knoxville: University of Tennessee Press.

———. 1991. "Ethnicity as Practice? A Comment on Bentley." *Comparative Studies in Society and History* 33(1):158–168.

Young, Sir William. 1971 [1795]. *An Account of the Black Charaibs in the Island of St. Vincent's (the Charaib Treaty of 1773, and other original documents)*. London: Frank Cass.

Index

Maximilian C. Forte is assistant professor in the Department of Sociology and Anthropology at Concordia University in Montreal, Canada. He is the founding editor of the *Caribbean Amerindian Centrelink* (www.centrelink.org) and *KACIKE: The Journal of Caribbean Amerindian History and Anthropology* (www.kacike.org). His published works on the Caribs of Trinidad have appeared in *Cultural Survival Quarterly, The Indigenous World, Indigenous Affairs,* and edited collections. He can be contacted at *mcforte@centrelink.org.*